# FADS *and* FOIBLES *in* MODERN SOCIOLOGY *and Related Sciences*

## *Books by* PITIRIM A. SOROKIN

*Crime and Punishment* (1914). In Russian.
*Leo Tolstoi as a Philosopher* (1915). In Russian.
*Elements of Sociology* (1919). In Russian.
*System of Sociology* (2 vols., 1920-21). In Russian.
*General Theory of Law* (1920). In Russian.
*Today's Russia* (1923). In Russian.
*Essays in Social Politics* (1923). In Russian.
*Leaves from a Russian Diary* (1924). Revised ed. (1950).
*Sociology of Revolution* (1925). German ed. (1928). Latvian ed. (1934).
*Social Mobility* (1926). Japanese ed. (in part, 1928). Chinese ed. (1930). Spanish ed. (1954).
*Contemporary Sociological Theories* (1928). German ed. (1930). Japanese ed. (in part, 1930). Yugoslav ed. (1932). Chinese ed. (1933). French ed. (1935). Second Chinese ed. (1936). Czechoslovakian ed. (1936). Spanish ed. (1951). Turkish ed. (1949). Polish ed. (in preparation). Ukrainian ed. (in preparation).
*Principles of Rural-Urban Sociology* (1929).
*A Source Book in Rural Sociology* (3 vols., 1930-31).
*Time-Budgets of Human Behavior* (1939).
*Social and Cultural Dynamics* (4 vols., 1937-41). Spanish ed. (in preparation). Hindustani ed. (in preparation).
*Crisis of our Age* (1941). Portuguese ed. (1945). Norwegian ed. (1948). Czechoslovakian ed. (1948). Spanish ed. (1948). German ed. (1950). Dutch ed. (1950). Finnish ed. (1952). Japanese ed. (1954).
*Man and Society in Calamity* (1942).
*Sociocultural Causality, Space, Time* (1943). Spanish ed. (in preparation).
*Russia and the United States* (1944). Portuguese ed. (1946). British ed. (1950). Japanese ed. (1953).
*Society, Culture, and Personality* (1947). German ed. (in preparation). Italian ed. (in preparation). Spanish ed. (in preparation).
*Reconstruction of Humanity* (1948). Japanese ed. (1951). German ed. (1952). Norwegian ed. (1953).
*Altruistic Love: A Study of American Good Neighbors and Christian Saints* (1950).
*Social Philosophies of an Age of Crisis* (1950). German ed. (1953). Spanish ed. (1954).
*Explorations in Altruistic Love and Behavior: A Symposium* (1950). French ed. (in preparation).
*S.O.S.: The Meaning of Our Crisis* (1951). Czechoslovakian ed. (in preparation).
*Estructura Mental y Energias del Hombre* (1952).
*The Ways and Power of Love* (1954).
*Forms and Techniques of Altruistic and Spiritual Growth: A Symposium* (1954).

# FADS *and* FOIBLES *in* MODERN SOCIOLOGY *and Related Sciences*

*by* PITIRIM A. SOROKIN

Gateway Edition

HENRY REGNERY COMPANY

*Chicago*

MANUFACTURED IN THE UNITED STATES OF AMERICA

*Library of Congress Catalog Card Number: 56-6176*

Gateway Edition, 1965.

# Preface

Any science, at any moment of its historical existence, contains not only truth but also much that is half-truth, sham-truth, and plain error. This has been especially true of the social and psychological disciplines, for the complexity of mental and social phenomena allows many a fallacy to be taken for the last word of science, "operationally defined, empirically tested, and precisely measured."

Even the sociology and psychology of today are not exceptions to this rule. They, too, contain verities; they, too, are contaminated by the diseases of sham-truth and error. Some of the ailments are well hidden in the recesses of their valid propositions while others infect their methods, techniques and tests.

The purpose of these essays is to expose the nonscientific and half-scientific elements in modern sociology and related disciplines. The operation is painful for the surgeon as well as for those who sincerely err in accepting sham-truth for verity. But, in spite of its painfulness, such an operation must be performed now and then to clear away the nonscientific parasites which, otherwise, progressively undermine the creative growth of these disciplines and their service to the society which supports them.

These considerations fully warrant the necessity of the cleansing operation. As to the irritation and distress which it is bound to provoke, especially among the devotees of the exposed half-truths and sham-verities, the author must humbly confess that he himself is also one of these "sinners." He, also, has been guilty of committing the blunders exposed in his book. If he criticizes others, he no less severely censures himself. It is hoped this confession may attenuate somewhat the irritation of all the "sinners" concerned. In addition, I regard the criticized scholars as the most eminent representatives of the respective currents of social thought. By specifically referring to these scholars, I show my high estimation of their works as being notably above the mediocre works in those areas of the psychosocial sciences which I have criticized. And after all, if the cleansing operation is performed competently, in the long run we will all benefit from it by freeing ourselves of errors mistakenly taken for truth.

In conclusion, it is my privilege to express my warmest thanks to the Lilly Endowment and to Eli Lilly for financial help in the preparation of this manuscript.

I would like to thank also all the publishers and authors who kindly granted me their permission to quote from their works and publications. In the "Notes" at the end of the book each of these publishers and authors is specifically mentioned. I am also deeply indebted to: *American Journal of Sociology, American Sociological Review, American Journal of Orthopsychiatry, American Scientist, Journal of Abnormal and Social Psychology, Philosophy of Science, Social Forces,* and *Sociometry* for the privilege of quoting the articles published by these journals.

# Contents

# FADS *and* FOIBLES *in* MODERN SOCIOLOGY *and Related Sciences*

# *Chapter One*

# Amnesia and New Columbuses

*Give to a Russian pupil, ignorant in astronomy, the map of the heavenly bodies; and next day he will bring it corrected.* F. DOSTOIEVSKY.

*Comment, voilá dix ans que vous avez des ailes, et vous n'avez pas encore volé.* H. POINCARÉ.

*More than twenty years elapsed after this diagnosis of Poincaré, and the situation remains the same.*
E. MEYERSON.

## 1. AMNESIA AND THE DISCOVERER'S COMPLEX

The terms "modern sociology" and "modern psychosocial science" refer to the state of these disciplines for the past twenty-five years or so. During this period, the first defect of these sciences has been a sort of amnesia concerning their previous history, discoveries, and achievements. A second foible is closely related to the first. Many modern sociologists or psychosocial researchers claim that they have made a number of scientific discoveries "for the first time in the whole history" of sociology or some other psychosocial branch of knowledge. For the sake of brevity, this foible can be called an "obsessive discoverer's complex" or just the "discoverer's complex."

The younger generation of sociologists and psychologists explicitly claims that nothing important has been discovered in their fields during all the preceding centuries; that there were only some vague "arm-chair philosophies"; and that the real scientific era in these disciplines began only in the last two or three decades with the publication of their own researches and those of members of their clique. Claiming to be particularly objective, precise, and scientific, our sociological and psychological Columbuses tirelessly repeat this delusion as a scientific truth. Accordingly, they rarely make any references to the social and psychological thinkers of the past. When they do, they hardly veil the sense of their own superiority over the unscientific old fogies. According to them, the discovery of the sociological or psychological "New World" was made not by a viking or a Columbus but by themselves, or by the members of their cult who just a few years ago crossed the Atlantic on the *Queen Elizabeth* or the *United States.* As a result, the indexes of their books list none, or very few, of the thinkers of preceding centuries, in contrast to a long list of "researchers" belonging to the author's "Mutual Back-Patting Insurance Company." Here are typical examples of this "amnesia" combined with the "discoverer's complex."

> The literature about groups goes back to the distant past. Careful research, however, has been known for only about a quarter of a century. . . . [Before this period there was only speculation and no "objective evidence."] Careful use of objective methods of observation, measurement and experimentation has accelerated rapidly within very recent years.[1]

This tune is noisily chorused by all the contributors to this symposium. The very title of R. B. Cattel's paper is "New Concepts for Measuring Leadership, in Terms of Group Syntality." According to the author these new concepts and measurements were "unfortunately neglected by psychologists and sociologists."[2] According to R. M. Stogdill "the pioneering work of Lewin, Moreno, and their followers" introduced scientific methods into the study of "leadership as a phenomenon of groups," while his own work opens "the study of leadership as an aspect of organization."[3] For H. H. Jennings a study of "interpersonal phenomena generated by the interaction between individuals" was begun by Moreno's "pioneering work undertaken in a public school."[4] S. Scheidlinger assures us that the unconscious was discovered by S. Freud.[5] Likewise, the papers of L. Festinger, J. Thibaut, J. R. P. French, S. E. Ash, R. L. Gorden, E. W. Bovard, Jr., S. Schachter, L. M. Killian, L. Coch, J. Levine, and J. Butler, M. Deutsch, R. F. Bales, and other contributors to the volume again and again state that until their studies

> there has been little in the way of explicit theorizing and virtually no experimental work with respect to the effects of cooperation and competition upon social process.[6]

or that

> the task of exploring many implications [of multiple-group membership] has only just begun.[7]

And so on, and on.[8]

In their peculiar vocabulary the apostles of Group Dynamics formulate their propositions as important verities which for the first time scientifically decipher the mysteries of what constitutes a social group and social organization, social "cohesion" and mobility, "group valence and locomotion," competition and cooperation, group hierarchies and power, group conflicts and agreements, group leadership and pressure. Rarely, if ever, do their references go beyond Freud, Lewin and Moreno. They never fail, however, to refer to the works of one another in the same group of new Columbuses in sociology and psychology, anthropology, or psychiatry. A lay reader unfamiliar with the historical A B C's of these branches of knowledge is led to believe that they did not exist at all in the past but emerged only during the last fifteen or twenty years. This "amnesia" has been noted, of course, by J. L. Moreno and other investigators. Confronted by the increasing tendency of others to appropriate various of his ideas and techniques, Moreno finally was forced to bring the matter into the open and explicitly show what was whose. Here are significant excerpts from his outline of the origin and development of sociometry, psychodrama, group therapy, and group dynamics.

> Besides the good genii who surround every pioneer, there is also a class of people who want to steal his ideas and make them their own. It would be harsh to call them intellectual thieves. They are usually honestly affected people. First they become friends and followers because an intellectual commodity cannot be stolen; it has to be absorbed. But once they believe that they master the new skill they prefer that the creator be dead. Indeed, they often deny his existence. . . .
>
> It is incredible and unfortunate that the people who steal your ideas become, in addition, also your personal enemies. . . .[9]
>
> Just as there are people who can have no children, so there are people who cannot create any ideas; therefore, they adopt them. . . . It is unfortu-

nate that these students of group dynamics have not only published distorted versions of my ideas and techniques, but they are practicing them on actual people in so-called research and training laboratories ["the Research Center for Group Dynamics, M.I.T.; the National Training Laboratory, Bethel, Maine; the Research Center for Group Dynamics, U. of Michigan, Ann Arbor"], receiving large fees and research grants without being properly trained for the job. . . .

By using a technique of quoting only each other, that is, those who belong to their clique, and not quoting any of my close associates or myself, their double game became the laughing stock of the connoisseurs and initiated in this new form of "interdependence." [10]

Further examples of the peculiar "amnesia" and of the "discoverer's complex" can be found in the monumental four volumes of the *Studies in Social Psychology in World War II,* by Samuel A. Stouffer and other distinguished contributors to these "epoch-making volumes" (as they have been called by some of the reviewers). In almost every paper of these volumes new discoveries are claimed and emphasized by the authors.

For the first time in history, a method of auxiliary referenda [Gallup's poll in the newspapers and Roper's poll in *Fortune*] was available to establish a new channel of communication between the people and their elected servants. . . .

For the first time these researchers "developed a new conceptual model, called scalogram," "the concept of principal components," "the theory of latent structure," "a concept of relative deprivation," and so on.[11] "The chapters in this volume contain a body of facts unique in the annals of war." [12]

Original and challenging as some of the new concepts here introduced may be. . . . Our purpose is to offer a new theory and its concomitant techniques. . . . This rather new approach seems to afford an adequate basis for the quantification of many types of qualitative data.[13]

And so on, throughout all four volumes.

If, instead of symposia, we take the works of single authors, we meet many similar claims, repeated and re-repeated ad nauseam, of discoveries made "for the first time."

We shall make an innovation which it is well to point out to the unsuspecting. In this book we intend to apply the methods of the exact sciences to

> the interaction of people. . . . [The author modestly adds that until his work] the most curious phenomenon in the history of human thought has been the consistent inability [of sociologists, psychologists, economists, political scientists, and so on] to apply the methods which have had such evident success in the physical science.[14]

Or

> The study of human groups is a part of sociology, but a neglected part. . . . Sociology . . . has only begun to study smaller social units. . . . [By his pioneering investigation of human groups the author aims] to reach a new synthesis.[15]

Or

> [Though Simmel and Cooley were interested in small groups, they could not, with their "primitive research methods," develop a theory of such groups. Therefore] sociological knowledge about the small groups remained stagnant. . . . Within the past decade or so, this condition greatly changed [and sociology of small groups has enormously progressed].[16]

Or

> To geographic distance the behavioral scientists have paid very little attention thus far.[17]

For any scholar moderately competent in history of sociology, psychology, or the related sciences, these statements are brazenly unprecise and grossly unscientific. As a matter of fact, all these "modern discoveries" were made long ago; and in the works of the previous thinkers they were, if anything, analyzed better, understood more adequately, and formulated even more precisely than in the recent works. But let us continue our collection of cases of amnesia and discoverer's complex. Since these diseases seem to be widely spread among modern sociologists and psychosocial researchers, and since they appear in so many diverse forms, a better knowledge of them will illuminate one of the characteristics of modern psychosocial disciplines. Anatol Rapoport confides that "the [operational] approach which we will use here is not old, certainly not more than a century old." [18] When carefully checked, his "operational philosophy and approach," so far as they have any definite meaning, are found to be at least twenty centuries old.

He also tells us that semantics and metalinguistics were discovered by A. Korzybski, B. Malinowski, and E. Shapir within the last thirty years.[19]

One has to know next to nothing about what Rapoport calls semantics and metalinguistics to make such a blundering statement. As a matter of fact, everything that is sound in Korzybski's semantics was very thoroughly discussed and formulated at least some 2000 years ago, especially by the great Buddhist logicians: Gothama, Dignaga, Vasubandhu, Dharmakirti,[20] and by other thinkers of India, China, Greece, Rome, and the Europe of the Middle Ages. Even the main motto of the contemporary semanticists that "the word is not the thing; the map is not territory" was coined by the above-mentioned Buddhist logicians. It needs no arguing, that for at least two millennia, epistemology has dealt with all the main problems of today's semantics, and dealt with them more competently than the modern semanticists do. Likewise, for centuries comparative philosophy and linguistics have studied substantially the problems of Rapoport's metalinguistics. Only an ignorance of these disciplines and of what they have been busy with makes a statement like Rapoport's possible.

Still another example is given by S. A. Stouffer. In his presidential address he tells us that "we have come quite a way in the last generation or two in the development of quantitative methods. We are even able to measure interactions and to some extent behavior patterns. . . . Indeed, the advances in techniques have seemed so rapid as compared with advances in sociological knowledge that some scholars . . . may yearn wistfully for a moratorium on technical progress to give our substantive knowledge a chance to catch up. The phrase 'he's a mere technician' is a not uncommon epithet."[21]

Unfortunately, when he tries to substantiate his claim, he fails to prove it. For anyone who has studied a history of inventions or of scientific discoveries, neither the thirty-nine propositions of Gillfillan nor J. B. Conant's twenty-one propositions in this field contain anything new: they merely popularize discoveries made long ago. Moreover, some of the propositions of Gillfillan and Conant have been shown to be wrong, while several important rules are entirely missed.

Stouffer has made other untenable statements: for instance, that "the habit of experimentation in medicine is only a few decades old." If consulted, any competent history of medicine would show that medical experimentation was already practiced in ancient Egypt, India, China, in Greece from the time of Hippocrates, in Arabic cultures, and, of course, in the centuries after the sixteenth. It is true this experimentation did not cover the whole field of medicine; but, being potentially unlimited, experimentation does not cover the whole medical field at the present time either. This, however, does not mean there is no medical experimentation now, or that there was none in past centuries.

All that remains from Stouffer's validation of his claim are the references to the "measurement techniques" of Bales and Lazarsfeld, of Merton and Guttman, of D. Thomas and S. Dodd, of Stouffer and his collaborators in the *Study of Social Psychology in World War II,* and of a few others. Later on, in chapters five and six we shall show that these "innovators" did not make any new discovery in mathematics or in the science of measurements at all. All they "discovered" consists of a mere variation in manipulation of questionnaire data, which variation is either inapplicable or fallacious or quite arbitrary. To be sure, during the last few decades several important discoveries have been made in mathematics, mathematical statistics, and mathematical physics, especially in the relativity and quantum theories. But these discoveries have not been made by sociological and psychological statisticians, with their limited mathematical knowledge, and with their routine statistical procedures. As to their techniques of measurement, further on, in chapters five and six, it will be shown that these techniques are mainly inept complications of the old techniques—complications, moreover, incapable of delivering the goods expected of them.

In addition, many of Stouffer's "new techniques of measurement" are wrongly set up at the very beginning of the measuring operations—start with wrong premises and continue with erroneous assumptions. His central "evidence"—"the measurement of role expectation"—gives an example of this sort of measuring technique. Its first defect is the very vagueness of the term "role." Its second error is the identification of "expected behavior" with "proper or obligatory behavior."

Like many others, Stouffer fails to see the profound difference between the notions of "expectation" and "obligation." Knowing that a high percentage of recidivists or drug addicts relapse into crime or the use of drugs, I expect many criminals or drug addicts to so relapse. This expectation does not, however, make their behavior "obligatory" or "proper" or noncriminal. On the other hand, if the recidivist or drug addict quite unexpectedly receives help and by virtue of that help is able to avoid a relapse, I can hardly call his behavior "criminal," "improper," or reprehensible in any way. Moreover, criminal law, clearly defining what actions are criminal and what are not, has little to do with any "expectation." The criminal code specifies an action as criminal regardless of whether it is expected or not; and all other actions—expected and unexpected—remain noncriminal. As a matter of fact, the term "expectation" is hardly even mentioned in criminal codes—either written or customary. There is no excuse for identifying the "expected" with the "obligatory" and the nonexpected with the reprehensible.

Third, there is no need to measure an endless variety of actions in order to find those with "role obligation." In the first place, no measurement can catch such a "fish." In regard to many actions—sometimes even our own—we cannot say whether we expect them or not. We simply do not know. Actions of this category form a large part of the total sum of human actions—and this sort of "fish" is entirely missed by our "precise" interviewers. Obviously it cannot be caught in the statisticians' measurement net of "expectations" and "role-obligations."

Again, in regard to the actions about which we may have some—now certain, now uncertain—expectation or nonexpectation, the Stouffer measurement net can, at best, catch only some utterances of the respondents regarding the sorts of role-playing they view as expected or unexpected. Being notably incidental, incessantly varying, and highly unreliable, these speech-reactions (their evanescent and unreliable character is further treated in chapters four, five and six) will not yield any fish of "obligatory role playing" or any "normal expectation" of "role obligation." An expedition of this sort goes to fish with the wrong sort of net and fish-measuring gadgets, to the wrong pond, where no "role obligation" fish can be found, and with quite unnecessary expenses. The members of the expedition should have asked for a competent guide before starting their adventure, for he would have told them that if they wanted to catch "obligatory fish" of different sizes and varieties they should have gone to the criminal and total law codes of the respective populations.

These codes give, first, a clear-cut definition of all actions as (a) lawful, or obligatory, (b) recommended, but not required and, (c) prohibited or unlawful—tabooed, sinful. They "measure" no less clearly the gravity of criminal actions by dividing them into the classes of the *felony* and *misdemeanor* in Anglo-Saxon law; of the *Verbrechen, Vergehen* and *Uebertretungen* in German law; of the *crime, délit* and *contravention* in

French law; of the *prestuplenia, prostupki* and *pravonarushenia* in Russian law. The codes do not stop at this division of criminal behavior into three or more classes. Within each of these classes, the gravity of criminal actions is measured in great detail by the kind of punishment specified for each such action, ranging from capital punishments of various kinds to imprisonment for different durations and under different conditions, and ending with different monetary fines. Each criminal and civil code has a long and detailed scale of such punishment-measures.

The law-codes go even further in their measurements, increasing the punishment for the same action if there are aggravating conditions, or decreasing it if the conditions are extenuating.[22]

In brief, since the remotest past, law-codes, whether written or customary, have been very precisely classifying, defining, and measuring the actions with which we are here concerned. So far as the sociologist's task is to study the social phenomena as they are given, including the objective measurements of these phenomena, he should take the phenomena and their social measurements as they are given, and should not replace the objectively given facts by his own fancies and subjective valuational measurements.

When an investigator deals with so-called "intuitive" or "unofficial" law convictions and actions, he should follow the same procedure of objective registration.

The above explains why Stouffer's "fishing expedition" for "the range of normal expectation of role obligations" cannot possibly succeed.[23]

These criticisms may sound harsh; but they are no harsher than the condescending superiority assumed by the measurers towards "philosophers speculating in their arm chairs,"[24] and towards the great social thinkers of the past, whom they regard as Stone Age "survivals."

But, let us go on with our investigation of the new Columbuses. If we believe many a recent text, we must conclude that the main scientific principles of the psychology of the unconscious and, partly, that of the conscious, as well as the scientific study of mental diseases and the basic therapeutic methods for them, were discovered by S. Freud, C. Jung, and by still more recent psychologists and psychiatrists.

> "In *recent years* scientific psychology has begun to explore the hidden regions. . . ."
>
> "The method of free association [was] *devised by Freud*. . . . The *first*

> *serious attempt* to embody this principle in a convenient test was the word association method, *first brought* into scientific prominence by Bleurer and Jung shortly after 1900. . . ."
>
> "The next important step came in 1921 when Rorschach published his work . . . and showed that perceptual and imaginative processes might be made the basis for a comprehensive diagnosis of personality." [25]

We are told further that scientific interpretation of dreams was begun by Freud in 1900 and continued by Klein, Malamud, Prince and others during the period 1920-30 and later. Then came the "Thematic Apperception Test" and other projective techniques using plays, puppets, drawings, painting, incidental movements and exclamations for diagnosis of personality, especially of man's unconscious, subconscious and preconscious "minds" and his "hidden repressions." Needless to say, all these principles and techniques were discovered at least two thousand years ago and were used by many a medicine man, yogi, saintly ascetic, and *spiritualis pater*. They were especially used by the founders of monastic orders of the East and the West.[26]

In the recent past before Freud, E. von Hartmann published his famous work, *Philosophie des Unbewussten* in 1869 (English tr. *Philosophy of the Unconscious,* London, 1930); E. Kraepelin published the classical and still unexcelled four volumes of his *Lehrbuch d. Psychiatrie* in 1883; and one of Freud's teachers, P. Janet, dealt with the unconscious and subconscious more thoroughly and scientifically than Freud himself later did.

Now one hears it said: "About four years ago, in 1949, we originated the phrase 'behavioral sciences.' " Again, "Stewart [John Q.] has initiated the concept of 'social physics.' " And, "Parsons and Shils have been concerned with social system." [27]

Without going far back, the author of these statements could have easily found that in the United States, in 1913, M. Parmelee had published a substantial volume entitled: *The Science of Human Behavior*. If he had undertaken a little study before making his statement, he would have found that the term "behavioral sciences" was used at least some four or five centuries ago. If he had glanced only through Chapter One of my *Contemporary Sociological Theories,* he would have learned that the concept of "social physics" was initiated in Ancient Greece and Rome, and that "social physics" itself had been brilliantly developed into a special branch of science in the sixteenth, the seventeenth, and the eighteenth centuries. Likewise, if he had condescended to glance through the volumes of my *Social and Cultural Dynamics,* he would have discovered that long before Parsons and Shils quite a few social thinkers, including myself, had been concerned with social system. Miller's statements are typical, in their gross incorrectness, of the statements of other pseudo-discoverers claiming that their propositions and theories have a monopoly on scientific preciseness.

The epidemics of amnesia and discoverer's complex have also infected modern anthropology. Even such notable anthropologists as Linton, Malinowski, Murdock, Kluckhohn, and others have not escaped the infection. They, also, repeatedly state that their theories were unknown "until very recent times" [28] or were discovered only by "the new science of anthropology." [29] As a matter of fact, the three basic needs of Linton (emotional response, security, and new experience) and the eleven biological drives of Malinowski ("impulse" of breathing, hunger, thirst, sex, fatigue, restlessness, somnolence, bladder pressure, colon pressure, fright, pain), which these authors put at the foundation of cultural patterns and social institutions, are merely variations of the ages-old theories of instincts and drives developed, "validated," and reiterated in many variants by a legion of thinkers of the past centuries, not to mention many predecessors in the twentieth century.[30]

The same is true of G. P. Murdock's "principle of limited possibilities" in the variation of cultural patterns;[31] of Leighton's "emotional uniformities";[32] of Kluckhohn-Kelly's concept of culture;[33] and of other theories of these anthropologists.

C. Kluckhohn in his *Mirror of Man* repeatedly tells us that until the nineteenth century no really scientific anthropological and sociological theories existed; that the multitudes of propositions in his book are rooted in well documented scientific data; that most of the verities seemingly discovered by history, archeology, sociology, biology, or psychology have, in fact, been discovered by recent anthropology; and so forth.[34]

The same can be said about the pretentious "discovery" of "the basic personality structure" by A. Kardiner and R. Linton.[35] H. Ozanne correctly appraises it (and several other of Kardiner's discoveries) as a vague variation of a very old concept "pilfered" from sociologists.[36]

The germs of amnesia and of the mania of new discoveries have also spread in the field of modern theoretical sociology. T. Parsons and E. Shils can be taken as representative victims of the epidemics discussed. Parsons, in the well-founded words of E. Faris,

> confidently believes that new knowledge has come into the world [with publication of Parsons' *The Social System*]. Unfortunately, he does not spell out clearly these revelations, and the reader is left to discover them for himself. He cannot mean "the clear establishment of the reasons why the mechanisms of behavior involve the non-rational process" for this, while accepted, was set forth by Sumner in 1909, emphasized by Dewey in 1922, made central by Mead and has long been familiar to us all [as a matter of fact, it was set forth already by Savigny and Puchta at the beginning of the nineteenth century, and still earlier by Plato, Ibn-Khaldun, Montesquieu, and others].
>
> Nor does he mean the doctrine of "optimization of gratification" for this is indistinguishable from hedonism of which he, himself, has expressed doubts.
>
> The proudest boast in Chapter XII is the discovery of the combination of interdependence and independence of personality, culture, and system (organization). This claim borders on the incredible. Fifty years ago Cooley spoke of society and the individual as like the player and the orchestra—two aspects of human life. Thomas taught that personality is the subjective aspect of culture. Dewey elaborated on this truth, and more recently Sorokin in 1947 has made the same point in words strikingly similar to those of Parsons.[37]

Similar criticism of Parsons' and Shils' *Toward a General Theory of Action* (Cambridge, 1951), is made by L. von Wiese.[38] Granting a sort of system to the conceptual framework of the authors, the eminent dean of German sociologists also notices a strange lack of references to their predecessors, in addition to a sterile scholasticism, the illegitimate use of terms borrowed from the natural science, a pedantic abstractedness, an arid vagueness "often taken for wisdom," and the premature "gray-hairness" of a hitherto young, fact-finding American sociology. Knowing well that Parsons was an instructor in my courses at Harvard and observing the essential similarity between Parsons' sociological framework and mine, Von Wiese particularly stresses a complete lack of references to theories of mine published many years before Parsons' work.[39]

On my part, in an unpublished mimeographed manuscript, *Similarities and Dissimilarities Between Two Sociological Systems,*[40] I have shown by a long series of parallel quotations from my works and the volumes of Parsons and Shils that their basic definitions and concepts are practically identical with mine; often they are identical even in wording. This identity is found in the conceptions of: (a) meaningful interaction as the basic social process; (b) the subjects of interaction; (c) the three-fold aspect of sociocultural reality: personality-society-culture; (d) the three forms of meaningful cultural patterns; (e) the concept of system, generally; (f) the concept of social system and its properties; (g) the concept of cultural system and its properties; (h) the concept of change of social system: immanent and due to external factors; (i) the personality system; and several other basic points.

Side by side with these basic similarities I indicated a multitude of dissimilarities mainly in secondary points. "Among many factors of these dissimilarities one is due to Parsons' incompleted transition from his previous, mainly M. Weberian, semi-nominalistic standpoint to the new one. For this reason 'the sins' of the previous framework continue to visit upon, to crop in, and to vitiate the new framework. Hence the peculiar eclecticism of his new standpoint.". . . Durkheim's successor at the Sorbonne, G. Gurvitch, finds Parsons' theories mainly "vicious circles and empty and pretentious verbal formulas," a mere "pile of disparate elements." [41]

Parsons lists the main contributions of his later works under four headings.[42] These claims have to be discounted also. I can convincingly show that, excepting for a multitude of logically poor and empirically useless paradigms and neologisms, there is absolutely nothing new in the sound part of Parsons' propositions. They all have been developed more scientifically and formulated more precisely by many previous sociologists, psychologists, and philosophers. Even my own humble analysis of these phenomena is possibly more precise, more detailed, more adequate logically and better documented empirically [43] than Parsons'.

Still other examples of loss of memory in regard to even recent events are given by many writers on social mobility. Most of them hardly ever mention their predecessors, including my *Social Mobility* which was published in 1927 and which, so far, is still "the only comprehensive work" in this field.[44] Yet they all use many of the basic concepts and generalizations given in my volume, without, however, adopting my practice of citing and giving credit to the main preceding investigators of the phenomena of social mobility. Even more, when any of these recent "researchers" do make reference to their predecessors they give the credit to other "researchers" who happen to be repeating, often verbatim, generalizations and uniformities formulated and corroborated in my volume (again without any reference to it).

An example of this "acute amnesia" is supplied by M. M. Tumin's paper: "Some Principles of Stratification." [45] Tumin starts his inquiry with the statement: "It is most curious that the basic premises and implications of the assumption [of universality and functions of social stratification] have only been casually explored by American sociologists. The most systematic treatment is to be found in the well-known article by Kingsley Davis and Wilbert Moore, entitled 'Some Principles of Stratification.'" [46]

The peculiar aspect of this statement consists in the fact that not only Tumin but also Davis and Moore seemingly suffer from the amnesia, for in their paper Davis and Moore also fail to mention my *Social Mobility* although they were formerly graduate students in my courses and well knew the volume. When, however, their "original" generalizations and "systematic treatment" of social stratification are compared with the discussion offered in my volume, it will be found that *Social Mobility* includes those generalizations and treats them in a much more developed form, buttressed by abundant historical, empirical, and statistical corroboration.[47]

With a few exceptions, like P. H. Davidson's and H. D. Anderson's *Occupational Mobility in an American Community* (Stanford University, 1937), most of the studies of social stratification and mobility which have appeared since the publication of my work have discovered hardly any new uniformity, or generalization, or significant principle that was not already formulated in my volume. Some of these studies—like R. Center's "Occupational Mobility," *Amer. Sociol. Review,* XIII (1948), pp. 197-203; or E. A. Suchman's "Social Mobility in the Army," (in S. A. Stouffer's *Studies in Social Psychology in World War II,* quoted, vol. I, chap. 6)—give new material but arrive at conclusions quite similar to those given in my work.[48]

The foregoing examples of "amnesia" and "discoverers' complex" can be multiplied *ad libitum.* Later on we shall see that almost all the new discoveries are either mere pompously worded platitudes, painful elaborations of the obvious, purely terminological innovations, or rediscoveries of a "sociological table of multiplication" initially discovered long ago.

## 2. Reasons for Amnesia and the Discoverers' Complex

What are the reasons for these "diseases"? Are they due to the modern scholars' ignorance of the history of the social and psychological sciences? Or do they represent an attempt at inflation of one's own achievements? If so, does this attempt mean, in Moreno's term, "intentional stealing" of the creative achievements of others, or a sort of a naive inflation of their own efforts by the mere disregard of the works of others? The bulk of these cases are probably due to the ignorance of our pseudo-discoverers, many of whom are newcomers from other fields. Having no preliminary training in sociology or psychology, they are often involved, as statisticians, say, in research projects of a sociological or psychological nature. Having had no occasion to make a serious study of these disciplines, the newcomers easily assume that there is hardly anything of real value which they need to study, and that with their "scientific" methods they are the pioneering investigators of these phenomena.

In this belief they are reinforced by the emergence of the *"omnibus researcher-professor"* exemplified by the "statistical omnibus researcher." The new and growing belief is that when one masters routine statistical method, he becomes competent to do research on any problem in any field, including the fields which he has not studied at all. This "omnibus-researcher" has already become an institution in psychosocial research and teaching and is widely used by government, business, and research institutions. The "omnibus-professor" is being appointed more and more often by universities for teaching psychosocial disciplines which he never studied, but which—as statistician, mathematician, or experimenter with rats and dogs—it is assumed he will be able to teach more scientifically than the scholars who have spent many years in these fields.

Along with the emergence of this new type of researcher, a peculiar creed has recently grown within the foundations, universities, and research institutions. It is the belief that *the less a researcher of psychosocial phenomena knows about these phenomena, the less partial he is and, therefore, the better his research or teaching*. However incredible this credo may sound, it not only does exist, but is already implemented in the policies of the foundations, universities, and other institutions. During the last few years, a number of persons, perfectly innocent of a serious knowledge of Russia, Japan, or Islamic culture, have been chosen for directorship or chairmanship in Russian-Japanese-Islamic research centers; statisticians, mathematicians, or specialists in rats' reflexes who have never seriously studied psychology or sociology, have been appointed chairmen and professors in these disciplines in a number of colleges and universities. With the emergence of the "omnibus researcher-professor" and of the peculiar *docta ignorantia* (quite different from the *docta ignorantia* of Nicolas of Cusa), the spread of amnesia and the discoverer's complex is quite natural.

The spread of these diseases among the younger generation of psychosocial scholars is also understandable. The prevalent training of our graduate students in these fields consists largely of learning various techniques and research-procedures: statistical techniques, the techniques of administering intelligence tests, temperament tests, projective tests, sociometric tests, and dozens of other tests that are taught and used at the present time. Learning these procedures and tests is a time-consuming business. It leaves little time for students to study seriously the proper fields of sociology or other psychological sciences. Their general knowledge of these sciences rarely goes beyond standard textbooks and a few monographs prescribed in their courses or necessary for their Ph.D. As a result, they receive the Ph.D. without having a substantial knowledge of their field. Repeatedly told by their professors that the tests and techniques are the most important and most scientific part of their discipline, and having spent most of their time in mastering these tests and procedures, the young Ph.D.s end with a firm conviction that they have a masterful knowledge of the whole field of sociology or psychology. When they have been so trained and when, after long and painstaking research, they happen to discover a "sociological table of multiplication," they are apt to believe they discovered it "for the first time in history."

This explains why in their publications there is an extreme scarcity of references to the basic works of their predecessors. This accounts also for the fact that "the major single source of data for introductory sociology texts" is other introductory texts. Some 37 per cent of all the references in 129 introductory sociology texts analyzed are to other introductory texts.[49] Elementary texts are easy to read; they can be mastered in a comparatively short time; and they supposedly give in a nutshell a knowledge of the whole field of sociology. In all these respects they are a God-given boon for the novices. Using the "short cut" they gain, in no time, the status of a competent, up-to-date scientific researcher or professor.

Another group—probably much smaller—of our pseudo-discoverers are the victims of ambitions far exceeding their creative potential and of our society's competitive mores and its cult of success. Driven by their Narcissistic complex and by the ever-operating social forces of rivalry, they are eager to overestimate their achievements, to advertise them as "discoveries made for the first time," and with a semi-rational naïveté they are apt sincerely to fool themselves and others with their claims. This class of would-be Columbuses contains an insignificant fraction of deliberate plagiarists. The majority are just the modern "business men in science." Using all the techniques of competitive business, our "business men in science" also use the techniques of modern advertising, of running down the products of their competitors and enhancing their own. For "business men in science" these techniques, including the unscrupulous ones, are as necessary as in other business fields for securing their means of subsistence, for obtaining the research funds, for promotion in a university or research institution, and for getting the prestige of a notable scientist or scholar.

The hypothesis that ignorance is the primary cause of amnesia is confirmed in a great number of specific amnesia cases. This hypothesis is reinforced by two specific techniques used by amnesics of this sort: (a) by "the technique of quoting only each other" and not quoting "the outsiders to the clique," as already noted by Moreno. The use of this technique is reconfirmed by the previously mentioned investigation of A. H. Hobbs. Analyzing 129 sociology texts Hobbs found a "mutual back-scratching . . . in citations. Authors tend to cite writings of their friends more frequently than they cite works of someone they do not know." [50] (b) The conjecture seems to be confirmed also by the technique of using new terms for old concepts to give them a look of originality. These and similar devices help to sell, especially to a credulous public, the old intellectual merchandise as the new.

Whatever the reasons, one can only deplore a wide occurrence of amnesia and discoverers' complex among modern sociologists and psychosocial investigators. These diseases do not increase our knowledge of psychosocial phenomena; nor do they facilitate making this knowledge of service to the needs of mankind. Amnesia and the delusion of new discoveries represent a disruption of the historical growth of sociology and the related disciplines. In a sense they cancel a large part of the knowledge of mental, social, and cultural phenomena accumulated by the experience and study of many generations of observers and thinkers. Instead of permitting the easy learning of a verity already discovered, these ailments force many a researcher to rediscover it by long, painstaking, and costly research. Considerable creative and cognitive energy is thus wasted.

Such is the first foible of modern sociology and the related sciences. Turn now to the speech ailments which afflict these sciences, ailments closely connected to the diseases we have discussed.

# *Chapter Two*

# Verbal Defects: Obtuse Jargon and Sham-Scientific Slang

*'Twas brillig, and the slithy toves*
*Did gyre and gimble in the wabe:*
*All mimsy were the borogoves,*
*And the mome raths outgrabe.*

*"It seems very pretty [Alice] said, but it's rather hard to understand! Somehow it seems to fill my head with ideas—only I don't exactly know what they are!"*
*And Humpty Dumpty said, "There are plenty of hard words there."*

LEWIS CARROLL, Through the Looking Glass.

"It is a matter of common observation that inherent intellectual inadequacy ('mental deficiency') is associated with corresponding difficulties in the acquisition of verbal tools for symbol formation and communication. . . . This difficulty is proportionate to the degree of intellectual defect."[1] According to A. Schopenhauer, clear ideas are usually expressed in a clear and intelligible language, while vague notions are communicated in obtuse and foggy speech. Amnesia and false pretensions at originality, poor logic and vagueness of ideas, together with a desire to cover these defects by "impressive verbal raiment," are responsible for numerous "speech disorders" among many modern sociologists and psychosocial scholars. The common trait of these defects consists of substituting vague, cumbersome, and imitative terms for the clearer and more comprehensible ones. This obsession has several forms.

One is a blind transference of terms and formulas from the natural sciences into sociology and the related disciplines. The net result of the transference is a distortion of the precise meaning the terms have in the natural sciences and a contamination of the social sciences by terms that now become either meaningless or vague. Being incomprehensible, such terms impress the uninitiated as exact and "scientific."

Another "speech disorder" is a ponderously obscure description of platitudes. Whether it is intentional or not, a ponderous and obtuse formulation gives platitudes an appearance of profundity and originality. It helps also to hide shallowness of thought.

The third "speech disorder" manifests itself in the introduction of many neologisms which hinder precise communication and the understanding of ideas.

As a result of these and similar "speech disorders," the language of modern sociology has become a sort of jargon devoid of elegance, as well as clarity. Here are some typical examples. A noted psychologist introduces the term "syntality" and explains that it means "the final performance of the group as a group." [2] Instead of clarifying the meaning given in ordinary terms, "syntality" needs a description in ordinary terms ("the final performance of the group as a group") to have any meaning at all. It does not add anything to this ordinary definition; it only increases the difficulty of understanding the author. It is a parasitic and disserviceable term.

"Synergy" is another term introduced by the same author. It means "the sum total of the *energy* which any group can command and expend," and is subdivided into "maintenance synergy," "effective synergy," and so on. In biology and organic chemistry the term synergy has a fairly precise meaning quite different from that given by this author. In his use, "synergy" does not clarify anything, but needs the help of ordinary terms to be intelligible—and so it is another useless, parasitic term. Moreover, its definition in ordinary terms contains the word "energy" which, according to the author, "cannot be precisely defined" [3] (although its definition in physics is precise). Since it "cannot be precisely defined," the whole definition of "synergy" becomes void and meaningless. And this applies also to the derivative "effective, maintenance, and other synergies." Here are other samples of propositions coined in a peculiar jargon by the author: "The satisfaction (reward) and punishment of *ergic* and *metanergic* motives, which concentrates on the drive phenomena ('valence' formulations may be regarded as an externalization of this formulation); and the energy expression formulation which directs attention to the work done in the motivation situation." [4] "And changes of goal under a leader can thus be measured by changes in the dimension of synergy, just as changes in the abilities by which goals are reached are measured in the remaining dimensions of syntality." [5] With all the respect due to the author, I cannot help stating that these impressive-sounding propositions are meaningless, since the terms "synergy," "energy," and "syntality" are undefined and void. If they mean anything, their meanings are very familiar platitudes concerning motivation, cooperation, influence of leadership, goal-directed activities of group, and so on. All these phenomena have been described in ordinary terms more precisely than they are described by the author. This cumbersome verbiage adds nothing to our knowledge of phenomena of leadership and of its measurement (if any adequate measurement of leadership is possible at the present stage of the social and psychological sciences).

*Group-cohesiveness* "refers to phenomena which come into existence if, and only if, the group exists." [6] How true! and what a beautiful sample of an obtuse tautological definition of "group-cohesiveness" this "precise" definition is! The authors seem to be unaware that the phenomena which they call "group-cohesiveness" have been excellently analyzed under the names of "group-solidarity," "group unity," "group-bonds" by a legion of eminent social thinkers. These thinkers, from Plato to Durkheim, have defined the nature, the forms and the factors of "group-cohesiveness" much better [7] than the whole fraternity of the "Group-Dynamics" has been able to do. Not mentioning any of their predecessors, our fraternity makes the supposed pioneering discovery of a "sociological table of multiplication," and achieves the astounding result of cumbersome tautologies like the one above. It is still more remarkable that these "pioneers" find a large number of followers who sincerely believe that "for the first time in history" "group-cohesiveness" has been discovered and has begun to be scientifically studied!

Let us continue our exploration of the "speech disorders" of these "pioneers." "*The valence,* or attractiveness, of any object or activity is a function of the needs of the individual and the properties of the object. [The group's] valence for any given person, then, depends upon the nature and strength of his needs and upon the perceived suitability of the group for satisfying these needs. . . ." "The valence or the attraction to the group is a function of the resultant forces acting on the member to belong to the group." [8]

We can pass by here without discussing the imitative character of these propositions which, contrary to the claims of the authors, merely repeat hundreds of similar statements made by the partisans of the Mechanistic or Physicalistic school in sociology decades and even centuries ago.[9] But two things have to be pointed out in these and hundreds of similar statements made by the partisans of Group-Dynamics. First, the term "valence" has a precise meaning in chemistry. It is the quality which determines the number of atoms or radicals with which any single atom or radical will unite chemically, and the combining capacity of an atom or radical compared with the standard hydrogen atom. As such, valence is precisely measurable in chemistry and its measurability is its main scientific function there. Valence in chemistry has nothing to do with "attractiveness," "needs," "desires" of an individual or group, just as the atom or radical has nothing common with the individual or social group. The use of this term in the above sense of attractiveness, etc., is an utter distortion of its chemical meaning, a sort of anthropomorphization of atoms and chemical elements and, consequently, a disservice to chemistry and to science generally. Secondly, this use of the term is also a disservice to sociology. The above quotations show that in order for the term "valence" to have any meaning in sociology, it has to be explained by the term "attractiveness," but the term "attractiveness" is not explained by the term "valence." For this reason, the authors again and again write: "the valence, i.e., attractiveness," "the valence or attractiveness," and so on. In short, the term "valence" is parasitic and useless in the field of the social and psychological sciences.

*"Location," "locomotion,"* etc. "What do we mean when we assert that a group does or does not 'get somewhere'? These terms seem to imply that a group can be said to have a location. . . . If a group does not 'get anywhere,' one would assume that it remained in the same location. . . . These vaguely conceived notions of 'location' and of 'preferred location' help us designate a class of phenomena for further analysis. . . . Whenever the group changes its location, we shall speak of group locomotion." [10]

"Another important source of forces to communicate are the forces which act on members of groups to locomote (change their position) in the group." [11]

"From the definition of promotively and contriently independent goals, it appears to follow that (a) any person, X, who has promotively interdependent goals with persons, A, B, C, etc., will come to have promotively interdependent locomotions in the direction of his goal with persons A, B, C, etc.; (b) any person, Y, who has contriently interdependent goals with persons A, B, C, etc., will come to have contriently interdependent locomotions in the direction of his goal with persons A, B, C, etc." "X has locomoted toward his goal. . . ." The implications of the cooperative situation are: "substitutability," "positive cathexis," "positive inducibility," etc.[12]

"Every psychological activity may be ordered to a *two-dimensional plane (surface)* where organism and goal represent certain spacial regions within *the surface*. . . ." "Psychological activity of all sorts will be ordered to a *path,* and may be said to represent *locomotion* in the psychological field." This psychological field is a "topological medium," with "fluidity," "cohesiveness," "permeability," "hodological space," etc.[13]

These examples make a detailed criticism unnecessary. The "disorderly character" of these obtuse lucubrations is obvious. First, none of these "locomotioning" authors has been able even roughly to define what he means by social or group space, by the location or position of a group, individual, or socio-cultural phenomenon in the socio-cultural universe. Second, therefore, the terms "locomotion," "fluidity," "vector," etc., are devoid of any clear meaning. Third, to give some meaning to them they have to translate each term into more comprehensible ordinary terms: "locomotion" is translated into "change of position," or simply social or cultural or environmental change, or a change within the group itself. As in previous cases, their terms are useless parasites hindering rather than helping the clarification and communication of ideas.

Fourth, so far as the term "locomotion" means a change in the position of a material object in physical or geometric space, it fails to cover most of the socio-cultural changes in persons or groups that do not manifest themselves in a change of their location in this geometric space. For instance, an emotional change in an individual from hate to love; or the social degradation of Czar Nicolas II from the position of czar into that of an imprisoned criminal in his palace, without any notable change of location in physical space. Fifth, so far as these terms are meant to cover all socio-cultural changes, they are entirely unfit for that purpose for the same reason for which the term "black" is unfit to cover all the other colors, "white," "red," "green," etc. Anyone who extends the meaning of "black" to cover all other colors, makes the term "black" meaningless. Meaningless become also the terms "white," "green," "red" and other colors. Anyone who extends the meaning of "locomotion" over all socio-cultural and psychological changes of and in an individual or group makes the term "locomotion" as well as the terms designating the "non-locomotional" changes devoid of any meaning. Insofar he makes disservice to the social and psychological sciences.

Sixth, the cumbersome and aesthetically ugly character of this sort of writing or speaking is obvious. Passages like the quotations cited above offer excellent material for comedy and satire. The comedy would run something like this: "After his deafness Beethoven locomoted himself in promotive interdependence with a few patrons in a contrient interlocking in regard to the non-cohesive and not cathectic critics, toward the goal-directed locomoted structure of his musical reflexes stimulated by the locomotion within the structure of his ears." Or "in March, 1917, the location of Russia locomoted on a two-dimensional plane (surface) from monarchy to republic, with positive cathexis and promotive inducibility of the Provisional government vectorized toward the goal of a democratic regime. In October, 1917, this locomotion was followed by a new locomotion in hodological space, fluid and permeable, along the dimension of Communism, marked by negative cathexis, and contrient inducibility toward a democratic structure of 'groupness,' 'we-ness,' 'valence,' and 'syntality.' "

After the preceding analysis, the following "operational definitions" and propositions speak for themselves, without lengthy comment.

"Cathexis, the attachment to objects which are gratifying and rejection of those which are noxious, lies at the root of the selective nature of action."[14]

> [Organism] "cathects particular objects. . . ." "Cognition and cathexis are simultaneously given and only analytically separable." "A cathexis cannot be evaluated except insofar as the object cathected is cognized in its patterned relationships to other cathected objects." "The shape of the cathexis belief attaching the various types of goal object (arrayed along a given generalization dimension) to the gratification end of a matrix. . . ." "A liked entity is said to have positive cathexis; whereas a disliked entity is

said to have negative cathexis." " 'Value' in one sense is synonymous with 'cathexis' and 'valence' and, in the other sense, with 'cathected entity' and 'object with valence.' "[15]

> With regard to the actor our interest is organized about the cognitive, cathectic and evaluative modes of his orientation.[16]

The meaning of the Greek word *kathexis* is "holding," "retention." This meaning was changed by S. Freud into the psychoanalytical meaning of the investment of emotional significance in an activity, object, or idea, and of the charge of psychic (libidinal) energy so invested. This Freudian meaning of "cathexis" is again changed by the authors quoted above, who have given the term a wide range of different meanings. In their use, it can now mean a mere liking of pleasurable things and the disliking of painful things or stimuli (or the old notion of seeking for pleasure and avoiding pain); and elsewhere it means something more complex: J. Bentham's "moral utilitarian arithmetic" as a rational (cognitive) evaluation of various phenomena from the standpoint of the comparative purity, duration, intensity, etc., of the pleasures and pains these phenomena produce. In one place, the authors' cathexis is something very different from cognition and evaluation; in another place it is something identical with them. And so on. Covering a wide range of different phenomena and processes, the term becomes extremely vague and foggy. In addition to these defects, the term in all the different meanings it is given by the authors remains purely parasitic: it does not help to clarify the meanings of other terms, but itself needs other terms like "attachment to the pleasurable and rejection of the noxious objects" in order to have even a vague and inadequate meaning.

Here are some further examples of "speech disorders" of various kinds.

> An *institution* will be said to be a complex of *institutionalized* role integrates which is of strategic structural significance in the social system in question.[17]

Besides "dumping together" a series of complex and poorly defined words, this definition of an institution has the additional striking virtue of being perfectly tautological: "institution" is "institutionalized role-integrates." A wonderfully elegant and precise definition!

Still more marvelous are the following "operational" definitions and statements.

> The images may be ordered, or located, quite differently along the respective different generalization dimensions of the different *matrices*. . . . The strength of the valence on the percept of, say, a given food will be a function of the general need-push for food activated by the given controlling matrix plus the degree of cathexis to the particular variety of food as determined by the shape of the generalization fork. . . .
> The strength of a field force is directly proportional to the product of the need-push and the determining valence in question and inversely proportional to the square of the behavior space distance between the region of the behaving self at the moment and the region of the corresponding valence. . . .
> In considering the operational identification of a locomotion it must be emphasized that . . . a locomotion is a purely hypothetical construct (an intervening variable). It is correlated with a behavior, but is not the behavior itself.[18]

Considering that neither matrix, nor valence, nor behavioral space, nor the field of forces, nor the force, nor the locomotion are even roughly defined, these "operational statements" become mere verbal effusions. They are of three kinds: (a) an imitation of the terminology of the natural sciences, especially of the Newtonian formula of gravitation; and, as we have said, it is an imitation which distorts the meanings of the natural science terms and renders these terms either meaningless or totally fallacious (so far as imitation of the Newtonian formula is concerned); (b) an unscientific predilection toward a use of vague and ponderous terms instead of the clearer, ordinary terms of the social sciences; (c) a most obtuse description of very familiar things much better described by the well defined terms of the social and psychological sciences.

The collection of examples of this sort of speech disorder can be increased by hundreds taken from the two volumes of Parsons and Shils. E. Faris gives a good satirical imitation of this manner of writing in the concluding paragraph of his review of Parsons' *Social System*.

> Knowing you to be an individual in whom the general value-orientation pattern of achievement-universalism, specifity, neutrality, and collective orientation is well established, I have long cathected you and still cathect. Let us look forward to an integration of ego (you) into a role complementary to that of alter (me) in such a way that the common values are internalized in ego's personality and/or alter's, and our respective behaviors come to constitute a complementary role-expectation-sanction system.[19]

## *Verbal Defects: Obtuse Jargon and Sham-Scientific Slang*

Crowning these speech and thought defects, here are a few further examples of perfectly useless home-made terms and of inadequate definitions of the basic psychological phenomena by authors infected by the "operational" and "imitative" speech disorders. "Adience" and "abience" instead of "love" and "dislike." "Enthropy" instead of "habit," "org" and "animorg" instead of "organism" and "animal organism."[20]

*"Consciousness* is an electron-proton aggregation." (A. P. Weiss)

*Consciousness* is "a complex integration and succession of bodily activities which are closely related to or involve the verbal and gestural mechanisms, and hence most frequently come to social expression." (K. S. Lashley)[21]

Emotion is "a particular stimulus-response relationship." (W. S. Hunter)[22]

According to G. Lundberg, the terms "fear," or "hate" can and should be avoided in scientific description; instead, the respective behavior can be operationally described as the "behavior of an object of specified characteristics reacting to a stimulus of specified characteristics within the specified field of forces."[23]

What a beautifully "precise" definition of "fear"! If I had not put at the beginning of these definitions the words "consciousness," "emotion" or "fear," nobody would even guess that such "rubber-stamped" phrases were operational definitions of these terms—to such an extent they are empty of any definite meaning. In a sense, everything in the known universe, including a typewriter, paper, a stone or a plant, is an electro-proton aggregation. Does this mean that typewriter, stone, plant and paper are "consciousness"? A frog or mosquito in action exhibits "a complex integration and succession of bodily activities which involve the vocal or gestural mechanisms." Does this mean that frog or mosquito is "consciousness"? The motions of a striking snake, a ruminating cow, or a buzzing bee show a "particular stimulus-response relationship." Does this mean the snake, the cow, or the bee are "emotions"? The motion of the moon or of a falling stone is "a behavior of an object of specified characteristics," etc. Are then the moon, the rain, the stone, or the bird "fear" or "hate"?

Here are a few further examples of "very, very scientific definitions" of things the reader must guess. A few lines further down he can find the answer and check whether his guess is correct.

X is "a system of energy operating within a field of forces."

Y is "both a mechanical system . . . and a semantic self."

Z is "an organism's selection of particular kinds of material operations to perform upon particular kinds of matter-energy in order to minimize the organism's own probable work."

W is "a movable mathematical point in time-space, in reference to which matter-energy moves in such a way that a physical situation exists in which work is expended in order to preserve a physical system from a final gravitational and electromagnetic equilibrium with the rest of universe."

In an experimental way I asked several scholars and intelligent laymen to guess what these definitions define, and in all cases they completely failed in their guesses.

Now it can be told that X is "organism" in the definition of G. Lundberg, Y is "an individual," Z is "mind," and W is "an organism"—all in definitions of G. K. Zipf.[24]

In the quoted remarks, our apostles of "operational preciseness" and "scientific adequacy" show their utter inability to form even a rough definition of psychosocial phenomena. The very fact that they coin descriptions of this sort in a firm belief they are scientific is a conspicuous "syndrome" of the disturbance of their thought and speech. If the syndrome were infrequent and limited to a few sociologists and psychologists, the matter could have been passed by without discussion and criticism: anomalies now and then occur in almost any field of human activity. Unfortunately, though, speech disorders of this sort are fairly common and during the last few decades have notably increased among social scientists and psychologists of the younger generation. For this reason, the disorders reveal a somewhat abnormal state in today's sociology, psychology, and related sciences. Truly creative minds in the younger generation of sociologists and psychologists have to be warned against this intellectual and verbal degeneration of research in their fields. It can lead only into a dead-end street.

Having thus pointed out two diseases somewhat external to the actual body of the psychosocial sciences, let us pass now to the "internal cancers" eating up the organism proper. These "cancers" are many. Their main forms are physicalism, thought phobia, quantomania, testophrenia, technomania, and so on. Let us examine briefly each of these diseases of the modern psychosocial sciences.

# *Chapter Three*

# The Illusion of Operationalism

*Doing nothing is better than to be busy doing nothing.*
*[Non-operating is better than mal-operating.]*

LAO-TSE

## 1. OPERATIONALISM IN THE NATURAL SCIENCES

Post-Newtonian classical mechanics has systematically used operational method in several ways, particularly for determining the position and motion of material bodies in space and time. Assuming space as isotropic and homogeneous, classical mechanics could determine the position and motion of a material point or body through reference to other material points or bodies, not by locating them in Newtonian "absolute space."

> It is impossible to imagine absolute space. Whoever talks of the absolute space employs words devoid of meaning. . . . Not only are we unable to know the absolute position of an object in space . . . and should talk only of its relative position in regard to other objects; but even the expressions: "the absolute distance of two points" are devoid of any sense; one should talk only about . . . the relationship between two distances.[1]

This relative space can have a meaning only when we have a unit for its measurement. Without such a unit and *the operation of measuring,* neither the position nor the motion of the body can be determined.[2]

> The position of a point (in space) can be determined but in relation to other points arbitrarily chosen as references. . . . In order to be able to refer to it, it is necessary to measure certain distances. To *measure means to take a meter and to cross (walk in) the space (along straight line).* Doing so they assume that the meter does not change in its length during this displacement.[3]

Here, as well as in the treatment of other problems of the natural sciences, the essentials of operational method are clearly defined.

In recent years P. W. Bridgman generalized the nature of operational method in the physical sciences. He contends that it is about the only fruitful method for construction of physical concepts and for scientific study of physical (and also social) phenomena.[4]

> The essential meaning of operationalism in physics is that physical concepts should be defined in terms of actual physical operations. On this view there is no meaning to a concept unless it represents an operation which can be performed in laboratory. Thus the term "pressure of gas" signifies nothing until an operation is described which constitutes the measurement of pressure. When one thinks of pressure one must think of some actual apparatus like glass and rubber tubing, some mercury and operations of using these until one gets a pointer reading called the pressure of gas. [The same standpoint is taken with respect to length, time, velocity, temperature, etc.] [5]

This means that operational method is experimental method *par excellence* and that experimental method in its pure form is identical with operational method. Its enthusiastic apostles contend that only operational method can yield valid results. They believe, further, that no contradiction or fragmentation of knowledge can ever arise in its use and results; that all valid scientific discoveries have been achieved through operational method; that it guarantees a fully adequate knowledge, and has only virtues and no drawbacks.

So heralded by Bridgman and others, operationalism has lured a legion of sociologists and psychologists, wearied by their fruitless search for an easy and reliable method of scientific research in their fields. Its apparent simplicity and prestige made it the God-given answer to their prayers. As usual, without the necessary study of the real nature of operationalism, of its real role in the progress of the natural sciences, of its limitations and doubtful elements, and forgetting the important role of pure intuition, deduction, and nonoperational induction in the progress of science and wisdom, our sociologists, psychologists, and anthropologists were converted into ardent operationalists and began *en masse* to apply operational method in their study of social, cultural, and mental phenomena. A sort of operational orgy rapidly spread throughout these disciplines. The expressions "using operational method," "operational concept and definition," "operational theory," and so on, have become magical catchwords monotonously canted for the resolution of all controversies. "The primary advantage of operational definitions lies in the unification of science and the resolution of controversy," states E. G. Boring. Operationism is "the revolution that will put an end to the possibility of revolution in psychology by its rigor of definition which silences useless controversy," cants another psychologist.[6]

Like devotees of any cult, the operationalists firmly believe in the infallibility of operational incantations. In spite of the fact that their operational manipulations often resemble the "scientific methods" of "the scientists" in *Gulliver's Travels,* they continue to sing their operational hymns and monotonously mumble their operational "mantras."

If the psychosocial operationalists had studied more carefully the nature, the role, the limitations and dangers of operational method in the natural sciences, and if they had a better knowledge of logic, mathematics, epistemology, and history of scientific discoveries, they would have avoided most of their blunders and have learned the following sobering verities about operational method in the natural sciences.

First, many experimental (operational) discoveries in the natural sciences have proved to be contradictory or questionable, and the contradictions and errors have ordinarily been removed only through use of the nonoperational methods of logical deduction and mathematical inference working in cooperation with supralogical and suprasensory intuition.[7] It happened, for instance, that the experimental results were contradictory and questionable in regard to: the Compton effect, the use of magneto-optic effects for chemical analysis and the detection of isotopes, the value of the charge on the electron, and so on. "Where in all this is the definiteness, objectivity, and freedom from inconsistency which are so loudly boasted for purely experimental operations?"[8]

Second, experiments or operations performed for the sake of experiments or operations are irrelevant and meaningless. Only experimental operations performed for the sake of proving or disproving certain ideas (which are nonoperational) can be of evidential value.

Third, any operational experiment deals with a narrow range of experience or reality. As such it can give but fragmentary results significant only from, and for, the standpoint of the operation performed. Experimental verification of the same hypotheses by the use of different operations yields equally fragmentary results and a different set of notions. As a result, in a study of the same problem there would be as many different results and concepts as there are different operations. None of them can give a general formula, concept, or uniformity valid for all the different operational manipulations used. Thus, the concept of the pressure of gas, operationally measured by the ordinary U-tube, is different from the concept of the pressure of gas as measured by an ionization gauge, since the operations are quite different. The concept of temperature would be different, if defined only through operational measurement by different thermometers. The difference between the respective operational procedures would make it impossible to set up an absolute thermodynamic scale of temperature independent of the particular thermometric substance and operations used. And so on.[9] Thus a strictly consistent use of operational method gives only bits of information and notions valid, at best, only for the specific operation used. In no way can the bits be of a general significance. In other words, operational method cannot yield any general formula, concept, or uniformity. Alone, it leads only to fragmentation of knowledge in the form of different operational concepts, theories, and causal laws.

> [If] a concept is synonymous with the corresponding set of operations, . . . there must be an infinitude of discrete concepts. Think, for instance, of all the different operations that have gone into a study of learning. To prevent senseless pluralism operations have to be grouped by classes, and there is ultimately no way of grouping them except by relational [theoretical] thought. The most austere operationist communicates not operations but a prior concept, for operational symbolizing depends upon prior ideas of entities and relations that are symbolized.[10]

Fourth, operationalism "implies the abandonment of the method of theoretical physics which has on the whole proved itself enormously successful in the description of physical phenomena." It is this—mathematical and logical—theorizing, in cooperation with intuition and imagination (tested *a posteriori* by experiment), that has contributed the most general concepts, theories, hypotheses, and uniformities in the physical sciences. This theoretical thought alone has been able to suggest, sift, reconcile, and generalize the results of operational experiments. For instance, in the cases mentioned

> the concept of pressure is derived from the theory of mechanics and it is on purely theoretical grounds that we decide that various methods may be used to assign numerical values to the symbol representing it. It has been and should be the physicist's steady purpose to keep the concepts from a too close association with a particular operation. . . .[11]

> Real entities have often been inferred from lacunae in natural order before their existence could be certified by the standards of empirical science. Elements were predicted from gaps in the periodic table, planets because of irregular movements of known heavenly bodies; radio waves owed their conception as real constituents of nature to the simplicity of the equations of electromagnetism which implied their existence. The most significant advances of modern physics were anticipated by conjectures. . . . Cases in point are the discoveries of the positive electron, the neutron and several types of meson. The whole case of the neutrino rests upon [theoretical considerations]: this particle simply *has* to exist if the principles of energy, momentum and spin are to be retained. Yet it has never been seen in the sense that other elementary particles have been observed.[12]

This does not mean emancipation of theoretical physics or any other science from the test of experiment. The intuitional principle must be tested and cleared by a logical or mathematical analysis of its meaning; then all the deductions from it must be inferred and these deductions must be verified (when possible) by an adequate experimental test.

> What we are insisting on is the right, which has indeed justified itself repeatedly in the past, of using in the construction of theories, concepts which are not defined directly in the terms of laboratory operations, [like the concepts of the potential energy function of classical mechanics, or the electric and magnetic fields in the electron theory of matter] concepts which are literally defined in terms of equations their representative symbols are assumed to satisfy.[13]

Even in the laboratory equations which constitute physical "laws," not all the quantities entering are operationally measurable. Thus in the law of motion for a freely falling body ($S = \frac{1}{2}GT^2$) the quantity G gets its meaning not from any direct or operational measurement, but solely because of its appearance in the formula. We must use the formula to calculate it—another indication of the importance of theory in every experimental operation.

Fifth, if the operationalists had really studied how an overwhelming majority of the most important scientific discoveries, technological inventions, the greatest religious, philosophical and ethical verities, and the highest artistic achievements really originated and grew, they would have learned, first, that they were born in intuition; second, that the intuitional idea was developed and elaborated by logical or mathematical thought which was used in making all the necessary deductions or consequences from the intuitional (or "postulational") principle; and finally, that in the field of science these deductions were tested by again rationally devised experimental, inductive, or operational method.[14]

In mechanics, out of the intuitional, unelaborated initial notions of space and time the more precise, sophisticated and abstract concepts of velocity and acceleration are constructed by logico-mathematical thought, and these and other deductions are tested by again rationally designed experiments.[15] The experimental or operational procedure (as a part of experimental method) is thus only a phase in this three-stage (intuitional, mathematico-logical, experimental) process of birth and growth common to practically all great creative achievements in all fields of creativity from science to religion and the fine arts.

We can sum up the situation by the statement that "though operationalism casts a valuable light on the problems of physics, it betrays certain weaknesses [and very serious limitations] which make its thoroughgoing application to physics of questionable utility. Certainly it would demand the complete scrapping of the well-recognized methodology of physics. The success already achieved by the latter will render most physicists cautious about sacrificing theoretical physics on the altar of operationalism." [16]

Without the cooperation of intuition and logico-mathematical thought, the operational procedures can not discover mathematical or logical inferences, and could not have discovered the bulk of the basic physical verities beginning with the Newtonian or Galilean laws and ending with the principles of relativity, quantum mechanics, uncertainty, and many of the concepts and equations of nuclear physics. To abandon intuitional insight and logical thought in favor of operational method would amount to castrating creative thought generally, and in science particularly. Without intuition and logic no real progress in science, religion, philosophy, ethics, and the fine arts has been or will be possible.

## 2. Sham Operationalism in the Psychosocial Sciences

If operationalism in the physical sciences is, thus, of limited value and applicability, its limitations in the social and psychological disciplines are even greater. This is confirmed, first, by the queer nature of what operational sociologists and psychologists claim to be their operational method. Even the operational physicists are surprised at the odd distortion of operational method made by their followers in psychosocial studies. Here are some typical examples of "operational definitions" offered by sociologists and psychologists.

*Operational definitions of "happiness or adjustment in marriage."* Clifford Kirkpatrick operationally defines "marital maladjustment" as "that quality in marriage which causes one close friend to classify the couple as maladjusted." Marital adjustment is crudely defined in a similar way.[17] Thus if a scholar wants to give an "operational" definition of happiness or "adjustment" in marriage, all he has to do is, first, to ask a friend of the married couple whether the marriage is "adjusted" or "maladjusted"; second, without any verification, to accept this opinion as valid and scientific; and, third, to build upon it a huge statistical superstructure of measurements and predictions of success or failure in marriage. This is a marvelously easy way indeed of finding a scientific answer to that troublesome problem of happiness or adjustment upon which "arm-chair philosophers" have wasted so much effort and thought! Following this "operational method" one can obtain an even more "precise" definition (and "measurement") of marriage happiness by asking the friend of the married couple more specific questions as to whether the marriage is "very happy," "happy," "average," "unhappy," or "very unhappy," and by, then, simply registering these precise revelations of the friend as an infallible scientific truth, exactly defined by the refined operational method!

Other investigators (L. M. Terman, J. Bernard, E. W. Burgess, L. S. Cottrell, and others)[18] use a somewhat different operational technique for their diagnosis of the "adjusted" or the "very happy," "happy," "average," "unhappy," and "very unhappy" marriage. Instead of asking the opinion of a friend of the married couple, these researchers prefer going and asking the married couple itself a lot of questions (by questionnaire or interview) as to whether their marriage is "very happy," "happy," "unhappy," and so on. Here, the investigators believe they have secured results of a very precise nature and of great scientific validity because of the infallibility of the untested and unverified answers given by the couple! Again, what a wondrous way of defining, diagnosing, and unraveling the mystery of happiness or unhappiness in marriage! One can but wonder why this easy "operational" method of securing valid knowledge was not discovered by the legion of social thinkers of the preceding centuries! One must also marvel why economists do not use this method to arrive at operational definitions of "capital," "surplus value," "economic equilibrium," "the law of demand and supply," "marginal utility," "the law of diminishing returns," and other basic economic concepts. To collect the answers to these questions from one person, or a few, is surely much easier than to follow the technique of painstaking mathematical, logical, and empirical analysis used by practically all eminent economists. One can still more deeply sympathize with a physician who uses a thermometer to determine his patient's temperature or a cardiograph to diagnose his heart-activity, instead of adopting the much simpler and more infallible operation of just asking the patient or his friend whether the former's temperature and heart-activity are "normal" or "abnormal." The same goes for the physicist, chemist, mathematician, and biologist who "perversely" prefer to spend their time and energies in using mathematical, logical, and experimental (instrumental) methods for defining their concepts, making their diagnoses, and unraveling their uniformities, instead of merely asking the opinions of a few—or many—persons about "quanta," "the principle of relativity," "the principle of uncertainty," or the composition of a certain chemical compound.

If the operational methods of the psychosocial operationalists quoted are scientific, then the integral methods of economists, physicists, chemists, biologists, and physicians are certainly unscientific, for the latter's methods and techniques have hardly anything in common with the "scientific," "operational" methods of the investigators of marriage "happiness" or "unhappiness."

Another example of operational method in the psychosocial sciences is given by the group of social scientists headed by S. A. Stouffer. In their study of correlation between the educational level of samples from the U.S. armed forces and their combat performance (in their results they applied the categories "below average," "average" and "above average"), they neither directly observed nor scientifically tested the combat performance of their samples, nor evaluated it themselves on the basis of any objective, verifiable data. Instead, they simply took the opinion of some army authorities without the slightest checking of its correctness.[19] Here, as in many other points of their study, they do not apply the most elementary rule of the scientist—not to accept any dogmatic statement without testing its accuracy. In place of this elementary scientific precaution, they simply swallow estimates made by largely unknown persons and arrived at by ways largely unknown to the authors.

Their acceptance of the combat performance variable is an "operation" of pure, unadulterated faith in the infallibility of evaluations made by largely unknown army authorities. Such a faith in no way differs from any dogmatic belief in untested propositions. In their naked reality these "operational rites" are but the *operations of collecting untested opinions* of either the married couples or their friends, or of the army authorities, or of somebody else. Instead of directly studying the phenomena, and in lieu of making their own analysis and definition of the phenomena, they simply "pass the buck" of study and definition to somebody else. The substitution of somebody else's opinions for a real study of the phenomena goes so far that many operationalists seldom come in direct touch with facts pertinent to the inquiry. They rarely observe the married couples or the combat performance of the soldiers. Even their "hearsay" material is ordinarily collected not by the investigators themselves, but by their assistants and hired pollsters. Imagine physicists or chemists operating in this fashion and then tabulating the collected opinions and giving the results in the form of various statistical tables and other paraphernalia to point to the "objectivity" of their "scientific" and "operational" techniques. Luckily there are no physicists or chemists of this kind. Unfortunately, in the psychosocial disciplines there is still a vast army of operationalists of this sort.

Besides the substitution of collected opinions for scientific study of the facts, the psychosocial operationalists unavoidably make other dogmatic assumptions and subjective evaluations. In the study of marriage happiness they assume that the answers to questions about "table manners," "kind of recreation of the spouses," "the ways of dealing with the in-laws," "frequency of kissing the spouse," and so on, are the criteria of marriage happiness or unhappiness, regardless of the manner of kissing or saying "good morning" or golf-playing. Our daily experience tells us that there are quite different types of kisses: the Judas kiss, the habitual kiss, the placating kiss, the deceiving kiss, and so on. For this reason, if, with ten couples, the frequency of kissing a spouse is the same, this in no way means the identity or equality of the kiss-unit among these couples. Therefore, it cannot be used as an identical quantitative unit of marriage happiness among all these couples. The same is true of other criteria of marriage adjustment. By equalizing all kissings, or all external table manners, among all the couples, our operationalists *make equal what is unequal,* and vice versa. Unfortunately, by these blunders the errors of our operationalists are not exhausted.

Having collected the *opinions* of their interviewees, and having accepted them as the true description or definition of the facts studied, the operationalists must tabulate these opinions, score them, find their interrelationships, and express these in the form of some equation or formula, such as a coefficient of correlation. All these operations inevitably involve a series of arbitrary (subjective) decisions. What weight or how many scoring points are to be assigned to each of numerous criteria of marriage happiness (to "table manners," to "kissing," to "golf or bridge playing," and so on) has to be and is decided quite arbitrarily by the investigators or by some "experts" to whom they may "pass the buck" of weighing, ranking, and assigning the score points. Moreover, since the "experts" do not have any objective basis for their assignments, their opinions remain as arbitrary as those of the investigators themselves. The same is true of the verdict of the queried majority, because what is true or false cannot be decided by majority vote. The history of science and human cognition is crowded with instances of ignorant majorities supporting false theories, wrong ideologies, and superstitious beliefs; and of creative minorities discovering new—and often unpopular—verities. Another series of arbitrary decisions has to be made at almost every step in "processing" the raw hearsay material into the "polished" form of precise-looking tables, numerical indexes, and so on.

"Operations" of this sort are a pure travesty of genuine scientific investigation.

*Another variety of operational definition in the psychosocial disciplines is represented by the concepts, definitions, and formulae transcribed and imported from the natural sciences.* In physics and other natural sciences these concepts, formulae, and propositions have definite meaning and precise measurability. Constructed for the study of physical but not psychosocial phenomena, the conceptual framework of the physical sciences is rarely applicable to the cognition, measurement, and prediction of psychosocial phenomena. For this reason, *many physical concepts and proposi-*

*tions "operationally transcribed and imported" into the psychosocial studies become meaningless.*

The "system of operationally defined concepts for sociology" of S. C. Dodd offers a typical example of such concepts. Following the poorest variety of the numerous examples of "social physicists" of preceding centuries,[20] Dodd introduces the concepts of "time, space, population," and "all characteristics of people or of their environment" as the basic concepts of his operational system of sociology. He does not derive these concepts from any operational procedure of his own, nor does he try to define them in any way; instead, he simply takes the terms with their symbols (like T for time) from the physical sciences and concludes that by such a transference he has satisfactorily solved the problem of operationally defined concepts for sociology. How "successful" this solution is one can see from Dodd's definitions of "the static and dynamic data," of "societal change," and "societal force":

> All static or timeless data may be represented by a zero exponent on the time component, . . . $T^0 = 1$. Dynamic data involve an exponent unequal to zero. Societal durations as in ages of institutions, of customs, or of persons, may be represented by an exponent of plus one, $T^{+1}$. Societal change, or process, always involves something happening in a period of time. The speed of such change, or process, is the amount of change divided by the period. Thus all change involves $1/T$ or $T^{-1}$.
>
> Acceleration is defined by dividing the speed, by the overall time period. The formula of it is $1/T^2$ or $T^{-1}$. A societal force may be defined as an acceleration of change in a population and may be measured, wherever the change is measurable, as the product of the acceleration and the population accelerated. In symbolic terms, if I represents the change, P, the population changed, and F, the societal force, $F = T^{-2}IP$ = societal force (Eq. 2).[21]

However impressive this simplified transcription of physical concepts and their symbols looks, in application to "societal" time, duration, change, acceleration, and force, these definitions are empty and useless. For *they do not give any real unit* for the measurement of societal change or of its acceleration, velocity or force. All these symbols ($T^0$, $T^{+1}$, $T^{-1}$, and so on) are no help at all for determining in what, for instance, the change of American culture during the last fifty years consisted, how great the "amount" of this change was, how fast it proceeded, and whether it was accelerated or slowed down. Likewise, Dodd's definition of societal force, having no real unit of force, is perfectly helpless in determining the extent of the societal force of religion, of the economic factor, of sex and hunger, of the law-norm and tragic drama, and in determining which of these "societal forces" is greater than the other, and under what conditions. Nor does it tell us what sort of "change in population" we have to measure: birth or death or marriage rates? suicide or morbidity? numerical increase or decrease of the population? changes in population density? intelligence? school education or criminality? changes in the population's racial, sex, and age composition? in the standard of living? religion? fine arts? laws? In brief, the supposedly "operational" definition of "societal force" is completely disoperative. Also empty of any meaning are such expressions as "the product of the acceleration and the population accelerated," and pseudomathematical "shorthand symbols" like $F = T^{-2}IP$. These terms cannot be solved by any mathematician because they do not contain any mathematical unit, number, or measurable quantity at all.

> Assuming that a social force is defined as F = PA [P is the number of people changed and A is the amount of acceleration; hence social force F = PA], how can one identify the existence of social force, such as the growing consciousness of war in this country, from this formula? The answer cannot consist of multiplying the number of persons in the United States (P) by some index of acceleration (A), such as the change in the number of war bonds sold, and stating that the result, F = AP, is the social force, consciousness of war. Yet, this or similar results are the only answers possible if we follow Dodd[22] [Shanas correctly remarks].

The same goes for others of Dodd's operational concepts and pseudo-equations, as well as for similar imitations of the physical sciences by a legion of psychosocial operationalists.[23] Further on, I shall give a more thorough criticism of this operational aping of the physical sciences. For the present we can pass on to a brief examination of the operational method in the psychosocial sciences as it is defined by the operational sociologists, psychologists, and anthropologists.

According to Dodd:

> A definition *(genus)* is an operational definition *(species and definiendum)* to the extent that the definer (a) specifies the procedure *(differentia)* including the material used for identifying or generating the definiendum, and (b) finds high reliability *(differentia)* for his definition.
>
> . . . A procedure may be defined as any human action (genus) to the extent that such action is a means to the end which is communicable by the

author. . . . Such communicated purposeful actions are called "a procedure." . . . "Reliability" may be defined as any index measuring the degree of agreement among reobservations of the same phenomenon. Unreliability is the lack of such agreement, or variation among reobservations. . . . The degree of reliability is measurable by some appropriate statistical index.

[Finally,] . . . the purpose here is to contribute to the general function of science—namely, the predicting and controlling of phenomena.[24]

A few brief remarks, plus a few examples of "communicated purposeful actions showing a perfect degree of agreement among the reobservations," netting non-sense, are sufficient to dispose of these cumbersome and foggy "operational definitions operationally defined."

First, let us dispose of predictability and control as the criteria of scientific propositions. Here, our operationalists repeat, in distorted form, A. Comte's statement: *"Savoir pour prévoir, prévoir pour pouvoir"*—without mentioning Comte, as usual. So far as predictability means a prediction of something in future time, it is no necessary criterion for scientific propositions. Statements like "Napoleon was defeated at Waterloo", "Julius Caesar was murdered", "Greece of the second century B.C. experienced a low birth-rate and depopulation"—and practically all accurate statements concerning the history of individuals, groups, nations, the earth, and the solar system—are statements about the past and not about the future. As such they do not predict anything, and do not have anything to do with prediction. And yet, even our operationalists cannot deny that most historical propositions are accurate and valid, that is, scientific.

Again, practically all the propositions of mathematics (like "2 plus 2 = 4") are timeless in their validity. They do not aim to predict specifically the future event or some future validity; they are valid for the past, the present, and the future. And here again, so far as our operationalists use prediction to mean specifically foretelling the future, none of the mathematical verities satisfy their operational criterion for scientific propositions. Therefore, the operationalists must either declare all mathematical propositions unscientific or abandon this criterion. In spite of their "reckless bravery" the operationalists dare not choose the first alternative; therefore, they have to abandon their "predictability" as the most important characteristic of scientific propositions. This argument will be further developed in a subsequent chapter on predictability and scientific theory.

This is still more true in regard to *control.* The essence and, if you please, the aim of all scientific propositions is to be true or valid, regardless of any efficacious control over the phenomena studied for our utilitarian purposes. Some scientific verities help in obtaining such a control, some others do not; and the non-helping verities remain as valid as the helping ones. Control is a by-product, not the essence, of scientific verities. A by-product cannot be regarded as the necessary criterion of verity. Most of the propositions of historical science give hardly any control over the historical processes. And yet, they remain scientific statements.

The tables of multiplication and all valid mathematical equations are scientific, no matter whether or not they are utilized for the purposes of control. The same is true of all verities. Many of them are not used for the purpose of control for a long time. And still, in spite of this, they remain valid. And *vice versa.* Many social phenomena have been subjected to very efficacious controls based on wrong theories and ideologies. In spite of their fallacious racial or Marxian ideologies, Hitler and Stalin efficiently controlled many political processes and the behavior of their subjects. And so did many a government, business concern, religious group, or labor union. To repeat, we must not take a by-product of a verity for its essence; nor should we elevate fallacious ideologies to the rank of the true theories merely because they help in the coercive control of social processes.

Again, *communicability* can in no way be taken for the inherent characteristic of the scientific proposition. It, likewise, cannot secure valid results in the pursuit of truth. Simple but invalid propositions are often more communicable than complex verities. Otherwise, we would not have millions of fallacious notions, beliefs, and superstitions endlessly flourishing in the course of human history. Particularly complex verities like most of the propositions of advanced mathematics, or those of the profound religious, philosophical, and aesthetic systems, are much less communicable to the large masses than vulgar art values and superstitious and primitive beliefs. As a rule, within a given time the less adequate and more primitive ideas in all fields of knowledge become more rapidly and widely diffused than the more complex and adequate theories in the same field. Elementary mathematics, physics, sociology, music and literature have been more communicable and have been more successfully diffused than advanced mathematics, physics, sociology, or more refined music and literature.[25] In spite of their lesser communicability, we cannot declare the more valid propositions (or more refined aesthetic achievements) less scientific and valuable than the more fallacious but more communicable propositions and achievements. Otherwise, to be consistent, our operationalists would have to give scientific priority to the more communicable but less valid propositions. In so doing, they certainly would have no following of real scientists and thinkers. Their only choice is to abandon their fallacy.

Finally, if Isaac Newton (or any discoverer of verity) just thought through his *Principia* but never published it, his principles of mechanics and calculus would still remain true, in spite of not being communicated to others. Communication is the process by which a discovered verity or falsity is socialized, but it is not the essence of either. Communication is the last of the three stages (conception, objectification and socialization) through which any new idea passes in its birth and growth in the empirical socio-cultural world,[26] but it is not the necessary trait of scientific verity. Here again our operationalists blunder in taking communication as the inherent criterion of valid propositions. Communication is not only something external to the verity but, as a matter of fact, is associated with error no less frequently than with truth.

Finally, Dodd's criterion of *reliability* for operational propositions is also unreliable in the form in which it is formulated. Ptolemy's cosmography was operationally tested and the solar system was re-observed many times by pre-Copernican cosmographers who, for many centuries, unanimously agreed on the correctness of the Ptolemaic cosmography. And yet, this agreement did not prevent the Ptolemaic system from being inadequate and "unreliable." A multitude of mathematical astrologers in Hellenistic Egypt unanimously ascribed an increase of sexual perversions to certain configurations of the heavenly bodies.[27] And yet, in spite of their unanimity and their complex mathematical calculations these *mathematici* were quite wrong. On the other hand, the cosmographic system of Aristarchus of Samos was nearer to the more adequate Copernican system. And yet, for centuries Aristarchus' system was regarded as wrong and was forgotten by almost all the Greek, Roman, and mediaeval cosmographers. Millions of believers in certain magical or miraculous phenomena, using the same magical operational procedures, observe and re-observe the same phenomena and unanimously agree on the perfect validity of their beliefs. Such believers have existed in all populations and at all periods of history.

And yet, we know that these "operationalists" have often been wrong. The history of human cognition is filled with facts of this kind. These facts demonstrate the essential inadequacy of criteria such as Dodd's for determining the reliability of propositions. Mere agreement among the observers and re-observers of the same phenomena does not guarantee the validity of their conclusions.

Still less reliable are the *statistical* coefficients of reliability stressed by Dodd and many other psychologists and social scientists. Later on, in chapters seven and eight, it will be shown that statistical formulae for determining the "significance" or "reliability" of quantitative propositions have very little reliability so far as the verity of a proposition is concerned. Their "misleading preciseness" often leads to wrong conclusions, especially in the investigation of causal and functional relationships between phenomena. This, in fact, is one reason why an enormous percentage of modern statistical studies in the psychosocial sciences have been either sterile or wrong in unraveling causal or probabilistic problems.

Another kind of defect in operational definitions is exemplified by S. A. Stouffer's definition of "opportunity" and especially of "the intervening opportunities" in the phenomena of migration or territorial mobility. Having designated by the symbols $\Delta y$ "the number of persons moving from an origin to a circular band of width $\Delta s$" and by $x$ "the number of intervening opportunities, that is the cumulated number of opportunities between the origin and distance $s$," Stouffer continues: "opportunities must be precisely defined in any employment of the theory. The particular operational definition appropriate will depend on the type of social situation investigated. This is the hardest problem in any practical application."[28] So far, neither the concept of "opportunities" nor that of "intervening opportunities" is defined in this operational definition. Or they are defined tautologically: "intervening opportunities are intervening opportunities," or what one finds in the social situation investigated. They seem to be somewhat more definitely symbolized by the formula: $\frac{\Delta y}{\Delta s} = \frac{a \Delta x}{x \Delta s}$ but as long as $x$ remains undefined, the formula remains indeterminate. This is confirmed by the fact that, in the actual computation of the expected and observed movement of families (not individuals) from one census tract to another in Cleveland, "intervening opportunities" are replaced by distance-measurements, in terms of distance bands, except that portion of the movement in which the factors of the $15 and $19 rentals are considered. Thus, the supposedly "new" factor of "intervening opportunities" turns out to be the familiar factor of distance and its attractions, and Stouffer's "new" formula becomes a mere variation of several familiar formulae of migration or mobility, in which, under the terms of "attractions" and "advantages," or, in negative terms, of "obstacles," the factor of intervening opportunities was well considered.[29]

The same can be said of the study in which M. L. Bright and D. S. Thomas tried to apply Stouffer's formula and technique.[30]

Now, why this quite familiar kind of statistical study is called "operational" is unclear. It has no specific traits distinct from those of the ordinary type of statistical study. Nor, as we have seen, can it claim to offer a new idea, a new method, a new formula, or any special superiority in comparison with many similar statistical studies. If anything, it is more indeterminate in the definition of its variables than many other studies, and yields as big a discrepancy between the calculated and the observed results. In addition, it clandestinely replaces its "intervening opportunities" by mere "distance."

To sum up: if the only reason for calling this sort of study "operational" is its *quantitative* character, then operational method is something very, very old because quantitative studies of psychosocial phenomena are very, very old. If "operational" means that a given study is *repeatable* in its data, method, technique, and reasoning, then many qualitative studies, even many fallacious ones, are also repeatable. For this reason, such repeatable studies—whether quantitative or qualitative, correct or fallacious—are also "operational" in this sense. Such repeatable investigations are again very old; therefore, "operational method" is also very old and cannot claim the privilege of being a new method and technique. If we take the "operational method" in all these senses, it becomes a sort of money, circulated on the intellectual stock market without its real value being known.

A further demonstration of the vagueness, meaninglessness, and defectiveness of operational method is given by Hornell Hart in his study: "Toward an Operational Definition of the Term 'Operation'."[31] Hart states that in some 140 papers on operationism the basic term "operation" remains operationally undefined and devoid of any precision. Hart groups various meanings of the term into the following four definitions: (1) "Operation: An action"; (2) P. Bridgman's definition: "Operation is . . . any conscious activity" which Bridgman later qualifies as "any consciously directed and repeatable activity"; (3) "any action of a biological organism, performed by voluntary (striated) muscles"; (4) "any physical or mental change which operator produces intentionally, in himself or in his environment."

Having "operationally" tested two groups of judges to find out which of these four definitions of "operation" is accepted as correct by the majority of the judges (80 per cent or more), he reaches the following conclusions: (1) the basic term of operationalists, "operation," remains either undefined by them or is given different meanings; this deprives the operationists of the right to claim a particular precision for their method, for their concepts, and for theories they have built by the operational method; (2) "the moderate operational definition [No. 4 above] is the most reliable," i.e., is accepted by the majority of the judges; (3) "Bridgman's definition [No. 2 above] is 'less reliable,' i.e., is accepted by lesser number of the judges than the moderate operational definition." (4):

> It seems reasonable to raise the question of whether any considerable number of those who have published or read articles on operationism in learned periodicals have understood each other more than a minor fraction of the time. The doubt arises persistently whether even the leaders have achieved, and consistently maintained, clearcut, operational concepts at crucial points.[32]

Many identify "operationalism" with "measurement." As we have seen, such an identification is untenable. According to some operationalists (S. Stouffer, K. Lewin, J. F. Brown, and many others) there are a number of qualitative phenomena which cannot be quantified and measured at the present time. In spite of being nonmeasurable and qualitative, such phenomena can, nevertheless, be studied by operational method according to these researchers. On the other hand, measurement of many social phenomena (like a census of population, births, deaths and marriages, or the computation of taxes, income and expense, of the size of military force or the number of genuflections or other religious and magical operations, short prayers or words pronounced) was practiced in the ancient past among several pre-literate groups, in Ancient Egypt, Babylon, China and

Rome. If operational method means measurement and computation, then its partisans must recognize its hoary age and abandon their claim to its being a newly discovered method. If they insist on its recent discovery, they cannot identify it with the operation of measurement. In both cases they become entangled in a series of self-contradictions which are, manifestly, illogical and contrary to scientific method. When, trying to escape these self-contradictions, they endeavor to measure the nonmetric and nonmeasurable qualities, to quantify the phenomena which are nonscalar (at the present time), they commit, as we shall see further, the grossest logical, mathematical, and empirical blunders.

Finally, when we examine operationalist methods and techniques for the study of empirical phenomena, as we did above, we find the operationalists using, as a rule, the nonoperational techniques and exploiting little of their magical operational approach.

When Dodd, Lundberg, Burgess, Stouffer, and others, turn to a study of human values, they do not show any trace of using operational method for either their classification of values, or the construction of their definitions, or for discovering the characteristics and interrelationships of their subject matter. Instead, they use, often in rather unskilled fashion, traditional Aristotelian logic (especially Dodd, who is fond of the Aristotelian formula for making definitions: *definitio fit per genus et differentiam specificam*—define by indicating the *genus* and the specific *differentia* of the species) and other common methods of scientific investigation with a special penchant for the questionnaire-interview technique and statistical "measurements." [33]

The same is true of practically all operationalists in the field of *Group Dynamics*.[34] Although they frequently declare their "oath of allegiance" to the operational method, their studies show hardly any traces of the operational virtue they so enthusiastically profess. The same can be said of a legion of operational psychologists, sociologists, psychiatrists, cultural anthropologists, "operational" philosophers, theologians, prognosticators, numerologists, and would-be directors of historial processes. Rarely does one find in their studies of socio-cultural and psychological phenomena a real use of operational method. And when some of them try to apply it, they most often come to grief. This infrequent use of their magical method, and the deplorable results when it is used, are further proofs of its limited applicability and of its almost unlimited danger in the study of psychosocial and cultural phenomena. Even when we identify operational method with experimental method, the applicability of a true experimental method in these fields is, as we shall see in all subsequent chapters, very limited. Most of the studies now euphemistically called "experimental" are in fact far from being such.

I, for one, cannot see how we can operationally define and study such phenomena as the state; the nation; Taoism or Christianity; Classicism or Romanticism in the fine arts; epic, comedy or tragedy; love or hatred; happiness or despair; or, as a matter of fact, any of the events of the whole past history of mankind. These historical events in all their uniqueness (for instance, the murder of Julius Caesar) have already happened and cannot be reproduced in any present or future "operational" setting. For this reason they cannot be "researched" operationally. On the other hand, the events of history and other phenomena indicated have been fairly successfully understood by the nonoperational methods: by supralogical and suprasensory intuition; by empathy and introspectively co-living the experiences of historical persons and groups (Cooley's dramatic method); by logical and mathematical analysis; by all the forms of empirical induction and observation—by historical observation and description (case method), by the collection and analysis of relevant statistical data, by direct individual-and-collective observation, and now and then by something similar to experimental method—and by the combined totality of all these approaches. That the operational approach can add anything to these nonoperational methods in the study of most mental and sociocultural phenomena remains very doubtful. The *onus probandi*—the burden of proving—the fruitfulness of operational method lies on the believers in this "new magic." So far they have been unable to submit even remotely significant evidence for the all-resolving, all-discovering and never fallible properties of their new idol. Until this is done, we must disbelieve their contention that operational dogma is *the scientific credo par excellence.* In its present form operationalism in psychosocial studies is either a meaningless term or a new term for very old methods.[35]

# *Chapter Four*

# Testomania

*. . . Man is a marvelous vain, fickle, and unstable subject, and on whom it is very hard to form any certain and uniform judgment.* Michel de Montaigne.

## 1. The Age of Testocracy

Half a century has elapsed since the publication in 1905 by Alfred Binet and Th. Simon of the first series of their intelligence tests.[1] Their pioneering endeavor started an epidemic of all sorts of tests of psychosocial properties of individuals, groups, and cultural phenomena. Hundreds of competent and incompetent psychologists, psychiatrists, anthropologists, sociologists, and educators began to manufacture their own tests and to apply them to hundreds of thousands of human beings, to social groups, and to cultural phenomena. Now and then the manufacturers of intelligence or aptitude tests did not know the ABC's of psychology or sociology; and once in a while they did not have intelligence enough to understand their own incompetence. In spite of these obstacles, multitudes of "testers" have succeeded in selling their products to their fellow-scholars, educators, governmental agencies, business and labor managers, and to the public at large. At the present time in the Western countries almost every individual is tested from the cradle to the grave, before and after the important events in his life. He is given a battery of various tests after his birth, in his nursery school and kindergarten, in his elementary school, high school, and college, before and after his draft into the armed forces, before and during his marriage, before and after his gainful employment, and so on, up to the tests preceding and following his death. His life-career is largely determined by these tests. Beginning with intelligence tests and ending with the tests of loyalty and subversiveness, various testers have replaced the old-fashioned angel-guardians that supposedly guided the life-course of each person. We are living in an *age of testocracy*. By their tests of our intelligence, emotional stability, character, aptitude, unconscious drives, and other characteristics of our personality, the testocrats largely decide our vocation and occupation. They play an important role in our promotions or demotions, and in our successes and failures in social position, reputation, and influence. They determine our normality or abnormality, our superior intelligence or hopeless stupidity, our loyalty or subversiveness. By all this they are largely responsible for our happiness or despair, and, finally, for our long life or premature death.

The enormous influence of tests and testers is primarily due to the supposedly scientific and infallible character of these tests. The testocrats have succeeded in selling their tests as strictly scientific, precise, operational and unerring. As such they are rarely challenged and hardly ever questioned.

The enormous demand has generated an abundant supply of quick, easy, and semi-automatic tests which can be applied to the structure and psychodynamics of any imaginable characteristic of a human being, social group, or cultural value.

Within the last three decades, in the United States alone, hundreds of different tests have been devised and administered.[2]

1. *Dozens of intelligence tests* representing, mainly, revisions of A. Binet's tests, by Thorndike, Terman, Miller, Otis, Pintner, Patterson, Coxe; the California Test of Mental Maturity, the Army General Classification Test; the tests of E. B. Green, L. Isserlis, S. S. Colvin, C. Burt, etc., etc.
2. *Personality Tests:*
   A. *Tests of various traits of personality:* aggressiveness, ascendance-submission, caution, compliance, confidence, conformity, conscientiousness, expansion-reclusion, decision speed, deception, honesty, incorrigibility, originality, perseverance, persistence, self-assertion, self-assurance, self-estimation and evaluation, social perception, social resistance, studiousness, suggestibility, trustworthiness, etc., etc.

B. *Tests of instincts and emotions:* strength of various instinctive drives and "prepotent reflexes"; emotional stability and instability, the particular kind of dominant emotion.

C. *Tests of moods, temperament, and will-power:* cheerfulness and depression, encouragement and discouragement, praise and reproval, will-power; extroversion and introversion, etc.

D. *Tests of attitudes, interests, preferences,* etc.: fair-mindedness, international and national preferences, money-mindedness, open-mindedness, public-mindedness, radical, liberal or conservative attitudes, race prejudices, religious beliefs, sociality, aesthetic and other preferences, etc.

E. *Tests of ethical judgements and actions:* ethical discrimination, ethical values, ethical perception and knowledge, practicing ethical precepts, etc.

F. *Tests of aptitudes, abilities, and of leadership* of a broad and very specific character, like those for the: architect, astronomer, contractor, accountant, airplane or automobile designer, ventilating engineer, sculptor, archeologist, adding machine operator, essay writer, plumber, carpenter, city planner, director of archeological expedition, department store manager, medical researcher, book reviewer, editorial writer, actor, paleobotanist, advertiser, etc., etc.[3]

G. *Tests of mental and moral normality and abnormality, personal adjustment and maladjustment of general and specific kinds.*

H. *Tests of potential general and specific criminality:* murderer, rapist, pickpocket, forger, etc.

I. *Tests of the types of personality:* introvert-extrovert; schizothymic-cyclothymic; endomorphic-mesomorphic-ectomorphic; genital-anal-oral-cutaneous sexual type; Nordic-Mediterranean-Alpine; theoretical-economic-aesthetic-domineering-religious, etc.

J. *Projective tests:* word-association, thematic apperception, Rorschach, dream-interpretation, etc., for testing the instinctive and the "repressed" drives and "complexes" like the Oedipus, Tetanus, fear of castration, penis envy, and other sexual and destructive drives in the unconscious region of personality.

K. *Specific tests* of: business ability and leadership; political ability and leadership; military ability of specified character; secretarial ability, scientific or artistic ability, up to the ability for successful performance of a most detailed given activity.

L. *Specific tests* as to whether a given criminal, if granted a parole, will or will not break it.

M. *Specific tests* of compatibility for the prospective bridegroom and bride, of prospective happy and unhappy, adjusted and maladjusted marriage.

N. *Sociometric and Psychodramatic tests.*

O. *Tests of Loyalty and Subversiveness:* in their Soviet, American (or Communist, Democratic), and other, variations.

This highly condensed list of the main types of existing tests gives an idea of their extraordinary number and variety. If I had attempted to give a detailed list of each of the existing tests, of their techniques, and of the literature on these matters, I would have had to write a few substantial volumes. The above list suffices, however, for our purposes. It shows that we do, indeed, live in an age of testomania and testocracy. Now we can raise the "sacrilegious" questions: Are these tests scientific? Do they unerringly test the presence or absence of the tested phenomena? Do they accurately measure their gradations or intensities? Are the tests' results as objective and free from subjective estimates and arbitrary interpretations as are the readings of a thermometer or a barometer?

## 2. Testing as a Universal and Perennial Social Process

Before answering these questions I must point out a few basic verities inextricably connected with our problems. These truths must be kept in mind in order that our questions concerning the modern tests can be correctly answered.

First, *the process of testing its individual members goes on incessantly in all differentiated, stratified and long-living societies.* In any such society its members are continuously tested, selected, and distributed among its various social positions: strata, ranks, occupations, and activities. Even in a pre-literate tribe only one member, or a few, can be its chief, medicine man, great warrior, priest, or a member of its ruling artistocracy. On the other hand, in any tribe there is a large stratum of members who, as slaves, "inferior," or unskilled members, discharge menial and often unpleasant work necessary for the existence and survival of the tribe. The members of any organized tribe thus are found to be distributed among its various positions, strata, and occupations, and this distribution and redistribution goes on as a continuous process.

The same is true of the more differentiated and stratified society, be it a nation, religious denomination, business concern, political party, university, or any organized group.[4] Some 160 million American citizens are distributed and incessantly redistributed among thousands of various political positions, from that of the President of the U.S.A. down to that of the prisoner condemned to the electric chair; among diverse economic positions, from that of a multimillionnaire down to that of a pauper; among occupational positions, from the tops of the professions and big businesses down to the bottom level of unskilled labor; and so on. The members of the Catholic Church are distributed among its strata, from the positions of the Pope and the cardinals down to those of ordinary parishioners. The membership of a university is stratified into the ranks of its president, deans, full-associate-assistant professors, instructors, graduate students, seniors, juniors, sophomores and freshmen, not to mention clerical and maintenance personnel, each member having his own functions, rights, and duties. The same is true of any organized group. The distribution of members is a perennial and universal characteristic of all organized societies.[5]

Second, *this distribution among, and selection of members for, different social positions is not a mere matter of chance but is based upon a variety of continuous testing processes going on in any organized group. The testing agencies and procedures widely vary from society to society, but in some form they function in all societies.* The reason for their existence is simple: in order to survive, any society must successfully meet all the challenges to its existence, and must satisfy all its basic needs. This can be accomplished only through a more or less wise distribution of its members in such a way that most of them, especially those in the ruling and leading stratum, successfully discharge their functions. Otherwise, if and when "an inborn ruler" is placed in the position of a slave and, *vice versa,* when brainless cowards are appointed as the chiefs of armed forces, when incapable managers are put at the head of big business concerns, and the stupid are made scientists and inventors, crooks and criminals, moral leaders, and so on—under these conditions none of the important social functions can be performed successfully. Such a society is doomed to an increasing disorganization eventually leading to its decay and extinction. For this reason all long-living societies have had a complicated system of tests that directly or indirectly probe the abilities of their members, select and distribute them, to some extent, according to the rule "everyone is to be placed according to his ability."

Third, *if not all the numerous tests in various societies have been testing adequately, and if not all the tested individuals have been placed ac-*

*cording to their ability, still, some of the tests in all long-living societies happened to be real in their probing efficacy, and a part of their members have been distributed according to their ability.*

Fourth, as to the character of the tests in such groups, they can be divided into four main classes. First, *continuous real institutional testing* of the members by the society's testing agencies. Thus in most of the societies the member's paternal family is taken as an indicator of his general physical, mental, and moral fitness. This family test is based on the assumption that a *good heredity and a good training* of the children of good parents provide a larger proportion of good children than poor heredity and poor training of the children of physically, mentally, and morally defective parents. Other agencies of continuous testing are: the school in all its forms, the religious organizations, and, finally, the economic and occupational organizations entered into by the members. Beginning with the nursery and elementary school and ending with college, schools continuously test, over a period of years, the character, temperament, health, and mental and moral qualities of each pupil. So, also, does the member's religious group in societies where religion is taken seriously, and where it efficiently controls the moral conduct of its members. Being for many years in daily contact with the member and observing his mind and behavior under most different life-conditions, the school and the church, through the leaders and co-members, cannot help but know him intimately and correctly diagnose his total personality.

The diagnosis based upon these real tests by the family, the school, and the church largely determines the social position of the member. If the diagnosis is negative, he is barred from occupying important positions in such a society. If the diagnosis is positive, he is admitted as a candidate for the upper and middle strata positions. After he enters his occupational activity, his occupational group continues the testing by observing his occupational work. If he performs this task well, he is promoted in his social and occupational ranks. If he fails, he is either discharged or demoted, or held at the lower rungs of his social and occupational ladder.[6] These tests by the family, the school, the church, and the social and occupational groups are *most rigorous real-life tests of the real mental and overt activities of the individual, given in real-life conditions.* In their totality they probe the total structure and psychodynamics of personality or its basic character. There is nothing artificial or fictitious in these institutional tests in contrast to the bulk of the modern "scientific" tests. The latter are mainly paper-pen tests, or vocal answers to questions dealing with imaginary, hypothetical situations or with mere wishes, preferences, and aspirations. They are neither continuous nor long-time tests, but are administered *ad hoc,* of a few minutes' or a few hours' duration.

Besides the real—*continuous institutional*—tests, all long-living stratified societies have had other real tests, namely: (a) crucial real tests, and (b) special real tests.

By the *crucial real tests* are meant life-tests, under crucial life-conditions, of the ability of the member to cope successfully with the crucial tasks of his social and occupational position. The commanding activity of a general planning and directing his armed forces during an important battle; the planning and carrying out of policy by a monarch or governing group during a great crisis; by the head of a business concern during a serious depression; by the pope or the highest religious hierarchy in the times of proliferation of great schisms and heresies; the fighting of competing champion boxers in their crucial match—these are examples of crucial real tests. In all such cases the success or failure in the crucial test largely determines the future social position of the monarch, the pope, the general, the business manager, the champion and the contender. Indirectly, the outcome often tangibly influences the well-being of the respective society, as does, for instance, the victory or defeat of the commander-in-chief of an organized group. Here the tests are fully real. They call for mobilization of the total ability of the tested persons. On the other hand, they are not continuous but of a short duration and occur only sporadically. There is no need to add that they are as adequate and scientific as any test can be.

Next to be mentioned are *special real tests for testing a specific ability in a person.* In practically all Oriental and Occidental monastic orders, at their heroic age, nobody was admitted to the membership of a monastic community without a severe and long testing of his aptitude for monkhood. An aspiring person was kept outside the monastery for several days, often being insulted and jeered at by the monks and the passers-by. If he successfully stood this test, he was admitted as a novice to a special part of the monastery, was stripped of all his possessions and clothes and given under the closest supervision of one of the experienced elders. As a novice, he was subjected to the severe discipline of a moral and spiritual re-education, and to fairly painful conditions of life, unrestricted obedience, and menial work. This testing of the novice continued for several years. During this period he was continuously instructed—by theory and practice—in the difficult duties of the monk; several times he was reminded about his complete freedom to either abandon his goal of monkhood or continue his preparation for it. If, and when, the novice successfully withstood these severe trials and impressed the elder, the abbot, and the monastic community positively, only then was he admitted to full-fledged membership in the monastery.[7]

Similar tests of specific ability are given in many vocational, occupational, and other groups. They differ from general institutional tests by their limited duration and by testing a specific ability in the person. From the crucial tests they differ by their noncrucial nature and much longer duration. Here the ability or its lack is not decided by one test, or a few, but by the totality of numerous performances of the testee during his period of probation. Like the institutional and crucial tests, this special testing is again fully real, even rigorously behavioristic, and free from the fictitious and conjectural elements of paper-pencil, speech-reactional, and "make-believe" tests of the modern psychosocial sciences.

Finally, side by side with these real tests, all societies have had also *artificial and magic tests* of various kinds. Playing-card tests, tea-leaf tests, coffee-ground tests, dream-interpretation tests, free-association tests, tests of specific bodily marks and peculiarities "as signs of the devil's (or the deity's) imprint"—all are examples of *artificial* tests. Augury tests, ritualistic ordeals in ascertaining the guilt or innocence of an accused party, various magical tests of the medicine man, shaman, or oracle; and tests by "God's judgments," are examples of *magic* tests.

In contrast to the real tests, the artificial and magic tests rarely test the individual directly. Instead, they are based upon a belief in the existence of mysterious or causal relationship between certain events or objects and the tested characteristic of a person. To certain phenomena—a tea-leaf configuration, a combination of playing cards cut at random, a certain cloud-formation, the pattern of flying geese, or the sinking or floating of the tested person when thrown into water—they ascribe a syndromatic or evidential value revealing the presence or absence of the tested trait in a person. It goes without saying that these assumptions and beliefs are largely arbitrary and devoid of an adequate basis. So, also, are the interpretations superimposed on these "omens."

The artificial and magic tests are usually *ad hoc* tests, administered from time to time, and of a short duration. A variety of these real, artificial, and magic tests have been practiced in all differentiated and stratified societies of the past and present. This means that the tests are not invented by the modern psychosocial sciences but are as old as human history itself. Their concrete forms vary in time and in space, but the testing itself is a universal and perennial constant.

After this excursion we can turn now to the discussion of the modern psychosocial tests

## 3. Defects of the Modern Psychosocial Tests

"Man (in good earnest) is a marvelous vain, fickle, and unstable subject, and on whom it is very hard to form any certain and uniform judgement," said Michel de Montaigne in 1580.[8] This fickle, unstable, and complex nature of man is the main obstacle to the validity of psychosocial tests of persons and groups. This obstacle is responsible for gross errors in the artificial "paper-pen" tests as well as for those in the real long-time tests of outstanding persons, administered by supposedly capable examiners, teachers, and observers. Thus, one of the greatest writers of the world, Leo Tolstoi, used to get "C" marks in his university courses on Russian composition. Somewhat similar were the grades received at an early age by the greatest poet of Russia, A. Pushkin, in the courses on Russian language and composition. Hegel's university diploma solemnly states that Hegel's performances were satisfactory in all courses except philosophy in which he was deficient. Sir Isaac Newton was graduated from his university with practically no honors. G. Vico, one of the founders of sociology and philosophy of history, in his competition for the university position, was voted down in favor of a mediocrity. Saint Thomas Aquinas was called "a dumb ox" by his teachers and fellow pupils. St. Ignatius Loyola was ridiculed as a queer ignoramus by many doctors and students of the University of Paris. Nothing great was expected from Verdi by the professors of Milan Conservatory. Not much was expected from Beethoven as a composer by his music teachers; even the great Haydn was skeptical about the musical genius of "this big Mogul" as he styled Beethoven. Teleman was twice preferred to J. S. Bach for the position of a musician. And so on, and so forth. Many other cases can be added to the list of similar misjudgments.

What is important in these cases is the fact that the blunders were made in regard to true geniuses by their competent teachers, relatives, and fellows who closely observed and tested them directly and continuously (by quizzes, examinations, actual performances, etc.) for many months and years. And the tests were largely real, based on the actual, overt performances of these incipient geniuses in the field of their training and creativity.

If such striking errors in testing and diagnosing emerging geniuses are possible, still more probable are similar blunders in testing the psychosocial traits of ordinary persons by ordinary testers and diagnosticians. This is well confirmed by daily misjudgments of students by their professors, of pupils by their teachers, of promoted and demoted employees by their employers, of the subordinate personnel by their superiors in government, of the elected representatives by the voting citizens, of instructors by the administrations of universities, of a bridegroom by his bride or *vice versa,* of a prize-winner and a prize-loser by their judges, of the applicants for grants by various foundations, and so on. Mistesting and misjudgment in these and many other evaluations are about as frequent and "normal" as sound diagnoses and evaluations.

If such is the situation in the field of the real tests, the results are bound to be still more blunderous with the artificial tests predominant in the modern psychosocial sciences and especially with the magic tests not totally absent in these disciplines. In spite of the supposedly "scientific" nature of modern tests, they are infested with many misjudgments and errors. A cursory survey of the main testing procedures confirms the accuracy of this sad statement.

The bulk of modern psychosocial tests use *three kinds of procedure:*

*Paper and pen answering of the testing questions.* The tests are presented in the form of direct questions, or that of multiple or alternative choices, or that of some other variety of the so-called "objective tests." Now the probing questionnaire or examination contains few questions, now many; it asks now for a short "gun-shot," now for essay type answers. Whatever the variations, the testing procedure consists of paper-pen operations.

*Vocal answers to vocal questions* presented in the form of oral examinations, interviews, and the various quizzes of the class-room or of the "give-away" programs of radio and television.

*Actual performance of the tested activities:* violin or piano playing by the tested musician; car-driving by the tested driver; the design and construction of a gadget by a prospective inventor; a sermon given by a prospective preacher; a lecture by a lecturer; carpenter-mason-electrician-mechanic operations by the respective persons; a poem, a novel, or a Ph.D. thesis prepared by the tested candidates; and so on.

Of these three kinds of tests only *"the actual performance test"* is a real test. Unfortunately, this sort of real test occupies a very modest place in the battery of modern "scientific" tests. The overwhelming majority consist of paper-pen and vocal tests. As a whole, they are partly artificial and partly magic; only in a small part are they real tests, and then they apply mainly to the elementary psychosocial properties of the individuals, like the threshold of sensation, rapidity of perception, intensity and duration of memory, and so on. Rarely, if ever, are the real tests applied to the complex, deep, and important traits of a person, like his creative capacity, character, moral stamina, integrity, and abilities.

The defectiveness of the artificial, pencil-paper, and vocal tests is notably increased by the conditions under which they are administered. First, they are, for the most part, not continuous but sporadic *ad hoc* tests, given only once or a few times to the tested individuals. Lack of repetition makes the results of such tests somewhat accidental, and unrepresentative of the knowledge or the traits of the testee. He may fail to answer the questions of such a single test, though he may know well the whole field of which the questions touch only a small fraction. He may be in a "blocked" state of mind at the moment of testing and, therefore, may respond more poorly than he would in his normal condition. Without numerous retestings, any single artificial test runs the risk of getting inadequate results.

Second, ordinarily these tests have a short time-limit: the persons being probed are told they have to answer the questions within one-half hour or an hour or a few hours.

Third, the time of testing is autocratically decided by the testers and not by the persons being tested. The last two conditions greatly add to the chance character of results. These conditions assume that everyone is capable at any moment of answering instantaneously all sorts of questions as they are announced; that there is no need to take into consideration temporary moods, indispositions, and blockings of the testees; that no time is necessary for warming up and for mobilizing the total knowledge of the testee. Likewise, such tests totally ignore the individual differences between persons who may be slow or fast in their testing operations; and so on. The examined persons must start instantaneously and hurry their answering; otherwise they are penalized for failing to answer all the questions asked within the prescribed time-limit. This means that the conditions of the pencil-paper and vocal tests are highly abnormal and do not give full opportunity to show who knows what and how much. They especially penalize those who are somewhat slow in the total mobilization of their knowledge and other potentialities, though the slow workers sometimes are superior to the fast ones. These three conditions of artificial tests make their results rather doubtful and inadequate.

Fourth, these inadequacies are inflated still more by the shortcomings of the testing questions themselves.

*a*) A notable number of such questions ask for wishes, desires, aspirations, preferences, tastes, and other subjective evaluations of the testees.

*b*) Another portion of the tests asks for hypothetical answers to hypothetical conditions—what would the testees do under such and such imaginary circumstances.[9] So far as questions of this sort do not ask for factual knowledge or facts generally, or for answers requiring a display of logical or mathematical thought, or real skill, or solid knowledge of the problem, the answers do not reveal the differences between the competent and incompetent, skillful and skilless, talented and untalented, virtuous and criminal, brave and cowardly, because the brilliant and the stupid all have their wishes, preferences, tastes, evaluations or wishful hypothetical answers to hypothetical questions about what they would do in such and such imaginary situations.

*c*) Now and then the answer which the testers consider correct is really a wrong answer. Due to their ignorance, the testers count such a wrong answer as correct, while the truly correct answer is counted as wrong. In this way an additional error creeps into the test's results. For instance, one of the standard tests for nine and ten year old pupils depicts a picture of a harp, a drum, a violin, and a piano, and the question asked is: "Find the three things that are alike and draw a line through the one that is not like those three." The tester's correct answer consists of drawing the line through the drum as a percussion instrument in contrast to the stringed instruments, harp, violin, and piano. This "correct" answer is in fact incorrect: a piano is as much a stringed as it is a percussion instrument. The authors of the *Studies in Social Psychology in World War II* have this question among thousands of others: "The heavy bombing attacks on Great Britain were part of an attempt by the Nazis to: (a) invade and conquer England; (b) keep England from helping Russia; (c) break down English morale so they would surrender." The authors consider that only the first answer is the correct one. On my part, and on part of any competent historian, all three answers are correct and *b* and *c* answers in no way can be marked and then tabulated as wrong answers.[10] If one carefully goes through many "standardized" test-questions, one easily finds similar errors.

*d*) A still more common defect of the tests is the vague wording of the questions, of the categories and characteristics asked to be indicated, defined or classified. Many wrong answers in written or oral tests are due to this logical and semantic carelessness of the examiners or testers. Often they are due also to the fact that the preferential choices are too few, too static, and too unqualified. For instance, in one of the best tests of dominant interests in personality, the question is often asked, whether a testee would prefer to read: (a) "the story of religion in America, or (b) the story of industry in America." My answer would be: (a) at some periods I do not want to read either one; (b) sometimes I prefer to read the story of religion; some other times the story of industry. Such an answer would hardly be counted, but it is the only one that correctly expresses my interests. The question, like thousands of similar questions, does not consider the changing stream of preferences and thereby contributes to the inaccuracy of the answers and of the results of the test. In experimenting with various testing schedules from this standpoint, I often find myself incapable of answering many a question or of checking the category to which I belong or the characteristic which I have. The questions, categories, or traits I speak about are not those which I am incompetent to answer, but those which are well within my knowledge and experience. My difficulty here is exactly due to the vagueness, ambivalence, poor classification, poor definition, the too "static" character, or the fallacy, of the questions themselves.

Such tests naturally cannot adequately test the probed characteristics of the testees.

*e*) The adequacy of the tests is greatly limited also by the predominant character of the tests. In testing intelligence or knowledge, most of the tests probe mainly the informational and memorized "capital" of the individuals, and much less their creative potentials, their specific abilities, and their capacity for logical, mature, and original thought. Most of so-called "objective" tests are of a "scatterbrained" type. Their questions ask mainly for various bits of information or for terms, concepts, definitions, and theories memorized from the texts, lectures, lessons, and especially from abridged "manuals" and "efficient" tutors drilling their pupils for examination. In this respect the tests differ little from "the empty-minded" tests of "Information, Please," Groucho Marx's tests and the moronic questions of the various "give-away" programs of radio and television. It is only natural that tests of this sort successfully moved from the realm of science into the field of entertainment and commercial advertising where, by their nature, they belong. If in both fields they reveal very little, at least in the "give-away" programs they are less boring and more lucrative than in the realm of so-called "scientific tests."

*f*) When these tests deal with psychosocial phenomena — for instance, when they probe the psychological, psychiatric, sociological, anthropological, economic, political, historical, philosophical, ethical, juridical or aesthetic values of the tested persons—the unreliability of the tests is still more increased for the following reason. In these fields there are few generally accepted concepts, definitions, theories, methods, uniformities, and values. In these disciplines we have, instead, different theories, approaches, generalizations, and values. Insofar as the testers are all too human, they are inclined to regard as correct only the answers and values which agree with their own "denominational creed." In this way new elements of subjectivity are introduced into the tests.

*g*) The damaging role of the enumerated conditions *(a, b, c, d, e, f)* is immeasurably magnified by the subsequent *interpretation and quantification of the test results.* The devotees of the psychosocial tests view them as if they were a sort of thermometer or barometer. By their tests they want to ascertain not only the presence or absence of a tested trait, but also to measure its magnitude or intensity and to score the results in exact numerical units. Unfortunately, before the testers can do this, they must interpret the results of their tests.

In contrast to the precise and direct indication of body temperature by thermometer, or of barometric pressure by barometer — indications that do not need any indirect interpretations — the results of the psychosocial tests, taken *per se,* are neither direct, nor clear, nor diagnostically meaningful. They acquire diagnostic meaning only when they are "interpreted" by the tester. And the "interpretations" are usually quite different from the empirical results as such. Empirically the results of a word-association test are but a number of various words uttered by the testee in response to the words of the tester. Perceptionally, the results of the Rorschach test are but a mass of various images evoked in the testee by the ink-blot of a Rorschach card. Neither the words nor the images have, *per se,* any meaning, diagnostic or otherwise.

They acquire such a meaning only through interpretation of these "syndromes" by the tester. Whether he wants it or not, he must *superimpose his interpretation upon the responses of the testee.* And these superimposed interpretations are quite different from the empirical or perceptional test-results. A patient tells correctly his dream of the night before to his psychoanalyst or psychiatrist. He relates that in his dream he was climbing a mountain; that when he was near to its peak he suddenly lost his footing and began to fall down; that this falling down evoked in him a mortal fear; and that in this state of trepidation he finally awoke. Such is the empirical content of the dream. To acquire a diagnostic meaning, it has to be interpreted by a psychoanalyst or psychiatrist. Is the dream a syndrome of some unconscious processes? If it is, does it manifest the Oedipus complex, or fear of castration, or some other "repressed" wish, or something else? Whatever the interpretation, its diagnostic character is quite different from the content and character of the dream itself.

These interpretations open the royal road for all sorts of arbitrary, fanciful, and subjective misinterpretations of the tests and their results. The very assumption that a dream is a syndrome of this or that subconscious process is already an arbitrary assumption quite different from the dream itself. That a given dream is a syndrome of a certain complex or repressed wish is again an arbitrary conjecture, devoid of scientific proof.

When carefully studied, most of the interpretations are found to be based not on a proven causal connection between the test results and the specific interpretation, but mainly on a dogmatic belief that the results are true syndromes or omens of certain entities and forces: repressed wishes, instinctive drives, various complexes, "native intelligence," "prepotent reflexes," dominant interests of a certain variety, and so on. This is confirmed by—among other things—the fairly frequent discrepancy between interpretations of the same results by different interpreters. To sum up: the interpretations import a large portion of nonscientific elements into the test results and thereby notably contribute to their invalidity.

*h*) Still greater distortion of the test-results is introduced by their quantification. Obsessed by metromania our testers indefatigably measure their test data and present them in the "exact" and "objective" form of numerical scores, indexes, and statistical tables, marvelously decorated with impressive-looking mathematical formulae and other simulacra of precise quantitative research. The manufacture of these "quantitative movies" is done so artfully that many a logically and mathematically innocent onlooker seriously takes this sham-quantitative appearance for genuine reality. A legion of psychosocial researchers sincerely believe that these impressive scores, indexes, rows of figures, coefficients of correlations, probable errors, standard deviations, coefficients of least squares, and so on, deliver in fact the objectively studied and exactly measured "diamonds of valid knowledge."

As a matter of fact, the bulk of these "diamonds" are merely the arbitrary, subjective, and often fantastic, assumptions of the testers dressed up in quantitative costumes. Our testing numerologists have as little relationship to real mathematics as did the various numerologists and astrologers (*"mathematici"* as they were called) of ancient and medieval times.

The bulk of the test data is qualitative and, so far, is untranslatable into quantitative units. They do not show how many score points each test-response has, nor which response has a greater and which a lesser number of score points. For this simple reason the points for each response cannot be counted; nor can they be added, subtracted, divided, multiplied, or subjected to any other mathematical operations.

This means that these quantitative units, or scoring points, with all the subsequent quantitative manipulations, are largely the arbitrary creations of the quantifiers. They decide how many score points are to be given to each of numerous responses of the testees, and which responses are to be given 10, 5, or 99 points. Their scoring becomes no less arbitrary if they decide to give an equal number of points to all responses. If, instead of scoring points, the testers decide to rank the responses, such a decision also remains arbitrary. The same is true of their placing each response in one of these ranks. If, instead of one tester, the ascription of points, weights, units, or ranks is done by five "expert testers" (and this subterfuge is frequently used) the quantification of five or five hundred pseudo-experts still remains arbitrary, since none of them has any objective basis for his numerological distribution of points or weights or ranks.

In later chapters, a great deal will be added to these remarks. For the present, the considerations we have taken up regarding the doubtful validity of the artificial psychosocial tests, and regarding the conditions (*a* to *h*) additionally damaging their adequacy, are sufficient to justify a strongly skeptical attitude towards the scientific nature of these tests. All in all, they are hardly more scientific than the old-fashioned tea-leaf or coffee-grounds tests. Modern testomania is mainly a new form of the old belief in omens. This verdict is well corroborated by a closer examination of the main modern tests and by an inductive testing of the tests themselves.

# *Chapter Five*

# The Fad of Intelligence Tests

## 1. General Defects of Intelligence Tests

Let us briefly examine, first of all, the so-called intelligence tests. After the pioneering tests of Binet, they spread with the rapidity of an epidemic. In the early stages, the enthusiasm of the testers was so great that they did not much bother themselves with such questions as: What exactly was that intelligence which they were testing and measuring? What was the meaning of their scores? Did the tests measure mainly the native or the acquired intelligence? — and a lot of other questions which should have been asked before embarking upon the testing crusade. Eventually the testomanic fever cooled off notably and these questions began to be increasingly asked. As a result, skepticism in regard to the infallibility of the tests started to grow. At the present time the situation can be summed up as follows:

*a*) Various testers have meant different things by "intelligence." Hardly any of them has clearly defined his meaning of intelligence, while many have not defined it at all and have measured something they did not know well. For E. L. Thorndike, intelligence was the individual's "native intellectual capacity," or his "general status and general capacity."

For F. N. Freeman, "intelligence was a somewhat more inclusive capacity than is implied when it is used as a name for our present tests . . . . The capacities measured by our tests include: sensory capacity, capacity for perceptual recognition; quickness or flexibility of association; imagination; span or steadiness of attention; quickness in response; . . . mental balance, co-ordination of the mental processes; reflection; mental control; mental adjustment; nonsuggestibility; . . . balanced and sane reaction to the entire world of things, ideas, and persons."

For S. S. Corvin, "An individual possesses intelligence in so far as he has learned to adjust himself to his environment."

For L. M. Terman, "If intelligence is the ability to think in terms of abstract ideas, we should expect the most successful intelligence tests to be just those which involve the use of language and other symbols."

For R. Pintner, "Because we are dealing with something which we hardly know how to define . . . , by intelligence tests I mean tests of general ability to do all sorts of things as opposed to educational and trade tests which are specifically made to measure the knowledge which an individual has been directly taught."

For V. A. C. Henmon, "The so-called general intelligence tests are not general intelligence tests at all, but tests of the special intelligence upon which the school puts a premium." [1]

Dissatisfied with such vague and contradictory definitions, some of the testers solved the problem by cutting the Gordian knot. They simply stated: "Intelligence is that which we test and measure, and that which we test and measure is intelligence."

W. I. Thomas and D. Thomas correctly sum up the situation: "There is no general agreement as to the nature of intelligence, and there is no scientific way of checking whether the tests measure what their sponsors claim." Intelligence scores "tend often merely to confuse the issues and add to controversy." "The result is a kind of reasoning in circles: tests are devised to measure intelligence the exact nature of which is unknown, and then intelligence is defined in terms of performance on the tests." [2]

Perhaps still more eloquent are the conclusions one of the most eminent pioneers of mental testing, E. L. Thorndike, reached in his later work. "Just what they measure is not known; how far it is proper to add, subtract, multiply, divide, and compute ratios with the measures obtained is not known; just what the measures obtained signify concerning the intellect is not known." [3]

Thus, as soon as the basic problem is raised as to what the measured "intelligence" or "mental capacity" is, the foggy and "mystical" character of this "something" becomes obvious. If the testers do not know exactly what they test and measure, their measurements and scores become also indeterminate in their meaning. The whole impressive quantitative superstructure of IQ's and other scores also becomes largely meaningless.

*b*) A similar deflation has occurred with regard to the early assumption that the tests were testing native intelligence or mental capacity. At the present time there is hardly any intelligence tester who adheres to this belief. Even such partisans of it as L. M. Terman have had to admit that the mental tests probe not only inherent but also acquired or learned intelligence. An ever-increasing majority of intelligence testers stress the role of learning and environmental factors in the test results. Many of them give to these factors a predominant role. Tested intelligence is increasingly regarded as the acquired, learned ability.[4]

*c*) Anyone who has experience in administering and scoring the tests knows that the scoring operations involve many an arbitrary assumption based mainly on the subjective decisions of the scorers.[5] What numerical value or weight-points are to be given to this or that answer; how many points are to be added or subtracted in quantifying this or that item; what mathematical or pseudo-mathematical formula is to be applied for the summation of arbitrary numerical points; what number of IQ points manifests "the normal," "the subnormal," or "the superior" intelligence; to what extent is the sample of tested individuals representative for a given group; and what are the criteria for a comparison of the results of one tested group with other groups? It need not be argued that such arbitrary assumptions notably decrease the validity of the intelligence tests.

These considerations justify a skeptical attitude toward the adequacy of intelligence tests. If the tests are looked upon as a sort of thermometer of mental capacity, it is a defective thermometer measuring something nobody exactly knows what. This conclusion is confirmed by an inductive test of the tests themselves.

## 2. Inductive Deflation of Intelligence Tests

*Terman's Test of Intelligence Tests.* One of the best inductive verifications of the value of intelligence tests is given by a foremost authority in the field, L. M. Terman. In 1921-22 Terman and his associates proposed "to sift a school population of a quarter-million in order to identify and study a thousand or more of highest IQ" or "to discover in the schools of California a thousand or more subjects with IQ's that would rate them well within the highest 1 per cent of the child population."[6] The investigators most carefully used not only the best intelligence tests (Stanford-Binet, Terman Group Test, Army Alpha Test, National Intelligence Test), but also the teachers' recommendations of the three most brilliant pupils in each school; the highest school grades; detailed information about the children's health and their racial, ethnic, home, occupational, and economic backgrounds; their character, interests, plays, books read, and so on.[7] On this basis, the investigators selected 1,070 children—prospective geniuses—with IQ's ranging from 135 to 200.

Twenty-five years later, in 1945, when the selected prospective geniuses had reached the mean age of 35, Terman and his associates made a careful, follow-up investigation as to how well the selected children fared, what happened with them, and to what extent they demonstrated their exceptionally high intelligence and potential genius. The results of this follow-up study help clarify our problem as to what extent the best mental tests really probe and measure the intelligence, giftedness, genius, abilities, and character of human beings.

Terman and his associates assert that their follow-up studies in 1940 and 1945 confirm their 1921-22 diagnosis of the children as potential geniuses and, through that, the adequacy of their tests and measurements.

But the main conclusion to be drawn from this painstaking study of would-be geniuses is that, *twenty-five years later, at the mean age of thirty-five, the 1,070 school children, selected by a battery of the best intelligence tests available, and certified by the tests as being the most gifted among some 250,000 school children in California, have not demonstrated any notable superiority over a typical sampling of children of the professional, semiprofessional, and business classes from which 81.4 per cent of them came.* (Only 6.8 per cent of the 1,070 children came from semiskilled and unskilled parents.)

I accept the factual results of the follow-up studies. *But exactly these results, plus other factual evidence,* force me to arrive at the above conclusion, which so sharply contradicts the conclusion drawn by L. M. Terman and his associates. First of all, about one-third of these would-be geniuses (called "group C") twenty-five years later showed themselves to be mental, occupational, economic, and social failures by all the standards used by Terman and his associates for evaluation of intelligence and achievements of human beings. Their achievements were, if anything, inferior to those of mental, occupational, economic, and social mediocrity. This fact clearly shows that the tests of intelligence and creativity, used by Terman and his associates, dismally mistested this part of their "gifted group."

In a milder form, the tests failed also in testing another portion of these would-be geniuses (called "group B"). Twenty-five years after their initial test their achievements were perfectly mediocre. In no way did they surpass the achievements of the rank and file of children from professional and business families.

This double failure is decisive evidence of the inability of the tests to really probe and measure the intelligence or the other mental properties of the individuals.

Finally, the fact that among 1,070 selected children there happened to be 150 individuals (called "group A") whose achievements were above the rank and file of mediocrity is due not so much to the selective adequacy of the tests as to a comparative abundance of individuals of high ability among the children of professional and business families, when compared with the children of skilled, semi-skilled, and unskilled families. These 150 gifted individuals came in almost all cases from the high-standing professional and business families. A purely random selection of 1,070 children from some 250,000 children of such families cannot help but pick up — side by side with children of low and mediocre intelligence — some children of high intelligence and ability. If one makes the selection on the basis of the children's school marks and teachers' evaluations, the chances of picking up 150 gifted children are still higher than in a random selection. Though Terman declared school marks and teachers' evaluations unreliable, he nevertheless used these marks and evaluations in selecting his 1,070 children.

Further on I shall give data on the comparative abundance of high intelligence in the professional and business strata. For the present, the foregoing considerations are sufficient to demolish the myth of the adequacy of mental tests.

Let us now glance at the relevant results of the follow-up study. In regard to physical traits, Terman's "gifted" group, as a whole, reveals hardly any characteristics clearly different from, or superior to, the traits typical of the professional and business groups of similar age and sex. If the average stature of the "gifted group" is somewhat higher than the stature of the general population, it is due mainly to the class composition of the group and not to its supposed giftedness. The professional-business classes, or the upper and middle strata of practically any population, are taller than its general population or especially taller than the lower classes.[8]

In regard to health and physical defects, the data are so uncertain that any accurate comparison with either the general population or with the unselected members of the professional and business classes is impossible, and is not seriously attempted by the authors. If such a comparison with the health of the general population had shown some superiority in the studied group, this would also be due mainly to its professional-business composition: the health and vitality of the upper and middle strata are generally better than those of the lower classes, or of the general population of the same society.[9]

As to mental health and nervous disorders, "The insanity rate in the 'gifted group' did not differ significantly from the expectancy for the generality."[10] The same is true of other mental disorders and mental health generally. The "gifted group" was not free from alcoholism, delinquency, and homosexuality, but, according to the authors, there is no reliable data for comparison of the rates in the gifted group and in the general population. The authors guess that the rates for the gifted group are possibly lower than those for the general population, but this wishful thinking is not supported by the necessary evidence. Moreover, the incidence of delinquency and alcoholism is generally lower in professional and business classes than in the unskilled, semiskilled, and skilled occupational groups.[11]

As to intelligence, the "gifted group" when retested in 1940 and 1945 showed a lowering by 10.4 IQ points.[12] Such an unexpected result is explained by "the errors of measurements," by "failure of the Stanford-Binet and the Concept Mastery tests to measure exactly the same functions," and by "maturational changes, environment, and education." These excuses are but a confession of fallibility in tests otherwise declared to be infallible.

The high school and college showing of the "gifted group" is declared to be superior "in comparison with the general population of whom only about 5 per cent graduate from college and only 30 to 40 per cent graduate from high school."[13] This comparison with the general population is again fallacious because the *unselected* children of the professional and business classes generally graduate from high school and college, receive high grades and honors, and yield real genius much more often than the children of the lower classes.[14] The alleged superiority of the "gifted group" ascribed by the authors to the selectivity of their tests, is, again, the general characteristic of children in the upper and middle class strata.

What is really surprising in the high school and college performance of the "gifted group" is the fact that a notable part (30 to 33 per cent) failed to graduate from college; and another part was perfectly mediocre in its school performance. The "gifted children" were not even all A or B students in high school; and in college only from 8 to 13 per cent had A grades, from 37 to 70 per cent had B grades, from 17 to 48 per cent had C or still lower grades.[15] No genius is necessary for becoming an A student in high school and college. Still less exceptional intelligence is needed to make B grades; and only a very mediocre ability is required to get C or lower grades.

With reference to the occupational and economic achievements of the "gifted group," only 48.3 per cent of its male members were, in 1945, in professional occupations; 32.0 per cent were in semi-professional and business occupations; and the remaining 19.8 per cent were in clerical, skilled, and semiskilled, gainful pursuits. Of the women members of the group, 42 per cent became housewives without employment outside the home. Of the fully employed, 27.8 per cent were teachers; 34.8 per cent were office workers or in business; 7 per cent were social workers; 2.7 per cent were in nonprofessional pursuits; and the rest were in secretarial and clerical work.[16]

In comparison with the general population, the "gifted group" entered the professional and business pursuits in a notably greater proportion, but in all societies the children of professional and business classes, or of the upper and the middle strata, enter these occupations in a much greater proportion than the children of the skilled, semiskilled, and unskilled classes that make up the bulk of the general population. When the "gifted group" is compared with the unselected college men and women, the difference in occupational distribution becomes slight, practically insignificant. Further, the very fact that a tangible portion of the "gifted group" did not succeed in entering professional and business pursuits but landed in the ranks of skilled, semiskilled, and unskilled labor, or in clerical and secretarial work, points out clearly the inadequacy of the tests in regard to this portion of the "potential geniuses." It does not require genius to enter business and the professions. For this reason even the more successful part of the "gifted group" does not prove the adequacy of the tests in selecting the most intelligent persons.

This conclusion is warranted also by the incomes of the "gifted group." The median annual income of men members of the group in 1940 was $2,373; in 1944 (with the war and the postwar decrease in the purchasing power of the dollar) it was $4,713. The range of income among the members of the group fluctuated between $1,500 and $84,000. The median annual income of women members of the group was $1,660 in 1940, and $2,550 in 1944.[17] These figures show a very modest financial success for the group as a whole. In comparison with the median income of semiskilled, unskilled, and possibly skilled labor, the income of the "gifted group" may have been slightly higher; but not tangibly higher than the income of the rank and file from the professional, business, and semiprofessional strata. Millions of ordinary Americans without any claims for genius were making $2,550 or $4,713 in 1944; and millions were making much greater income—if amount of income is an important symptom of genius. [If it is, then Mozart, Schubert, Rembrandt, Beethoven, Vico, St. Pachomius, St. Francis of Assisi, Buddha (after leaving home), and the like, should be put into the class of morons—which shows how questionable are the criteria of genius used by the authors of this study.]

We can pass by several other "evidences and tests" offered by the authors as corroboration of the claim that their "gifted group" is gifted indeed. Tests (like Strong's) of occupational interest, or of the number and kind of avocational interests; tests of reading habits or self-ratings in various other interests, most frequently read magazines, or political party affiliations, and so on—these tests do not and cannot test the high or low ability of a person or of any "gifted group." Such tests are irrelevant in this matter. Nobody as yet has proved that a strong occupational interest is a uniform sign of genius, because there is many a mediocrity as deeply interested in his work as a genius. Still less proved is the idea that a genius usually reads *Time, Reader's Digest,* and *Life,* and that ordinary men and women do not read these magazines; or that 33.7 per cent of men of genius read detective stories, and only 2.2 and 3.0 per cent read essays and poetry; or that genius is interested mainly in sports and photography

(61 and 30 per cent, respectively, of the "gifted group"), and very little in writing (10 per cent) and arts and crafts (3.4 per cent); or that genius is most closely associated with the Republican party (39 per cent), much less with the Democratic party (23 per cent), and hardly ever with any kind of "Radicalism" (1 per cent) or with being politically "Independent" (only 2.8 per cent).

How irrelevant all these "tests" and "syndromes" of genius are is well attested to by such facts as that an overwhelming majority of the founders of great religions and higher ethical systems, or of the most eminent social thinkers (whose works make up the content of texts on the *History of Political Theories,* or the *History of Social Thought*) have been "Radical" and "Independent." Otherwise, these men would not have been imprisoned, banished, persecuted, and executed by the existing governments and powers. Otherwise, among all Christian Saints 37 per cent would not have died the martyr's death.

The same is true of many poets, artists, writers, and scientists. At least some 40 to 50 per cent of these men and women of real genius, whose names have entered the annals of history, have been "radical," "independent," and "subversive" from the standpoint of existing governments and "conservative" political parties.

Somewhat more symptomatic is the rate of divorce and separation in the "gifted group." In 1945, 12.94 per cent of married men and 14.42 per cent of married women had been divorced once; 1.18 per cent of men and 1.52 per cent of women had been divorced twice; and 0.29 per cent of men and 0.38 per cent of women had been divorced three or more times. Even if these rates of divorce are somewhat lower than those of the general population (though this is uncertain), they show that a tangible portion of the gifted men and women were incapable of successfully marrying and staying married, that they failed to manage ably this important function in human life.

To sum up: By no stretch of imagination or of standards of genius is the "gifted group" as a whole "gifted" indeed. It is, rather, a group typical of the professional and business classes of the same age, sex, and other conditions.

Now turn to "group A." This is the top part of the whole "gifted group." The performance of 150 members of this "group A" is much better than that of 430 members of the mediocre "group B" or of 150 members of the near-failure "group C." The achievements of "group A" are certainly considerable and superior to those of the rank and file of the members of the professional and business classes. However, these achievements still fall short of those of real genius. They are similar to those of a comparable group of the American Rhodes Scholars. At the average age of 35 only 4.7 per cent of group A are listed in *Who's Who in America,* and only 12.7 per cent in the *American Men of Science.*[18] To be listed in *Who's Who* or in *American Men of Science* is a real distinction. However, even this distinction has only a very remote relation to real genius.

Does the presence of the 150 talented members of group A among the 1,070 selected children with IQ's of 140 to 200 prove the validity of the intelligence tests used to select them? Are these 150 talented persons picked up exclusively through the selective power of the tests, or do they happen to be included in the 1,070 children through the operation of other factors quite different from the battery of tests used?

Since the majority (about 79 per cent) of the 1,070 supposedly "gifted" children showed themselves, twenty-five years later, either as mediocrities (group B), or even near-failures (group C), the tests evidently erred grossly in testing the intelligence and abilities of the children. For this reason alone, the inclusion of group A in the selected group of 1,070 supposedly "gifted persons" cannot be due either exclusively or mainly to the tests. This is shown also by the IQ's given to the children of group A and group C by the tests in 1922. The mean IQ by the Stanford-Binet test was 155 for group A and 150 for group C; by the Terman Group Test the mean IQ for group A was 143.2, and for group C 142.3. By Parent-Teacher Ratings the mean for group A was 3.5 and for group C 3.8. In other words, according to the tests administered in 1922 there was practically no difference between these contrasting groups: the children who, twenty-five years later, turned out to be members of the near-failure group C, were as intelligent as the children who eventually made group A.

For an explanation of how the talented members of group A happened to be picked up, side by side with the mediocre and submediocre children of the whole group of 1,070 "would-be geniuses," we have to look for other than the test factors.

The most instrumental factor in this matter is the much greater abundance of high intelligence, talent, and genius in the professional and business-managerial classes in comparison with the lower strata of skilled, semiskilled, and unskilled classes that make up the bulk of the general population. The professional and business-managerial classes in America, corresponding to the upper and the middle classes in other societies, have supplied the overwhelming majority of great geniuses and creators in practically all countries.

In England "the upper and professional classes, composing only 4.46 per cent of the total population, produced 63 per cent of the men of genius, while the labor, artisan, and industrial classes, composing about 84 per cent of the population, produced only 11.7 per cent of the greatest leaders of Great Britain."

According to F. Adams Woods, among the royal families studied we have one genius in every 32 monarchs. According to my own study of 352 monarchs, one monarch of unquestionable mental superiority occurs in every 7 monarchs.

In France "the nobility produced literary geniuses two and one-half times more than the high magistrature; six and one-half times more than liberal professions, twenty-three times more than the bourgeoisie, and two hundred times more than the labor classes." Of illustrious French scientists 35 per cent were produced by the French aristocracy, 42 per cent by the professions and the middle (business) class, and only 23 per cent were from all the lower classes which composed from two-thirds to three-fourths of the population.

In Russia from 80 to 90 per cent of eminent scientists, scholars, artists, men of letters, and leaders in other fields came out of the professional, governmental, and business-managerial classes.

The situation has been similar in Germany and in practically all countries studied.

In the United States, the professions produced 43.1 per cent of the leading men of science, while the professional class forms only 3.1 per cent of the total population. The American *Who's Who* lists one person for every 32 persons in the clergy, for every 70 persons in professions, for every 124 in business, for every 1,100 in farming, for every 2,470 in skilled and semiskilled occupations, and for every 75,000 in unskilled labor.

The American professional class produced 32.8 per cent of the eminent men of letters; the business class 15.1 per cent. Taken together these two classes produced 47.9 per cent of all the eminent American men of letters.

Of 476 American captains of industry and finance (multimillionaires)

79.8 per cent came from professional and business families.[19] From the same classes came 62.7 per cent of the National Leaders of Labor and Radical Movements in the United States and the majority of the National Farmer Leaders.[20]

These figures clearly show an extraordinary abundance of high creative ability and genius in the upper and the middle classes which in America are the professional and business-managerial strata. This abundance, rather than the tests, is responsible for the inclusion of the talented "group A" in the otherwise little-gifted group of 1,070 children selected by the tests of Terman and his associates.

This hypothesis is supported, first, by the occupational, educational, and economic status of the parents of group A and group C. Of group A, 149 members of the 150 came out of professional, business-managerial, comparatively rich and well-educated parental families, while only 17 per cent of 150 members of group C came from professional and business parental families, and these families were poorer and less educated than the parental families of group A. If we have one person in *Who's Who* for every 32 clergymen, every 70 persons in professions, and every 124 businessmen, a purely random selection of 1,070 children from these classes cannot help but pick up a number of talented persons, side by side with the mediocre and submediocre. And the number of gifted persons of the group A kind in this randomly selected 1,070 children is likely to be no less than the 150 found in group A. This conclusion is confirmed by the following computation. Out of 1,070 children of supposedly high intelligence, selected by the tests in 1921-22, only 7 were listed in 1945 in *Who's Who* (4.7 per cent of group A). On the basis of the above-mentioned ratios of one person in *Who's Who* per every 32 clergymen or per every 70 professional persons, or per every 124 business persons, out of 1,070 children selected at random from the professional and managerial-business classes we could expect (according to the formula of probability: p = 1/32 or 1/70 or 1/124 of 1,070) 33 (if all 1,070 were clergymen's children); 15 (if they were professional children); or 8 (if they were businessmen's children), to eventually be listed in *Who's Who*. Any of these numbers is larger than the 6 or 7 who succeeded in entering *Who's Who* from the 1,070 children selected by Terman and his associates. Readily admitting that after 1945 an additional number of Terman's group A would enter *Who's Who*—admitting even that the number of

*Who's Who* persons from the Terman group would eventually double and reach 14, 15 or even 20—these numbers are still not greater than the 33, 15, and 8 resulting from a random selection of 1,070 children of professional and business classes.

If, instead of a random selection, we selected 1,070 children from the professional and business classes on the basis of their school marks and teachers' evaluations (which were used also by Terman) but did not use any of the intelligence tests, the proportion of gifted children, and of eventual candidates for *Who's Who,* would probably increase still more.

Thus, as soon as the intelligence tests are really tested, they turn into a set of paper-pen operations hardly testing, and still less measuring, either intelligence or other mental properties of human beings. Their testing adequacy is mainly a fashionable myth, believed in by their devotees but largely devoid of objective foundation.

*Test of the Tests by the OSS Assessment Staff.* This conclusion is confirmed by inductive tests of other current tests of intelligence, character, ability, and other psychosocial properties of individuals. Let us examine, for instance, the adequacy of a whole battery of tests performed by the Assessment Staff of the Office of Strategic Services.

During World War II the Office of Strategic Services gathered together a large staff of notable psychologists, psychiatrists, and social scientists to devise the best methods for testing the various abilities of the prospective agents of the Office of Strategic Services, in order to place each agent in the position most suitable to his ability. This extraordinary staff of scientific experts devised a battery of the best tests available in the light of the modern psychological, psychiatric, and social sciences. A special country estate forty minutes outside Washington was assigned for the testing and assessing operations of the staff. The estate "provided ample space for setting up all sorts of stressful situations, indoors and outdoors, to test intelligence and stamina of the candidates" [21] for the important positions in the OSS. The staff tested and assessed intensively 5,391 recruits, each person being studied for a three-day period during which he lived with the testing experts. To the credit of the staff it should be mentioned that its battery of tests included, besides current paper-pen, vocal and similar tests, several real tests like placing the testee in an actually dangerous situation and observing his ability to cope with it. In many respects the whole testing procedure was more sound and realistic than most of the ordinary tests of psychosocial qualities in individuals. To the further credit of the staff, two additional facts should be mentioned. First, the staff's awareness of the inadequacy of the tests for discovering specific abilities and for predicting how the testee would act under different and scantly predictable conditions.

> How can a psychologist foretell with any degree of accuracy the outcome of future meetings of one barely known personality with hundreds of other undesignated personalities in distant undesignated cities, villages, fields, and jungles that are seething with one knows not what potential harms and benefits? Fortune—call the old hag or beauty what you will—can never be eliminated from the universe of human interactions. And this being forever true, prophetic infallibility is beyond the reach of social scientists.[22]

Second, still greater credit is to be given to the staff for its decision "to embark on an extensive program to check the ratings and recommendations of assessment." "The final result [of the checking] was a decrease, rather than an increase, in degree of certainty" in regard to the adequacy of the tests.[23] The checking of the ratings and assessments was done on the basis of the actual performance of duties by 2,748 testees sent overseas for this purpose. They were assigned the positions corresponding to the abilities discovered and assessed by the tests. A good or bad performance of the duties assigned to the testees in their overseas service was appraised by the Overseas Staff Appraisal, the Theater Commander Appraisal, the Reassignment Area Appraisal, and the Returnee Appraisal.[24] These appraisals of the actual performance of the assigned work by the testee during several months or a year of his service were done in the terms of ranking the performances as: (1) outstanding; (2) high average; (3) low average; and (4) unsatisfactory. Appraisals were made of several specific characteristics of the testees, as well as of their overall performance.

The essential results of this checking of the adequacy of the assessment tests are as follows: "None of our statistical computations demonstrates that our system of assessment was of great value."

The coefficients of correlation between the assessments of job rating (through the battery of tests) and appraisal ratings of the actual performance of the testees run between .08 and .37 for the testees of testing center S and between .15 and .52 for the testees of testing center W.[25]

The coefficients of correlation between the assessment ratings and Returnee Appraisal are .19 and .21. Still lower are the coefficients of correlation between the assessment and appraisal of specific traits in the testees: intelligence, emotional stability, leadership, and social relations in their actual performance.[26]

This courageous test of the tests shows again the striking inadequacy of the tests in discovering and measuring the general character and the specific psychosocial abilities of human beings.

The totality of the considerations, and the inductive evidence given in this and other chapters, is sufficient to warrant the following conclusions: first, intelligence tests are very inadequate and highly unreliable; second, their infallibility is largely a myth; third, their "precise" measurements are only a pseudo-mathematical screen hiding the arbitrary assumptions of the metromanic numerologists; fourth, therefore, these tests should not be given as great a practical importance as they enjoy at the present time. If the current overvaluation of the tests is continued, one of its results will be an increasing misselection and maldistribution of individuals in various social strata and positions. As a consequence of the maldistribution and misselection, the creative activities and the total life of respective societies will be progressively deteriorating and disintegrating. Such is the penalty for an inflated testomania in our age.

These conclusions concern not only intelligence tests, but all the psychosocial tests mentioned above and those to be analyzed in the next chapter. Turn now to an examination of the "projective methods" and other psychosocial tests.

# *Chapter Six*

# Projective and Other Psychosocial Tests

## 1. Projective Methods

Under the influence of Freud the projective or "indirect" tests play now as important a role as the intelligence tests. Like the latter, the projective tests represent a sort of cult, with its own credo, ritual, priests, and a large crowd of devotees. The prestige of the cult is high and is crowned by the halo of scientism. Sigmund Freud is its Messiah and prophet; psychoanalysts are its apostles; the psychoanalytic couch is its altar; the mentally ill are its beneficiaries and victims. Its Gospel is the Unconscious, the omnipresent and omnipotent Sexual Libido. Its fellow-travelers and propagandists are many psychologists, psychiatrists, sociologists, anthropologists, journalists, ministers, businessmen, little bureaucrats in big foundations, and all sorts of highbrow sophisticates and credulous suckers. The practical role of this cult is enormous; and the influence of its apostles and devotees is gigantic.

Yet, when carefully tested, the projective methods are found to be even more inadequate than intelligence tests.

The projective tests aim to diagnose the hidden, unconscious regions of personality. The devotees of these tests believe these regions are inaccessible for "direct" or conscious methods of exploration. The individual cannot know his own unconscious drives, "complexes," "repressions," motivations or the type of his basic personality hidden in his unconscious. Only indirect, projective tests, analogous to X-rays, are assumed able to penetrate these dark caverns of the unconscious and to bring to light a correct picture of what is going on. The main projective methods are: the test of free association and free word association, certain methods of dream-interpretation, the Rorschach and the thematic apperception tests, those of story-completion and verbal summation, the tests through interpretation of plays, drawings, paintings, and other art-expressions, the doll and puppet tests—and a few other similar rituals. Critically examined, these tests are full of holes. They are based on unproven theories and doubtful assumptions. The nature of the tests is largely indeterminate. Interpretations of their results are quite arbitrary. There is little demonstration of their validity. What the tests really test remains largely unknown. Even the interpretations of their devotees are so different from, and so contradictory to, one another, that only a very credulous person can accept them as exact revelations of the properties they supposedly probe. Here is a condensed corroboration of these criticisms.

First, the tests presuppose a dyadic personality structure consisting of two strata: conscious and unconscious (or subconscious or preconscious). Most of its devotees adhere to the Freudian conception of the unconscious. This concept of personality structure is grossly defective. It puts into one unconscious class two entirely different orders of mental phenomena: the unconscious that lies below the level of the conscious, and the supraconscious that lies above the class of the conscious mentality. The supraconscious is the highest creative and cognitive class of mental phenomena. It is the source of all the greatest creative achievements of genius. The unconscious is the lowest stratum of mental phenomena common to all species endowed with instincts and reflexes.[1]

If we assume for a moment that the projective tests really probe the unconscious, it is evident that they cannot test the basically different phenomena of the conscious and the supraconscious orders. Meanwhile, being indiscriminately applied to the unconscious and the supraconscious the tests deliver results in which the "syndromes" of the unconscious, the conscious, and of the supraconscious are hopelessly mixed up, distorted, and made impossible for scientific analysis and objective interpretation. For instance, all projective tests give an exceptional significance to the *"common"* and the *"uncommon"* associations, perceptions, images, vocal reactions, reaction-time; to *"usual"* and *"unusual"* themes; and so on. In this way the tests try to diagnose the "normal" and the "abnormal" personality or mental process. Now, the uncommon or abnormal reactions may be due to a disorganization of the unconscious mechanisms, to a disorderly state of the conscious mind, or to the supreme organization of the supraconscious. Creative genius differs from the common norms as much as an insane person or uncreative moron. The original responses of a genius to the tests are likely to be as "unusual" and "uncommon" as the subnormal responses of a mentally defective person. Since the supraconscious is not distinguished from the unconscious, the basically different abnormalities of a genius and of a schizophrenic are dumped into the same abnormal class. As a matter of fact, many a psychoanalyst has many times declared genius as a form of insanity and insanity as a form of genius. The same fallacious theory of the unconscious as the main stratum of human mentality has been applied in innumerable psychoanalyses of great geniuses by the devotees of the projective tests. Their theories interpret practically all great creators, from Buddha and St. Paul to Beethoven and Leonardo da Vinci, in terms of Oedipus, Narcissus, or Tetanus complexes, this or that form of libido, various "repressions," and other factors of the disorganized unconscious processes. As long as these fallacious theories of personality structure remain the basis of the projective tests, they are bound to yield the grossest blunders in diagnosing the psychodynamics and personality structure of the tested individuals.

The second blunderous assumption of the tests is the Freudian conception of the unconscious, shared in a diluted form by many non-Freudian psychologists and psychiatrists. Freud viewed the unconscious now as (a) identical with the vital energy of an organism, but more frequently (b) as libidinal, sexual instinct, in its genital, anal, oral, or cutaneous forms, and finally (c) as a combination of two primordial drives: the sexual and death-destructive instincts. In conformity with these assumptions most of the partisans of the projective tests look for, and expect to find, mainly instinctive or "repressed" sexual complexes, destructive-masochistic or sadistic drives, and one of the basic sexual types of personality. Directly and indirectly these assumptions predetermine the nature of the projective tests and the interpretations of their results. Dogmatic assumptions of this sort prevent their devotees from testing the validity of their preconceptions and tests. They remain blind and deaf to all the factual and logical evidence that decisively contradicts their assumptions.[2]

For this reason, if even the projective tests were indeed testing the dark regions of the unconscious, they are bound to extract mainly sexual and destructive "ore" which they put there beforehand. With their assumptions they cannot help but interpret this "ore" mainly in terms of the preconceived—diluted or straight—Freudian credo. This credo views man as an autoerotic, sadistic, and masochistic creature since infancy charged with an incestuous drive, among boys to seduce their mother, and among girls to seduce their father. Due to this drive boys are filled with a fear of castration by the father, and girls with a fear of destructive punishment and with an envy of penis. Since the parental and social taboos prohibit a satisfaction of these incestuous desires, these wishes are removed from the conscious region of individuals and are sunk or "repressed" into the unconscious. The repressed wishes make the life of such persons painful and lead now to sadistic and masochistic actions, now to suicide, and most frequently to neuroses and other disorders of mental life. Only a psychoanalyst through his projective tests is capable of bringing to light these complexes, and through that to "redeem" and bring to sanity the mentally sick persons.

The devotees of such a conception of the unconscious and of human nature generally, cannot help but believe that their tests dig these very complexes out of the caverns, nor can they help but believe in their sexual and destructive interpretations of the excavated "ore."

Third, a very doubtful assumption with regard to the validity of the tests is the belief that casual associations of images, or the words with which a testee answers the probing words of the tester, adequately reveal either a specific hidden complex or the over-all basic personality of the testee. The same assumption is made in regard to the testee's responses to the Rorschach ink-blots or the pictures of TAT tests, or the incidental drawings, paintings, treating dolls, unconscious gestures and mumbled words of the testee. These beliefs are no more valid than the ancient beliefs in the diagnostic, revealing, and predictive efficacy of randomly thrown playing cards or dice cubes, of randomly spread coffee-grounds or tea-leaves, or of a configuration of clouds or flying geese. As a matter of fact, tests with tea-leaves or coffee-grounds tests are essentially similar to the Rorschach tests. Very similar to their modern variations are also the ancient forms of the "free association" and "dream-interpretation" tests. Practically, I do not find any single modern projective test that in a similar form has not been used over the millennia by shamans and medicine men, by priests and "spiritual fathers," by the tests of the monastic orders, and often by judges and courts. A list of the various tests used for designating heretics, persons possessed by the devil, or suspected criminals contain all the contemporary projective tests and several additional ones.[3]

If we do not believe in the validity of the ancient projective tests, we have no reason whatever to believe in their modern slight variations. If we are entitled to be skeptical of a causal relationship between the randomly opened cards and unconscious complexes of a certain kind, or between the randomly spread tea-leaves and the future behavior of a testee, we have no more reasons for believing in a causal connection between the responses to the ink-blots and this or that "repressed" complex; between the manner of handling a doll and the basic type of personality structure or the future conduct of the testee.

Several additional reasons can be added in favor of this healthy disbelief in the magical powers of the projective tests. By observation of others and of ourselves, we know well that our spontaneous associations, words uttered in answer to the tester's words, images aroused by pictures or clouds or ink-blots or tea-leaves—that these reactions change from moment to moment, that they depend upon innumerable internal and external conditions, that depending on these conditions we respond quite differently. In view of these ever-changing responses, we cannot assume that, out of hundreds of different responses, exactly the response given to the tester at a given moment under the highly abnormal conditions of being pestered by the tests (blocked by the testing situation, sometimes hypnotized, often shocked by insulin, stupefied by barbital or other drugs, and "abnormalized" in many other ways) is the adequate response that reveals our hidden drives, emotions, and complexes or the form and content of our basic personality structure. To believe this is equivalent to a belief that out of hundreds of various chance-possibilities the tester always hits the lucky chance. *An elementary knowledge of probability theory decisively repudiates such a belief.* If projective tests reveal anything, they reveal the utter credulity of the testers themselves.

The uncertainty of the tests is increased still more by the pseudo-mathematical operations of scoring the points of various tests and factors in a complex system of total scores and factors. In the Thematic Apperception Test an investigator has to decide what weight or score he gives to each of the categories of stories (traced to books or to the testee's own experience, or to his fantasies); how many points to give to each story in each of these categories and to each of the subtopics in each story; and whether to give any weight to the emotional or other traits of the narrator; and so on. There is no objective basis to determine the comparative weight or score to be given to each of these "components" or "variables." The score is arbitrarily determined by the tester and on the basis of these subjective estimates he constructs a chart or statistical table that is nothing more than an objective-looking screen hiding a set of arbitrarily made scores. In the Rorschach tests the investigator arbitrarily decides, first of all "the location" of the ink-blots—whether the whole blot or its small detail—is chosen for testing and then for interpretation; whether the shape, or shading or color or movement or all of these characteristics of the blots are given particular importance; whether the content of the response or its originality, slow or fast reaction-time, or some other characteristic, is viewed as especially significant. After these questions are arbitrarily decided, there comes the problem of scoring each of these "variables": what score or weight is to be given to each of these "indicators" (W, D, Dr, F, F-plus, F-minus, C, FC, CF, M, T, etc.) in the total "complex-indicator" that supposedly reveals to us the basic personality of the testee. All these questions have to be, and are, arbitrarily decided (including the question of whether greater frequency of certain responses is more "syndromatic" than a lesser frequency). The final, objective-looking diagnosis is again a mirage.

Still greater invalidity creeps into the tests through interpretation of their results. In contrast to the clear indication of temperature by a thermometer, the tests do not give direct answers to questions asked about the properties of the testee. In order that the results of the tests can answer these questions, the responses of the testees need to be interpreted by the tester. And the meaning of an interpretation is entirely different from what the test results are in their physical, sensory, or perceptual forms.

As soon as we enter the phase of interpretation, we find ourselves in a region of shadows and all sorts of fantasmas and spooks about which nothing certain can be stated, and still less can be proved. The distance between the perceptual data of the tests and their diagnostic or revealing meaning is so great that dozens, even hundreds, of different interpretations are possible for bridging the test results with their diagnostic meanings.

Take, for instance, the dream tests. Nobody, as yet, can validly interpret exactly what a dreamless or a dreamful sleep means. No one exactly knows the diagnostic meaning of each of the thousands of different dreams, coherent or incoherent, one has throughout his life, especially the dreams having neither sexual nor fearful content. Instead of a generally accepted theory of dreams, we have dozens of mutually discordant theories, each of which in its claims to general validity is contradicted either by solid factual evidence, or by the contradictory logic of the theory itself. Thus Freud's theory of the *latent* content of dreams as the fulfillment of wishes is contradicted by the fearful and painful dreams. This contradiction forced Freud himself to limit his theory by considering the dream as an "*attempted* wish-fulfillment." In its turn, this new theory is also contradicted by many dreams free of any attempted fulfillment of wishes. The revised theory then had to be limited by the new theories of "distortion" of wishes in a finished dream, by the hypotheses of "condensation," "displacement," "secondary elaboration," "modification by environmental stimuli," and by a host of reservations, qualifications, reformulations, and substitutions.[4] As a result, Freud did not give any consistent theory of dreams. Instead he gave several self-contradictory conjectures. Of these conjectures his sexual interpretation of dreams is actually the only one used by Freud and the Freudians.

Being in accord with Freud's own sex-obsession and his pan-sexual metaphysics, this sexual theory claims that "the majority of the dreams of adults deal with sexual material and give expression to erotic wishes."[5] By this theory almost all dreams are produced by repressed infantile sexual wishes: whatever image one sees in dreams is a symbol of sex. Thus Freud assures us that "the male genital organ is symbolically represented in dreams in many different ways": the penis is symbolized by the number three, by sticks, umbrellas, poles, trees, knives, daggers, lances, sabers, guns, pistols, revolvers, taps, watering-cans, springs, reptiles, fish, cloaks, hats, lamps, pencils, penholders, nail-files, hammers, balloons, aeroplanes, Zeppelins, and flying in dreams means penis-erection. The female genitalia appear in dreams as pits, hollows, caves, jars, bottles, boxes, chests, coffers, pockets, ships, cupboards, stoves, rooms, doors, gates, wood, paper, tables, books, snails, mussels, mouths, churches, chapels, apples, peaches, fruit, thickets, landscapes, various types of machinery, and so on. Scenes of sliding or gliding, falling out, extraction of teeth, dancing, riding, climbing, experiencing some violence, stairs, steps, ladders, ties, underlinen and linen signify the sexual act and its different forms. And so on.[6]

This enumeration shows that practically anything which appears in dreams is a symbol of sex, sexual organs, normal and abnormal forms of coitus, and so on. The utterly unscientific character of such an interpretation is obvious. Using this method one can claim with an equal right that almost all dreams deal with eating, or drinking, or praying, or fighting, or breathing, because whatever appears in dreams is but a symbol of a dogmatically assumed eating, drinking, praying, and so on. In their foolish fancy such theories are in no way more crazy, arbitrary, and unscientific than Freud's pan-sexual interpretation of dreams. One should wonder, not at the sex-obsessed Freud setting forth theories of this sort (there is no scarcity of dogmatic ideologists manufacturing all sorts of foolish ideologies), but at the fact that a legion of gullible psychologists, psychiatrists, sociologists, anthropologists, journalists, and even ministers of God, can seriously accept these phantasmagorias, and sell them to the public as the last word of science.

This does not deny that a portion of dreams have sexual character. This character, however, is discovered not by the doubtful projective tests, but by the direct (introspective) experience of persons having such dreams, and by direct (conscious) questioning and observation of the behavior of others. Combined, these direct tools explore our unconscious and conscious regions much more adequately than the fanciful and unverifiable interpretations of the devotees of the projective creeds.

With proper modification, these conclusions are applicable to all diagnostic interpretations of dreams, as well as to the results of other projective tests where, too, an enormous amount of arbitrariness or subjectivity is unavoidable. This accounts for the frequently contradictory interpretations of the same results by different testers.

The totality of the considerations given is sufficient for us to conclude that the projective tests are not the royal road to the unconscious; they are not the magic tools that open the secrets of the basic structure and dynamics of human personality. If we reject the "testimony" of tea-leaves, playing cards, cloud configurations, or dreams, interpreted by soothsayers, medicine men or oracles, for the same reason we must be skeptical of the testimony of ink-blots, pictures, dreams, dolls, or incidental words no less arbitrarily interpreted by the modern believers in these omens.

## 2. Inductive Deflation of Projective Tests

These conclusions are well confirmed *inductively* by a few experimental studies of the diagnostic and predictive adequacy of the projective tests. These experimental studies show at least three things: first, that the projective tests often fail to register the strongest—conscious and unconscious—drives, emotions, or complexes dominating the total personality tested; second, that the direct, conscious methods often reveal the unconscious drives better than the indirect, projective methods; third, that the projective tests often deliver misleading results.

Here are examples of these failures.

A group of scientists of the University of Minnesota carried on, during World War II, an experimental study of starvation on 36 conscientious objectors kept for six months on a semistarvation diet. The diet was so meager that the human guinea pigs lost one-quarter of their initial body weight. During these months they were in a state of continuous hunger. As a result, their thinking, feeling, and striving were constantly centered on food and phenomena connected with it. Food-images and associations became obsessive,[7] striving for food imperative. Body and mind were dominated by the quest for food. Even when our 36 conscientious objectors intentionally tried to free themselves from the persistent obsession with food, they could do it only for a few moments, after which the obsession returned. The significant fact in this study is that, in spite of the incessant striving for satisfaction of their food-drive, the projective tests failed to register this drive. The tests of free word association, first-letter tests, analysis of dreams, the Rorschach test, the Rosenzweig P-F test, all failed to register this prepotent drive, with exception of the free association test which gave a slight indication of it.

Allport is right in saying that "here is a finding of grave significance. The most urgent, the most absorbing motive in life failed completely to reveal itself by indirect method" (by the projective tests). "It was, however, entirely accessible to conscious report."[8]

Other studies reveal similar failure of the tests in performing their revealing and diagnostic tests. The Rorschach testers, asking a testee what he sees in an ink-blot, now and then are answered by an "astounding": "Just an ink-blot." The story is told of a patient who said that an ink-blot made him think of sexual relations. The clinician, thinking to tap a buried complex, asked him why. "Oh," said the patient, "because I think of sexual relations all the time, anyway." "The clinician scarcely needed a Rorschach card to find out this motivational fact." [9] Testees whose hidden complexes are expected to be uncovered by their "imaginings" about a picture shown to them, now and then respond by an accurate, matter-of-fact description of the picture-detector. These and similar cases show that the projective tests fail even to "penetrate" the "resistances" of common sense. If the testees were not forced by the tester to give some interpretations, images or associations, if they were not hypnotized, drugged, shock-treated, and abnormalized in various other ways, then such common-sense responses as "I see only ink-blots" would have been incomparably more frequent. On the other hand, if the responses are given under abnormal conditions—and most of the testees are subjected to some sort of abnormality by the testing procedures—the responses become abnormal responses incapable of revealing the normal state of the conscious and unconscious regions of personality.

Numerous cases of lying, hypocritical, and mischievous responses, in which the testees intentionally falsify their reactions, add to the incertitude of the tests. For instance, in the word association test they may intentionally respond to the word "white" by "holy mackerel" instead of a spontaneous "black." Sometimes, knowing the sexual preoccupation of a psychoanalyst, they mischievously give him a bizarre sexual interpretation of a Rorschach card or a picture. Often, by the tester's suggestions and innuendoes, they are artificially induced to respond in a manner pleasing to the tester. In these and similar ways the responses are almost always distorted to some tangible extent.

When they are spontaneous indeed, the direct, conscious reactions of normal testees coincide—contrary to the claims of the testers—with the testees' indirect responses to the projective tests. The studies of J. W. Getzels and several others demonstrate this.[10] When the direct and projective responses do not coincide, the reason for the discrepancy often lies in the difference between seemingly identical questions, or in neurotic conditions in the testees, or in abnormalization caused by the projective procedures, or in several other conditions. In most discrepancies of this sort, the conscious answers to the direct questions are more significant than the indirect responses to the projective stimuli. Among other advantages of direct answers, is the fact that their "interpretation" is less hazardous and arbitrary than "interpretations" of the indeterminate projective results.

Inductive verification of the projective tests increasingly shows their limitations and dangers, especially when the tests are given a preponderant significance in comparison with the conscious responses of the testees and objective observation of their overt behavior. This explains the growing trend toward the total or integral method of investigation and diagnosis of personality.[11] This method consists of four combined methods: (1) fullest collection and analysis of the conscious vocal answers of the testees to the questions of the investigator, especially of the testees' "confessions," "autobiographies," spontaneous and thoughtful accounts of what, how, and why they think, say, and behave as they do; (2) an objective observation of the testees' overt actions and behavior; (3) very cautious and limited use of the projective methods as supplementary to the other methods; (4) when possible, reinforcing these three methods by an approach which can be called "suprasensory-intuitional." It is the method of a true seer or a true genius that reads correctly the supraconscious region of personality and grasps, in a "twinkling of an eye," the most important essentials of the supraconscious, conscious, and unconscious regions of human beings,[12] the essentials of the soul, mind, and bodily behavior. Representing supreme insight, this method unfortunately is accessible only to a genius or seer. It can hardly be learned and fruitfully used by the ordinary investigators, devoid of the grace of genius. Herein lies its limitation. This limitation has to be emphasized in order to prevent a legion of "unanointed" and "unelected" fools to think of themselves as geniuses capable of reading the minds and souls of other human beings.

Only the integral method can give a roughly adequate understanding of the total personality of human beings. Taken alone, each of the four methods is inadequate and can lead to a series of gross errors. The integral method was successfully used by practically all the great "readers" and educators of human beings: by Homers and Shakespeares, Bachs and Beethovens, Platos and Shankaras, Patanjalis, and al Ghazzalis, by the founders of all the great religions, by the great moral educators of humanity, including the founders of monastic orders, like St. Pachomius, St. Basil the Great, St. Benedict, St. Francis of Assisi, to mention but a few names.[13]

These seers and geniuses revealed to us the infinite richness and complexity of the total human personality much more adequately than all the psychoanalysts, psychologists, and mental testers taken together. While the latter "explorers" hardly even scratched the surface, the seers and geniuses opened to us the sublimest heights and most unfathomable depths, the divine and the devilish forces in man, the dazzling multicoloredness and the monotonous aridity, in the total personality, with the how and why of its psychodynamics. Exactly because they understood the total personality so well, they were able to invent efficacious methods for spiritual, mental, and moral transfigurations of millions of human beings, and also for the alleviation of their mental troubles and disorders. When we turn to their sayings and writings, we find indeed a clearly outlined integral method of diagnosing human personality.[14] They clearly state that for a full comprehension of every human being one must use: (1) the method of suprarational, inspired intuition for understanding the supraconscious region; (2) the methods of conscious, sincere interrogation, free communication of souls, confession, examination of conscience, etc.; (3) the method of careful observation of the overt behavior for comprehension of the conscious and unconscious regions; and (4) a real, often experimental, projective method for bringing to light some of the "sins" hidden in the deep recesses of the unconscious.

For this purpose, the seers analyzed dreams, incidental vocal reactions, spontaneous actional gestures, various postures, the details of facial expressions, the facts of *acidie* or depressive moods, and other "troublesome syndromes" of a brother-monk, or of any person seeking freedom from his sins, peace of mind, salvation of his soul, and union with God. Especially rich in various "projective" methods was the arsenal of the eminent "spiritual fathers." Each monk freely chose his *pater spiritualis* for his life-long moral and spiritual guidance. Each spiritual father likewise freely accepted this tremendous responsibility before God and the monastic community, at the cost of perdition of his own soul. By this acceptance the *pater spiritualis* became responsible for all the misdeeds, evil thoughts and sinful wishes of his disciple as much as for his own. This all-embracing union for life and death, for salvation and eternal damnation, was based on complete mutual sincerity, trust, and devotion. The disciple's soul and mind were unrestrictedly open to his spiritual father, and no secret could be kept from him. On his part, the spiritual father incessantly probed every dangerous "syndrome" of his disciple, if he was unaware of it. Together they labored to get to the roots of the hidden soul sickness. In their "psychoanalysis" the spiritual fathers elaborated a rich assortment of projective methods for diagnosing, curing, and regenerating their disciples.

As any ingenious art of great virtuosi, this assortment does not lend itself to a standard classification and standard use by the ordinary craftsmen, just as an excellent knowledge of the rules of musical composition does not make a Beethoven or Bach out of the competent professor. As with all creative giants, the great spiritual fathers created their masterpieces regardless of, and contrary to, some of the standard rules. However, "by their fruits, ye shall know them": by their fruits we know Beethoven and Mozart; by their fruits we know also the great achievements of the great spiritual fathers, including their system of projective methods. Reading their writings and their monastic rules, studying their doings and sayings, their diagnosing and curing of many persons, we get a glimpse of their artful projective techniques as well as of their total, integral system of cognition, diagnosing and helping human beings.[15]

If in this supreme form the integral method is hardly accessible to the rank and file of psychologists, psychiatrists, and other scholars of personality, in its standard form it is accessible to all of us. As a matter of fact, in this ordinary form it has been widely used by many a sound and expert psychiatrist, educator, and psychologist. They rarely, if ever, gave an exclusive importance to the existing "projective" methods. Systematically improving the integral method and each of its component parts, we can notably refine our knowledge, diagnosis, and therapeutic treatment of the total personality. The integral method prevents us also from making many blunders bound to be committed through use of only one of its component methods.

### 3. Other Psychosocial Tests

If intelligence and projective tests are inadequate, many of the various psychosocial tests are still more questionable. Most of these tests represent variations of paper-pen and speech-reactional operations which are believed to reveal the presence or absence, and the extensity and intensity of the tested traits. There is as little foundation for belief in such magic as in the cases of intelligence and projective tests.

Thus, measurement of a weak reaction to an imaginary mild rebuke hardly measures the traits of *ascendance-submission*. An arbitrary measurement of difference in mental work under "normal" and again under "distracting" conditions, observed once or twice for a period of a few minutes, hardly measures *aggressiveness*.

The ratio between the attempted and the rightly or wrongly solved items of an intelligence test does not measure *caution*.

The length of time during which a child tries to open a box with an interesting object within cannot be taken as an adequate test of the child's *compliance*.

Only a testomaniac can believe that the longer one can stand on his toes, the greater is his *general perseverance*. From this standpoint the trained ballerinas or boxers must be the most persevering persons, while the untrained Schuberts and Mozarts, or Newtons and Kants must be diagnosed as the least persevering persons in any field of activity.

Only an enthusiastic devotee of tests can believe that a number of conventional preferences in a multiple-choice paper-pen test, administered once or a few times, measures one's *conformity*. Only a gullible simpleton can believe that a more frequent withdrawing of one's hand from an apparently dangerous situation, after the experimenter's assurance that it is harmless, demonstrates the *greater emotional instability* of the subject in comparison with a person who withdraws his hand less frequently. If this test indicates anything, it indicates the greater *caution* of the first subject rather than his emotional instability.

Likewise, the 120 questions of the Woodworth Personal Data Sheet, or the paper-pencil data of the Pressey XO tests, or Allport-Vernon-Lindzey's test of dominant interests, or the "mind-reading-graphological" items of J. Downey's Will-Temperament tests, or the Landis-Gullette-Jacobsen emotional tests, or Bernreuter's personality inventory—these and similar tests hardly even scratch the emotional, volitional, and temperamental equipment of the testees. At best these tests, including the better ones, like the Minnesota Multiphasic Personality Inventory, are but poor snapshots of "something" as it is caught at a given moment. Meanwhile, this "something"—this configuration of our associations, interests, emotions, moods, ideas, wishes, memories, or whatnot—is incessantly changing, and due to the continuous change we have no certainty that the snapshot catches exactly that configuration which is typical, basic, permanent and, therefore, truly characteristic of the testee's personality.

These and dozens of similar qualifications are not considered at all in questions of this sort. For this reason, they cannot be answered correctly, or, if answered, the answers cannot be typical and truly characteristic of the basic interests of the testee. Furthermore, many of the tests are based upon questionable premises and, now and then, wrong assumptions. For instance, Downey's Will-Temperament tests presuppose the validity of very doubtful "graphological" and "mind-reading" beliefs. For this reason their results are void.

Further, almost all tests assume that the actual behavior of the testee will be similar to the imaginary behavior described in his vocal and paper-pencil answers. The general assumption that one practices what he preaches is largely untenable: there are few, if any, individuals whose actions are identical with their vocal or written answers to the questionnaires and interviews. Some discrepancy between one's preachings and one's actual behavior is a fairly universal uniformity, so there is no guarantee at all that the testees have acted and will act exactly in accordance with their test answers. This discrepancy alone greatly invalidates the results of the "snapshot" tests.

Moreover, as mentioned before, these results *per se* are meaningless. To be diagnostic or meaningful they require interpretations and often measurements. In their turn, these operations make necessary a multitude of arbitrary rankings, estimates, weighings, and scorings. In most cases quantifications of essentially qualitative data are based on purely arbitrary assignment of ranks, scoring points, weights, and numerical values. Consequently, the results of the tests are predominantly subjective and dogmatic indicators of nobody knows what qualities and intensities. No wonder that almost all of these tests come, flourish for a short time, and go with the wind into oblivion.

To continue our examples.

Only a very gullible researcher can believe that creative originality, or aggressiveness, or submissiveness, and so on, can be measured by a cephalic index, or by the color of the skin, eyes and hair, or by height and weight, or by any other anatomical trait. Only very uncritical scholars can contend that this or that anatomical characteristic is evidence that a given person is a potential murderer or rapist or pickpocket; or that endomorphic, mesomorphic, or entomorphic somatic types are closely associated with sociality, aggressiveness, or some other psychosocial characteristics. Still more untenable are the dianetic theories of "the bank of the reactive mind," "engrams," and the methods of "recall" for diagnosis of "cleared" and "uncleared" persons, and for curing of the "uncleared" patients. The same goes for various "astrological" theories and their "horoscope tests," as well as for diverse "karmic" beliefs, diagnoses and tests. To a lesser degree, the various "geographic" interpretations of personality are also inadequate. On the other hand, there is a certain grotesqueness about the diagnostic theories that interpret the structure and psychodynamics of personality, society, and nation by a single narrow factor, such as the way in which infants are swaddled, or trained in micturition and defecation; and so on (the Freudians, M. Mead, G. Gorer, J. Rickman, and others). Not denying a small role to these factors, nevertheless the "swaddling theories of personality and historical processes," and the "micturitional-defecative philosophies of history" are phantasmagoric in the all-powerful and decisive role they ascribe to these factors.[16]

And yet, such theories, diagnoses, and tests proliferate luxuriously in the modern psychosocial sciences. Only a testomaniac can offer twelve vague and doubtful paper-pencil tests as a valid measure of *general originality,* regardless of what sort it is and in what field, regardless of whether it is the pathological originality of a schizophrenic or the creative originality of a genius. Only credulous persons can believe that the cephalic index accurately measures the general creativity of a person. Much better is the psychodramatic test of *spontaneity-creativity* or *constructive originality* of J. L. Moreno. By spontaneity Moreno means the impromptu "response of an individual to a new situation, and the new response to an old situation" in the surprise situations created on a psychodramatic stage; and by creativity he means the spontaneous response which is "adequate." Moreno's tests register the actual behavior of the testee in experimentally created, real situations. These tests record the spontaneity trait much better than most artificial tests. However, in testing *creativity* they are also not wholly adequate. If creativity means an *adequate* spontaneous response to any surprise situation, then the criteria of spontaneity—like instantaneity, flexibility, and novelty of the response, rapid warming-up, dramatization of the routine, and so on—cannot be an adequate measure of creativity. Such criteria of creativity are biased in favor of "good mixers," "energetic go-getters," "cynical turncoats," agitated devotees of the "do something" school, Pareto's persons with a dominant "residue of combination," and "manipulators" (regardless of the adequacy of their "doings" and "being in motion"). And the criteria are biased against "poor mixers" like Beethoven, lonely souls like Pascal, "nonsocial" geniuses like Newton, recluses like St. Anthony, and generally slowly ripening and introvert creative geniuses. "The flexibility and momentary responses ('warming up') of the first type of persons are not necessarily more creative or a more adequate response than inflexible and 'conserved' responses of the second type. The principle of adequacy of response and of its creativity is something fairly neutral to the flexibility-inflexibility, 'conserved-deconserved,' 'agitated action and nonaction on the spur of the moment,' and other symptoms of genuine spontaneous behavior. . . . Only so far as psychodramatic tests of the spontaneity-factor exhibit the *adequacy* of the response; only when one is tested for this adequacy many times and given all the time needed to develop his real spontaneity—only thus far are these tests reliable indices of genuine spontaneity-creativity."[17]

Moreno's tests of spontaneity-creativity are more adequate than practically all of the mechanical, artificial tests combined. Moreno's tests probe the well outlined traits of real spontaneity-creativity, tested by actual behavior, in real situations, created on a psychodramatic stage. As such they are nonmechanical and not limited to paper-pen operations. And the more adequate they eventually become, the less mechanical and artificial they are bound to be. Even at present, Moreno's concepts of spontaneity-creativity define and test these phenomena more adequately than most of the current tests of "originality," "creativity," high intelligence and genius.

If creative originality could be detected and measured by these current "easy" tests, if they could certify the specific abilities and disabilities of the tested persons, the most difficult problem of selecting and distributing individuals among various occupational and social positions would be excellently solved. Everyone could be placed in the position corresponding to his ability. The whole society would immensely benefit from such a scientific distribution. The total set of correctional and educational institutions would be radically remodelled and simplified. The total creative output of society—its economic, political, scientific, technological, religious, ethical, and artistic achievements—would increase immensely and through this increase of creativity almost all the problems of the society and mankind would be constructively solved.

Unfortunately, such a utopia cannot be achieved through these tests. As is shown above, the tests, beginning with intelligence tests and ending with automatic tests of creativity, are fallible. If they, being defective, are actually made the basis for selecting and distributing individuals among the multitude of social positions, they are bound to misplace the members of a society rather than place them according to their abilities. Through their mistesting and misselection they would likely aggravate rather than alleviate the defects of the existing selection and distribution. By this aggravation they would decrease rather than increase the total well-being of a society.

For the foregoing reasons, healthy scepticism and great caution are needed in regard to these artificial tests. As merely supplementary tools they can be used. As the main tests to determine who is what and for what positions he is fit or unfit we must still rely on *real life-tests of the integral type:* a study, through inspired intuition, of the supraconscious potential of each individual; a long-time, continuous study of his conscious vocal and written mental processes, and of his behavioral performances and achievements at home, in school, in his occupational pursuits, and in his interactions with various persons, agencies, groups, and institutions; and a similar, long-time study of his unconscious region as it manifests itself again in his speech-reactions, in his writings, and in his overt actions. This continuous study may be somewhat supplemented by the real tests, which probe this or that quality through challenging experimental situations. The artificial, semiautomatic, or even semiexperimental short-time tests should not be given too important a role. At best they are but the supplementary tools for the integral study of that most complex and most mysterious cosmos: human personality. Above, I gave several cases of spectacular misjudgment of great creative geniuses. These misjudgments were based on long-time continuous and careful observations by many judges: their teachers, comrades, and relatives, their professors, professional critics, and other experts. If gross blunders are possible with real tests in regard to the first class geniuses, or in regard to the nonentities—glittering mediocrities and smart alecks often elevated by "experts" to the rank of geniuses—it is still more probable that blunders will be made by the manufacturers of the various mechanical, artificial, and easy tests so fashionable at the present time. These tests are still mainly the manifestations of a raging testomania rather than adequate scientific tests. Caution and skepticism—and once more, caution and skepticism—are prescribed in regard to them for any prudent society and for any real scientist and scholar.

# *Chapter Seven*

# Quantophrenia

*Life is much too involved to be fully accessible to mathematics.* E. SCHROEDINGER.[1]

## 1. THE QUEEN OF SCIENCES AND THE CULT OF NUMEROLOGY

Already in ancient Egypt, Babylonia, India, China, and Pythagorean Greece, the logical elegance of mathematical thought and its fruitfulness in the analysis of empirical phenomena were fully acknowledged. Since that time, mathematics has rightly been called "the queen of sciences." Mathematical reasoning has played the royal role in the development of science and rational thought itself. Mathematical analysis has been largely responsible for a good share of scientific discoveries and inventions. Finally, mathematical calculations have been the main basis for most of the accurate predictions of various phenomena.

In the ancient civilizations mathematics was used for theoretical and practical purposes, not only in the field of physical and vital problems, but also in that of psychosocial problems. Population-census; calculation of taxes, wealth and income; computation of armed forces; measurements of the durations of various cycles in the life-spans of individuals and groups; psychosocial predictions based on astrological and other calculations—in these and more complex forms, quantitative data and mathematical analysis were applied to the field of psychosocial phenomena. Since that time, mathematics itself has continued to develop, and with its progress the quantitative approach to the study of psychosocial matters has also grown. Though this latter growth has been much more modest than the use of mathematics in the field of physical phenomena, it has, nevertheless, contributed a great deal to our knowledge of the psychosocial world.

The mathematical study of psychosocial phenomena was especially cultivated in the seventeenth and the eighteenth centuries. Spinoza, Descartes, Leibnitz, Newton, Weigel, Malebranche, Cumberland, Berkeley, Hobbes, and others, began to build a universal quantitative science, *Pantometrika* or *Mathesis universae,* with its branches of *Psychometrika, Ethicometrika,* and *Sociometrika* designed for investigating psychosocial phenomena along the lines of geometry and physical mechanics. "All truths are discovered only through measurement," and "without mathematics human beings would live as animals and beasts," were the mottoes of the Social Physicists of these centuries. Together with "cameralists" and "political arithmeticians" they began a mathematical analysis, measurement, and interpretation of psychological, social, political, economic, ethical, and religious phenomena.[2]

During the subsequent centuries these efforts have been continued. At the present time quantitative study of psychosocial phenomena is one of their main methods of investigation. So long as the method is genuinely mathematical and is applied to those psychosocial facts which lend themselves to quantitative analysis, it proves fruitful and deserves ever-increasing cultivation. But when the true quantitative method is replaced by pseudomathematical imitations; when the method is misused and abused in various ways; when it is applied to phenomena which, so far, do not lend themselves to quantification; and when it consists in the manipulation of mathematical symbols in a vacuum or in the mere transcription of mathematical formulae on paper without tying them to the relevant psychosocial units—then the approach misfires. Under these conditions, use of mathematical method becomes a mere quantophrenic preoccupation having nothing in common with mathematics and giving no cognition of the psychosocial world.

During the last few decades, to the detriment of the psychosocial sciences, this metrophrenic preoccupation has grown rapidly in the field of psychosocial studies and now threatens to drown in its murky waters many a nonquantitative investigation as well as many an investigation which is truly quantitative. The tidal wave is at present so high that the contemporary stage of the psychosocial sciences can be properly called *the age of quantophrenia and numerology*. This disease manifests itself in many forms and in every region of sociology, psychology, psychiatry, and anthropology:

*a*) Ever-increasing numbers of quanto- or metrophrenic studies are published in the journals of these disciplines. According to the metrophrenics, only the papers containing measurements and numbers are regarded as scientific papers. Each quantitative study is considered as a sign of the progress of the psychosocial sciences toward an "objective," "exact," and "mathematical" phase in their existence, toward a maturity approaching that of the physical sciences.

*b*) The same is true of the books, texts, and monographs dealing with psychosocial phenomena. They also become increasingly numerological and metromanic.

*c*) The prestige of truly quantitative and, even more, of metrophrenic research has grown so high that an ever-increasing number of researchers in our sciences now believe that quantitative research is the only truly scientific investigation of psychosocial phenomena, and that all nonquantitative studies are either merely "arm chair philosophy," or "subjective speculation," or at best "an inexact, superficial, and unverifiable literary exercise."

*d*) Similar misevaluation has spread among governmental agencies, business corporations, big and small foundations, universities, and other institutions that furnish the funds for research in the "behavioral" or psychosocial disciplines. In these institutions, the officials who decide on the grants for research in these fields are increasingly recruited from statisticians and numerologists as the "best" experts in the psychosocial sciences. An ever larger portion of the funds is granted for quantitative research projects. The support of quantitative research, regardless of whether it is truly quantitative or merely metrophrenic, has gone so far that qualitative research projects now have only a slim chance of being supported in many research-financing institutions. Almost all such research projects are ruled, offhand, as nonscientific and not worthy of support by agencies.

*e*) A similar trend is under way among journalists, reviewers, and even ministers and the public at large.

*f*) Accordingly, the prestige of the statistician, the pollster, the builder of "mathematical models" or "mathematical robots," the numerologist and the metrophrenic manipulator of numbers is now far above that of qualitative scholars. Of all the courses in the departments of the psychosocial sciences, a course in statistics is often the only one required from all students in these departments. Being ignorant in the history, theory, methods, and other fundamentals of sociology and psychology, they still can get their Ph.D. with high honors if they know elementary statistics. Without passing a satisfactory examination in statistics, they can hardly graduate or receive an advanced degree, in spite of an excellent knowledge of the history, theory, and methods of these disciplines. Likewise, without being trained in statistics, there is an ever-decreasing chance of their becoming instructors or professors of the psychosocial sciences. These disciplines have become territories dominated by an occupational army of statisticians, bookkeepers, accountants, numerologists, and metromanics.

We shall turn now to substantiation of the above charges.

## 2. Sham Mathematics in the Modern Psychosocial Sciences

The first variety of quantophrenic obsession in modern psychology and sociology is represented by those allegedly quantitative studies which have no relationship to true mathematical method. Here are a few examples of the *substitution of shorthand symbols and empty formulae for the true mathematical ones.*

In his quantitative study of interaction as a specific social energy, Lysen tells us that: (1) the social ties can be either positive or negative, and (2) that the interacting agents may be either qualitatively equal (inorganic ties) or unequal (organic ties). Expressing both criteria "mathematically," Lysen denotes the quantities of social energy by the symbols: $a$, $b$, $c$, and its qualities by those of $x$, $y$, $z$. Having obtained his symbols, Lysen proceeds to use them in the following manner: (1) $ax = bx + cx$ means a horde or the sum of persons devoid of social consciousness and held together only by instinct; (2) $ax = bx — cz$ means the negative social ties or social conflicts; (3) $ax = by \times cz$ means the positive organic ties or collective consciousness of the interacting individuals; (4) $ax = by : cz$ denotes the negative organic ties or the sum of interacting persons aware of subordination, dependency, etc.[3]

No lengthy comments are necessary in order to see—besides poor classification and analysis of interaction phenomena and group structures—the sham-mathematical nature of the shorthand symbols, which hinder rather than help Lysen's verbal definitions of social energy, positive and negative ties, and types of groups. His *ax, by, cz,* etc., do not mean anything clearly defined; neither do they mean any measurable quantity or definite quality; his signs of "=," "+," "—," "×," and ":" are perfectly arbitrary and do not mean at all what they mean in mathematics. Why, for instance, is a group with collective consciousness denoted by the symbol of multiplication $(by \times cz)$, while a horde is denoted by the sign of addition $(bx + cx)$? Or why is the group with domination-subordination expressed by the equation $ax = by : cz$, while the group with social conflicts is defined by the equation $ax = bx - cz$? Why division in one case and subtraction in the other? These formulae, symbols, and equations are nothing but a logical mess, mathematical nonsense, and empirical rubbish.

Another example of sham mathematics is given by many of the shorthand formulae of K. Lewin, J. F. Brown, and others. For instance, Lewin expresses the notion that "the variety of behavior increases during childhood with normal development" by the following formula: $var(B^{Ch}) < var(B^{Ad})$ "where *var* means variety; $B^{Ch}$ behavior of the child; $B^{Ad}$ behavior of the adult." Or, "we call the totality of these factors the life-space (L Sp) of an individual and write B = F (P,E) = F (S Sp)" (B means behavior, P person, E environment).[4]

Lewin's works are full of these homemade shorthand symbols. Having no relationship to mathematics, his cumbersome hieroglyphics serve no useful purpose whatsoever.

S. C. Dodd supplies another set of sham-mathematical symbols. Like other formulae of this sort, they do not serve even the pedagogical function of aiding in the understanding of Dodd's verbal statements. Dodd's basic "S-theory" is an example of his formulae. Here is its essence.

> The generalization, "People's characteristics and environments change," can be more rigorously stated as: "Any quantitatively recorded societal situation (S) can be expressed as a combination of:
>
> 4 indices [I], namely: of time [T], space [L], a human population [P], and indicators [I] of their characteristics; each modified by:
>
> 4 scripts, namely: the exponent [$I^s$], and descripts denoting a series of classes [$I_s$], of class-intervals [${}_sI$], and of cases [${}^sI$]; all combined by:
>
> 8 operators (;), i.e.: for adding [+], subtracting [—], multiplying [×], dividing [÷], aggregating [:], cross-classifying [: :], correlating [.], and identifying [′]."

The S-theory is a system of hypotheses which assert that combinations of these basic concepts [in square brackets] will describe and classify every tabulation, graph, map, formula, prose paragraph, or other set of quantitative data in any of the social sciences.[5]

Here is the master formula of the S-theory:

$$S = {}^{s}_{s}(T;L;P;Ipp,\ I_r)^{s}_{s}.$$

Here S stands for recorded social situations; T, denotes time; L, distance; P, number of people; Ipp, indices of population's characteristics; $I_r$, residual characteristics.

We should not be surprised at the sharp reaction of an eminent mathematician to this metrophrenic abracadabra.

> There is no more pathetic misapprehension of the nature and function of mathematics than the trite cliché that mathematics is a shorthand. . . . Mere symbolization of any discipline is not even a respectable parody of mathematics. . . . For all its symbols, a theory may take the name of mathematics in vain. . . . The S-theory has yet to take its first step toward generative mathematical symbolism. . . . No reckless abuse of the mathematical vocabulary can [of itself] transform a theory not yet mathematical into anything more substantially mathematical than a feeble mathematical pun. . . . [Dodd's] "Research Suggestions" contain several queries relating to possibilities for mathematical developments, for example, "Can dimensional analysis of societal situations be used, as dimensional analysis is used in physics?" with a citation of P. W. Bridgman's (sic), *Dimensional Analysis*. Offhand, a mathematician would say, probably not, at least until someone can give a meaningful answer to such exactly analogous questions as, "How many yards of buttermilk does it take to make a pair of britches for a bull?" Such queries as some of these in "Research Suggestions" may seem profound to the mathematically uninitiated; to at least one mathematician by trade they seem profoundly pretentious. . . . There is no mathematics in the book. As for the "geometric technique consisting of translating S-theory into terms of vectors with their points, lines, and angles," it seems to fritter out in a new "verbalistic nebulousness," evaporating finally in an unimplemented aspiration for a mathematical theory of human relationship.[6]

Any competent mathematician would give a quite similar appraisal of the logical, mathematical, and empirical blunders stemming from such an "operational" abuse of mathematics and physics.

A few additional comments on the sociological aspects of Dodd's "shorthand system of sociology" will round out the appraisal.

*a*) Contrary to Lundberg's statement that in the terms of the equation S = (P:I:T:L) "all societal situations and behavior can be described" [7] this formula, as well as all of Dodd's derivative formulae, can hardly describe any societal situation, if by scientific description is meant the description that really gives the essential traits of the phenomenon studied. In the first place, the sign ( : ) denotes "aggregation." What an "aggregation" of (P:I:T:L) means remains unknown because Dodd does not clarify at all the meaning of his: Time, Location, Population, Population's relevant characteristics, and especially of his "class-intervals," "cases," "aggregation," "cross-classification," "correlation" and "identification." All these terms have such various meanings,[8] and are so haphazardly dumped together in the S-theory, that no definite meaning can be obtained from such formulae. At least, the above formula—"social situation is equal to the population aggregated with indicators of its characteristics aggregated with time and all three aggregated with location"—has no meaning for me nor, I believe, for anyone who tries to decipher its meaning.

*b*) Taken at its face value, the formula is so wide and vague that all "societal situations" slip through its network. The categories of time and space are the categories applied to all empirical phenomena: physical, biological, and social. Therefore, these categories do not give any of the *differentia specifica* of any societal phenomenon. Still less do they give it to the specific social situation. Likewise, the category of "Population" is so general that by itself it does not indicate any specific population or the interacting subjects of any given social situation. What is really most important for description or definition of the given social situation, namely "the characteristics of the given population," are not differentiated or classified at all. Instead, they are just dumped together under the category of "population's characteristics." For these reasons, the general category of "population and its characteristics" is meaningless.

*c*) If Dodd sees the main virtue of his S-theory as its universality and applicability to all societal—and even the nonsocietal, physical, and vital—phenomena, then his formula is too narrow. So far as by "population" he means human population, his formula is inapplicable to all nonhuman phenomena. If one is ambitious to give a shorthand universal formula applicable to all phenomena, then the formula A = APh is the most universal, because in it A means all phenomena of any time and timeless, of any space and spaceless. But being most embracing it is void of any definite meaning and, as Hegel correctly put it, is equal to "nothing." Similarly, the S-theory in its application to societal phenomena is void of any definite meaning and is equal to "societal nothing."

*d*) If the S-theory means the *Kategorienlehre,* a system of the most general categories of human thought, it is but a defective variation of either the Aristotelian system of categories: (substance, quantity, quality, relation, time, place, action, passivity, plus position and state), or the Kantian, Hegelian, Spencerian, and other systems of categories. Logically, Dodd's categories represent a hash of some of the general categories mixed up with very narrow sub-sub-sub-subcategories, notions, and even with operational procedures like addition, division, correlation, etc. This mixture makes the S-theory unfit for classifying and describing empirical societal situations and human behavior.

*e*) If we try to use the formula as a classificatory framework, most of the societal situations, social processes, and forms of behavior cannot be pigeonholed as "indices, scripts, and operators." Creative activity, or acts of love, hatred, fighting, praying, working, crying, rejoicing, and so on, do not find any allotted place in the S-theory. These and thousands of other forms of behavior are neither addition, subtraction, multiplication, division, nor correlation, aggregation, cross-classification, and identification. If we try to put these acts into one of the "operator's" pigeonholes, each of the operators loses its meaning and becomes void. The same is true of societal situations. Most of them (like wedding, love-making, execution of victims, religious service, the classroom situation, reconciliation, domination, battle, and so on) do not fit any of the pigeonholes and so cannot be described and classified by the S-theory. This means that it is glaringly inadequate even as a classificatory framework.[9]

*f*) Finally, it has been shown that the S-theory and its formulae are but a most cumbersome variety of homemade shorthand. No mathematician can operate with these signs. Of course, one can transcribe these signs in various combinations, can put the signs of plus or minus, aggregation or correlation between T, L, P, or I, but all such formulae would remain mere abracadabra.

These criticisms are sufficient to show the mathematical, logical, and empirical inadequacies of the S-theory and its formulae. They are but one of the conspicuous syndromes of the raging quantomania in the psychosocial disciplines.

The given examples of sham mathematics are typical for a large number of similar "researches" in modern psychology, sociology, and related sciences. The sooner these sciences free themselves from this variety of metrophrenia, the better. Turn now to other varieties.

### 3. The Transcription, Distortion, and Bootlegging of Mathematical Formulae into the Psychosocial Sciences

Another variety of metrophrenia consists of transcribing mathematical formulae and the concepts of physics and chemistry and trying to apply them to psychosocial phenomena. This sort of operational procedure consumes the energies of a considerable number of "researchers" in the modern psychosocial disciplines. As a hobby this preoccupation is innocent enough to be passed by without prosecution. The situation, however, changes notably when it is claimed that the transcription is not mere recreation but a revolutionary introduction of mathematical method into the undeveloped social and psychological sciences in order to usher them into the kingdom of the exact physical sciences. The importance of the claim leaves us no choice but to examine carefully the substance of this contention.

To begin with, the transcription and importation of mathematical notions into the psychosocial disciplines are not revolutionary but very old operations. They are almost as old as psychosocial thought itself. We find them in old Hindu, Buddhist, Babylonian, Greek, and Roman treatises on psychosocial phenomena. In the seventeenth and eighteenth centuries, under the names of "social physics," "social mechanics," "social geometry," "Pantometrika, Sociometrika, Psychometrika, Ethikometrika" and *mathesis universae,* the transcription, importation, and application of the concepts of mechanics and mathematics flourished luxuriously. Since that time these "operations" have been continuously performed by a legion of social and psychological scribes hoping to establish a new "social physics," "social mechanics," "social geometry," or "social energetics."

Contrary to their claims to being revolutionary, contemporary "social physicists," econometrists, psychometrists, sociometrists, and ethicometrists are merely continuing centuries-old operations. Their claims are without any foundation whatsoever.[10]

Now, let us see whether many modern quantifications consist merely of such operations, and whether these operations are fruitful in the cognition of psychosocial phenomena. Of recent attempts, the operations of A. Portuendo y Barceló, S. C. Haret, M. Lins, K. Lewin, and J. F. Brown are typical examples of this form of metrophrenia. Y Barceló borrows G. Cantor's "arithmetic space of *n* dimensions" and rechristens it as "the parameter of *n* psychological dimensions." The "material point" of mechanics is rebaptized as "the individual" as a "psychosocial point." $X_1$, $X_2$, $X_3$, etc., now denote "the values as *n* coordinates of this psychosocial point." Since mechanics has "vector with two senses," social mechanics also has "vector with two senses." Since in mechanics there are "inertia," "rectilinear and uniform motion," "state of being at rest," "velocity," "equilibrium," and "equality of action and reaction," y Barceló merrily introduces them in his "social mechanics," without clarifying what these terms can mean in the realm of social and psychological phenomena.

If, for instance, one attempts to get the meaning of "the uniform and rectilinear motion of the individual," one can get hardly any. By this statement y Barceló does not mean "uniform and rectilinear motion of the individual" in physical space, but the psychological changes within an individual or group. In such a context, "rectilinear and uniform change with a constant velocity at any given moment" can have hardly any clear meaning, or can have any meaning, if you please. What is "rectilinear psychological change"? What is its "constant velocity"? The formula for velocity (S/T) again can hardly be applied to such a change, because we do not have the units of distance. What is "inertia" in a psychological sense? What is the individual's or group's "state of being at rest"? A motionless, actionless, breathless, sleeping state? or what? What is equilibrium in a psychosocial sense? [11] Finally, what is the psychological meaning of the "law of the equality of the action and reaction"?

> Each time as an individual receives a psychological action tending to change his status at rest, or in movement, this individual exerts, in his turn through reaction, another action equal and opposite and applied to the point whence the action emanates.[12]

Now what may this poor transcription of the law of mechanics mean psychologically or sociologically? Does a person X murdered by the individual Y exert upon Y "action equal and opposite" to the murder-action of Y exerted on X? Is the action of X imprisoning Y equal and opposite to the action of Y exerted upon X? Is the action of lecturer X equal to the reaction of student Y falling asleep during X's lecture? If in these interactions, each action and reaction are equal to each other, then what action-reactions are unequal? It is enough to pose these simple questions to see how empty of psychosocial meaning this law of mechanics is.

In short, the industrious transcriptions of y Barceló distort the precise meanings of the concepts of mechanics and add nothing to our understanding of social and psychological phenomena. The same criticism applies fully to similar transcriptive quantification of psychosocial phenomena by S. H. Haret, P. de Miranda, M. Lins, K. Lewin, J. F. Brown, and others.[13] We can take the efforts of Lewin and Brown as another example.

> In our definition of the psychological field [their terms "field" and "field-theory" are again taken from physics] as a space construct, space must be understood in its post-Riemannian sense.

Psychology is now turned into "psychological field," as a construct to which all psychological activity (that is, behavior) may be ordered. Having obtained their psychological "spatial field," the authors proceed to transfer verbatim the terms of geometric space: direction, vector, sense, magnitude, distance, continuity or discontinuity, liberty or restriction. They add to these physical concepts their own homemade terms: "path," "locomotion," "mobility," "fluidity," "permeability," "cohesiveness," "purpose," "goal," and a few other terms entirely alien to the Euclidian, Lobachevskian, Riemannian or post-Riemannian concepts of space—and thus distort the space-concepts of physics or mathematics. The same is true of the space-notions of "Group Dynamicists" and other physicalistic social researchers.

Are these transcriptive operations fruitful? Do they give some cognitive advantages in the study of psychological and social phenomena in comparison with the "ordinary" concepts and referential principles of "traditional" psychology or sociology? The reader can judge for himself from what is given above and from a few examples which the authors supply to "demonstrate" the fruitfulness of their borrowed concepts in the field of psychology. The authors instruct us that, like the space of mechanics, with its vector, direction, and magnitude, "The points in the psychological field are associated with both direction and magnitude, but these may for the present only be nonmetrically defined."

By their statement that space, vector, and magnitude—according to their usage—are nonmetrical, the authors make the terms practically void of significance; for when magnitude, vector, and direction cease to be measurable, they become mere qualitative notions of an indeterminate nature. By dequantifying these borrowed concepts the authors also distort the meanings of the terms in physics. The dequantification of their concepts is sufficient evidence of their uselessness for any metric analysis of psychosocial phenomena.[14] Depriving the borrowed terms of their metric character—that is, of their main function—the authors are forced to reintroduce the traditional concepts of psychology under the terms of physics and mechanics. So the above quotation is continued, as follows:

"The behavior of an organism may be said to be directed towards a goal." By this statement the authors introduce a notion entirely alien to geometry or physics. In addition, they commit a factual error by assuming that all behavioral acts have a goal and are purposeful, while in fact only a part of our actions have a goal or purpose as an intentional future objective to be achieved through purposeful motivation. The greater part of our overt actions are neither purposefully motivated nor have they a goal as an intentional target to be achieved in the future. Instead of purposeful motivation for the sake of such and such a goal, a part of our actions are performed because of such and such stimuli operating in the past and immediate present, or because of such and such a habit built in the past, or as unconscious, reflexological and instinctive actions which, by definition being unconscious, do not have any consciousness of goal or purpose, and so on. This assumption that all behavioral actions have a goal or are purposefully motivated is an error perpetrated by many psychologists and sociologists.[15]

Let us continue the "revelations" of the authors.

> The *force* behind the behavior may be said to have a magnitude. . . . Whenever an organism behaves psychologically, it may be said to be behaving in a psychological field [note the tautological definition of "psychological behavior" as "behavior in a psychological field." Truly wonderful logic!]. The goal which it is trying to find is to be ordered to a *point* within this psychological field. The force which is causing the behavior is ordered to a vector within this psychological field, as is its present position.[16]

And so on and so forth. Without adding a scintilla to our knowledge of psychological phenomena, these incantations commit one error after another in the process of rechristening psychological terms as terms in mechanics and retranslating mechanical terms into psychological ones.

Translating physics' term "direction" into that of "goal" and "goal" back into "direction," the authors distort the meaning of both terms, because the term "direction" in mechanics has nothing to do with, and is never used in the sense of, the term "goal"; and the term "goal" has nothing to do with that of spatial "direction" in physics. The goal of Mr. X to become a millionaire or of Y to get his Ph.D. degree has no spatial "direction," and is free from any spatial connotation: latitude, longitude, altitude, etc. If these goals are called "spatial directions," the expression becomes meaningless. On the other hand, "directions" in mechanics are always "directions in space," clearly defined and exactly measured. As such they have no "spaceless goals," "spaceless aims to be achieved," "ambitions to be realized," "purposes to be accomplished."

The same can be said of "vectors," "nonmetric magnitudes," and other terms borrowed from mechanics and inaccurately translated into psychological terms, which, in turn, are erroneously retranslated into the terms of mechanics. Therefore, "revelations" like the statement that "every psychological activity may be ordered to a two-dimensional plane (surface) where organism and goal represent certain spatial regions within the surface" are senseless verbiage. Or like the statements that "psychological activity of all sorts can be ordered to a *path,* and may be said to represent a locomotion in the psychological field."

When authors begin to use pseudomathematical signs like A, B, C, and D, and, in their homemade terms of "locomotion," "path," "direction-goal," "vector," "fluidity," "cohesiveness," and so on, begin to describe a football game between Harvard and Yale, they fail in their simple task to such an extent that, if they had not mentioned in advance they were going to describe a Harvard-Yale football game, nobody would be able to guess what the authors were talking about or what psychological phenomenon they were describing. I made an experimental test of this. I read the authors' description to my class and asked the class what psychosocial phenomenon was being described. None could guess that it was a description of a Harvard-Yale football game.

To sum up: Lewin's and Brown's transcription of the terms of mechanics and geometry into psychological terms, and *vice versa,* is a fruitless preoccupation adding nothing to our knowledge of psychological phenomena. Its sterility is aggravated by many errors inseparable from this sort of operation. In its essentials the effort of Lewin and Brown is a poor variation of hundreds of similar efforts undertaken before and after their "field theory" and "topological" psychology, and, like the other variations, it retards rather than promotes our knowledge of psychosocial phenomena.

The above cases give a fairly clear idea of this variety of metrophrenia. Since we shall deal with many similiar theories in subsequent chapters, we can stop our criticism at this point and pass on to an examination of other forms of the quantophrenia.

### 4. The Cult of Numerology

The next variety of quantophrenia is represented by a multitude of numerological studies. The fault of the psychosocial numerologists consists, not in their passion for counting and the manipulation of numbers, but in their three dogmatic assumptions: first, that counting and the manipulation of its results is the only—or the best and surest—method for discovering uniformities in psychosocial phenomena; second, that the results of the counting can be generalized far beyond the phenomena counted, and can be expressed in quantitative formulae as either universal or significant uniformities; third, that these numerological operations permit one to define precisely and quantitatively many a fundamental category, entity, and relationship otherwise not clearly definable. Due especially to the second and the third assumptions, psychosocial numerologists differ notably from sound quantitative investigators, as well as from other metromanics.

As to the counting, when psychosocial phenomena have measurable units, the counting and sound mathematical analysis of these units can, indeed, yield important results valid now only for the universe of the counted phenomena, and now for a large part or for the whole class of these phenomena. Repeated censuses of a population give us a fairly accurate knowledge of its size and density, its sex-age-occupational-religious-educational-economic composition, its birth-death-marriage rates, its life-expectations, and hundreds of other characteristics. The censuses supply us also with knowledge of thė quantitative changes the population has undergone in each of these traits in the course of time. By similar countings we obtained a vast body of quantitative knowledge of many less tangible—static and dynamic—properties of psychosocial phenomena. Now and then the counting and simple mathematical analysis of its results have even yielded some uniformities in the relationships of the phenomena studied. These uniformities are hardly ever of an unlimited kind, valid for all times and all classes of psychosocial facts. They are always limited uniformities valid only for a certain class of phenomena, under specific conditions. In spite of such limitations, these temporary and localized uniformities have a great cognitive value. Theoretically and practically they are a sort of a rough map guiding us through at least a large area of the unknown psychosocial jungle.

The trouble with the numerologists begins when they forget these limitations and begin to believe in the infallibility of the counting and the various mathematical operations, in the unrestricted validity of their formulae, and in claims that their numerological procedures have a monopoly for valid and precise cognition of the psychosocial world.

As our first example of numerological studies, we can take G. K. Zipf's *Human Behavior and the Principle of Least Effort,* and also his *National Unity and Disunity.* As usual in this sort of investigation, the book opens with grandiose claims of "establishing the Principle of Least Effort as the primary principle that governs our entire individual and collective behavior of all sorts," of demonstrating "an orderliness, or natural law, that governs human behavior," and of being "able to make predictions" and to make life "more agreeable for all concerned." [17]

Already at this point two things are to be noted. First, Zipf makes hardly any reference to Ernst Mach and several others who, decades earlier, introduced and clearly defined in physico-mathematical terms "the Principle of Least Effort." Here the already discussed "amnesia" of the younger generation of psychosocial researchers clearly shows itself. Second, Zipf's logic, whether in the definition of his main "principle of least effort," or of "an individual," or "mind," or "organism," or of any basic concept he deals with, is so lopsided and confused that a logically minded reader can hardly follow him. His "definition" of the Principle of Least Effort is arrived at by the following "demonstration" of "the economy of words." On the part of a speaker the principle of "economy of effort" requires that one word should refer to *m* distinct meanings. This Zipf calls the "Force of Unification." On the part of the auditor "the economy of effort" requires that there be one distinctive meaning for each word. This is called the "Force of Diversification." In using language a person automatically seeks a balance between these conflicting forces. This semantic balance, describable by a simple equation, supposedly demonstrates the "principle of least effort," because effort is minimized when the number of different words ($n$) evoking $m$ number of different meanings is a minimum.[18] This principle is thus a natural law in the use of speech.

But this definition and demonstration of the "natural law" of "least effort" hardly defines or demonstrates anything. To begin with, if a word has several different meanings, it is either meaningless or completely vague in its content. As such it cannot do its work of conveying one definite meaning to the auditor. At best, the auditor must make many unnecessary efforts to single the intended meaning out of the word's plurality of meanings. Unnecessary effort does not mean the economy of least effort, but its denial. Thus Zipf's principle of unification, in his own formulation, is already a negation rather than a confirmation of the principle of least effort. Since the auditor has to exert unnecessary effort to choose one meaning out of many, and since he may choose a perfectly wrong meaning for the word, "the principle of diversification" is uneconomical and wasteful, especially when a wrong meaning is chosen. If Zipf's definition of the principle of least effort defines anything, it defines the principle of uneconomical, wasted effort.

Add to these defects the double meaning the author gives to his definition: now it indicates what the use of words *should be* to conform to the principle of least effort; now it is used in the sense that the *actual use of words* by human beings conforms with this principle and makes it a "natural law" governing our real speech-behavior. When viewed from the standpoint of the ideal "should be," the definition, as we have seen, does not at all define the principle of least effort. If it is viewed as a description of the actual speech of human beings, it is utterly fallacious. If it were correct empirical law, we should conclude that all human beings are impeccable logicians and first-class orators always using the very minimum of words in their conversations, always choosing the best word and the most adequate meaning of the many possible meanings of each word. In brief, the actual speech of human beings would be the most economical and precise speech possible. The fallacy of such a generalization is obvious.

Since the basic principle of the work is so glaringly misdefined, the whole structure built on it is inevitably misconstructed and falls to pieces at the slightest touch of a critical finger. Zipf's definitions of an "individual," "mind," "organism," "system," "mathematical point," and his manipulations with these terms, display rather pathetically the "disorders of logic and speech" discussed in the preceding chapter. Here is a typical example of Zipf's definition of something. The reader is invited to guess what it is.

> [X] is a movable mathematical point in time-space, in reference to which matter-energy moves in such a way that a physical situation exists in which work is expended in order to preserve a physical system (continual as a whole but not continual as to its parts) from a gravitational and electromagnetic equilibrium with the rest of the universe.[19]

In an experimental way I read this definition to several persons, including four biologists, and asked them to guess what the definition defined. None of them was able to guess it correctly. As a matter of fact, most of the scholars and scientists to whom I read it refused to guess at all, stating that it was gibberish, a senseless collection of various terms, mainly physico-mathematical. Now it can be told that this "precise" and terribly "scientific" definition defines "Organism." Still more incoherent are the definitions of "mind," "individual," and so on.[20] To sum up: the logical, theoretical part of the work is mainly nonlogic and vague verbiage.

Turn now to the "numerological" part. Taken at their face value, Zipf's arithmetic exercises in the counting of various items are not entirely valueless and are, anyhow, less objectionable than his logical wanderings. The objections arise when he begins to force his figures to fit his preconceived "laws" and to extrapolate their significance far beyond their legitimate limits. Manipulating various numerical data, such as the populations of cities, the dollar values of sales by various trading corporations, the number of employees of business establishments, etc., he formulates his *"rank-size rule"* or uniformity. This "rank-size rule" was much more cautiously formulated several years before by A. J. Lotka. On the basis of his study of the urban population of the United States, Lotka concluded that the product of the rank of the city and its population is very roughly constant. In a less cautious manner and in a more generalized form this uniformity is repeated by Zipf. The essentials of this rule are derived as follows.

Taking, for instance, the 1940 census of the urban populations of the United States, and arranging the cities into the ranks: 1, 2, 3, etc., according to the size of their populations, we find that New York, with 7,450,000 population, occupies rank number 1; Chicago with 3,400,000 is of rank 2; Pittsburgh with 670,000 is of rank 10; Nashville with 167,000 is of rank 50; Utica with 100,000 is of rank 92; the cities of the rank 199 have 50,000 population; of the rank 2,042 have 5,000 population; and so on. Multiplying the size of the population by the city's rank we have: New York 1 time 7,450,000; Chicago, twice 3,400,000 or 6,800,000; for Utica we get 9,200,000; for Philadelphia 5,794,000; at rank 412 it is 10,300,000; and so on. From these figures Zipf concludes that there is an empirical uniformity or natural law by which cities competing with each other attract and hold the population. Indirectly this uniformity in some way also testifies to the validity of the principle of least effort, though an adequate theoretical explanation of this uniformity so far is lacking.

A closer examination of these data suggests, first, that the rank-size rule is a fairly loose rule: since the product of the size and the rank of the cities varies from 5,794,000 to 10,300,000 or within a ratio of 5 to 9, it is difficult to claim such a product constant. Such a constancy seems to be notably inconstant. It becomes much more variant if we take the population of the cities in 1840. Then the product of the rank and the size of only the 17 biggest cities fluctuate from 391,114 (New York) to 67,050 (Chicago)—that is, our constant for New York is six times larger than that for Chicago. In this case there is hardly any possibility of talking even about a loose constant. The rank-size rule simply does not exist for 1840. It is even less in evidence if we take the census data for 1790, 1800, and other years of the census. If the rule is tested on the cities of other countries, there is practically nothing left of the rank-size rule. For these reasons the uniformity claimed is at the best only a very loose, temporary, and local semblance of uniformity. As such it has hardly any relationship to the principle of least effort. In addition, what it really means and to what factors it is due remain unknown.

What is said of the rank-size rule in regard to the distribution of city populations can also be applied to other rank-size uniformities given by Zipf: the amount of the gross sales of 100 retail business corporations with gross sales above $25,000,000 in 1948; the number of employees of business establishments in the United States; and a few others. Here, even in the figures of Zipf the variation of the "constant product" of rank and size is so great that he himself is obliged to acknowledge its inconstancy.

If we make a slight change in the way of ranking the figures in each of these series—and such a change is as legitimate as the arbitrary ranking selected by the author to fit the figures to his preconceived rank-size rule—then even the ghost of the author's uniformities vanishes in the air. On the other hand, if one juggles almost any series of figures as they are juggled by Zipf, and calls widely varying products of size and rank "constant uniformity," one can discover a legion of "uniformities" of a nonuniform kind. An additional curiosity about these numerological manipulations is that the author is uncertain what to do with these uniformities, what they mean, and to what factors their existence is due.

The manipulations are called numerological because they are identical with a multitude of numerological "discoveries"—both very ancient and more recent—of preconceived uniformities in various sets of figures. For instance, in ancient India, Babylon, China, Persia, Greece, Rome, Medieval Europe, and the Islamic world, many efforts were made to discover and to prove the existence of certain periodic cycles in the life of the world, of social processes, of every individual. The greatest of these is the ever-repeated "elemental" cycle of 311,040,000,000,000 mortal years in the life of the whole universe. In the life of mankind we have the great periodic cycle (kalpa) of 4,320,000 mortal years divided into four subperiods: the creative Krita Yuga (1,728,000 mortal years), the Treta Yuga (1,296,000 mortal years), the Dwapara Yuga (864,000 mortal years), and the Kali Yuga of decay and disintegration (432,000 mortal years) which mankind entered at the beginning of the fourteenth century, and in which humanity is destined to stay until the Kali Yuga runs its course. "There are infinite successions of these four ages." Then we have various cycles of "the great year" (the *annus magnus*) whose duration, according to different authors, is 20,250,000; 760,000; 21,000; 10,000; 7,500; 4,800; 3,600; and so on, mortal years.

Side by side with these, the numerologists "discovered" a legion of shorter periodicities especially connected with various "sacred," "astrological," and "magic" numbers: 3, 7, 9, 16, 27, 30, 54, 59, and so on.[21]

Each of these periodicities was causally associated with many changes, carefully outlined by the numerologists, in the life of either the whole universe, or mankind, or the nation, or the individual. In "discovering" and "demonstrating" the validity of these periodicities the numerologists manipulated sets of various figures in a way similar to that of the modern numerologists. This is why I call the operations of Zipf and of many others numerological, but not mathematical.

Zipf's valiant effort is typical of a great many numerological "researches" blossoming now under the impressive label of "quantitative," "mathematical," "precise" research. Because of the proliferation of the cult of numerology it is necessary to mention it as a special form of the metrophrenia we have been discussing.

Criticism of numerological manipulations does not concern those quantitative studies which often sum up results in the form of a mathematical formula, without extrapolating it beyond the facts studied, and with a clear indication of the main assumptions made. Consequently, there is no objection to Lewis F. Richardson's formulae summing up the relationships between the frequency of "fatal quarrels" and their magnitude or the quantitative analysis of a pacifying role for common language, government, religion, or local contiguity.[22] Similarly, my criticism does not concern such formulae as $y = 22.92 + 0.884X$ summing up the relationship between the delinquency rate of a Chicago district and the proportion of the delinquents in that district who were recidivists.[23] Or E. C. Young's formula $M = k(F/d^2)$ [24] concisely describing *one* of the fairly general uniformities in migration or the territorial mobility of individuals in certain rural-urban regions or countries. Or W. Firey's formula on the deprivation of a social system from its overall optimum functioning, or the best proportional satisfaction of its important needs: $D = k(d - x)^{2m} + F$.[25]

These and many other mathematical formulae are free from numerological vices, if they are not extended beyond the samples studied and are considered just as abbreviated symbolic expressions of the results found in that particular investigation. In their turn these formulae have their own shortcomings which will be discussed further.

For the time being we can here end the discussion of the numerological type of quantophrenia.

## 5. Sham Quantification of Nonscalar Qualitative Data

Perhaps one of the most notable manifestations of metrophrenia is the increasing trend toward unrestrained quantification of all qualitative data, no matter whether or not they lend themselves to such an operation. What is still more symptomatic in this enterprise is the very high scientific prestige these attempts have acquired in the opinion of quantitatively minded psychosocial scholars. Consequently, these attempts deserve to be briefly examined.

The passion for quantifying all sorts of qualitative data has manifested itself in many fields: in measuring the intensities and qualities of beliefs, emotions, intelligence, ideologies, attitudes and public opinion; in the quantitative theories of "factor-analysis"; in the construction of "mathematical models"; and in exploring general methods for correctly translating nonmetric qualities into scalable ones. In previous chapters of this work we have already discussed the attempts to measure intelligence, emotions, unconscious drives, and attitudes. In subsequent paragraphs we shall examine the methods of mathematical models and other approaches of quantification. At this point we shall concisely discuss a few studies on the general methods for quantifying qualitative data. Among the recent investigations of this problem L. Guttman's "scaling" or "scalogram" method (supplemented by E. A. Suchman's "scalogram board" for practical convenience) and P. F. Lazarsfeld's theory of the continuous "latent classes" offer possibly two of the best general methods for scaling apparently unscalable phenomena.[26]

As to the success of these efforts the matter could be foreseen in advance: if the quantified qualities have units, they can be measured or scaled and the measurements expressed in numbers. If the scaled qualities do not have units, they cannot be adequately scaled and measured. If, in spite of this, the "unitless qualities" are quantified, the resultant measurements are bound to be fictitious rather than real, arbitrarily superimposed upon the phenomena rather than giving objective measurements of them. The reason for these statements is well expressed by the eminent physicist, P. Appel:

> In mathematical formulae the letters designate numbers; these formulae can be applied only to the measurable quantities which can be expressed

by numbers. In analytical geometry, *x, y, z* designate numbers. The parameters *x, y, z* in the equations of mechanics are numbers.

Where there are no units and numbers, all the formulae and equations are either void or represent a subjective ranking, weighing, and scoring by the devotees of a misplaced quantification.

This conclusion is confirmed, perhaps contrary to their own wishes, by the results of Guttman's, Lazarsfeld's, and Suchman's explorations. To begin with the "scalogram-board"—merely a convenient device for arranging individuals and answers in ranking order of frequency—in Suchman's own opinion its use is limited, first, to unidimensional phenomena and, second, among these, to a very small fraction of objectively scalable phenomena, which can be scaled without any "scalogram-board." For application to all nonscalable qualitative data the "scalogram-board" is useless. Even the simple operation of arranging data in ranking order of frequency on a "scalogram-board" involves "weighings," "solid streaks," "correction of errors close to center," "combining of categories," "choice of cutting points," and other arbitrary arrangements well hidden behind objective-looking tables and diagrams.[27]

Still less successful are the attempts at "scaling" comparatively simple qualitative phenomena such as the opinions, emotions, wishes, and attitudes expressed by the armed forces in their answers to the various questionnaires of the investigators.

> A question which is often asked is, "how often do you find scales in practice?" Quite obviously, if the rigid parallelogram pattern required of a scale did not occur empirically, then the theory would have little practicality. There is a real question, then, as to whether scales occur frequently enough to be applicable to the study of social attitudes. . . . The bulk of social phenomena is too complex for one to expect many aspects to be scalable. . . . [During their study of its applicability] it was a much more frequent experience *not* to find a series of items scalable, [though] there were enough instances of scalable areas to warrant further research.[28]

When, however, these few allegedly scalable areas of opinion-attitudes are carefully examined, one finds that their scalability is due, not to objectively existing units or ranks in the phenomena studied, but to the fact that in their questionnaires the authors had already arbitrarily arranged the scalability of the answers. Their questions ask not only positive or negative answers, but answers ranked in terms of "very much," "some," or "little," or in even greater detail. Having predetermined the answers by ranking in this way, the authors simply count the number of answers in each rank and thereby get their "ranking" or "scalability" of various intensities of this or that opinion, belief, emotion, wish, or attitude. In the answers they get exactly those ranks, units, or intensities which they put into their questions. This is fictitious scalability, created and superimposed upon the phenomena by the free act of the investigators. Without any study, it assumes the existence of the scalable ranks "very much," "much," "some," and "little" in attitudes or beliefs, regardless of the existence or nonexistence of such ranks in the experience of the respondents. Even more: it also predetermines the number of these ranks or intensities in the experience of the answering persons. The questionnaires themselves already contain the main answers to the questions of scalability and the number of its main ranks. These answers are: (1) the studied phenomena are scalable; (2) the number of main classes on the scale is exactly the same as indicated in the questionnaire—three, if the questions are: "very much," "some," "little"; five, if the subdivision is given in five ranks; and so on. Such a prearranged scalability in no way demonstrates an objectively existing scalability of qualitative emotional, volitional, affective, and intellectual experiences in the respondents to their questionnaires. If anything, this substitution is liable to introduce into the study a large element of error, of untested, arbitrary, and subjective opinions of the researchers.

This conclusion is directly corroborated by the authors' own data. Where they ranked the questions more loosely, leaving a larger margin for the choice of the respondents, they find that the answers do not quite fit the scale. For instance, the questions about fear are coined in the following way.

> How often have you had these reactions when you were under fire? Check one answer after each of the reactions listed to show how often you had the reaction.
>
> Violent pounding of the heart
> Sinking feeling of the stomach
> Feeling weakness or feeling faint
> Feeling sick at the stomach
> Cold sweat
> Vomiting
> Shaking or trembling all over

Urinating in pants
Losing control of the bowels
Feeling of stiffness

The answer categories for each of the above were: "Often/Sometimes/Once/Never/No answer."

The authors state that all categories except "cold sweat" fit into a scale pattern and that the coefficient of reproducibility is .92. The frequencies ranged from 9 per cent of the respondents who reported "urinating in pants" to 84 per cent who experienced "violent pounding of the heart." "The rank order of the dichotomized symptoms permits one to predict, for example, that if a man experienced 'shaking or trembling all over,' he must also have experienced 'sinking feeling at the stomach' or 'violent pounding of the heart' . . . . The symptoms come from a single universe and permit a rank ordering of respondents along a single continuum. There is an intrinsic interdependence among the different fear symptoms which permit them to be ordered *from more to less severe.*"[29]

Now let us note a few revelant things in these results and in the conclusions of the authors. First, "cold sweat" does not fit the scale. Its nonfitting means that either it is put at a wrong rank among the intensities of fear, or the whole scale is conjectural. Second, not only various symptoms of fear, but practically all the important changes in an organism come from one universe and are mutually interdependent: this simple truth is nowadays accepted by not only "the holistic" biologist, but by practically all other competent biologists as well. It is also a basic characteristic of all social and cultural systems vs. congeries.[30] Likewise, competent physicians and biologists can tell that without pounding of the heart hardly any "shaking and trembling all over" is possible. No special "scalogram" or "latent structure" theories are necessary for the discovery of these familiar truths. Third, from the fact that various changes in an organism or sociocultural system are interdependent, it does not follow that these changes are necessarily scalar in their intensity, or have a definite time-order in their manifestations. No biologist or physician would claim that all the important changes in an organism when it passes from childhood to adolescence (increase of weight and stature, change of glands and other organs, emotional, and mental changes) are scalar in their intensity or in the time-order of their appearance. No uniformity exists even in regard to the time-order of walking and talking in the growing child: some begin first to walk and then to talk; others first develop talking and then walking. No biologist or physician would also try to scale from most to least intense such sickness-changes as the common cold, disorders of digestion, the straining of an ankle, a slight bruise, or cancer, heart disease, tuberculosis, and so on. Though all these changes are interdependent and come from a single universe, it is neither objectively possible nor practical to order these hundreds of changes in a continuous scale, from the most intense or important to the least intense or important.

For similar reasons, from the fact that various fear symptoms "come from the same universe" and are interdependent, it does not follow that these symptoms can be rigidly scaled from more to less severe, or from "feeling of stiffness" to "violent pounding of the heart," as they are scaled in the above scale, or that a time-order of fear symptoms uniformly begins with violent pounding of heart and ends with "losing control of the bowels" and "feeling of stiffness." There is no objective basis for believing that a "feeling of weakness" is a more severe symptom of fear than "sinking feeling at the stomach," or that "urinating in pants" is a more intense symptom of fear than "vomiting," or "shaking and trembling all over," and that the degrees of intensity separating each adjacent class of fear symptoms is exactly the same between all adjacent classes of fear symptoms. Moreover, several of these fear symptoms occur simultaneously, and fear symptoms vary with different individuals.

Likewise, there is no objective evidence that, except for "pounding of heart," which is the most general symptom of fear (as well as of hate, intense love, fatigue, excitement, etc.), one can predict, on the basis of this scale, that if one experiences a "feeling of stiffness," one necessarily experiences all the preceding, less severe symptoms of fear. This rigid scaling of intensities of fear symptoms is arbitrarily superimposed by the authors on various manifestations of fear, and in no way can serve as a solid basis for predictions. In other words, the authors did not succeed in objectively ranking the symptoms of fear. As a matter of fact, they give hardly any evidence that their scale of fear symptoms is a scale of fear intensities. What they really supply is the percentages of soldiers in their sample who experience each of these symptoms and the frequencies of occurrence of each symptom; and nothing more. It is obvious that neither the percentages nor the frequencies have any relationship to the *intensity* of fear: they do not measure fear severity, nor do they give a scale of fear intensities.

By substituting the percentages and frequencies for intensities, the authors committed the error of identifying two different phenomena: the *frequency of occurrence* of each fear symptom with fear *intensity*. From the fact that the common cold occurs much more frequently than cancer, it does not follow that the common cold is a more severe sickness than cancer. From the fact that only 9 per cent of soldiers "urinate in pants," while a larger per cent vomit in fear experience, it does not follow that either one of these phenomena is a more severe form of fear than the other. These considerations show that the authors' scale of fear symptoms is not a scale of the intensities of various manifestations of fear.

As we have seen, Guttman's premise, that fear symptoms as well as other qualitative data all come from the same universe and are interdependent, does not entitle him to infer that all fear symptoms are scalable in their intensities. Nor are the premises themselves adequately formulated. Not only do all fear symptoms come from the same universe, but all the important changes in an individual, or in an organism, or in a mechanical, biological, and sociocultural system are interdependent and come from the same universe. His formulation of this general proposition is similar to the proposition that "all Camel cigarettes attract one another in a direct ratio of their mass and in inverse ratio of the square of their distance." Such a proposition is inadequate, because Newtonian law tells us that not only Camels but all material bodies gravitate according to this law. To apply it only to the Camel is to be guilty of logical and factual inadequacy.[31]

These remarks indicate the inadequacy of Guttman's very premises and of his inferences from these premises. If his premises and inferences are wrong, his attempt to scale the intensities of fear or of other qualitative phenomena also becomes inadequate.

These criticisms are still more applicable to Lazarsfeld's hypothesis of "latent continuum structures" which serves as the main premise for his belief in the scalability of qualitative data or phenomena. This hypothesis consists of a postulation that "there exists a set of latent classes, such that the manifest relationship between any two or more items on a test can be accounted for by the existence of these basic classes and by these alone. . . . Any attitude has thus two aspects—one associated with the latent classes, and one which is specific to the item." In contrast to Guttman, for whom an attitude is an empirically observed response, for Lazarsfeld attitude is an inference from the latent classes, themselves inferred from the manifest data. "The latent continuum is [thus] a hypothetical construct." [32]

Here we have an instructive example of how sheer metaphysics gets into the modern psychosocial sciences. "Sheer metaphysics," because Lazarsfeld has neither mathematical, nor logical, nor empirical grounds for his postulation that all or many manifestly nonscalar items represent in reality a scalar *continuum,* and that when all the latent classes of this *continuum* are considered, the apparently discontinuous or nonscalar items become continuous and scalar. Mathematics operates with continuous as well as discontinuous functional equations, like $B = 1/A$ or $B = \sqrt{A^2 - 1}$. Therefore, mathematically, Lazarsfeld has no ground to assume that qualitative data are always continuous in their manifest and latent classes. Like almost all theories of "social physics" Lazarsfeld's theory is based on largely antiquated physical and mathematical theories. It completely ignores the quantum theory and modern microphysics. The very essence of the quantum theory is the principle of discontinuity, of the "quantum jumps" in the transition of small constellations of atoms from one level of energy to another. It is so discontinuous that even the term "moving" or "motion" can hardly be applied to it.

If the principle of discontinuity is the governing principle here, then there is no basis for believing that psychosocial phenomena cannot be also discontinuous and unpredictable. So far as Lazarsfeld's postulate ignores the Planck-Delbrück-Heitler-London-Schrödinger "solidifying forces of molecular model," and so far as it ignores the quantum theory of modern physics, it is without a serious grounding in physics and mathematics.[33]

Logically, Lazarsfeld's theory is circular. If empirical data can be collected for its confirmation, the latent *continuum* is proved empirically; if the empirical data contradict the existence of the scalar latent *continuum,* then the contradiction can be accounted for by assuming that some of the latent classes are missing which, if discovered, would fill the gaps and thus confirm the postulate. In this respect it is identical to the "infallible" hypothesis of a "latent *continuum*" of ghosts or "hidden forces" whose inscrutable ways are made responsible for anything and everything that happens in the manifest empirical world.

Lazarsfeld's theory is also not supported by empirical evidence. "The ugly empirical facts" (to use the expression of T. Huxley) are stubborn and cannot be "ordered" to behave according to his postulate. In trying to quantify nonscalar phenomena, he is forced to create "quasi-scales" that by definition are arbitrary and fictitious. As such they are not scales at all. The very introduction of the "quasi-scales" is a frank confession that quantification of his qualitative data is impossible. The whole hypothesis of "continuous latent classes" is useless for quantifying qualitative data.

In regard to both Guttman's scalogram and Lazarsfeld's latent classes, S. A. Stouffer is correct in saying: "there is still relatively little which is not controversial" in these hypotheses.[34] G. Murphy puts the matter more emphatically: "there is every reason to believe that none of the rather complex social attitudes . . . will ever conform to rigorous measurement."[35]

The net result of these attempts to quantify qualitative data wholly confirms the propositions set forth at the beginning of this section. If even such "high priests of quantification" as Guttman and Lazarsfeld failed in their tasks, the lesser devotees of the cult can be expected to fail doubly. As a matter of fact, most of them are even unaware of the gross blunders they commit in their indefatigable quantification, in their scaling of unscalable phenomena, in their ranking of unrankable items, in their combination and measurement of utterly uncombinable and incommensurable variables. For instance, in the problems of multiple causation they seem to find no difficulty in combining, scaling, and measuring the comparative conditioning power of such incommensurable variables as flora and fauna, the range of temperature, the health-age-sex composition of the population, its dominant religion, the influence of its political regime, its technological factors, even its hobbies. With their scanty training in mathematics and logic, they do not see any difficulty in such problems, and continuously "solve" them with their "home-made" mathematics, logic, and technique. They probably would not find any difficulty in combining and measuring the comparative conditioning efficacy of such variables as: a horse's tail, a bee's buzzing, a bird's flying, man's breathing, religious preaching, an atomic explosion, a nervous breakdown, and what not.[36]

It is needless to repeat that this sort of quantification has no relation to real scientific scaling, ranking, and measurement. The fashion of pseudoquantification can hardly be accounted for apart from the epidemics of quantophrenia now raging among psychosocial investigators. Infected with the fever of this epidemic, they sincerely believe their great mission is to promote the psychosocial sciences to a higher level of scientific preciseness; they have even convinced many a nonscientist. They cannot for long, however, fool history and science itself. With the multiplication of their efforts, the fallacious components of these quantifications become more visible. More obvious also become the real fruits of such endeavors. As we shall see further on, these fruits are either inedible or harmful. In spite of gigantic labor, energy, and funds, this Sisyphean enterprise has not yielded any important valid theory, or any set of fruitful hypotheses or crucial facts. It has not discovered any significant uniformity or techniques or a new scientific method. It has yielded, at most, perhaps a few semi-correct observations of tertiary importance. It is high time to cease these pseudoscientific preoccupations.

# *Chapter Eight*

# Quantophrenia (*Concluded*)

> *We must beware of confounding the degree of precision with the certainty of science itself. The certainty of science and our precision in the knowledge of it, are two very different things. A very absurd proposition ($S_{\Delta} = 3_{\Delta}$) may be precise . . . and a very certain proposition may be wanting in precision of it, as, for instance, when we assert that every man will die.*
>
> A. Comte.[1]

## 1. Mathematical Models

As mentioned before, any genuine mathematical study of psychosocial problems can only be welcome. None of the criticisms of sham mathematical investigations can be addressed to real mathematical research in psychosocial phenomena. In contrast to the pseudomathematical investigators, mathematicians well realize the enormous difficulties and the limited possibilities for applying mathematical tools to the analysis of social and psychological facts. The leading mathematical sociologists acknowledge that "no one can deny this fact [of nonamenability of social phenomena to mathematical treatment] in the past," but they hope that "it is legitimate to challenge such a pessimistic extrapolation into the future," though such an optimistic opinion is "also nothing but a statement of belief."

They do not deny that the essentially qualitative nature of certain psychosocial phenomena makes mathematical analysis difficult. They point out, however, that "such branches of mathematics as Boolean algebra, topology [analysis situs] may well be said to deal with qualitative, rather than quantitative, relations." Now, many social phenomena are quantitative in their nature and permit one to build from quantitative postulates a systematic theory "which not only enables him [the mathematician] to describe correctly already known quantitative relations, but also to predict new relations which have not yet been observed."

They readily admit that "the mathematics used" for analysis of psychosocial facts is often "too elementary," that many equations inferred "are of little practical value, partly because of the generality of their formulation, partly because of the mathematical difficulties involved in their solution"; that many assumptions are "only the artefacts used for mathematical expediency," "too simple and hardly corresponding to reality," "purely imaginary cases which due to the intentional oversimplification have no real existence"; that many an inference does not fit or fits poorly the observed empirical facts; that postulates and other assumptions often do not lead to correct prediction, or do not give a basis for prediction at all; that in other cases the predictions and conclusions are valid "only with the particular set of assumptions made. A change in any of the assumptions may change the results." And so on.[2]

These and other limitations are responsible for the hitherto modest contributions of mathematical investigations to our knowledge of the what, how, and why of psychosocial facts. These contributions have been much more tangible in the field of mass-quantitative than in the field of singular or qualitative psychosocial phenomena. Having measurable units, the large samples of quantitative phenomena more easily lend themselves to mathematical analysis. This explains why mathematical study of the phenomena of population (density, size, migration, incidence of crime, etc.) has been fairly successful, not only in establishing empirical or statistical "semi-uniformities" but in formulating "mathematical models" as postulational systems of closely related equations well fitted to the observed phenomena and, with some limitations, capable of predicting their future empirical course.

Much less successful, so far, has been the mathematical attack on singular and qualitative psychosocial data. It has given five different results, none of which can be called very fruitful. These results are as follows.

*a*) In many investigations the intended mathematical study degenerated into either a pseudomathematical "shorthand," or a mere transcription of mathematical symbols, which we have already discussed. The above has shown the sterility, sometimes even harmfulness, of this sort of "research."

*b*) Other mathematical studies changed into routine statistical investigations dealing with empirical items according to the standards of somewhat elementary statistics. Mathematical statistics represents a genuine mathematical method, but the routine type of statistical operation has only a remote relationship to it. The next section of this chapter discusses both these forms of statistical study in some detail. Here it suffices to say that a part of the routine statistical studies has contributed something to our knowledge of the psychosocial world, while another part has been fruitless or misleading. Fruitless or fruitful, the *routine kind of empirical statistical studies is not identical with a strictly mathematical analysis of the respective items.* This latter analysis ordinarily starts with a few axioms or postulates and infers from them a series of equations which in their totality make a self-contained mathematical system. In mathematical analysis there are "usually three main steps or levels: (1) the mathematical system; (2) the identifications of coordinating definitions; (3) the specific applications." [3] Only the last of these steps has to deal with empirical data, in order to find out how well the inferred equations agree with the observable facts.

In contrast to this, the routine statistical investigation does not postulate any axioms or derive a series of equations from the postulates. It simply counts its items, classifies them, sometimes discusses the representativeness of its sample, computes percentages and, sometimes, the coefficient of correlation, and the like. To these and similar operations it limits its task. For these reasons, the substitution of a routine statistical study for a mathematical one is, in a sense, evidence of the failure of the mathematical attack, regardless of how fruitful the statistical substitute may be. Such substitutions occur fairly frequently.

*c*) The third outcome consists of the elaboration of an irreproachable mathematical system with all the main equations inferred and many subsystems consistently derived. From a purely mathematical standpoint, such a system is an example of logical elegance. However, since the qualitative variables are not concretely measurable, or lack the minimum of measurable items, such a model is left in a sort of vacuum. It remains a beautiful blueprint of a marvelous building for whose construction the necessary material is unavailable. In mathematical economics, sociology, and psychology, there are many mathematical systems or models of this type. Sometimes their authors use fragments of measurable items in their equations, but they warn us that these items are used as illustrations and nothing more. However much one can admire the impeccable elegance of such an abstract model, it contributes little to our knowledge of the phenomena studied.

*d*) Much more helpful are those mathematical models which have a minimum of measurable empirical material for application to actual situations. Through their equations they point at unsuspected relationships between empirical variables. Within their specified conditions they often predict accurately a future course for the variables. For examples of this type of mathematical study of psychosocial phenomena we can cite N. Rashevsky's best models in the quoted works; Neumann and Morgenstern's models of economic behavior; Bush-Mosteller's, S. Karlin's, H. G. Landau's, H. D. Landahl's models for simple learning and imitation; A. Rapoport's model of rumor-spread; L. F. Richardson's models dealing with foreign policies and fatal quarrels; and S. C. Dodd's model of airborne leaflet communication.[4]

In spite of a considerable potential value, the actual contribution of these models to the understanding of psychosocial phenomena is still very limited. By their logical nature, they are built upon specific axioms or postulates, and throughout the whole process of mathematical inference they have to make additional assumptions of an empirical nature. For this reason, their equations remain valid in regard to the empirical facts studied *only within the limits of these postulates and empirical assumptions.* If the empirical phenomena do not correspond to these assumptions, the models become inapplicable to reality. They cease to serve as a precise, generalized description of the respective facts and their relationships; nor can they accurately predict new relationships. To illustrate this we can take the admirable model of games and economic behavior by von Neumann and Morgenstern. Their inferences and equations fit the actual economic behavior only under the following assumptions of their model: utility is a linear quantity; there is transitivity of preference among the utilities; means are scarce and transferable; individuals are rational; they have an equal access to information; individuals conform to certain accepted standards of behavior; individuals carefully plan a rational strategy for their economic actions; and so on. If the individuals happen to be not only rational but also nonrational and irrational, as human beings are; if they do not have an equal access to information; if they do not always conform to the accepted standards of conduct and do not always take into consideration the reactions of other individuals—then most of the equations of the model lose their applicability. The same can be said about practically all mathematical models of this type.

By its very nature a good model can be constructed only upon a limited number of specific postulates and empirical assumptions, which often are only a few out of many relevant empirical conditions. For this reason, actual applicability, and especially the heuristic and predictive ability of mathematical models in regard to empirical phenomena, has been very limited. So far, the models have tried to "catch up" with the nonmathematical studies of empirical phenomena rather than lead such studies to a new and wider horizon. It is possible that with a refinement of mathematical tools their contributions to sociological and psychological knowledge would increase. But this desideratum still remains in the realm of hope rather than in that of actual reality.

*e*) When the assumptions of a mathematical model grossly differ from the actual empirical situation, the conclusions and predictions of such a mathematical theory become empirically erroneous. The model becomes misleadingly "precise"; it turns into a "rigorous" fallacy parading in the guise of exact knowledge. Being a professor of mathematics, August Comte well understood this danger.

> The possibility of applying mathematical analysis to the study of phenomena is exactly in proportion to the rank which they hold in the scale of the whole. . . . *We must beware of confounding the degree of precision with the certainty of science itself.* The certainty of science and our precision in the knowledge of it are two very different things (often confounded). A very absurd proposition may be very precise [for instance, 2 + 2 = 7] . . . and a very certain proposition may be wanting in precision in our statement of it as, for instance, when we assert that every man will die.[5]

Unfortunately, mathematical sociology and psychology are contaminated by models of this kind. In several models of Rashevsky, of von Neumann and Morgenstern, and of other mathematical "modelists," one frequently finds wrong empirical assumptions leading to fallacious conclusions. Rashevsky's "Outline of a Mathematical Approach to History" can serve as an example.[6] In spite of the most commendable purpose and rigorous mathematical logic of this study, its fallacious empirical assumptions strongly vitiate its conclusions and predictions.

First of all, the author seems to be unaware that his main thesis is not new. It is as follows: "the specific shore line does sufficiently strongly affect the distribution of the population, and hence the structure of the social communication net, to account for the observed differences in the rates of cultural development" of the greatly contrasting cultures of the pre-literate peoples, of the Orient, and of the West. Among the many historians, social geographers, and sociologists who stressed this factor and the related factor of the great rivers as the means of interaction and communication,[7] Leo Metchnikoff in his *Civilization and Great Historical Rivers* made this emphasis especially strongly. A severe criticism of these theories has shown their gross mistakes and their inability to account for notable differences in cultures, or for many other psychosocial phenomena the theories claimed to explain. If Rashevsky had studied these criticisms, he would hardly have made his basic empirical assumption.

In the second place, other empirical assumptions of this study are also fallacious—for instance, its "linear" conception of primitive, Oriental, and Western cultures, as well as the specific characteristics ascribed to each of them. If the "primitive" and some of the Oriental cultures were the cultures of unlimited ignorance and superstitions, as Rashevsky paints them, these cultures and peoples simply could not survive: if in primitive conditions one does not know what plants or animals are edible, what grounds are good for hunting, what use can be made of a stone or stick or animal, or how to protect oneself from inclemencies of climate, dangerous animals, or human enemies, and so on, one cannot survive even a few weeks. On the other hand, we know well that many of the greatest discoveries, such as the domestication of fire and animals, which plants and animals are edible and which are not, the principle of lever, the invention of many "primitive" weapons and tools, elementary mathematics, astronomy, meteorology, biology, and medicine, various forms of social organization, not to mention many forms of the fine arts—that these and other great discoveries and inventions were made by "primitive" peoples in the "prehistorical" period of humanity.

There is no need to insist on the fact that up to the fifteenth century A.D. the torch of scientific, technological, and cultural advancement was carried not by the European, but by the Oriental cultures and peoples. While

Europe was still in a preliterate stage, the great cultures of Egypt and Babylonia, Assyria and Iran, Sumeria and the Hittite Empire, China and India, Creto-Mycaenae and Arabia, emerged and flowered for centuries, even millennia, before Europe entered the ranks of the great cultures. The shore lines of the primitive, the Oriental, and of the European populations changed little during these centuries and millennia. If the much longer shore line of Europe accounts for the emergence and leadership of Europe during the last five centuries, why did not this favorable shore line produce European leadership during the earlier millennia? If the poorly developed shore line of the Oriental populations is responsible for their cultural backwardness during the last few centuries, why did not this factor inhibit the marvelous blossoming of the great Oriental cultures during the preceding millennia? With the main shore lines remaining little changed for centuries, why has the leadership in various fields of culture shifted from country to country, from nation to nation, from group to group even in the European population?[8] These "ugly facts" demolish Rashevsky's assumption that the shore line variable is the main factor in cultural progress.

Empirically incorrect, also, is Rashevsky's subassumption that after the fifteenth century A.D. the Western population became entirely scientific, rational, free from "religious and other superstitions," from the ideas of "inequality of men, from all forms of slavery, serfdom, and limitations of freedom." The reality, unfortunately, is very different from this utopian picture.

Having started with such mistaken assumptions, Rashevsky makes additional errors in the course of his mathematical analysis: (1) his notion of the actual role of population density is too simplistic; (2) he holds too one-sided a theory of the role of cities in the production of nonconformists, and in the diffusion of their influence; (3) he dumps together various, often opposite, types of nonconformists: nonconformists as protectors of the superstition and ignorance of a minority, together with the nonconformists who are creators of new values; (4) he fails to distinguish the positive and negative roles of a well-developed network of communication, used now for broadcasting scientific and other great values, and now for disseminating ignorant ideologies and vulgar values; and so on, including his incorrect assumptions concerning migration and mobility. Due to these fallacies, the conclusions of Rashevsky's mathematical analysis do not account satisfactorily for the main problem of the study, nor do they discover new empirical relations hitherto unknown, nor can they predict correctly the future course of the scientific and cultural development of mankind.

Wrong empirical assumptions are responsible, also, for the poor fitting of the von Neumann-Morgenstern model of economic behavior to the observable economic actions. With a reasonable degree of certainty we know that there hardly ever existed an individual whose economic behavior was entirely rational, entirely free from irrational and nonrational components. In assuming the contrary, the authors develop equations hardly applicable to the actual economic phenomena. The same is true of their assumptions of an equal accessibility of information to all individuals, of utility as a linear quantity, and so on.

The charge of being inapplicable to actual economic behavior and processes can be made against other mathematical models, insofar as their assumptions are empirically inadequate. Unfortunately, almost all mathematical theories contain such assumptions. For instance, several of the mathematical models of learning and imitation assume the empirical correctness of C. L. Hull's theory of learning. Other models accept as valid the punishment-reward theory of learning, or the incidental results of a single pseudoexperimental study of imitation skillessly done by an undergraduate student, or the results of a similar investigation by another student of the effect of reward on imitation, and so on. By uncritically accepting the results of a single, incidental empirical study, without consulting the main body of the existing investigations of the same problem, and by elevating the incidental results of such a study to the rank of assumptions on which their own analysis is based, mathematical modelists introduce suppositions which are bound to vitiate their conclusions. No wonder that many mathematical models turn out to be inapplicable to empirical reality and render but little service to our knowledge of the what, how, and why of the phenomena studied. As long as mathematical modelists continue to make such uncritical assumptions, the nonmathematical investigators of empirical phenomena are justified in their cautious attitude toward these theories and conclusions.

Finally, the mathematical study of psychosocial phenomena most frequently assumes the character of some sort of statistical investigation. Let us now glance at the forms and fruits of a statistical exploration of the psychosocial universe.

## 2. Statistical Methods

There are statistics and statistics. And there are diverse statistical methods and diverse cognitive tasks to be solved by statistical study.

*a*) We can mention, first, the unambitious or routine variety of statistical study. It consists of merely counting the items investigated, as exemplified by a population census; of counting the objectively given divisions of the population: its age, sex, race, occupational, religious, urban-rural, and other classes; of computing the changes which the population undergoes from year to year, or from census to census; of translating the absolute figures into the percentages; and so on. By simple arithmetical operations statistics of this sort deliver the desired quantitative information. Providing that the counting is done carefully, and that the whole universe of the items studied is counted, the results are fairly accurate for the moment of the census-taking.

In spite of their elementary character, these statistics have given us valuable quantitative information about a multitude of psychosocial phenomena. They have possibly delivered a greater amount of correct information than the more ambitious forms of statistical research. On the other hand, the quantitative knowledge supplied by elementary statistics is strictly informational—they do not pretend to give general uniformities, or formulae describing causal relationships, or to answer the basic question *Why*. Further, the results of this sort of statistical study are accurate only in a local and temporary sense, only within the universe of the counted items at the moment of the counting. They cannot be extended over other sets of the same categories of items, or be applied to the same items at a different time in their existence. The birth, death, marriage, and unemployment rates obtained by the census of 1950 cannot be extended as correct for 1955. The percentages "for and against" Senator McCarthy given by the polling of February 15, 1954, cannot be assumed to be correct for March 15, 1955. The rates and percentages change incessantly, now gradually, now abruptly. Those that are correct for Massachusetts or Cambridge are not necessarily correct for other states or cities of the United States; still less are they correct for foreign countries and cities. Herein lies a great limitation of "unambitious" statistics. If, in a sampling operation, we extend the results over the whole class of the items we have sampled, we run the risk of introducing errors into our data. And the larger and more heterogeneous the whole class studied, and the smaller the sample, the less representative the latter becomes and the greater the risk of error grows. If "every observation, every measurement, introduces error," and "if a measure without error is an absurdity," [9] to extend the results of a sample study over the whole class of the sample-items makes the introduction of errors doubly certain.

The same is true about extending census results beyond the moment of the given census. Now and then, mainly for practical reasons, we need to know some of the statistical figures, rates, and percentages. Mainly for practical reasons, also, we need to have a sort of repository of this informational material. Beyond these needs, the informational statistics cease to be scientifically valuable. As a resident of Winchester, Massachusetts, I may need to know the Winchester population figures, its sex-age-economic-occupational-political-religious composition, its school enrollment, the budget of the town, and so on. Not being vitally connected with many other towns, I am not interested in them nor have I a serious reason to burden my memory trying to learn this sort of information about them. For similar reasons I do not need to memorize the endless statistics of all the "Year Books," the "World Almanacs," the annual reports of business corporations, public opinion polls, and similar repositories of the local and evanescent statistics. The only thing which I need to know in regard to these endless statistics is where to find the needed data about this or that item. Otherwise, all these figures contribute little either to my intellectual development or to my understanding of the sociocultural universe in its basic aspects.

So much about this "humble" or "bookkeeping" variety of statistical study. In no way can it replace either the nonstatistical exploration or the mathematical analysis of interhuman phenomena.

*b*) Other statistical studies set forth on much more ambitious tasks, and correspondingly use more refined procedures of statistical analysis. The ambitious tasks of such "high-brow" statistics are: discovery of the degree of stable association or causal and probabilistic relationships between the variables studied; the existence or nonexistence of uniformities in the field explored; analysis and measurement of the factors involved; computation of probabilities and predictions of various sorts related to the empirical data; and so on. These tasks are the basic objectives of any scientific exploration, and especially of "generalizing sciences." They go far beyond the tasks of the "counting" statistics. The methods and procedures of the "ambitious" statistics imperceptibly pass into mathematical methods of inquiry regarding the what, how, and why of the phenomena investigated.

Judged by its fruitfulness in the study of physical phenomena, the method of mathematical statistics has proved to be very valuable. It has rendered an inestimable service to the physical sciences and partly to the biological sciences. However, the situation changes sharply when we examine its achievements in the psychosocial disciplines. So far, in the study of psychosocial phenomena its fruitfulness has been very modest, in spite of the enormous energy, labor, and funds invested.

The *statistical exploration of causal, functional, or probabilistic (chance) relationship* between psychosocial variables can serve to show the limited value of the method. A most frequent procedure for establishing these relationships is correlational statistics. In the earliest correlational studies the technique of computing the ordinary, partial, or multiple correlations was regarded as a marvelous key unlocking the secrets of causal or associational (chance) relationships. If the coefficient of correlation (r) happened to be "significant" (for example $r = .7304$),—followed by the "trimmings" of "standard deviation," "probable error," and other paraphernalia of statistical "scholastics"—it was considered as serious evidence of the close association of, or causal relationship between, the variables. If the coefficient was not "significant" (say, $r = .1036$), it was accepted as evidence of the lack of a stable or causal relationship between the phenomena studied. Generally, the coefficients of correlations were looked on as exact indicators of relationship. Sociologists, economists, and psychologists were proud of using correlational statistics as an instrument which, they felt, raised psychosocial research to the exact and objective level of the physical sciences.

Inspired by this belief, an avalanche of correlational studies started and covered the whole field of psychosocial phenomena. The mass-production of various coefficients of correlation began and has continued without abatement up to the present time. Ideologies glorifying statisticians and depreciating "arm-chair philosophers," praising the statistical measurements of causal relationships and condemning the "speculative yarns" of the nonstatistical scholars, sprang up and have become widely diffused throughout the psychosocial disciplines, among business and governmental bodies, among foundations and universities, and in the public at large. The "golden era" of the "statistical cult" dawned on the unenlightened psychosocial sciences.

While this was going on, and while coefficients of correlations were being manufactured in ever increasing volume, something unexpected began to happen with the correlational "revelations" and their coefficients. They started to misbehave, first of all, in the form of *striking discrepancies between two or more coefficients of correlation dealing with the same variables;* second, *in their failure to register a stable causal or functional relationship where such a relationship has been ascertained by different methods, including the experimental one, and in their indication of a "highly significant" association between the variables where it is denied by a more convincing body of evidence.* Both forms of coefficient misbehavior increasingly testify to the inability of correlational statistics to perform its "detective function": to uncover and measure the hidden causal, functional or chance relationships among psychosocial phenomena, and to perform this task without gross blunders. Found fallible in this function, correlational statistics has also shown itself wanting in its *predictive task.* As a result, its earlier glorification has tended to fade, and its weaknesses have begun to be more and more emphasized. Its halo, however, is still bright in the eyes of the "clerks of psychosocial research" for whom its automatic operations are a God-sent substitute for thought and for the highly difficult art of scientific investigation, although the real masters of scientific study of the psychosocial world are fully aware of the limitations and defects of correlational statistics.

Following are some typical examples of the failures of this method. First of all let us take the *striking discordancy between various coefficients of correlation dealing with the same or essentially similar variables.*

A multitude of correlational studies investigated the *relationship between intelligence and criminality, in some 163,000 cases all in all.*

> C. F. Chassell has carefully summed up the results of the bulk of such studies. In the first place, the results of various studies are contradictory, some exhibiting a positive and others a negative relationship between these variables, some a close and others a very remote relationship. The coefficients of correlation between these variables range from minus .52 to plus .76. . . . About as contradictory and discordant are the coefficients of correlation between *delinquency and illiteracy, deliquency and amount of*

*schooling, criminality and school progress, delinquency and educational achievement; intelligence and morality.*[10]

Thus, after a multitude of painstaking correlational studies, the contradictoriness of their "exact" coefficients of correlation leave us as ignorant as ever about the real relationship between these variables of criminality-delinquency and intelligence. The hopelessness of the situation is aggravated by the fact that these studies do not give to us any objective basis for deciding which of these discordant coefficients are valid, and which are not. The discordancy washes away the significance of these studies and damages the validity of their method, the reliability of their coefficients of correlations, and the accuracy of their predictions.

It is similar with statistical studies of the comparative IQ's of the sexes and of different ethnic groups, nationalities, and so on, together with the factors responsible for these differences. Some of the studies find boys' intelligence higher; some others, girls' intelligence. Some studies support the primacy of innate or hereditary factors, while others confirm that of environmental factors. The dispute among statistical investigators of these problems still goes on as strongly as among "the speculative arm-chair philosophers."[11]

Similarly discordant are the coefficients of correlation concerning the role of similarity and dissimilarity, agreement and disagreement in choosing the marriage mate or in happy and unhappy marriages. Some of the studies show a predominant role for similarity ("like begets like"), while others exhibit the dominant role of dissimilarity, with a wide range of coefficients in both cases.[12] The same is true of the role of agreement and disagreement of husband and wife in happy or unhappy marriages. Sometimes two studies by the same authors display quite discordant coefficients of correlation between identical variables.[13]

No less discordant are the coefficients of correlation between non-battle casualty rates and willingness for combat, ranging from minus .82 to minus .07; or between non-battle casualty rates and confidence in combat skill ranging from plus .18 to minus .74.[14]

If we turn to the coefficients of correlation between such seemingly "solid" variables as economic prosperity or depression (measured by various business barometers) on the one hand and the rates of marriage, birth, death, and divorce on the other, we find again a sharp discordancy in our "precise and objective" coefficients. The discrepancy ranges all the way from a claimed increase of death rate in depression periods, through G. U. Yule's statement that "there is no evidence that death-rate has tended to rise in time of depression" (in England and Wales since 1850 to 1925), to M. B. Hexter's minus .361 between the death rate and unemployment, and up to W. Ogburn and D. Thomas's coefficients: plus .63 (for the United States, 1870-1920), and plus .30 (for England, 1854 to 1913) showing an increase of death rate with an increase of prosperity.

No less contradictory are the coefficients of correlation between economic prosperity and birth, marriage and divorce rates. They, also, range from high positive to "significant negative" correlations. The same is true in regard to the discordant coefficients of correlation between economic variables and suicide, pauperism, criminality, migration, revolutions, wars, and other phenomena.[15]

If there were a real need I could go on and on, filling pages and pages with the contradictory and discrepant coefficients of correlations between practically all sorts of variables studied. With a reasonable degree of certainty I can state that if there exist three or more correlational studies of the relationship between the same or essentially similar variables, these studies will probably give essentially discordant, and often contradictory, coefficients of correlations or contingency between the variables.[16]

From this account, one can see that, instead of being infallible indicators of the degree of association between the variables studied, the coefficients of correlation or their substitutes are like a set of faulty watches giving different time readings all the way from 12:01 A.M. to 11:59 P.M. None of these watches is reliable. Before using them one must send them to the watchmaker.

With slight modification these conclusions are equally applicable to practically all other statistical methods of factor-analysis, of establishing causal relationships, of discovering and formulating constant or universal uniformities and other basic discoveries of scientific knowledge regarding the what, how, and why of psychosocial phenomena. All of these "exact" measurements and formulae are but other varieties of the above set of watches showing discordant time readings.

This is even more true in regard to a legion of *percentages* dealing with rapidly changing situations and fleeting phenomena. At best, percentages of this sort give but "momentary snapshots" of ever-changing configurations. More often than not they fail to deliver even these snapshots in a correct form, or fail to inform us which of several discrepant snapshots is the correct one. To illustrate this, we can take almost any percentage of the Gallup and other public opinion polls or the vast collection of percentages given, for instance, in the earlier-quoted *American Soldier* by Stouffer. Whether the public opinion polls concern percentages of votes for the Republican and the Democratic parties, or percentages dealing with the popularity ("for," "against," and "no opinion") of Senator McCarthy or the attitude towards Russia, each polling of the same item within the same sample of a population shows different percentages from polling to polling. Each polling then gives but a momentary snapshot of "public opinion" at the moment of polling. For any other moment the snapshot would be incorrect and misleading. In addition, we know well, especially after the grossly erroneous prediction of the Truman-Dewey presidential election results, that the snapshots of the pollsters—due to poor sampling, to the insincerity of some of the polled persons and their ever-changing opinions about the polled items, to the complexity of the factors involved, and so on—depict the situation distortedly even for the moment of the polling. As a result, the real cognitive value of the percentages "for and against" is exceedingly meager, often zero or of negative order.

With slight modification this conclusion applies to most of the percentual snapshots of "opinions," "attitudes," "wishes and aspirations," preferences and plans, and other evanescent and fleeting phenomena. In the *American Soldier* we read, for instance, that the percentages of privates ready for further combat according to the degree of their vindictiveness is, in Division A, 26, 25, and 21; but in Division B the corresponding percentages are: 67, 67, and 59.[17] Granting that the authors were able to establish objectively the "high," the "intermediate," and the "low" degree of vindictiveness (though for such a scaling they have only the answers of the soldiers to the prearranged questions), why such a great contrast in the percentages of these two divisions? The reasons for the contrast not being given, we can ask: which of these two sets of percentages is more typical for the majority of the privates of the American army? If this is unknown, then what is the cognitive value of these percentages? If we question other divisions, would we not get different percentages for each division, or subunit, spread over a still wider range? As a matter of fact, 568 infantrymen give only 2 per cent to the vindictiveness-incentive among all the incentives for combat.[18] Can we be sure that the percentages of Divisions A and B would not change if the questioning of them were repeated, and if they were polled before and after combat, or after a victorious battle and a disastrous one? Is it not highly probable that the repeated polling of the same divisions in contrasting situations would yield different percentages in each polling? The net conclusions of the above are: that the two sets of percentages reflect at best "the speech-reactional state of mind" of the questioned privates of Divisions A and B at the moment of questioning; that the percentages are likely to fluctuate widely even for these divisions when polled under different conditions; that it remains unknown which of these two sets, if any, is typical for the majority of the privates of the U.S. Army; that neither of the sets can be generalized beyond the polled samples of Divisions A and B, and even for these divisions beyond the moment of the polling. One can memorize thousands of such percentages and yet remain an all-around ignoramus incapable of using even these percentages for any theoretical or practical purposes.

This can be said, for instance, of the percentages derived from the question: "Generally, from your combat experience, what was most important to you in making you want to keep going, and do as well as you could?" Of 568 infantrymen questioned, 39 per cent mentioned "ending the task"; 14 per cent, "solidarity with group"; 9 per cent, "sense of duty and self-respect"; 10 per cent, "thoughts of home and loved ones"; 6 per cent, "self-preservation"; 5 per cent, "idealistic reasons"; 2 per cent, "vindictiveness"; 1 per cent, "leadership and discipline"; and 14 per cent, "miscellaneous."[19]

If one replaces these percentages by others notably different, his figures would still be about as "valid" as before. The questionnaire presupposes in the infantrymen a higher ability to analyze the motivations of their combat behavior than is often present even in the psychologist-experts. Even for the experts it is not easy to distinguish such an incentive as "idealistic reasons" from "sense of duty and self-respect"; or the incentive of "cannot let the outfit down" from "doing my part, my duty"; or "kill or be killed" from "anger, revenge, and fighting spirit." It is puzzling, also, that only 6 per cent of the combatants mentioned "self-preservation," as an incentive. It is hard to believe that the active combatants had either time or desire or knowledge to answer carefully these and hundreds of other "sophisticated" questions they were required to answer by their military superiors.

The absurdity of the method of direct questions has been recognized; but its temptations are not always resisted.[20] With great force this observation can be applied to the answers of these combatants pestered by the endless questions they were commanded to answer. If even "under the most favorable conditions, a man . . . quickly tires of a subject and then he is likely to say anything which will secure his escape from the irritating [questions]," [21] under front-line conditions our soldiers still more eagerly would say anything to escape the endless irritating questionnaires.

To sum up: it is doubtful that these percentages give a snapshot of the incentives of the questioned men accurate even for the moment of the questioning. In all other respects its cognitive and practical value is negligible. The percentages neither "enrich" our mind, nor do they move our heart. Descriptions of incentives in the great war novels, like Tolstoi's *War and Peace* or Stendhal's *La Chartreuse de Parme,* or in the recent books of Ernie Pyle or Bill Mauldin, give not only a more vivid, more significant, but also more accurate picture of the motivations studied.[22]

If these snapshots are taken repeatedly with the same sample under about the same conditions, they can trace the main line of change or main fluctuations of "public opinion" or other evanescent psychological phenomena. In that case the cognitive value of statistical snapshots naturally increases. But even the repeated polls would supply us only with knowledge of the fluctuations within the period studied. They cannot be extrapolated beyond this period into the future or extended over unpolled groups. They cannot give us a solid basis for predicting future trends; nor can they disclose to us the causal or associational network of the variables or the factors of the fluctuations within the studied period. When used for the purposes of either prediction or causal analysis, a series of statistical snapshots of incessantly changing "opinions," "beliefs," "wishes," etc., are likely to yield fallacious predictions and wrong factors about as frequently as correct ones.

### 3. Additional Shortcomings of Statistical Method

*a*) *Quantitatively Disguised Subjectivity.* When a statistician starts to poll the opinions and other "states of mind" of his respondents, he has already injected a first dose of his own subjectivity into his apparently objective quantitative study. It is introduced through the character of his questions, their wording and their organization into a certain number of classes. If the same investigators of the same "states of mind" of the same respondents classify the items in their questions differently, the results of two pollings are likely to vary a great deal. We saw above how widely divergent the percentages of the incentives of vengeance and hatred were in three different samples. The same authors supply an excellent example of notably different results when the classifications in two questionnaires are different. In one questionnaire the prayer incentive was not classified at all. Therefore, it did not get any percentage. However, in the second questionnaire referred to, the authors of the *American Soldier* classified the incentives into the following five classes: (1) prayer; (2) not letting the other men down; (3) ending the task in order to return home again; (4) hatred for enemy; (5) realization of the objectives of the war. The results of this polling in four army samples were as follows:[23]

From 57 to 83 per cent of the respondents (in four samples) stated that prayer "helped a lot."

From 56 to 85 per cent of the respondents said the thought that they "could not let the other men down helped a lot."

From 28 to 53 per cent mentioned that the incentive "to finish the job in order to return home helped a lot."

From 21 to 46 per cent indicated that "hatred for the enemy helped a lot."

From 19 to 34 per cent of the respondents stated that the thought of "what we are fighting for helped a lot."

Because of the different classification of incentives these two questionnaires resulted in very different pictures. In the first polling, prayer as a motivational factor was totally absent; in the other polling, it was about the most important incentive "to keep fighting even when the going was tough." While "self-preservation" drew some 6 per cent of the answers in one polling, in the other polling it was totally absent. While the "hatred and vengeance" incentive gave only 2 per cent of the answers in one polling, in the other it was mentioned by 21 to 46 per cent of the respondents.

To sum up: the difference in the prearranged classifications of the incentives studied yields quite discordant pictures of their natures and percentages and clearly demonstrates that a great deal of subjectivity is almost unavoidably injected into supposedly objective investigations and precise measurements, at the very start of such studies, even at their planning stage. This dose of arbitrariness predetermines and distorts the results of statistical pollings, questionnaires, and interviews. If the questionnaires on incentives had been made by differently-minded psychologists, sociologists, philosophers, or moralists, classifying the incentives into radically different classes, the discordancy of the results would have been still greater than it is in the two sets of pollings by the authors of the *American Soldier*.

A second dose of subjectivity is injected into these studies through the *wording* of the questions. I indicated above that vague, overlapping, and too "sophisticated" wording of the questions concerning incentives could hardly be answered intelligently by the combatants. Besides vagueness in wording, the *different wording* of essentially the same questions is another channel through which subjectivity unavoidably gets into the statistical polls of "states of mind." The authors of *American Soldier* stress this fact and give examples of the vitiating of results through this sort of subjectivity. Asked how necessary is it for the war effort to have women in the Army, 39 per cent of 3,400 enlisted men answered "not necessary." This per cent increased to 43 when they were asked to express their agreement or disagreement with the statement "Being a Wac is bad for a girl's reputation" (43 per cent agreed with it). The percentage increased to 57 when they were asked whether they would advise a girl-friend to join or not to join the Wac (57 per cent said they "would advise her not to join"). When the same question concerned the respondent's sister, 21 years or older, 70 per cent answered they would advise her not to join. Finally, 77 per cent disagreed with the statement that "a woman can do more for her country in the Wac than she can by working in a war industry."[24] Differently worded, these questions ask essentially the same question: the advisability of having women in the Army for the war effort. The positive answers, however, systematically decrease from 61 to 23 per cent as the questions proceed to be increasingly "closer" to the respondents, as we pass from women generally to the girl-friend and sister of each respondent. This illustrates how strongly the wording of the question influences the answers, and how easy it is to get a quantitatively precise but misleading account of the investigated state of mind through poorly worded questions. Deficient wording is unfortunately fairly frequent in this sort of statistical study.

A third way of introducing a very large dose of subjectivity into the statistical exploration of uniformities, and especially of the factors, in the relationship of variables, is the unavoidable "weighing," "evaluating," "scaling," "ranking," "scoring," and "correcting" of the raw data obtained, or the "fitting" of them to this or that formula. In the preceding chapters it has been shown that these operations are unavoidable in all statistical studies of qualitative phenomena that do not have "natural quantitative units." It has been also shown that all these operations are arbitrary and subjective to a large degree.

When one keeps in mind all these ways in which subjective elements infiltrate the objective-looking results of statistical inquiries, he is not surprised at discrepancy in the conclusions reached by different statistical studies of the same problem; and he no longer feels obliged to accept the statistical findings as infallible. The discrepancies in coefficients of correlations and in other results of statistical studies, and the unavoidable infiltration of subjective elements into such studies, fully warrant at least as strong a skeptical attitude towards most statistical findings about qualitative, fleeting, and little "measurable" psychosocial phenomena as we have in regard to "philosophical" conclusions about these phenomena reached by way of "epistemological," "phenomenological," or "logical" analysis or of an "intuitional" grasp of these problems. None of these methods is infallible and self-sufficient. Each requires after-testing confirmation on the part of all the other methods, and statistical method is not an exception to this rule. Therefore, a sound skepticism in regard to it is not only permissible but quite necessary.

*b*) *Fallacies of statistical method resulting from its uniform application to psychosocial systems as well as to psychosocial congeries.* The bulk of modern psychosocial statisticians claims that they are following the methods and principles of the physical sciences, and are trying to build "a natural-science sociology and psychology." This claim is partly correct, so far as a poor imitation of a somewhat superseded Newtonian macrophysics is concerned. From the standpoint of this macrophysics it seems to be reasonable to view everything real, including the causal uniformities, as objectively given in time and space. "Elementary particles [then] were conceived as balls, hard and impenetrable, made of electricity which is the prototype of matter, and attracting or repelling each other by virtue of the charges they carry. Physics was in its infancy; the physicist was playing marbles."[25]

The Newtonian concepts and laws were so simple that their projection into the external world as objective realities was natural. "The laws and concepts were identified with the real world, 'real state.' [Newtonian] objects, events, measurable properties and states appeared to be objective and real." "Processes were transformations of objects in time." And so on.[26]

Our "natural science sociologists and psychologists" try to build their disciplines according to the model of this Newtonian macrophysics. They seem not to have noticed that the development of the physical science in the twentieth century, especially after the emergence and growth of quantum microphysics, has made this Newtonian physics if not obsolescent then, at least, inadequate.

During the twentieth century several basic principles of physics, including that of causality, have undergone a revolutionary change. Among other things, the transformation of the causality principle has been so great that some physicists call it "the causal catastrophy."[27] The causality of the older physics was viewed as being of mechanical and deterministic character, objectively functioning in the external world, and possessing its own laws and uniformities. When these laws were discovered, they enabled us to predict the future state of a material body or particle on the basis of its known present state.

In the views of modern physicists this "monotypic" causality is replaced by three different substitutes: by the principle of the uncertainty and unpredictability of the future state of a single atom or particle or of a small aggregation of atoms and particles—the electron, the proton, the photon, the neutron, the positron, the meson, the neutrino, the antiproton, the antielectron, the antineutron, the antineutrino; by statistical laws or probability uniformities observable and predictable in the large aggregations of atoms or particles, viewed otherwise as chance phenomena; and by immanent "laws of direction" (A. Eddington), or "self-regulation producing orderly events" (E. Schrödinger), or "conscious, active, voluntaristic decision" (H. Margenau), or "free will" (M. Planck), in regard to biological organisms, conscious personality, and sociocultural systems. A knowledge of the nature of the biological, or the personal, or the sociocultural system and of its immanent "laws of direction" and "self-regulation," or of its "conscious decision," allows one, to some extent, to predict the future state of the system, in spite of the fact that some of these systems represent very small aggregations of atoms, like genes that contain in themselves the "plenotype" of the future organism transmitted from generation to generation.

A few comments on these three substitutes of the superseded monotypic causality of the earlier physics are in order.

1) The microphysical world of the single atom or particle or the small aggregation of atoms and particles is called "the Microcosm of Lawlessness," the realm of discontinuity and indeterminism. The categories of "continuous path," and "continuous motion," are not applicable to it. Nor is it possible to determine simultaneously the position and momentum of the particle, or certainly predict all its future continuous states. It is a world of unpredictable "fireflies" most fancifully appearing and disappearing, either irregularly replacing or mysteriously transforming into one another. "No theory has yet been proposed to render the vagaries [of the single atoms or particles] understandable in detail, none is able to predict them. . . . Indeed Heisenberg's principle says precisely that such predictions are impossible. . . . Man's inability to trace the path of atomic objects is grounded in something far more serious than ignorance; its roots lie in actual indetermination of perception. In the case of an ordinary firefly, observed as moving from its scintillations in the dark, ignorance of intermediate positions does not prevent their interpolation and hence a construction of its path. The situation with respect to the atom is completely different; interpolation will not work however cleverly it be conceived." [28] "In the microscopic world of modern physical science systems such as electrons, atoms, molecules, and photons . . . their historical continuity is broken in many processes, e.g., in the emission and absorption of radiant energy, in radioactive transformations, and in pair formation. . . . Their states are not projectable into the external world as the real states of individual systems. . . ." Neither are they totally predictable. Discontinuity and ambiguity mark the microscopic subatomic world. "There is no generally accepted operational test for reality." [29]

The moral of this microphysics for psychosocial statisticians and "natural-science sociologists and psychologists" is that their hunt for causal or statistical uniformities in the field of unique or rare psychosocial phenomena, is likely to be a search for something that really does not exist at all, whether in the unique or rare perception, emotion, or other inner experience, or a unique, or rare creative or criminal action in the life of an individual or a unique and rare historical event. Being a unique or rare phenomenon or a unique aggregate of a few phenomena, such an object of study does not lend itself to a causal, experimental analysis, because all inductive methods—identity, difference, concomitant variation, and so on—require for inductive inference at least two or more phenomena of the same kind. Being unique phenomenon it makes an application of inductive methods impossible; being rare phenomenon it makes the application very difficult. Still less possible is an application of statistical method to such unique or rare phenomena for the discovery of statistical laws. For discovery of such laws, statistical method demands a mass observation of large aggregates of similar phenomena. Statistics can hardly have the smallest foothold on the ground of unique or rare phenomena. Nor can this method predict the future states of a rare or unique psychosocial phenomenon, especially by an observer external to it.

Statistical methods cannot predict even the states of single units in the predictable mass phenomena. Predicting an increase of suicide rate in a large population, statistics cannot predict precisely who of the individuals A, B, C, M, N, · · · X will contribute to the increase of the rate, or whether you and I will be included among its victims. Or suppose that statistics show that 72 per cent of paroled criminals with a certain background and certain characteristics make good. This prediction does not, however, insure that J. Brown who has the above background and traits will necessarily make good his parole, or that M. Jones who has a different background and different traits will necessarily violate his parole. Generally, the future states of the single units of fairly predictable mass phenomena remain largely unpredictable.[30] For these reasons, unique or rare psychosocial phenomena cannot be viewed as causally determined, or as possessing the chance uniformities of large aggregates observable by statistical procedures. When the unique or rare psychosocial phenomena are mere congeries unrelated to one another either causally or correlationally or otherwise meaningfully, when they are not a part of a meaningful psychosocial system, such phenomena fall within the psychosocial realm corresponding to microphysical phenomena. As in the physical microcosm this psychosocial realm is a world of discontinuities, irregularities, ambivalences, uncertainties, and unpredictabilities. As such it may be studied by the methods of "quantum sociology" and "quantum psychology," homological to those of quantum mechanics. Statistical methods cannot be applied to, and if applied cannot yield fruitful results in, investigation of the unique or rare psychosocial congeries. The fruitlessness of innumerable attempts only confirms this conclusion. Such is the practical lesson suggested by modern quantum physics in regard to this realm of the psychosocial universe. This lesson informs us also of the new limitations of statistical methods in regard to this class of psychosocial phenomena.

2) We pass on to psychosocial phenomena which are repeated in time and space and lend themselves to statistical mass observation. They can be studied statistically and, now and then, inductively or experimentally when the rules of induction can be applied to their study. (Later on it will be shown that the overwhelming bulk of what is now called "experimental" or "inductive" study is neither experimental nor inductive. These terms are greatly misused and abused in modern sociology, psychology, and related sciences.) This part of psychosocial phenomena is the proper field of statistical study. It corresponds to the ever-repeated macrophysical phenomena of large aggregates of atoms susceptible to mass observation by statistical and inductive methods. These methods often discover chance uniformities in the relationship of such phenomena. On the basis of the discovered uniformities, their future states can often be predicted, with varying degrees of accuracy. The ever-repeated mass phenomena of births, deaths, marriages, divorces, suicide, morbidity, migration, crime, wars, revolutions, mobility, stratification, organization and disorganization, integration and disintegration, increase and decrease of governmental control, economic prosperity and impoverishment, demand and supply, antagonism and solidarity; phenomena of habit-formation, the conditioned reflex, perception, the biopsychological drives of sex, eating, drinking, repeated emotions, wishes and motivations, and so on—all are examples of macrocosmic, repeated, frequent, mass-scale psychosocial phenomena. Statistical methods have been applied mainly to this sort of psychosocial phenomena and in their study these methods have been moderately fruitful.

Since the relationships among these phenomena are viewed as chance relationships—now more uniform and stable, now more variant and capricious—a statistician can take any sets of these phenomena as his variables, and can try to find out how closely the sets are associated with each other and what, if any, uniformities are given in their relationship.

Likewise, the chance character of these phenomena and of the dynamics of their states allow the statisticians to observe, on a mass scale, what are the main states through which a set of phenomena passes in the process of its existence; what, if any, are the time-order uniformities in the succession of these states; what, if any, are the repeated cycles and trends in the succession of the states; how rigid or invariant are the time-order uniformities, cycles, or trends in the incessantly changing states; and what are the factors or the independent variables associated with these dynamic uniformities. For a study of static and dynamic relationships among these vast congeries or chance aggregates of psychosocial phenomena statistical methods are the proper ones. Providing that statisticians do not forget the limitations of their methods and do not apply their tools to a study of unique, rare or single phenomena as well as "the meaningful psychosocial systems" (to be discussed on the following pages); providing, further, that the statisticians do not try to count, measure, and scale the uncountable, unscalable, and nonmeasurable qualitative phenomena; assuming that they do not consider their chance uniformities as invariant causal laws and do not extrapolate their findings far beyond the samples studied; in brief, assuming that the statisticians bear in mind all the discussed limitations, uncertainties, and errors of a misused statistical method—with these conditions, statistical methods are the main methods for investigating static and dynamic relationships among macrocosmic mass congeries or chance aggregates of psychosocial phenomena.

3) Finally, we come to the third class of biological and psychosocial phenomena, to *the class of biological and psychosocial systems or unities.* It has been briefly mentioned that the modern physicists sharply separate this class both from the phenomena of "the lawless physical microcosm"—single atoms and particles or small aggregations of them—or from chance macrocosmic phenomena and their relationships. While the subatomic phenomena display discontinuities, irregularities, and uncertainties; and while the large macrophysical aggregates manifest statistical uniformities and orderly relationships which are, however, chance uniformities and chance relationships; biological and psychosocial systems, no matter how small an aggregation of atoms they represent, display orderly relationships and static and dynamic uniformities quite different from the above two classes. Physicists call these relationships and uniformities by terms ranging from "the inner law of direction" (A. Eddington), and "a mechanism

producing order from order" in contrast to a chance, "statistical mechanism producing order from disorder" (E. Schrödinger), all the way up to the order determined by a "free will" (M. Planck), by "conscious, voluntaristic decision" (H. Margenau), and by "conscious mind" or Athman as a part of the superpersonal Cosmic Mind or Cosmic Self or Brahman (E. Schrödinger).

As an example of this class of biological and psychosocial phenomena we can take Schrödinger's analysis of genes and organism. Genes represent very small aggregations of atoms. As such, genes belong to a microphysical world and should display the discontinuity, uncertainty, unpredictability and "lawlessness" of microphysical phenomena. Instead of these characteristics, genes appear to be highly integrated systems. They contain in themselves a "plenitude pattern" or the "plenotype" of the respective organism—the totality of its hereditary characteristics. Even more, genes preserve their specific individuality unimpaired from generation to generation of the respective organisms. Amidst ever-changing environmental conditions they carry on their integrity and the plenotype. Through this "plenotype" they predetermine the essential characteristics of an organism. Instead of chaotic lawlessness, they display orderliness, regularity, and predictability for the anatomical and physiological, and, indeed, for all the main states of the life cycle of the organism. Thus "incredibly small groups of atoms, too small to display exact statistical law, do play a domineering role in the very orderly and lawful events within a living organism." And "an organism's astonishing gift of concentrating a 'stream of order' on itself and thus escaping the decay into atomic chaos, seems to be connected with . . . the chromosome molecules which doubtless represent the highest degree of well-ordered atomic association known."

In the physical world there is nothing like this "organism's orderliness" that "displays the power of maintaining itself and producing orderly events." This orderliness is guided by a "mechanism" entirely different from the "probability mechanism of physics." In this sense life is fundamentally different from physical phenomena,[31] and living matter involves, in addition to the known "laws of physics," other laws hitherto unknown. In other words, a biological organism is a system that bears in itself the reason of its individuality and perpetuation, of self-directing orderly change. Its essential traits are determined by its genes, and its life career consists largely of an unfolding or realization of its potentialities. In the preservation of its life integrity, and in passing through its life career's determined phases, it has a tangible margin of autonomy from all external forces. It does not easily dissolve into atomic chaos. The external forces can hinder or facilitate a full realization of its potentialities (its hereditary "plenotype"); in exceptional cases they can destroy an organism; but they cannot radically change its inherited properties and the succession of states or phases in its life history. They cannot produce a cat from the fertilized egg of a cow, or change the states of the human organism's development from childhood through youth and maturity to old age into a reverse sequence of these phases. Its orderliness and development is "a living potentiality (life, soul) in a state of incessant becoming that fulfills its unique life-course or Destiny in the Time-process, never reversing its Direction, and flowing from the past through the present to the future. . . . It has destiny as an organic necessity of potentiality passing into actuality." [32]

Spengler's characterization of biological and psychosocial unities is very similar to that of Schrödinger and other microphysicists. My own definition and analysis of organic and psychosocial systems are practically identical with those of the physicists. Here, as in other basic problems, the sociologists and psychologists who are opposed to the noisy imitators of the natural sciences are in fact in a much greater agreement with the physical sciences than the devotees of "natural-science sociology and psychology."

What Schrödinger and other eminent physicists say of a biological organism can be said of any integrated personality, organized group, and unified cultural system.[33] Whether we take an integrated personality whose "self," values, and ideas are unified into one consistent system; whose overt actions and material instrumentalities practice what his values and ideas preach; whose "self" controls his conscious and unconscious drives; or we take an organized social group, be it a harmonious family, a school, a business enterprise, the state, an occupational union, a political party, a religious organization, or any organized group with a clear-cut distribution of rights and duties, functions, and roles among its members, with a set of consistent values for whose realization the group is organized; or we take a consistent system of scientific, philosophical, religious, ethical, legal, aesthetic, and other cultural ideas and values articulated by the material vehicles of the system and operated by its human agents—these personal, social, and cultural systems are similar to Schrödinger's organism in many respects. In contrast to an unintegrated personality, an unorganized social group and eclectic cultural congeries, each integrated personality, organized group and unified cultural system has its own reality, individuality, and interdependence of its important parts upon one another, of each part upon the whole, and of the whole upon its parts; each system maintains the continuity of its existence and "sameness" despite an incessant change of its elements; all important parts of each of these systems change in togetherness; each system immanently self-directs the main phases or states of its life career; in its functioning and changes each system has a margin of autonomy from all environmental forces, and the better the integration, the larger the margin; each system is selective in what it takes from its environment; no matter how small the system is, it displays most of the characteristics of Schrödinger's organism.[34]

> Whether the system is scientific or religious, aesthetic or philosophical, whether it is represented by a family, a business firm, or a state, it bears within itself the seeds of incessant change, which mark every action and reaction even in a fixed environment. . . . The whole series of changes the system undergoes throughout its existence is to a large extent an unfolding of its inherent potentialities. From an acorn can spring only an oak. From the seeds of any organism can emerge only the respective organism. In spite of the vicissitudes of their subsequent life-history, the main phases of life of an organism are mainly the result of the inherent properties of the seed. The same is true of sociocultural systems. For instance, the course of the change of a family is different from that of a political party or state; of a musical system is different from that of a scientific or ethical system. The forms of change of a "univariant" sociocultural system are different from those of "bivariant" or "multivariant" systems; the forms, phases, rhythms, periodicities, and directions of their quantitative and qualitative changes differ in each system according to its nature. In this sense any personal or sociocultural system largely molds its own destiny.[35]

The above gives some idea of how different the realm of unified biological, personal, and sociocultural systems is from those of microphysical and macrophysical phenomena, or from unintegrated personal and sociocultural congeries. In perfect agreement with modern physicists, we find statistical methods little applicable to "microphysical"—unique and rare—psychosocial phenomena, especially for the purposes of discovering statistical uniformities in their static and dynamic relationships. In full agreement with modern physicists, we find, too, that the best field for statistical study of psychosocial phenomena is the realm of large aggregates or "vast dumps" of personal, social, and cultural congeries: congeries of ideas, values, emotions, wishes, actions; unorganized, disorganized, and "atomized" plurels of individuals; congeries of cultural objects, phenomena, and events not bound together into one whole by meaningful, logical, and aesthetic consistency, or by causal interdependence of the type "when A is given B is given," and "when A (or B) varies B (or A) varies also"; congeries of psychosocial phenomena "united" only by spatial adjacency in a "psychosocial dump" or by mechanical proximity of the type occurring when a page of Plato's *Republic* is glued together with a page of a Sears-Roebuck catalogue. All psychosocial congeries are chance phenomena, and as such can be studied statistically. A statistician can take any congeries or any "part" of a congeries as his variable and try to find out whether there are statistical uniformities in its relationship to other chance variables. In the realm of psychosocial congeries he has full liberty to operate as he pleases, to combine any congeries-variables, and to use his tools in exploring any part of any dump of psychosocial phenomena.

Finally, again in full agreement with modern physicists, we find that in regard to biological, personal, and sociocultural systems statistical methods are either inapplicable or are greatly limited in their service. The order and uniformities of these systems are not of a chance character, but of an organic and meaningful nature inherent in the systems themselves since the moment of their inception and emergence. The knowledge of personal, social, and cultural systems—of their nature, their structure, their static and dynamic uniformities—is obtainable not only through external-sensory observation by one outside the systems, and not only through logical analysis and mathematical (statistical) calculations by the observer, but especially through direct cofeeling and coexperiencing the system's psychosocial states, and through direct intuition, and identification of the knower with the known, of the cognizing subject with the cognized system. A scientist observer who has never experienced joy or sorrow, love or hatred, religious or aesthetic bliss, justice or injustice, creative or dull moments, certitude or doubt, can never obtain even the remotest knowledge of these living, feeling, wishing, emotional, and thoughtful states. With all his statistical, logical, observational techniques he can get only shadows of the dead shells of these meaningful, living miracles. He hardly can even count, classify, and analyze these phenomena because in order for his countings, classifications, and analyses to be accurate, he must be able to distinguish joy from sorrow, religious ecstasy from sex-drive, love from hatred. If he has never experienced these states, he simply cannot distinguish them from one another and, therefore, cannot classify them into adequate classes and count the identical units in each class.

The same is true of social systems. Only through direct empathy, coliving and intuition of the psychosocial states can one grasp the essential nature and difference between a criminal gang and a fighting battalion; between a harmonious and a broken family; and, generally, the essential nature and differences of various groups from one another, or diverse states of similar groups (e.g., the familistic, the contractual, and the coercive family).

The same can be said of the nature and differences of religious, scientific, aesthetic, ethical, legal, economic, technological, and other cultural value-systems and their subsystems. Without the direct living experience of these cultural values, they will remain *terra incognita* for our outside observer and statistical analyst. He can meticulously count the number of the measures of a Bach suite, the number of G or F notes in it, the number of different rhythms or tempi, and so on; and yet, if he is "musically deaf," he cannot obtain even the remotest idea of the suite. The same can be said of a form-and-color-blind statistician studying Raphael's painting or Michelangelo's sculpture. All his measurements and logical analyses will not avail him in understanding the "essence" of the paintings or sculptures. Without a still largely mysterious and indescribable inner experience, called "understanding" and "thinking through," no idea or thought, beginning with "two plus two make four" and ending with the most complex systems, can be understood, comprehended or known, despite all sorts of observation and statistical measurement. These methods are useless in understanding the nature and difference between, say, Plato's and Kant's systems of philosophy, between the ethics of the Sermon on the Mount and the ethics of hate, between Euclidean and Lobachevskian geometry, and between different systems of ideas generally. Only after successfully accomplishing the mysterious inner act of "understanding" each system of ideas or values, can one classify them into adequate classes, putting into one class all the identical ideas, and putting into different classes different ideas or values. Only after that, can one count them, if they are countable, and perform other operations of a mathematical or statistical nature, if they are possible. Otherwise, all observations and statistical operations are doomed to be meaningless, fruitless, and fallacious simulacra of real knowledge.[36]

Such is the first limitation of a fruitful applicability of statistical methods to the study of psychosocial systems.

The second limitation consists of a considerable narrowing of the statistician's liberty in the selection of variables for his analysis. In regard to congeries of psychosocial and cultural phenomena, he can select from the "dump" of congeries any set or bits of the "dump" as his variables and can study their interrelationship. His freedom of choice among congeries-variables is theoretically unlimited.

But the situation with regard to a statistical study of the systems is very different. Here one's choice of variables is greatly limited. A statistical biologist cannot select for his variables, say, the leg of a horse and the digestive organ of a bird, which are heterogeneous parts of different biological systems. Nor can he expect any fruitful results from a statistical study of the relationship between a bee's buzzing and a fish's swimming, which are heterogeneous functions of different organisms. Let us assume that a biologist is unaware of the unity of an organism and of the heart and stomach as its organs. And let us suppose, further, that he gets many three-quarters of hearts and as many halves of stomachs of the same kind of organism. And let us now imagine that he takes these parts of the heart and of the stomach for his variables and sets forth on a study of their relationships. The absurdity of such statistical research is obvious. A statistician can study the relationships between the heart and digestive organ in the same organism or in a series of organisms, but he cannot arbitrarily cut the system and its subsystems into a minced meat of slices and cubes, and then fruitfully study their interrelationships with one another.

Fortunately, there are no biologists doing studies of this sort, but there still are many psychosocial researchers who commit exactly these blunders in their statistical investigations of psychosocial systems.

> Without realizing at all the fundamental difference between the psychosocial systems and congeries, the rank and file of statistical factorial analysts unhesitatingly take any psychological, social, or cultural phenomena, and treat them simply as "variables," regardless of whether they are congeries or systems and subsystems. They handle all psychological, cultural, and social phenomena as congeries.[37]

As a result, the psychosocial sciences are filled with contradictory theories about various "independent" and "dependent" variables, about the "primary" and "secondary" factors of this or that psychological, social, or cultural phenomenon. They are filled with fallacious uniformities supposedly describing relationships between diverse variables. They are full of statistical studies in which the problems are, generally, wrongly set and wrongly "solved." A few familiar examples illustrate this criticism.

Instead of an investigation of the social and cultural systems, subsystems, and congeries of whose agglomeration Yankee City (Newburyport)[38] consists, W. L. Warner and P. S. Lundt first arbitrarily cut its population into six slices (upper-upper, lower-upper, upper-middle, lower-middle, and so on). By such slicing they cut across many of the social and cultural systems of the city, dumping into the same stratum various cuts of diverse mutilated systems,[39] and distributing into diverse strata various cuts of the same system. If anything, these operations are even worse than that of the hypothetical biologist taking as his variables three-quarter sections of hearts and halves of stomachs. Having done their slicing into six strata, our authors devote the whole volume to the study, statistical and otherwise, of their relationships. No wonder they failed to find any uniformity, or to describe adequately the *modus vivendi* between their slices. This failure is frankly acknowledged by the authors themselves in the preface and introduction to their second volume. They say that, contrary to their expectation, members of the same stratum neither thought nor behaved in a similar way, nor had a similar system of values and style of living, nor had any particular solidarity with one another.

In their second and third volumes the authors tried to remedy the failure, but instead of improving the situation they only aggravated it. They took 357 associations in the city and arbitrarily ranked them into 19 strata. Artificially distributing these strata in lateral extensions of each of the previous six strata, they obtained 54 still more artificial positions. Not satisfied with these "cubes," they divided all the families of

Yankee City into twenty-four classes and converted them into fifty meat balls ("positions"). Next they took all the "cliques" of the city and grouped them into thirty-one slices (strata). Finally, grinding the six classes, nineteen associational strata, twenty-four family ranks, fifty positions and thirty-one clique slices into minced meat, they obtained, in a somewhat mysterious way, a grand total of 89 meat balls ("positions"). Having obtained these 89 meat balls, they laboriously proceeded to describe them and to analyze their interrelationships. Should we wonder that the results of the study were about nil, so far as the real structure of Yankee City and the interrelationships among its social and cultural systems were concerned? The whole laborious "research" and its numerous statistical tables are a glaring example of how a study of social systems and their agglomerations ought *not* to be made. What Warner and Lundt achieved was a parody of scientific and statistical investigation. Their operations are not those of anatomists, but of butchers. The main reason for all their blunders is an ignorance of the profound difference between systems and congeries, and their treatment of sociocultural systems as congeries. The authors also make some valuable contributions in these volumes, but precisely in the nonstatistical parts of the study.

In modern sociology, social psychology, and anthropology there are many studies of cities, communities, towns, and agglomerations of social systems suffering from similar butcher methods. No wonder, again, that except for informational bits and ends, these studies have not yielded a real knowledge of the structure of the communities, or any significant uniformity in their network of relationships.

Another famous example of the wrong classification of cultural phenomena into false unities is given by Danilevsky's, Spengler's, and Toynbee's unification of an enormous number of cultural phenomena into the pseudosystems of "civilization" or "high types of culture," or "culture-historical types." In the whole of human history Danilevsky finds ten great civilizations or systems: Egyptian, Assyro-Babylonian, Chinese, Hindu, Iranian, Hebrew, Greek, Roman, Arabic, and Germano-Romanic or European. Spengler finds eight great culture-civilizations; Toynbee increases their number to twenty-one. Each civilization-culture is considered by the authors as a unity or system. Each civilization-culture is born, grows to its maturity, and then declines and dies.

When each of these "civilizations" is properly analyzed, it is found to be not a unified system, but a vast conglomeration of diverse systems, subsystems, and congeries; in this conglomeration many a system is in a congeries-relation to other systems; many isolated congeries (single cultural phenomena) are scattered over the whole cultural or civilizational "dump." In brief, none of the Danilevsky-Spengler-Toynbee "civilizations" is a unified cultural system, but a vast cultural dump. Not being an integrated system, a civilization cannot be born, or grow, or die, as one system. What has not been integrated cannot disintegrate. These authors united into one civilization a series of different sociocultural systems and congeries, and put into different civilizations various parts of the same cultural system. These blunders are due to the lack of a clear distinction between sociocultural congeries and systems.[40]

Further examples of this same situation are presented in dichotomic theories of cultural "lead and lag," and in the factorial theories of Karl Marx and Max Weber, to mention but a few. The essentials of the theories of cultural lead and lag (K. Marx, T. Veblen, L. Weber, A. Weber, R. M. MacIver, W. Ogburn, F. S. Chapin, and others) consist of a division of all cultural phenomena into two main classes: material and nonmaterial. Further, the theory contends that in a change of the total culture the material culture uniformly leads, while the nonmaterial culture lags, that the material culture is "the independent variable," while the nonmaterial culture is the dependent function of this factor. Among various "proofs" of this theory, a considerable body of statistical data has been offered to support it.

When one tests the theory carefully, he finds it vague and ambiguous. So far as the theory is clear at all, it is untenable. Apart from its vagueness, its first blunder consists, as we have said, of dividing all sociocultural phenomena into material and nonmaterial classes. Whatever the authors mean by these two classes—and there is a considerable variation in meaning among the proponents of this theory—neither of them is a unified sociocultural system or variable, but a peculiar concoction of the parts of different systems and of many congeries. In addition to this absence of unity, most of the sociocultural systems that do exist are butchered into two parts, and these parts are placed in the two different "systems" of material and nonmaterial culture. In order to see this double blunder, imagine for a moment a biological theory that divides all life phenomena into two classes: the material life made up of all the physical organisms, and the nonmaterial life composed of all the functions of organisms (blood-circulation, breathing, eating, drinking, digestion, micturition, and so on). Suppose, further, that the material life phenomena "lead" while the nonmaterial life phenomena "lag" in the process of life transformation; that the material life determines the nonmaterial one. This hypothetical theory is fairly close to the sociological "lead-lag" conjectures, and these conjectures are about as erroneous as the imaginary biological theory.

The point is that all empirically grounded sociocultural phenomena have their "nonmaterial" and "material" components. Their nonmaterial components are represented by their meanings, values and technical rules. Their material part consists of the totality of the material objects, instrumentalities, and vehicles in which the meanings, values and technical rules are incorporated, and through which they are objectified, materialized, and communicated to others. Thus, a religious system consists of the totality of the nonmaterial beliefs, values, and ritual rules, and of the totality of material temples, buildings, religious pictures and sculptures, objects of the cult, books, financial funds, land, and other earthly possessions of the religious body; of behavioristic ceremonies and rituals performed according to the technical rules of each religious service; finally, of the "material" members of a given religious organization, like the Roman Catholic, or the Mohammedan religious body.

Similarly a scientific system consists of the totality of the nonmaterial theories, values and technical rules incorporated into the material educational and research institutions, with their material buildings, laboratories, libraries, museums, behavioristic actions of teaching and researching according to the technical rules of scientific methods, carried on by "material" individuals and scientific organizations. A legal system consists of the totality of the nonmaterial laws, regulations, and technical rules of "due process of law," and of the totality of the material law books, court buildings, prisons, gallows, police and judges, and overt ritual of detection, arrest, trial, and so on. The same can be said of all sociocultural systems. Each of them is made up of nonmaterial and material components. Each of them has also its own "technology" of how to carry on scientific research, to perform a religious service, to compose music, to proceed with a court trial, to paint a picture, to write a play, or to manage a business.[41]

In short, this dichotomic theory, with its "leading" material and "lagging" nonmaterial variables, becomes either meaningless or untenable in its general form. It utterly violates the scientific rules for classification of phenomena into adequate classes and for logical formation of class concepts.

The theory would be more logical if it claimed that in the change of a sociocultural system its material part uniformly leads and its nonmaterial part lags in the process of change. Being logically better, this variation of the theory is, however, also untenable because it is violently contradicted by the relevant facts. If anything, it is the nonmaterial theories, ideologies, beliefs, ideas, values, and technical rules—not the material part of a system—that ordinarily initiates the change. Now and then there are exceptions to this rule, but these exceptions in no way reverse it.[42]

There are still other variations of the lead-lag theories, according to which either the scientific or the religious or the economic system leads the change of the other systems in the total culture. However, these variations are also invalid since each of them is sharply contradicted by a large body of factual and logical evidence.[43]

The preceding excursion shows the error of statistical or other investigations of the static and dynamic relationship in and among the systems when these systems are treated as congeries or isolated variables. The error ensues when the variables are chosen blindly, without consideration of whether they are independent congeries or inalienable parts of living systems.

As a third example of the blunders ensuing from disregard of the profound difference between psychosocial systems and congeries—from statistical treatment of systems as congeries and of congeries as systems—I shall mention the error of taking *a part of a system as an independent variable* (or the cause or predominant factor) *and the whole system as a dependent variable* (or effect or conditioned phenomenon). If a hypothetical biologist declares that a mustache, or the color of the eyes, or an arm, or a single gland, or a sex-organ, or any other part of an organism is the primary factor or independent variable determining the total anatomical structure, and all physiological functions of all the organs and of the whole organism, the fallacy is glaringly obvious.

If, further, our hypothetical biologist declares that one of the above parts of an organism is responsible for all the anatomical, physiological, and psychological changes which the organism undergoes in its passage from childhood to adolescence, to maturity and to old age, the absurdity of such a theory regarding the main factor of the organism's dynamics is still more obvious. The error of both biological theories consists in taking a part of the organism as the factor determining the whole organism, in making the part greater and more powerful than the whole system of which the factor is only one of many parts. In application to a concrete biological system the fallacy is so evident that this sort of theory does not exist in biological science.

In regard to discrete sociocultural systems the fallacy is not so clearly visible. Therefore, factorial theories of this sort still proliferate in the field of the psychosocial sciences. Owing to an ignorance of the basic difference between sociocultural systems and congeries, most statistical, or nonstatistical, sociologists, social psychologists, historians, anthropologists, economists, and political scientists take for their "preponderant" or main factor either the economic, or technological, or scientific, or religious, or philosophical, or legal, or artistic variable, and through their "pet factor" they try to account for the structure and dynamics of the other classes of sociocultural phenomena, often even for the statics and dynamics of the total sociocultural universe in which the main factor operates. While in a study of sociocultural congeries such a setting of the problem of the factor(s) is legitimate, in an investigation of sociocultural systems it is as fallacious as the approach of our imaginary biologist. As a matter of fact, most of the factors picked up by recent theories are not congeries but either part of a system, or a system as a part of a larger supersystem. Thus the religious variable, claimed by many theories to be the preponderant factor in economic, scientific, legal, ethical, and other classes of sociocultural phenomena, happens indeed to be a system in a larger supersystem of several Oriental and Occidental total cultures. The same is true of fine arts phenomena: painting, sculpture, architecture, music, literature, and drama. Likewise, in several cultures the legal and ethical systems happen to be the parts of a larger supersystem (Ideational, or Sensate, or Idealistic). The same goes for science, philosophy, economics, politics, and technology.

In regard to the Greco-Roman and the Western cultures, and more cursorily in regard to the Ancient Egyptian, Chinese, and Hindu cultures,

I have shown in considerable detail that their language, science, technology, philosophy, ethics and law, painting, sculpture, architecture, music, literature, many of their economic and political phenomena, and many of their social groups—that each of these classes has been not a mere statistical plurel or a conglomeration of congeries, but an integrated system of which the parts were bound together by the ties of logical or aesthetic consistency and of "causal"—or empirically observable—interdependence.[44] In the same work it is shown that practically all these systems—scientific-technological, religious, philosophical, artistic, ethical, economic, political, and social—have been mutually interdependent systems or parts of a still larger supersystem.

Like the parts of a system, all these systems have been bound together into a supersystem by the same double ties of meaningful consistency and "causal" interdependence. The mutual integration of these systems into a larger supersystem has been the reason for their changing in "togetherness" in the course of time. When the Ideational form of one of these systems rises, the Ideational form of the other systems and of their supersystem rises also. When the Ideational form of one of these systems declines, the Ideational form of the other systems and of their supersystem declines too. A rise or decline of Sensate form in one of these systems is paralleled by the rise and decline of this form in the other systems and their supersystem. It is true that the degree of interdependence among these systems and the synchronism of their change vary somewhat: some of the systems display a closer interdependence and a stricter synchronism of change than the others. In spite of such variation from system to system, both remain quite tangible in all these systems. Observable, also, remains their meaningful "causal" unification into a supersystem, with its three-fold interdependence: the dependence of each important part upon the other important parts of a system or supersystem; the dependence of each part upon the whole system or supersystem; and the dependence of the whole system or supersystem upon all and each of its important parts.

In the light of these statements, the errors of such factorial theories become perfectly visible. Marx and other partisans of an economic interpretation of history take the economic subsystem, expressed as "the means and instruments of production," and make it the main factor of change and structure for all the other systems, including the "superstructure of ideology and religion." When Max Weber takes his factor of *Wirtschafts-ethik* and religion as the preponderant factor, and tries to interpret through this "independent variable" the static and dynamic properties of other systems (including the economic one) and of their supersystem, he again commits the error of conditioning the whole system by its part. No wonder, therefore, that we have a plethora of discordant, even contradictory, main factors or independent variables for historical processes. No wonder, either, that the relationship of the same variables is often expressed in contradictory equations. According to Max Weber, E = f(WER), "the economic variable is the function of the independent variable of *Wirtschaftsethik-Religion*." According to Marx, WER = f(E), "ethics and religion are the functions of the economic factor." Since each of these variables is taken as an isolated congeries, without any regard to its being part of a system, or a system in a supersystem, it is not surprising that Weber and Marx came to opposite conclusions in their study of the relationship between the economic and the religious variables. For Weber, Protestantism is the preponderant factor of Capitalism. For Marx, Capitalism is the factor of Protestantism. No wonder, either, that both conclusions are wrong. The economic factor did not generate Protestantism, nor did Protestantism generate Capitalism, but both of these systems, together with the scientific, philosophical, aesthetic, legal, ethical, and political systems, changed interdependently as parts of the rising Sensate supersystem in European culture. In the three-fold interdependence of a system or supersystem each part is the cause and effect of the other parts and of the whole system, and the system itself is the cause and effect of its parts. Any attempt to replace this three-dimensional interdependent change by the simplistic theory that a part of a system is the factor of change in all the other parts, and in the whole system, is logical and factual fallacy.

Forgetting this truth, and starting their study with the wrong assumption that all variables are congeries, and disregarding the possibility that the variables are part of a system, a legion of factorial analysts pick up the most diverse variables as main factors and arrive at discordant but equally wrong conclusions. Their theories duplicate the hypothetical theories of our imaginary biologist. Having observed the anatomical, physiological, and psychological changes of an organism passing from childhood to adolescence, to maturity and to old age, and (hypothetically) not being aware of the three-fold interdependence of each part upon the other parts, of each part upon the whole organism, and of the organism upon its parts, one of the biologists ascribes all these changes in all important parts of the organism to the "factor of mustache," another to that of "increased weight," the third to a change in the pituitary gland, the fourth to an increase of muscular power, the fifth to an awakened libido, and so on. In this hypothetical case we have no difficulty in seeing the utter fallacy of these phantasmagorias. In factorial analysis of psychosocial and cultural phenomena the obvious error of the above-mentioned "mustache," or "pituitary gland," or "libidinal" philosophies of history and of sociocultural structures is still not clearly visible to many social scientists. It is high time that such factorial "sociologies" and "philosophies of history" were removed from the field of living science into the museum of human blunders.

Finally, psychosocial and cultural systems tend to lead statistical studies to fallacious results through the many-foldedness and discreteness of their manifestations. Take, for instance, only one of many manifestations of the United States (as a sociopolitical system): the cold war with Soviet Russia. Empirically this cold-war activity of the United States manifests itself in a long series of diverse actions and heterogeneous events scattered over the whole world; in a feverish production of various bombs and armaments; in an increased draft of youth; in lending and granting financial aid to various allies; in increased taxation; in full employment; in building military bases in all parts of the world; in a multitude of diplomatic communications; in endless speeches of politicians; in stimulation of patriotism and loyalty; in witchhunts for subversives; in limitation of freedom and the inalienable rights of the citizen; in establishment of the "Voice of America," and other propaganda agencies; in an increase of "religious" prayers to God to punish the atheistic Communists; in a purge and burning of subversive books; in an enormously increased movement of ships and airplanes; in wholesale murder of the inhabitants of the ocean where bomb experiments are carried on; in best-selling records for a certain kind of books, and in a poor-selling record for other kinds; in a total destruction of many cities and villages, and in millions of killed and mutilated victims, in the Korean and other "police actions." And so on and so forth, up to a notable change in radio, movie, and television programs, and up to an increase of fear and insecurity in millions of human beings. These and thousands of other phenomena, scattered over the whole planet, are manifestations of the cold war activity of the United States, and this activity is only one of many activities of this sociopolitical system.

If we had not known that the United States is an organized sociopolitical system, and that all these activities are the war activities of the United States, we could hardly even guess that all these heterogeneous activities, events, and objects are mutually connected to one another as the cold-war activities of one and the same sociopolitical system. Without this knowledge, no statistician or experimentalist could discover the close association between, say, the rise of Senator McCarthy, the radioactivity of Japanese ships, the discharge of a French marshal from his high position, bloody massacres in Indo-China, the oratory of Vishinsky or Lodge in the United Nations, Tito's purge of his opponents, the suicide of Secretary of War Forrestal, the increased price of coffee, the Republican victory in the presidential election, an increased birth-rate, the appointment of Madam Luce to the Italian ambassadorship, the enormous increase of violent deaths among participants in the Korean war, the sensational success of Billy Graham's revivals, and thousands of other manifestations of the cold-war activities of the United States.

If a shrewd statistician could guess that there was a relationship between several of these variables and began a study of them, he certainly would not be able to discover by his statistical procedures the tangible association and interdependence between them, not to mention the relationships between these and thousands of other "variables." His methods are inadequate for a mathematical analysis of the relationships among such a gigantic multitude of heterogeneous variables as the cold-war activities of the United States. Even in his study of the relationships of a few variables, he is likely to get wrong results, if he takes these variables as congeries isolated from the rest of the war activities of the United States. We already know that the relationship between the same two variables is very different when the variables are congeries, and when they are parts of the same sociocultural system. As a matter of fact, many statistical studies have yielded false results for precisely the reason that they treated their variables as congeries while they were in fact the parts of a system. The previously discussed discrepancy and contradiction between coefficients of correlation, or of other indices, concerning the same variables have often been due to this mistake of treating the parts of a system as isolated congeries and, more rarely, of treating congeries as parts of a system.

The preceding lines sketch out an additional way in which errors infiltrate into a statistical investigation because of the many-foldedness of the manifestations of sociocultural systems. If statistical and even inductive researchers do not keep in mind the profound difference between the world of psychosocial congeries and that of systems, and if they handle the systems as congeries and congeries as systems, they are bound to arrive at fallacious conclusions and misleading formulae.

### 4. Conclusion

In the last two chapters the main virtues and vices of mathematical and statistical methods in the study of psychosocial phenomena have been concisely outlined. The outline shows that, when competently used in the investigation of those phenomena that lend themselves to quantitative analysis, these methods have rendered valuable services to our knowledge of the psychosocial universe. Potentially, the value of these methods is much greater than their actual value so far demonstrated by the existing studies. This actual value, especially in studies of uniformities, factors, and causes, has been, so far, fairly modest. The modesty of the results has been notably diminished by a "quantophrenic" misuse and abuse of mathematical and statistical methods. In the totality of various quantitative researches this "quantophrenic" part, unfortunately, is large. Since the catch-phrase: "precise, quantitative research" has become a sort of mania with the rank and file of researchers; and since a mechanical performance of quantophrenic statistical operations does not require discerning, logical thought, long training, and a solid scientific background, or a spark of genius, the rapid recent spread of thoughtless statistical research is quite comprehensible.

In the raging epidemics of quantophrenia everyone can be a "researcher" and a "scientific investigator," because everyone can take a few sheets of paper, fill them with all sorts of questions, mail the questionnaires to all possible respondents, receive the answered copies, classify them in this or that way, process them through a tabulating machine, arrange the results into several tables (with all the mechanically computed percentages, coefficients of correlation, Chi-Square indices, standard deviations and probable errors), and then write a paper or a book filled with the most impressive array of tables, formulae, indices, and other evidence of an "objective, thorough, precise, quantitative" research. These are typical "rites" in "contemporary quantitative research" in sociology, psychology, and other psychosocial sciences. They can be "officiated" over mechanically by a rank and file slightly drilled in the performance of these "rites." Hence, the rising tide of quantophrenic studies in these disciplines. If, however, we can fool ourselves with these simulacra of "precise, scientific research," we still cannot fool the objective record of history. The Nemesis of such simulacra is sterility and error—and this Nemesis is already walking abroad among the contemporary psychosocial sciences. As we shall see further on, in the chapter entitled "In the Blind Alley," in spite of our narcissistic self-admiration, of the enormous energy and funds spent in the pseudomathematical and statistical research, its achievements have been singularly modest, its sterility unexpectedly notable, and its fallacies surprisingly numerous. If we want to move along the royal road of creative psychosocial science, we must get away from the region of sham-mathematical and pseudostatistical "dirt-roads" where we largely move in circles.

# *Chapter Nine*

# The Grand Cult of "Social Physics" and "Mental Mechanics"

> *A science of history must not follow slavishly the pattern of physical science; such a science must strike out on its own along paths hitherto uncharted by existing disciplines.*[1] H. MARGENAU.

## 1. SIMULACRA OF "NATURAL SCIENCE SOCIOLOGY AND PSYCHOLOGY"

As mentioned before, most of the defects of modern psychosocial science are due to a clumsy imitation of the physical sciences. "Testomania," "quantophrenia," "operational method," "disorders of speech," "amnesia" and other diseases which will be further discussed in this chapter are manifestations of this slavish obsession. It is clumsy for several reasons. The sociological and psychological devotees of "natural science sociology and psychology" are usually deficient in their knowledge of physical science. Their "social physics" and "mental mechanics" are built not so much along the theories of modern physics as along either their own "home-made" pseudophysics or of a largely obsolescent mechanics. On the other hand, the natural scientists, anxious to help the psychosocial sciences to become the *alter-ego* of physical science, often know little of sociology or psychology. In both cases the results are deplorable. There are a few exceptions to this rule; now and then there appear thinkers competent in both the physical and the psychosocial fields. But such exceptions are very rare, and in no way annul the regretful rule.

Another reason for the failure lies in the very nature of the slavish imitation of physical science by psychosocial scholars. They seem to forget the cardinal fact that none of the established natural sciences has reached its maturity by merely imitating another science, especially when it is quite different. Each of them has built itself—in its basic concepts, uniformities, methods, and techniques—by following its own path corresponding to the nature of the phenomena studied. The basic concepts, laws, methods, and techniques of physics are different from those of chemistry or biology; and vice versa. Still more is this true in regard to psychosocial phenomena. Their main component—"the immaterial meanings, values, and inner human experience"—makes these phenomena radically different from the physical ones. There is no reason to expect that by plunging the conceptual network of physics into the basically different psychosocial ocean one can catch big psychosocial fish, and can learn the uniformities of their behavior. The big psychosocial catch usually slips through the meshes of the physical net, and the fishing "social physicists" get only a physical mud mixed up with dead shells of psychosocial phenomena.

These two reasons sufficiently account for the fruitlessness of the centuries-old attempts to build a "natural science sociology and psychology." The modern attempts are no exception to the rule.

In the preceding chapters we have seen the conspicuous clumsiness of these endeavors in several fields of investigation: in the "discovery" of a table of multiplication or of America long after they were discovered; in a childish and useless borrowing of the terms and notions of physics; in testomania; quantophrenia; operational method; and so on. In this chapter we shall examine additional examples of the slavish imitation discussed. As before, our criticism will deal with the imitations at the level of basic problems, not with unimportant details.

## 2. Experimental Method

In the chapter on Operationalism the outstanding importance of experimental method in the progress of the natural sciences has been duly stressed. Though it has not been the only way to a discovery of the most important uniformities and generalizations of the natural sciences, nevertheless, its role has been exceptionally significant and fruitful. This success warranted its application to the study of psychosocial phenomena. If experimental method has been so fruitful in the field of the physical sciences, it is bound to be fruitful also in the psychosocial disciplines. Hence the innumerable instances of its use in all sorts of psychosocial research, and hence its popularity in modern sociology and psychology.

If the so-called "experimental sociologists and psychologists" were using a real experimental method, in genuine experimental conditions, their valiant efforts could only be welcome, and no objection could be raised against their experimental procedures. Unfortunately, the real situation is very different from this. Owing to the great complexity and variability of psychosocial phenomena, to the difficulty of isolating and controlling the conditions studied, to legal and other prohibitions against experimentation with human beings, the possibility of applying a genuine experimental method to the study of social and psychological facts has been very limited, especially in an investigation of important psychosocial problems. Hence the regretful fact that *most of the numerous "experimental" studies in sociology and psychology are, rather, pseudo-experimental, and have a very remote relationship, if any, to real experimental method.*

Hardly any of these "experimental" studies satisfies the canon of inductive inference according to the methods of agreement or difference or concomitant variation, etc.[2] If in simplified terms "the fundamental rule of the experimental method is to vary only one condition at a time and to maintain all other conditions rigidly constant," then none of the experiments analyzed in F. S. Chapin's or E. Greenwood's books[3] are real experiments. Except for purely physiological experiments, most of the "experimental" studies of strictly psychological phenomena are also spurious, so far as their experimental character is concerned.[4]

The great bulk of sociological and psychological "experiments" consists either of a matched comparison of the experimental group with a so-called "control" group, or in observation of the same group before and after exposing it to the conditions or agencies experimented with. There may be different degrees of matching; in its search, the experiment may move from a cause to its effect or from an effect to its cause; the experiment may be done only once, or it may be repeated; but whatever the variations, the essentials of the majority of psychosocial experiments consist of the two procedures mentioned above: comparison of an experimental group with a control group not exposed to the experimental variable; and observation of the same group before and after its exposure to the experimental conditions studied. Both procedures fail to meet even in a rough way the conditions of a real experiment. In actual *comparisons of the "experimental" with its "control" group an experimenter never deals with two groups identical in all respects except the characteristic under study*. Two groups perfectly matched, in as many as ten of their important psychosocial characteristics—say, IQ, sex, age, race, nationality, religion, education, income, occupation, and residence—still remain profoundly different in hundreds of important traits: in their ethical and legal convictions, aesthetic values, scientific preferences, philosophical outlook, temperament, emotionality, prevailing moods, favorite sports, food and drink, in their preferences between blondes and brunettes or between short and tall stature, in their likes and dislikes of certain movies and television programs, and so on. In most of the experiments the actual matching of two groups rarely goes beyond matching in two to five traits. Rarely, if ever, are the groups matched in ten important characterists, as in our hypothetical case. This means that the compared groups are matched only in a few properties out of hundreds of traits in which they differ from each other. Even more: in spite of an apparently perfect matching of the above ten psychosocial traits, the matching in each of these traits is never perfect. A grossly apparent similarity in sex or age or occupation or religion or political party in no way excludes profound differences between the matched individuals or groups in each of these "similarities."

If five hundred persons are classified as "Roman Catholics" in religion, as "Republicans" in their political affiliation, as "University Professors" in their occupation, this does not mean that they are identical in their religion, political party and occupation. There is little similarity between the "Roman Catholicism" of a Chinese convert and of a Jesuit bishop, of the members of the "Catholic Worker" and Cardinal Spellman, of Senator McCarthy and J. Maritain, of the French Catholic "priest-workers" and the leaders of the Knights of Columbus. Likewise, the left-wing Republicans are very different from the right-wing Republicans, and "the Republican party" means something very dissimilar to hundreds of factions within the party. Still greater is this dissimilarity among the Professorial occupational group. This common term factually covers the enormous differences between the full, associate, and assistant professors, the illustrious and the little known, the well-paid and the poorly paid professors, the conservative and the radical professors, the physical and the social science professors, professors of unimportant and of important universities, and so on. The same is true of any other characteristic in which the experimental and the control groups are supposedly matched. Instead of an identity of the groups compared in a certain trait, the term "matched in their age or sex or income" really covers profound differences between the groups in each of these characteristics. Factually, almost any matching is a mere illusion of superficial similarity hiding a set of important differences in the matched variable.

This is especially true of the kind of matching ordinarily done in psychosocial experimental studies: it is almost always performed haphazardly and superficially, mostly through merely registering the answers of individuals asked about their religion or age or occupation or income or any other trait. Rarely, if ever, do the investigators check, or try to find out what an individual really means by his religion or political credo or standard of living; what is the real content of his terms, and how each of these variables manifests itself in his ideology, emotions, desires, and overt actions.

To sum up:

*a*) In experiments of this sort we have group A with hundreds of characteristics: a, b, c, d, n, m, k, l, · · · S · · · x, y; and group B also with hundreds of characteristics: a′, b′, c′, h, g, i, p, e, q, · · · z.

*b*) The experimenters assume that if they match groups A and B in a, b, c, then the groups become identical in all their traits except for the experimental variable S which becomes responsible for all the differences between groups A and B.

*c*) These assumptions are unwarranted because even the matching in a, b, c, is rarely achieved; instead of identity in these matched traits we have, as a rule, only an apparent similarity of *a* with *a′*, *b* with *b′*, and *c* with *c′*.

In addition to the experimental variable S, A and B remain different in hundreds of other characteristics: h, g, i, p, e, q, · · · z for B and d, n, m, k, l, · · · S · · · x, y, for A. In this ocean of differences the role of S factor cannot be isolated and studied experimentally. Neither the method of agreement, nor of difference, nor of concomitant variation, nor of residue, is applicable to such heterogeneous groups. They remain unmatched and different groups in which nothing is matched, nothing is constant, and nothing is rigidly controlled. Such comparison of two groups has no relationship to a real experimental comparison. Nor does it allow one to infer any valid conclusion in regard to the investigated variable S. No matter how much we vary it, the variations do not permit us to ascribe to S any specific effect or difference between groups A and B, or to view such a difference as an "effect" of "cause S."

The attempt to discover the real relationship between an independent and dependent variables is a very difficult and risky operation, even in an incomparably simpler constellation of variables. Suppose we notice that water boils now at 99, now at 100, now at 101 degrees centigrade. Suppose, further, that we do not know the real factor of the fluctuation of the boiling point and set forth on the task of finding out this factor experimentally. At first glance the task seems to be very simple. All that we need to do is to apply the inductive canon of agreement, or difference, or concomitant variation. But as soon as we start our experimentation we are faced with enormous difficulties. Which of hundreds of possible factors shall we test experimentally? The size of the water container? or its form? or the thickness of its walls? or the glass-iron-brass material it is made of? Perhaps the intensity and the kind of heat that heats the water have something to do with it? Or perhaps sunny or cloudy weather is responsible for the fluctuation? Since we do not know the real factor, we do not have any guide for picking up the real culprit out of hundreds of equally possible factors. Thus we are forced to try, one by one, many possible conditions without any certainty of putting our finger on the real "cause." In some experimental problems these blind trials end in a blind alley. In others they have a "happy ending," but after many failures made before the discovery of the real factor. This sketch of the preliminary stage of experimentation already shows the enormous difficulties confronting the experimenter in this simple task.

Now, suppose that after many unsuccessful trials we happened to boil water on the top of a mountain and then at the bottom of a valley. We noticed that on the mountain top it boiled at 99° while at a low elevation it boiled at 101°. This observation may easily suggest the hypothesis that the factor of altitude is the answer to our inquiry. To test the hypothesis we eagerly repeat the experiment and, assuming that the barometric pressure happened to be the same, we find out that our second and third experiments confirm the first one.

Suppose, now, that another scientist repeats the experiment and, due to the same barometric pressure, observes the same results as the first experimenter. Under such circumstances it is quite natural for both experimenters to conclude that their repeated experiments conclusively prove altitude to be the factor responsible for boiling point fluctuation—at high altitudes water boils at 98 and 99, and at low altitudes at 100 and 101 centigrade.

Until another experimenter comes along and repeats the experiments—by chance under different barometric pressures—and gets different results, the hypothesis that the altitude factor is the cause of variation of the boiling point would be accepted as an experimentally proven discovery. Even when it is disproved, another false hypothesis is likely to replace it, before the real culprit—barometric pressure—is discovered. Before its discovery many a failure, false clue, and wrong conclusion are bound to happen—even in a comparatively simple experimental study like this one where most of the conditions can be rigidly controlled, and induction-canon can be applied much more easily than in complex problems.[5]

In the incomparably more difficult experimentation with psychosocial problems, the probability of futile experimentations, false clues, and false conclusions is immeasurably greater. Especially in comparisons of "experimental" and "control" groups, where an experimenter is confronted with hundreds of possible factors, where groups differ from each other in hundreds of traits, where few, if any, of the variables are constant or controllable, where neither the rule of agreement, nor of difference, nor of concomitant variation, nor of residue, can really be applied. Only through an infinitely long series of trials and errors or through sheer luck or fortunate intuition, can an experimenter in these problems discover the real truth. In the overwhelming majority of experimental investigations he is likely to become lost among the multitude of possible factors, or to end up in a blind alley, or to mistakenly discover that an innocent bystander is the real culprit.

This analysis shows why the method of a superficial matching of "experimental" and "control" groups or persons or situations is not experimental at all, and has little chance to discover the real relationships among the variables studied.

The same is true of an "experimental" study of the same group or of the same individual before and after exposure to the experimental variable. As an example of such an "experimental" inquiry we can take the work of C. I. Hovland, A. A. Lumsdaine, and F. D. Sheffield: *Experiments on Mass Communication.*[6] The purpose of their investigation was "the measurement of changes in knowledge, opinion, or behavior produced by a film or other communication device." The experiment consisted of showing the orientation film series *(Why We Fight),* training films, and general interest films to several groups in the Army, and in getting their answers to the questionnaire partly before, but mainly after the showing of the film, and in comparing the answers of these "experimental groups" with those of Army groups, called "the controlled groups," which did not see the films.

The questionnaire, pompously called "the measuring instruments," was of the multiple-choice-fact-quiz and "agree-disagree" type. The difference in the answers of "the experimental" and "the control groups" or in the answers of the experimental groups before and after showing the films was considered as the index of the effects of the films.[7] In particular detail the effects of the film *The Battle of Britain* were studied.

Thus, instead of groups identical to each other in all their traits, except the showing or not showing of the films, we have several randomly picked groups different from one another in hundreds of characteristics. In the totality of these differences, the difference in the exposure or the nonexposure to the films is but a drop in an ocean of differences. An investigator does not have any ground to ascribe to this drop all the differences in the answers to the questionnaire by "the experimental" and "the control groups."

As to the differences in the answers of the same group before and after the exposure to the films, an experimenter again has no objective basis for ascribing the differences to the factor of the film. We know well that our speech reactions are incessantly changing. "Delicious" is our vocal opinion about a piece of stale bread when we are hungry; "inedible" is the opinion about the same bread after a good dinner. If the same group is questioned, say, three times about the same matters of a more or less complex character; and if each questioning is separated from the others by one week or one month; and if during these weeks and months several events vitally important for the group occur; then without any exposure to the films or other experimental condition there will be a number of differences in the answers of the group to the same questions repeated three times.

And the longer the time interval between each questionnaire operation, the more eventful the period, the greater the differences in the answers to the same questionnaire. Since, under life conditions which are ever-changing, especially for combatants, opinions rapidly change, and since the second and the third questioning by itself is one of the factors changing our answers to the same questionnaire (because the second reaction of even an amoeba or a paramecium to the same stimulus under the same conditions differs from the first reaction), we do not have any basis for ascribing the before-and-after differences to the films or to any other experimental factors, except for some obvious differences following from the mere fact of seeing the films and being, therefore, able to describe its character, its actors, its setting, and so on—which remain unknown to the persons who did not see it. Differences of this sort are, however, so obvious that no experimental or other study is needed to "discover" them. If I did not see the film *Roman Holiday,* I naturally do not know its plot and moral, the actors, the scenery, and the words, and do not get some information which the film gives. If you saw it, you naturally learned these traits and can describe them.

These conclusions are well confirmed by the "experimental study" discussed. It could not and did not yield any new significant knowledge, generalization, or fruitful observation except platitudes of the above kind. In the statements of the authors, *The Battle of Britain* "had marked effects" on men's factual information (as any film does), but it had no, or little, effect on "men's motivation to serve as soldiers, which was considered the ultimate objective of the orientation program." These platitudes are augmented by other painful elaborations of the obvious, like: "men who liked the film were most affected by it" (the statement is not only obvious, but practically tautological), or "those with greater intellectual ability [measured by their college, high school, grade school education—which measurement is not necessarily identical with 'intellectual ability'] learned more from a given exposure than those with less ability" (what is meant by "learned more" is not elucidated); or "active participation of the audience improved their learning"; or the factual information learned from the film tended to evaporate with lapse of time, and so on.[8]

With slight modification, the above conclusions are applicable to practically all "experimental studies" of psychosocial problems by comparison of "the experimental group" with "the control group," or by comparison of the same group before and after its exposure to the experimental factor. Such studies are hardly experimental at all. Among these sham-experimental investigations, especially poor are those which compare groups on the basis of "vocal reactions" to questionnaires, interviews, and quizzes. Further recent examples of sham-experimental exercises are given by practically all the "experimental operations" of the members of "Group Dynamics": John Thibaut, John R. P. French, Jr., S. E. Asch, R. L. Gorden, E. W. Bovard, Jr., L. Festinger, S. Schachter, K. Back, L. M. Killian, J. Levine, M. Deutsch, R. F. Bales, F. L. Strodtbeck, T. M. Mills, H. H. Kelley, K. Lewin, R. Lippitt, and others.[9] None of their pretentiously called "experimental" research is experimental at all. At best they represent an arbitrary mixture of observations, statistical manipulations, obtuse formulations of platitudes, and rediscoveries of "tables of multiplication" which were discovered centuries ago, the mixture being peppered by ambitious and amnesiac claims to an epochal significance for their experimental achievements "establishing for the first time in human history" the science of group-dynamics and group-structure. All these Gargantuan claims can be humorously dismissed. What remains after removing the façade is the all too familiar nonexperimental operation of interviews and questionnaires, sent out, filled by respondents, then summarized in an unnecessarily complex statistical form, and presented with all the pomp and circumstance of modern advertising as an epoch-making experimental research.

The same can be said of the bulk of similar "experimental" studies in psychology and education, cultural anthropology, and other psychosocial disciplines. The term "experimental" is a misnomer for these studies.

We should not be surprised at this conclusion because in the much simpler experimental studies of medical science the proportion of pseudo-experimental investigations also happens to be very high. Berkson's, Magath's, and Hurn's studies of counting red cells with the hemocytometer have shown a discrepancy, between first and second counting, of from 66 to 85 per cent deviation from the usual standards. Birkelo's investigation of the interpretation of chest X-rays by five X-ray specialists discloses the discrepancy between 59 and 100 films found to be positive for tuberculosis (out of 1256 films). Belk and Sunderman reported a high per cent of discrepancy in biochemical analyses of the same solutions by 59 clinical laboratories. O. B. Ross's analysis of 100 articles in five leading American medical journals shows that in 45 per cent of the studies actually no real controls were used, in 18 per cent the controls were entirely inadequate, in 10 per cent no real control was possible, and only in 27 per cent were the experiments really controlled.[10]

The pseudo-experimental nature of psychosocial studies is one reason why the results of two or more "experimental" investigations of the same problem are dissimilar and sometimes contradictory. For instance, my own and J. B. Maller's semi-experimental investigations of the intensity of solidarity or mutual aid in its relationship to social distance have shown that the intensity of solidarity, friendship, or mutual aid tends to decrease with an increase of social distance between the persons or groups involved.[11] On the other hand, B. A. Wright's study yielded quite different results: in her experiment the school children tended to help the strangers in preference to helping their friends. In other words, in this experiment the intensity of solidarity tended to increase with an increase of social distance between the parties concerned.[12]

A similar discrepancy of results can be found practically in all "experimental" studies of psychosocial phenomena, beginning with the simple ones like perception, reproductive imagination, emotionality, socialization, social facilitation, and aptitudes, and passing to the more complex problems of the factors and forms of delinquency and criminality, religiosity or atheism, sex-freedom or sex-restraint, marriage and divorce, birth-rate and suicide-rate, "autocratic and democratic" regimes, factors of creativity and mental dullness, of wars and revolutions, of the effects of poverty and wealth, and so on. A notable discordancy in the results is to be expected each time when we have several "experimental" investigations of seemingly the same problem, and when the problem is more or less complex. It is only when we have just one or two such studies that the discrepancy may be absent.

Another reason for the discrepancy of the results is the lack of distinction between the variables as congeries and as parts of a sociocultural system. In the preceding chapters this gross blunder has been already discussed. At this point it is enough to mention that many "experimental" studies are guilty of this error. Since in their setting they indiscriminately treat their variables as isolated congeries, and since their "experimental" and "control" groups are now the real organized groups, now semi-organized groups, now unorganized aggregates, now pure nominal plurels,[13] and since in most of the cases their groups are incidental, loosely united by superficial ties, an experimentation with these basically different variables, groups, and nominal plurels cannot yield identical or similar results. This striking carelessness in taking basically different groups and variables for identical ones is sufficient in itself to destroy the last vestiges of experimental conditions necessary for any experimental study. Together with the discussed nonexperimental nature of the matched comparisons of experimental and control groups, these two sins of psychosocial pseudo-experimental research are amply sufficient to divest these studies of all experimental characteristics. The two reasons also fully explain why the results of several experimental studies of the same problem are and must be discordant.

The third, ultimate, reason for the discrepancy of the results may be an objective lack of uniformity in a few of the experimental phenomena studied. If aggregations of a few atoms in subatomic physics display a lack of uniformity either in their "motion," or "appearance and disappearance," or in their transformations, we have no valid reason to deny dogmatically that a similar irregularity, diversity, discontinuity, and variability cannot occur with a few cases of psychosocial phenomena studied experimentally. In contrast to statistical method which deals with large masses or vast aggregations of phenomena, experimental method deals always with only a few "crucial" cases. An ideal inductive method applied in a pure experimental setting needs only two cases for inductive inference according to the rule of agreement or difference or concomitant variation. Like a small aggregation of atoms or particles in quantum mechanics, a small aggregation of experimental psychosocial phenomena may be "lawless." This hypothesis is at least as probable as the opposite belief in rigid uniformities pervading all psychosocial phenomena and their interrelationships.

This hypothesis has to be mentioned as a possible ultimate reason for discrepancy in the results. However, it is unnecessary for explaining the discordancy of experimental results in the psychosocial disciplines. The preceding demonstration of the pseudo-experimental nature of allegedly experimental studies is sufficient reason for the discordancy and doubtful validity of the "discoveries" of our experimenters. Since in their "experimental phenomena" many variables remain unknown; since among the known ones the majority are neither constant, nor identical, nor controlled; and since the experimenters are guilty of nondiscrimination between congeries and systems, or between organized, unorganized, and nominal groups; no identity of the results of repeated experimentations, and no valid generalization, can be expected.

Even in experiments roughly approaching the real experimental method, the results obtained cannot be automatically extrapolated far beyond the cases studied, and cannot be raised to the level of a universal uniformity covering all cases of the relationship between the variables under experiment. Unfortunately, this sort of extrapolation and generalization is a fairly common procedure among contemporary psychosocial experimenters. Having done mostly pseudo-experimental "research"—by the easiest and least reliable method of the questionnaire—on a few dozen individuals arbitrarily ranked on a scale of one or two variables, and, after numerous and largely arbitrary statistical manipulations, having obtained some results, the "experimenters" do not hesitate to claim for their results universal validity concerning either "social cohesion," or "social deviants," or "lecture vs. group decision in changing behavior," or what not.[14] No careful experimenter can allow himself this sort of extrapolation and generalization.

If the devotees of sham-experimental procedures have been proud of them and if, in spite of all the evidence to the contrary, they will continue their operations for some time, one of the reasons for that enthusiastic stubbornness is their adherence to the popular cult of "social physics" and "mental mechanics." Until the cult runs its course, and until its sterility and harmfulness become evident to the rank and file of investigators, it will noisily continue to advertise its doubtful virtues, to recruit its devotees, and to obtain large funds from various private and public sources. In due time, however, it will blow itself out.

The practical conclusion of this analysis is that we should by all means use a real experimental method in our studies wherever it can be applied, and the more it is used the better. But we should not fool ourselves and others with sham-experimental procedures. They do not and cannot contribute to the real knowledge of psychosocial phenomena. If anything, they corrode the real experimental method and psychosocial science itself.[15]

## 3. Recent "Social Physics" and Physicalistic Psychologies

The preceding chapters have shown a powerful invasion and diffusion of imitative "social physics" and "mechanical psychology" in the field of the psychosocial sciences. Beginning with a fruitless imitation of the terms of physical science—like "valence" instead of "attractiveness," "locomotion" instead of "change" or "transformation," "social atom" instead of "individual," "dimension" instead of "aspect," "cohesion" instead of "solidarity," "field" instead of "class or category of phenomena"—and ending with the transcription and importation of the methods of "operationalism," "mathematical and mechanical models," "experimental method," "mechanical tests," and the total formulae of macrophysics—in these and other forms the trend toward the construction of "a natural science sociology and psychology" has been spreading. Most of the theories examined above—Dodd's, Zipf's, and others; most of the psychological tests analyzed; most of the pseudo-experimental procedures mentioned—all are, to a great degree, manifestations of the same infectious fad of building up the psychosocial sciences as the *alter ego* of the physical sciences. The cult of "social physics," and "physicalistic psychology" as a science of mental processes different from the physiology of the nervous system, has been growing indeed among modern sociologists and psychologists, and there is no clear sign, as yet, of its recession.

In this section we shall examine a few additional "credos" of "the physicalistic denomination" in the psychosocial sciences, and some of the rituals of its scientific research.

We shall begin with a "manifesto of physicalistic sociology" by P. W. Bridgman. Although he is an eminent physicist, he unfortunately knows little of sociology or psychology. As a result, his manifesto is marked by the same characteristics which usually stamp the credo of a person who invades a science little known to him; that is, by the traits of incompetence and error, and, of course, by the discovery of the table of multiplication long after it had been discovered.

The book opens with a repetitious proclamation of the all too familiar credo of physicalistic sociology, that the same principles which physics has discovered to control any valid reconstruction of its concepts also control any valid reconstruction of social concepts, that the physical approach [to social problems] thoroughly justifies itself, and that the operational method of studying social phenomena is the only reliable method. And so on, and so forth.[16]

The bulk of the book deals with the concepts and methods of physics, with the insistent advice to sociologists to follow this approach.

The last part of the book is devoted to a discussion of social concepts and problems, such as duty, rights, morality, politics, and economics.

Our eminent physicist seems to be unaware of the fact that his manifesto of physicalistic sociology is but a repetition of hundreds of such manifestoes promulgated by the partisans of "social physics," and "social mechanics" of the preceding centuries.[17] Consequently, Bridgman's credo does not have even the fascination of novelty. As for his discussion of social problems—duty, rights, morality, the "intelligent individual," society, and so on—his naive theories, utilitarian and otherwise, are in about the same position among sociological and ethical theories as would be the theories of a "home-made" physicist who offered to modern physics an atomic theory similar to that of Democritus and Leucippus. Bridgman seems to be unaware of the enormous amount of study these social and ethical problems have received over the centuries. No wonder that his reconstruction of sociology along the patterns of physics does not go beyond purely wishful analogies and stops short before it even clears the ground for the proposed magnificent palace of "social physics."

The attempt of a group of recent social physicists led by John Q. Stewart, an astrophysicist of Princeton, goes somewhat further. Like other physicalistic sociologists this group also assumes that sociology must pass through stages of evolution analogical to those of physics; and that the former must follow the methods and concepts of the latter. In these and other assumptions the group uses the familiar analogical arguments, open to criticism at all points of their presentation. Fortunately the group does not stop at these misleading analogies, but tries to discover various uniformities of psychosocial phenomena, and to describe them in terms of physical science. Let us glance at Stewart's social physics, its methods and uniformities, and the other results of the group's labor.

> Our immediate quest is for uniformities in social behavior which can be expressed in mathematical forms more or less corresponding to the known patterns of physical science. Social physics so defined analyses demographic, economic, political, and sociological situations in terms of purely physical factors: time, distance, mass of material, and numbers of people, with re-

> course also to social factors which can be shown to operate in a similar way to two other physical agents, namely, temperature and electrical charge. . . . Social physics describes mass human relationships in physical terms, treating large aggregations of individuals as though they were composed of "social molecules"—without attempting to analyze the behavior of each molecule.[18]

Among other things, the declaration clearly states that Stewart regards all psychosocial phenomena as congeries, and does not make any distinction between congeries and systems, between an unorganized aggregation of individuals and the organized social group or system. Noting this basic error, let us follow Stewart's development of his "social physics." He views the social universe as six-dimensional or made up of six "social quantities" or "fundamental categories": "distance, time, mass, temperature, electric charge, and number of molecules," whatever social interpretation is to be given to each of these "dimensions" or "social quantities." We are told further that "this list [of six dimensions] makes social physics in its dimensional structure isomorphic with physical science," that is, "there is a complete and trustworthy analogy between two or more situations" which entitles one "to transfer equations from physics to politics."[19]

Having thus outlined the framework of social physics, Stewart proceeds to round up various social uniformities and to interpret them in terms of his six-dimensional categories. As the most important example of uniformities, Stewart takes Zipf's "rank-size rule" (discussed above). He extrapolates it much further than Zipf did, and in his enthusiasm he forgets to mention even those exceptions to the rule which Zipf mentions. Above, in the chapters on Quantophrenia we saw that the rule is at best purely local, temporal, and in no way as general as even Zipf claimed. However, when Stewart is confronted with the task of interpreting the rationale of this "rank-size rule," he completely fails to give any adequate explanation of it. "The rank-size rule is not at present derivable from general principles, and requires much more study before it will lead us to its underlying rationale—which then would fairly claim the dignity of being a law of social physics." Here we have "the widespread mathematical regularity for which no explanation is known."[20]

Thus, as soon as the occasion for an explanation of the rank-size rule arises, Stewart's categories prove themselves helpless and devoid of heuristic value. As any real explanation consists in indication of "the principle of sufficient reason" for the phenomena studied, the failure of Stewart's categories to do so is sufficient reason to demote them from the rank of universal categories in social physics to that of parishional notions, or even to exclude them from the scientific realm altogether. The failure leaves to Stewart only one way out of the difficulty, namely, issuing a big check for the unknown bank of the future where "some day, somehow, by some bank" the check of "social physics" will be redeemed "after much more study." This hope for the future banks where all doubtful checks of the present will be fully paid is also very familiar. However, it has nothing to do with a real scientific theory, which does not ask one to "believe in its future promises" but, so far as it claims recognition at present, pays its checks any time, anywhere, from its present capital of evidence.

Let us now glance closer at the social meaning of the six categories, and at how they work in the "scientific cognition" of social phenomena. First, we note that the time-dimension is taken by Stewart in the sense of the uniform, evenly flowing, infinitely divisible time of macrophysics ("watch time"). Here he seems to be unaware that this macrophysical time is only one of the sociocultural "times" and is in no way identical with the various "qualitative social times," which are neither uniform nor infinitely divisible. Being a mere variety of empirical "tempus" tied up with ever-changing sensory phenomena, Stewart's time entirely misses two fundamental forms of time which the mediaeval scholastics called *aeternitas* and *aevum*. *Aeternitas* deals with eternal or unchanging forms of being, while *aevum* is a category for semi-eternal forms of being like the truth of scientific propositions, which in their potentiality are viewed even by the scientists themselves as tending to be eternal and invariant (otherwise the true propositions would not differ from ever-changing fallacies).[21] The moral of these remarks is that, in limiting his "time" to "clock time," Stewart cannot "locate" in the time-process or measure in time-units a large part of the sensory-empirical—and even more of the nonsensory—sociocultural phenomena. His macrophysical time net is, for instance, particularly unable to catch and measure the "eternal or semi-eternal" values of the sociocultural universe. It also cannot catch many microphysical phenomena.

His other five "dimensions-categories-social quantities" are still worse for cognitive purposes than his "time-dimension." What, for instance, can be meant by "social mass," or "social electric charge," or "social temperature," or "social distance"? If they mean exactly what "mass," "electric charge," "temperature," and "distance" signify in the physical sciences, no "social physics," "social mass," "social distance," etc., are needed. The physical sciences take good care of "mass," "electric charge," "temperature," "distance," etc., whenever and wherever they are found, even in the human universe. If they mean something different from the categories of physics, then one has to show what each term really means, and one has to explain why it is named by a term from physics, and why the whole discipline is called "social physics."

In Stewart's use these terms do, in fact, mean something quite different from their meanings in physics. Thus, his "electric charge" does not really mean an electric charge at all, but "desire"; the term "mass" means "the bodies of the people and of their domesticated animals, their stocks of harvested food, their clothing and personal equipment, artificial housing, buildings, and ships, plants of all sorts, the weight of material that had to be moved in constructing trails, roadways, railways, mines, harbor improvements, airports, dams. It includes water being circulated by pumps, and the mass of the tilled soil." Quite a "mass" indeed! After finding such meanings for "electric charge" and "mass," we are not surprised at the meaning of "social temperature" which signifies the "level of activity" of people and the intensity of their interaction; or by the meaning of "distance" which is very distantly related to the "distance" of physics. On the other hand, several terms from the psychosocial sciences are given no less surprising physicalistic meanings; for instance, "the politico-economical concept of liberty" is viewed as a form of "social entropy."[22]

The above shows that Stewart's "social physics" has no relation to physics at all. His physicalistic terms are likewise total strangers to the similar terms of physics. The categories of "desire," "population and material culture" ("social mass"), "intensity of interaction and level of human activity," and so on, are just the ordinary notions of the traditional psychosocial sciences, and do not make these sciences "physicalistic" at all. For Stewart's sociology the term "social physics" is a complete misnomer. It only confuses the innocents, by distorting the terms and concepts of physics as well as of the psychological and sociological sciences. In brief, this sort of "social physics" is a big liability rather than an asset.

Taking now Stewart's categories in their real meanings: "desire," "level of activity," "the population and its material culture," time, distance, etc., we can easily see that this framework of categories is neither adequate logically nor fruitful empirically for the most economical analysis of the bulk of sociocultural phenomena. It is certainly more clumsy and defective than several conceptual frameworks of general sociology. In addition, it combines several incommensurable notions like "desire" and "social mass," or (in Stewart's letter) "time" and "reason," "distance and authority," and so on. In this respect the framework is an abortive bastard of pseudophysics and pseudosociology.

Unsatisfactory, also, is each of Stewart's dimensional categories. For instance, one can hardly use his category of "social mass" as an instrument for analyzing and measuring psychological and sociocultural phenomena. By itself this "social mass" is made up of so many different and difficult to measure (and partly immeasurable) quantities, that it is doomed to be largely an undefined, unmeasured, and indeterminate variable or category.

One of the components of the "social mass" is "the bodies of the people." Now, suppose we find that one group of 100 individuals has the total weight ("social mass") of 10,000 pounds (because it has many babies and children), while another group of 100 individuals has the total "social mass" of 16,000 pounds (partly because it has few babies and the grown-ups are fatter and heavier). What sociological significance can such a difference in the total weight have? And why is it important to know this "social mass," especially if we pay no attention to the age-sex-health composition of each group, its somatotypes, its morbidity and intelligence? If we pass from this component of the "social mass" to such components of it as "the mass of tilled soil" (not the acreage), we are confronted at once with the problem of how to measure this mass of tilled soil. By acreage, one or two or five feet deep? Stewart takes a one-foot depth. We can ask why one foot, but not two or ten? Even if we grant him his one-foot depth, what is the particular importance of such a mass measured and computed? Why is it more important than the fertility of the soil or the average amount of crop produced per acre?

Is not the whole of the "social mass" an incomplete and cumbersome and very inadequate expression of material wealth or capital, more easily and accurately measured by economics? Why does Stewart's "social mass" give importance to mere "weight" and "bulkiness" of plants, buildings, tilled soil, amount of food, clothing, equipment, "roadways," "railways," and so on, without any consideration of their quality at all? The ruins of a mediaeval castle would weigh more than a dozen modern houses; an old siege machine weighs more than a small atomic bomb; a haystack weighs more than a box of vitamins or highly concentrated food; the assortment of instruments of a jazz band weighs more than one Stradivarius violin; thousands of factory-made pictures weigh more than one sketch by Raphael or Dürer; four standard old-fashioned records weigh more than one long-playing modern record; a fat person weighs more than a "wiry individual." Does this mean that the group that possesses these heavy masses is more advanced, more creative, more civilized than the group which has the "lighter" "masses" of an atomic bomb, vitamins, Raphael's picture, one Stradivarius, as Stewart seems to think? Shall we call a person who has a large library of detective stories, comics, grade-school texts, and popular magazines more cultured than a person who has only a few books like Plato's *Dialogues,* Kant's *Critique of Pure Reason,* Homer's *Iliad,* Shakespeare's Tragedies, and Dante's *Divine Comedy?*

These questions make clear that Stewart's "social mass" cannot serve either as an index of material wealth and prosperity, or as a measure of standard of living, of cultural and social creativity, or of cultural and civilizational levels, or of hardly any other important sociocultural state of a person or group. As an index of these and other cultural and social states it is incomparably more primitive, misleading, and unscientific than the current indexes of standard of living, or wealth, or creativity, or cultural advancement. If, then, the "social mass" is perfectly useless for all these purposes, for what is it valuable? Why does one have to undertake an astronomical load of work to obtain even the roughest measure of Stewart's "social mass"? Is it because the term sounds so similar to the "mass" of physics? Of course, one is entitled to undertake whatever inquiry he pleases—for instance, to compute the total number of leaves on all the trees of the American continent, and to find out how they correlate with the total number of sand grains on all the shores of the Americas. There is no objection to that sort of "scientific research." On the other hand, hardly any serious scientist would be willing to waste his life-time in such "researches," and such a research can hardly find a high estimate on the part of scientists and the intelligent public at large. Stewart's "social mass" looks like this sort of inquiry. Being an astronomer he shows a meager knowledge of the psychosocial sciences. He assumes they have hardly ever studied the problems of his social physics. His paper is interspersed by his semisatirical remarks that "spaces which separate people are airily ignored" (by the social scientists); that "demographers had never introduced a term to measure the influence of people at distance"; that "the concept of demographic field" was unknown to social scientists; that they did not study intensively the phenomena of interaction; and so on. I can positively assure the author that not only all psychological and sociocultural phenomena discussed by him have been studied by the psychosocial sciences, but that the latter have investigated these problems with incomparably greater care, adequacy, objectivity, and quantitative precision than Stewart's amateurish smattering does. Economics has handled and measured "natural resources," "wealth," and "capital" much more accurately than the "social mass" of Stewart does. Sociology has studied demographic phenomena, the phenomena of interaction, "the influence of people at distance," social migrations and mobility, the levels and forms of cultural and social activity, and so on, again so much better that any comparison with Stewart's superficial utterances in these matters becomes superfluous.[23]

If, instead of assuming the superiority of his social physics, Stewart had seriously studied economics, demography, sociology, psychology, philosophy, and previous attempts to create "social physics," he would hardly have come out with his amateurish "social mass," "social temperature," "desire," and other dimensional categories. If a future social physics is going to be built on this sort of conceptual framework, there is hardly any future for it.

What is said of Stewart's "social physics" can be said, with still greater reason, of other modern "social physics," "social mechanics," "topological psychologies," "physicalistic politics," "field-theory economics," and so on, and so forth. In spite of my criticism of Stewart's endeavor, his social physics is better than most of the other physicalistic speculations of our time. Wherever and whenever the psychosocial problems lend themselves to real measurements, to real homological treatment, it is advisable to use such measurements and homologies; but they in no way eliminate direct study and measurements of these phenomena by means of a conceptual framework and the methods built by these sciences in accordance with the nature of the phenomena studied. A mere transportation of the terms, concepts and methods of physical sciences into the social and psychological disciplines, and a mere analogical reasoning, has not yielded, and cannot yield, any fruitful results in cognition of the psychosocial universe of man and of the total man himself.

Now we can turn to the fashionable cult of *"robot psychology" or physicalistic studies of psychological phenomena.* The preceding chapters have already dealt with many of the ritualistic procedures of this cult: with mechanical tests which supposedly automatically reveal and measure intelligence, emotions, temperament, opinions, attitudes, aptitudes, types of personality, unconscious drives, and complexes, and what not; with statistical operations processing their "hearsay stuff" through the "purgatory" of a miraculous "chi-square" or "coefficient of correlation," correcting it by the fanciful ranking and scoring of the physicalistic researchers, and through these rites never failing to eliminate "probable errors," and always delivering to us "objective, quantitatively-precise knowledge" of all the mysteries of the human soul and mind; with "mathematical models of robots," and pseudo-experimental studies of mechanical man and his "mindless mind," "emotionless emotions," "will-less will," with all "the invariant variations" of man's behavior and psychological processes. Most of these psychological investigations are but diverse manifestations of the same physicalistic epidemic among modern psychologists. The same is to be said of the now about dead "behavioristic psychology" of John Watson's type; about the unhesitating extension upon man of conditioned reflexes or the mechanisms of learning observed in rats, mice, dogs, rabbits, or other animals. The same goes for the still more mechanistic interpretation of man's psychology and behavior by the principles of cybernetics, with its "feed back" and extension of control and communication in the machine upon man, or dianetics with its mechanical "engrams" automatically registered and forever stored in the vaults of the "bank of the reactive mind" (quite different from the "analytical mind"); or somatological theories of man's psychology as a mere epiphenomenon of endomorphic, ectomorphic, or other somatic types invented by somatologists. Finally, the direct and purposeful study of man's psychology and behavior by the method of other "mechanical models" and "robots" is a still more conspicuous example of the "robot psychology" of our time.

In this section we shall briefly examine a few additional examples of this physicalistic psychology.

As before, I shall take better rather than poorer samples of the respective studies for my criticism. J. S. Bruner and his collaborators have made several studies of perception as influenced by the needs and values of an individual. Though these studies repeat and confirm the results of many previous studies,[24] nevertheless, Bruner's careful investigations are a valuable contribution to our knowledge in this field. A tendency toward using mechanical models was present even in these studies, but it did not occupy much space, and, therefore, did not harm the essentials of Bruner's inquiries. However, in one of his later studies[25] this tendency became quite prominent and, as a result, sidetracked the main issue and undermined the scientific value of the study. The problems of this study are: "are members of a group able to perceive their feelings for each other more accurately than may be predicted by chance," and what is the relationship between accuracy, mutuality, and "congruency" in this perception?

For clarifying these problems the researchers used three voluntary discussion groups, members of each group meeting for 12 two-hour sessions. After each meeting members were asked to indicate, without restriction on number, those in the group they liked best, and those they liked least, and then to guess which members they thought liked them best and least. With this material at hand, the investigators proceeded to find out, first, if the accuracy of a member's perception of another's feeling for him exceeded chance level.

> In order to test this question it is necessary to determine what might be expected to occur by chance in a group. One can do this by constructing groups of robots according to the following specifications. For each member of a human group a robot is constructed. Each robot is matched with his human counterpart in terms of number of choices and number of guesses. The robot is, of course, "forbidden" to respond to himself or to the same members twice, and is not permitted either to choose or reject the same person, or to specify another as both choosing or rejecting him. Within these boundary conditions, the choices and guesses of the robots were allocated in the group by means of a table of random number.

Such is the robot model. The first criticism of this procedure is that the whole "group of robots" is introduced quite uselessly. It does not play any functional role in the investigation of the question discussed. The whole matter as to whether the accuracy of perception by one member of another member's feeling for him is higher or lower than perception on a chance level is decided by "the combined chi-square measure for the deviation of three human groups from the chance level (measure of the deviation being 14.1 which, with 3 df, yields a *p* value of less than .01)." The only reason for introducing the robot models seems to be their current fashionableness. Otherwise, this model is quite unnecessary for determining the deviation in accuracy of the actual perceptions from those calculated at chance level.

This criticism is, however, a minor one. Much more serious are those defects of the study which seem to be motivated by a desire to make it "mechanical," in line with the fashionable "robot models."

The point is that the very problem—does accuracy of perception of another member's feeling exceed chance level?—is wrongly set forth and is ambiguous in its meaning. What indeed may be the meaning of "chance level" in cases of this kind? Does it mean the perception of another's feeling in a situation where individuals do not know one another? If so, then there is, as yet, no group of members or robots at all; instead, we have just a collection of total strangers. Since they do not know one another, they can hardly have any definite likes and dislikes in regard to one another. Does "chance perception" mean perception at the first instant of their meeting? If so, then it is not a chance perception, but that of strangers at the first instant of their meeting. If chance perception means an equal distribution of likes and dislikes among all the members of the human or the robot group, it is again not a chance configuration, but quite a specific one, namely, an "equal distribution"—which is even less a chance matter than an "unequal distribution" and is much less frequently found than an unequal distribution of choices and guesses. Both forms—equal and unequal—can in no way be identified with chance distribution of likes and dislikes. The same is still more true of the specific distribution of choices and guesses assigned to the robots by the investigators. Why is this notably crystallized and very specific distribution viewed as chance level distribution? No logical or mathematical reason is given by the authors for this assumption, and hardly any such reason can be given for its identification with chance choices and guesses.

Since it is not a chance distribution of likes and dislikes, it cannot be used as chance-matter and so serve for calculating—with a chi-square formula—the deviations of the actual choices and guesses of the members of the groups from the chance-level. Whatever deviation is actually found is not deviation from a chance-level but from the specific, crystallized form assigned to the robots by the investigators. For this reason, one of the main objectives of the study becomes void.

These considerations make comprehensible the next blunder of the study—the familiar blunder of an atomistic approach to the study of social groups and their relationships. As in almost all studies of "the small groups" (to be discussed further), the authors seemingly fail to realize that in a study of interaction phenomena (including the mutual feelings of the interacting parties), one cannot take just any collection of individuals as the general type of a group and, by studying their interaction, derive some general uniformities applicable to all or to many groups of the same size. If we take the following groups consisting of four individuals: a harmonious family (father, mother, and two children); a four-member discussion group made up of randomly picked previous strangers who have met in twelve one-hour sessions; a four-member group consisting of Senator McCarthy, Mr. Cohn, and two "subversives"; a four-member group of previous strangers who have just met in the smoking room of a railway car—though each of these "groups" consists of four individuals, none of them can be taken for a "chance group." Without any questionnaire one can state that the configuration of choices and guesses concerning mutual likes and dislikes will be quite different in each of these groups.

In the last group, the total strangers in the smoking room, there will be a perfectly amorphous configuration, because the individuals have not had time, as yet, to crystallize their mutual perceptions (of likes and dislikes) in regard to one another. In the Senator's group there will be a fairly accurate mutual perception of the feelings of each of two parties, and a clear-cut rejection of the Senator and Cohn by the subversives, and vice versa. In the harmonious family there will be an accurate perception of the mutual feelings of each member, and no rejection or dislike of one member by the others; instead, there will be only mutual likes, but of different quality between the parents and the children, and between each member in regard to the others. In various discussion groups of the same size and with the same number of sessions there will be a considerable difference in the distribution of the choices and guesses, depending upon the kinds of members, the nature of the problems discussed, the position of the discussing parties, the private or public character of discussion, and several other conditions. No uniformity of choices and guesses can be expected even in discussion groups of the same size and the same number of meetings.

This means that any research into the accuracy with which the members of an incidentally picked discussion group perceive their interrelationships, or into the configuration of the members' mutual likes and dislikes *aimed at a discovery of some uniformities in these relationships,* is a hopeless, and wrongly set, enterprise. Since the configuration decisively depends upon the social nature of the group (the family, the group of various kinds of adversaries, the group of superficial friends, the group of mutually indifferent persons, and religious, aesthetic, discussion, and other groups), upon the importance and the nature of the values involved, upon the length of the interaction, and on several other conditions, there is no reason to expect any uniformity in the accuracy either of the perception of mutual likes or dislikes, or of the choices and guesses. And, especially, there is no reason whatsoever to generalize the configuration of relationships found in one of the discussion groups to cover all groups of the same size and number of sessions, or even to cover any other discussion group. Only by fallaciously assuming that all individuals are identical atoms and that there is no basic difference in the nature of the groups, including their networks of likes and dislikes, and that the duration and intensity of interaction does not change the relationship of the members to one another—only with such entirely erroneous assumptions can one expect some uniformity of choices and guesses. Otherwise, with the real, profound differences in the psychosocial structure and dynamic functions of various groups, the existence of such a uniformity would be equivalent to the fallacious postulate that entirely different causes produce identical results and different results are produced by identical causes.

This analysis is sufficient to show why the atomistic approach of the authors is wrong in its very inception, and why the results of their study cannot be extended to apply to other groups. Even more: their conclusions concerning the relationship between the variables of accuracy, mutuality, and congruency cannot be applied even to the three discussion groups studied if the relationships are studied not on the basis of the sixth or seventh session, but on that of either the third or tenth or twelfth. At best, the conclusions reached by the authors are correct only in regard to the configuration in these groups at the moment of the sixth or seventh session. Such is the Nemesis of the mechanical, atomistic, "robot-model" approach to these psychosocial phenomena. No "chi-square" or other statistical formula can save such studies from this Nemesis.

These criticisms are corroborated by the conspicuous discordance in the results of various atomistic studies of the same problems in somewhat similar groups, mainly discussion groups. For instance, the results of studies by Bruner, Borgatta, Ausubel, and Dymond, to mention only a few recent investigations, are far from being identical; they are even, in part, contradictory.[26]

If to these studies of somewhat randomly picked individuals, artificially and superficially united into a semi-nominal group, we add the studies of well-structured or organized groups of various kinds, from the same standpoint of accuracy, mutuality, confidence, congruence, self-rating, rating by the others, popularity, and so on, the divergency of results becomes enormous and rules out any possibility of extending such results over any large number of groups, or of taking them as indicating a general uniformity. They become perfectly idiographic, valid only for the group studied at the moment of its investigation, a mere "case-study," devoid of any general significance and more dull and vague than a description of the case by a competent novelist or an imaginative participant-observer.

There are three additional errors which atomistic studies of social groups commit at the moment of their inception rather than at the stage of their accomplished organization or structuring:

*a*) An implied assumption that all social groups are of the same type as the semi-organized and semi-nominal group of individuals incidentally picked and artificially brought together either by order of the army authorities (Borgatta's "group"), or by some pretext—such as "discussion"—devised by the investigator to fool the members of the "group" as to why they are brought together and are interviewed and tested, or asked to fill questionnaires. In many cases the investigators fail in this "deceit" and vitiate the results of their study at its very start.

*b*) Our atomistic researchers set up a method which contradicts the methodological principle of Aristotle: if one wants to study the properties of the oak, one should investigate not only the acorn (the oak at its inception), but especially the fully grown oak, because a study of the acorn cannot give most of the important anatomical and physiological properties of the oak. This important advice is largely neglected by our atomistic-statistical researchers.

*c*) Being preoccupied with their "robot-models" and atomistic-statistical operations, our investigators pay little attention to the nature of their variables. They all operate with the variables "leadership," "friendship," "confidence," "popularity," "mutuality," "expansiveness," and so on, without any serious analysis of what they mean by these terms. If in the social sciences the meanings of these terms were well established, and if each of them did not have several essentially different forms, the undefined use of these term-variables by our atomistic investigators would have been justified. As a matter of fact, none of these terms has a generally accepted meaning, and several important studies of friendship, or leadership, or sympathy, or acceptance-rejection, show that each of the terms has different forms, which in no way should be used interchangeably.[27]

Paying no attention to these basic problems, hardly ever even mentioning the existence of these problems, and rarely referring to the most important studies of these phenomena, our atomistic investigators study relationships between largely undefined and unknown variables. As a result, their coefficients and numerical indices are only apparently precise.

These considerations show the drawbacks of the mechanistic-atomistic approach to the study of groups. If a small part of the time, energy, and funds expended in these fashionable pursuits were given to a more thoughtful analysis of group phenomena, to becoming acquainted with the classical studies of these problems by earlier investigators, the results would have been much more fruitful and our knowledge of the social universe would have been enriched much more than it has been. There are now so many of these fashionable studies that they impose a heavy burden on our memory and thought. They increasingly become a liability rather than an asset in the psychosocial sciences. For real progress in these disciplines a clearing out of such "weeds" is one of the important jobs at the present moment.

## 4. Cybernetic Models

The most recent variety of mechanical models to appear in the psychosocial disciplines is possibly the cybernetic model. The term cybernetics was coined by an eminent mathematician, N. Wiener, and it means a science of "control and communication in the animal and the machine," including man and social organizations.[28] As to the importance of cybernetics for the engineering sciences, F. D. Barrett and H. A. Shepard are essentially correct by stating that "cybernetics owes many of its elements to the practical science of communication engineering," and that "for communication engineers there is nothing revolutionary in cybernetics as it applies to their own work. For biological and social scientists, however, cybernetics presents a new point of view and system of concepts for studying the organism and its relations with other organisms and with the inorganic environment." [29]

Before testing the last part of this quotation—the alleged new point of view given by cybernetics to the biological and social sciences—let us hear a little more about the contributions of cybernetics to these disciplines, first of all from N. Wiener himself.

> It is my thesis that the operation of living individuals and the operation of some of the newer communication machines are precisely parallel. Both of them have sensory receptors as one stage in their cycle of operation. [In man and machine there is a special apparatus for collecting information from the external world. In both the external messages are transformed by an internal mechanism "whether it be alive or dead."] . . . In both of them, their performed action on the outer world . . . is reported back to the central regulatory apparatus. . . . In every chapter, we are studying either those respects in which the machine duplicates man, or those aspects of man which are clearer in view of our study of the machine, or both.[30]

These few lines clearly set forth the mechanistic character of this approach and the almost complete identification of man and machine, so far as they represent mechanisms of communication and control.

In spite of an important reservation, the same standpoint is particularly stressed by another leader in the field of cybernetics, D. M. MacKay. Comparing the brain with machines, particularly electronic computing machines, he contends that suitably designed mechanisms can imitate human behavior and can work internally on the same principles as the brain works.[31]

Cybernetics' main contributions to the psychosocial sciences consist, according to the claims of its leaders and followers, in clarifying the nature of information, the methods of its transmission, the mechanism of using information for controlling purposes (of a given organism by messages coming from other agencies, and of the agencies by the messages of a given organism), and in providing "a new frame of reference for considering some long-standing philosophical problems": free will, consciousness, teleology, scientific method, etc.

In the present fad of imitating the physical sciences, cybernetics has naturally been picked up and introduced into the psychosocial disciplines by many sociologists and psychologists anxious to follow each latest rippling in natural sciences.[32]

Now we shall ask two questions about cybernetics' contributions to the psychosocial sciences: first, is its point of view really new in these sciences? and, second, how fruitful have the contributions of cybernetics been to these disciplines?

The first question must be answered negatively. We already know that theories of similarity, and sometimes identity, of man and machine are very old in the history of sociophilosophical thought. They were already voiced by several Hindu, Buddhist, Greek and Roman thinkers. In Europe, these theories were systematically developed by Descartes, Hobbes, Pascal, Leibnitz, Malebranche, Spinoza, Condillac, and many others. The following short quotations show this in a nutshell.

> "The animal body is a machine simultaneously hydraulic, pneumatic, and pyrobolic, a sort of a natural automaton which infinitely surpasses artificial automata," says Leibnitz.
>
> "One can well compare the nerves of the human machine with the tubes of the machines of these fountains, his muscles and tendons with other engines and springs . . . Further, respiration and other functions are similar to the motions of a clock," says Descartes. "The body of a living man differs from that of a dead man only as much as a watch or any other automaton when it is wound up differs from the same watch or automaton when it is broken."
>
> *"Quid est core nisi elastrum, quid nervi nisi chordae, articuli nisi . . . rotulae,"* states Hobbes.
>
> Condillac compared man with a marble statue organized inwardly like a human being and completely dependent in its sensations and notions upon its sense organs and the messages from the outside world.[33]

Similar theories of man-machine have continued to appear up to the present time. The notions of cybernetics are only one of the latest variations on this old theme. Cybernetics' logic of similitude or identity, as applied to man and machine, is also very old—it is the logic of a misleading analogy: "man has nose and dog has nose; therefore, man is identical with dog."

When the man-machine theories are seriously examined, they show themselves either quite superfluous or wrong. One of the foremost authorities on the brain, Sir Charles Sherrington, calls the human brain "the greatest mystery," and finds completely misleading all the comparisons of the brain with even the most complex computing machines.

> There is an ingenious mechanical invention of these latter days, which has recently been challenging comparison with the human brain. It is so designed that it computes and performs arithmetic operations more speedily than can a man. Professor Geoffrey Jefferson . . . has done our public the service of revising the analogy drawn between such a machine and the human mind. In a weaving shed the machinery weaves faster than can a human hand, but to liken the loom to the human hand, apart from one very limited meaning, is erratic and misleading. Between the calculating machine and the human brain there is no basic similarity. . . . The brain is a mystery —it has been—and still is. . . . The facts we know concerning the brain have indeed greatly multiplied in recent years, but they all fail to give a key to the mystery of how it creates—if it does create—our thoughts and feelings; that is . . . our mind.

Sherrington indicates several other "mysteries" of the brain that make it entirely different from any machine.[34]

From another standpoint, the profound difference between man and machine is also stressed by one of the leaders of cybernetics, D. M. MacKay. Like an electrician arranging a complete array of lamps and wires for an electric advertising sign, a competent cyberneticist can hypothetically arrange a complete chain of physical causes of human actions. The array of the lamps and wires *per se,* however, is not "an advertising sign," and has no bearing on the advertised meaning, "The Club of Good Fellows." Similarly, the operations of communication machines are not identical to the meaningful communications of human beings. As a matter of fact, the total operations of any machine are devoid of meaning whether it is scientific, or religious, or aesthetic, or even "absurd meaning." The machine's operations are just certain "motions" of its various parts, prearranged and determined by human beings. These motions have meaning only insofar as it is imputed to them by man. It does not "exist" in the machine or for the machine, but only for the men and in the men who superimposed the meanings upon these motions and made the machine an instrumentality for manifesting and communicating their meanings. "I believe most seriously that man is 'more than' the physical organism which we can describe in observer language. . . . This implies not necessarily that there must be gaps in the physical account of his activity, but that man has other '*aspects*' that are neither revealed by, nor are contained in, the physical man." [35]

It is precisely the psychosocial aspects of man, his meaningful behavior,[36] communication, and control, which are neither revealed by, nor can be explained by, a physical account of some of his physical operations. These aspects cannot be caught in the cybernetics net: they slip between its meshes. To be caught, they require a "psychosocial meaningful net." So much for the first question.

The answer we have given largely predetermines the answer to our second question: how fruitful have been the contributions of "social cyberneticists" to the psychosocial disciplines? So far, their contributions to our knowledge of psychosocial (not physical) phenomena have been almost negligible. Beginning with the sociological excursions of Wiener and other leaders of cybernetics, and ending with "the missionaries of cybernetics" among the social scientists (K. Deutsch, L. K. Frank, R. D. Luce, A. Rapoport, A. Bavelas, C. W. Churchman, Fano, and others), cyberneticists as such have contributed hardly any significant new theory, or discovered any new uniformity. Their cybernetical interpretations of psychosocial facts have hardly ever gone beyond superficial or misleading analogies. Even when they undertake an experimental study of social communication and control, their painstaking "experimentation" either entirely misses the psychosocial aspects of the problem or yields painfully achieved platitudes and/or doubtful semi-truths.

S. C. Dodd's "experimental" study of message-diffusion and of its effectiveness can serve as an example of cybernetic investigation (though he does not call it "cybernetic") that almost entirely misses the psychosocial aspects of the problem. The objectives of his study are: how *fast* message-leaflets, dropped from an airplane on an inimical, neutral or friendly target population, might spread; how *fully* through the population a message might diffuse; how the leaflets should be worded to achieve maximal *effectiveness*. For solving these problems the leaflets were dropped upon eight supposedly similar towns. One town got one leaflet for every four inhabitants; the next town received one leaflet per two persons; the next town one leaflet per one person, and so on, doubling the ratio up to thirty-two leaflets per person for the eighth town. Three days later the interviewers questioned fifty per cent of the households of the target populations, to find out who knew the message, when it was first heard, etc. In another experiment, aimed at finding out the effectiveness of different wordings of an appeal to give blood, twenty-eight versions of such an appeal, each version in 1,000 leaflets, were dropped by an airplane over a town of 1,500 inhabitants. Then the interviewers, through a census of the households, determined which leaflets had been seen and remembered. A few additional leaflet-droppings were made to determine the roles of distance and time in the "diffusion and effectiveness" of a message. These are the essential characteristics of Dodd's "experimental" studies of the diffusion and effectiveness of a message.[37]

Dodd's description of the experiments—with their formidable apparatus of airplanes and other means, all described in Dodd's ponderous language with its scientific terminology and a multitude of coefficients of correlations and other indices—impresses the novice as a careful experimental investigation. A discerning scholar, however, is likely to be impressed by the following three features of the investigation: (a) by its substitution of the physical spread of leaflets, dropped from an airplane, for their social diffusion; (b) by its painful demonstration of platitudes; (c) by its almost complete by-passing of the real objectives of the study. As a matter of fact, these experiments were not so much a study of social uniformities in the diffusion and multiplication of a message as of the physical laws of falling bodies (leaflets), discovered by Galileo, developed and precisely known to the physical sciences. No amateurish experiment by a sociologist is needed for a formulation of the physical laws of falling bodies and of their spread over the area where they are dropped. Nor is any experimental study needed to prove the platitude that in a town over which thirty-two leaflets per person are dropped, a greater number of people will see the falling bodies than in a town over which only one leaflet per four persons is dropped. A few drops of rain are uniformly noticed by a smaller number of people than a cloudburst. Nor is experimental study needed to prove that, other conditions being equal, the greater the distance between the falling leaflets and the population, the smaller the number of people seeing the falling or fallen leaflets. And these are the main results of these formidable experiments.

The real social diffusion and the effectiveness of the message contained in the dropped leaflets are hardly touched in the study. The effectiveness or controlling power of a message, in this case an appeal to give blood, means its acceptance by and its realization in the actions of the persons whom the message reached. Dodd and his collaborators did not make any attempt to find out how many persons, among those who saw the leaflets, gave their blood as a result of their seeing and reading the appeal in the leaflets. Moreover, the authors did not try at all to find out how many persons agreed with and accepted the leaflet message. All that the experimenters did was to drop the leaflets and then find out how many persons saw them, or heard of them from people around the area where they fell, —now with respect to populations receiving a downpour of leaflets (32 per person), and now a few leaflets (one per four persons). Such a study hardly touches at all the real problem of the "genesis, multiplication, mobility, and diffusion of sociocultural phenomena in space or time"; [38] and still less does it deal with the effectiveness or controlling power of a message or any sociocultural factor over the mental states and overt behavior of individuals and groups, over social institutions, and over other cultural phenomena.[39] Since the study does not deal with the social diffusion and effectiveness of a message, it naturally does not give any single uniformity or generalized formula. When Dodd attempts to give a theory of the factors of diffusion, he delivers in sham-mathematical form a most vague metaphysics. In all these respects the study is largely fruitless.

A. Bavelas' cybernetic study of communication and control is also one of the best of its kind.[40] It can serve as an example, not of a by-passing of the social aspects of the phenomena, but of the experimental rediscovery of centuries-old platitudes, and of the unwarranted generalization of the results obtained. A. Bavelas, assisted by H. J. Leavitt and S. Smith, experimented with five persons charged with jointly solving certain problems. The five persons as a group did not discuss the problem in advance but sat in separate cubicles communicating with one another exclusively by written messages. Each member was given a card with certain signs. Each member was permitted to exchange an unlimited number of written messages with the others, informing them what signs were on his card and passing along the information he received. The problem to be solved consisted of identifying one sign that appeared on all five cards.

Three main communication arrangements were used in the studies.

*a*) A circular arrangement of the five cubicles in which each member could directly communicate with one other member on his right and one on his left, while for communication with the other two members he had to relay his message through one of his immediate neighbors. In this circular arrangement each of the five members was in an identical position as to the easiness of communication with his four fellows.

*b*) The second arrangement was a straight-line distribution of the five cubicles. In this arrangement the person at the middle of the line was in a much more advantageous position than the other members: he could communicate directly with his two neighbors, and could reach the other two by only one relay. The members at the ends of the line were in the worst position: they could directly communicate with only one neighbor, and had to use from one to three relays to exchange their messages with the others.

*c*) The third arrangement was an inverted *Y* pattern by which one person at the fork of the *Y* could communicate directly with three members, while the other four could do so only with one member. The results of this experiment were: the nondemocratic arrangements of the straight line and of the inverted *Y* led to a faster solution of the problem, and to fewer errors, than the democratic, circular arrangement; the person who was in the advantageous position in the nondemocratic arrangements became the leader; in the circular, democratic arrangement all members were happy with their task, but in the nondemocratic arrangement only the leader was satisfied, the other members soon becoming apathetic and somewhat unhappy with their work. Such are the essentials and results of this experimental study of social communication and leadership.

In contrast to Dodd's study, which by-passed the psychosocial aspects of the diffusion and effectiveness of a message, Bavelas' experimental investigation deals indeed with the psychosocial aspects of communication and "leadership." Bavelas' study is the nearest possible approach to genuine experimental research, and this experimentation is marked by the comparative simplicity of the experimental arrangement. In these respects it is unquestionably superior to, and more significant than, the Dodd study.

In spite of these virtues in Bavelas' experiments, their positive results are somewhat disappointing. No experiments were needed to arrive at the conclusions that in the circular arrangement all members are on a par with one another in the ease of communication with the other four members, that in the straight-line and the inverted *Y* arrangements one member would be in a more advantageous position than the others, and that the others would be in an unequal position with respect to ease of communication. No experimental study was needed for these discoveries, because they are clearly contained in the very nature of the circular, straight-line and inverted *Y* arrangements. The experimental proof of these "discoveries" is a mere demonstration of the tautology that A is A, and B is B.

It is regretful, also, that Bavelas did not study the history of this problem of arranging communicating members. If he had, he would have seen that his problem was well known to hoary antiquity, that many arrangements had been widely experimented with, and systematically used, since ancient times, by various religious, magical, philosophical, educational, political, theatrical, military, and other groups. In their practice we find not only the circular, the straight-line, and the inverted *Y* patterns, but several others: two parallel straight lines opposing each other; a radial arrangement converging on one point in front of the members, toward a preacher, officiating priest, lecturer, or leader; a square arrangement, and others.[41] In some religious and military groups we find a most complex combination of arrangements. After all, architects building a lecture hall or church or business establishment; educators anxious to convey their messages to the pupils; military strategists anxious to have a well-disciplined army capable of performing complex maneuvers and ever open to the instantaneous communications of its commanders, especially on a battlefield—these "social engineers of communication" have dealt with this problem for centuries and millennia. They carefully studied and selected their patterns because they were aware of the important role of the arrangement for the accuracy, effectiveness, and velocity of communicated values in their groups. A good textbook in military art contains an enormous fund of tested scientific propositions in this field. The same is true of the Constitutions of various monastic orders, and so on.

These facts testify that Bavelas and other investigators of communication are not raising a new problem, nor are their studies opening to us a new perspective, or new methods or verities. In comparison with the enormous experience accumulated by centuries of incessant experimentation with variously arranged communication systems, the experiments of Bavelas and other cyberneticists are but a drop in an ocean. The availability of this enormous fund of accumulated experience does not allow any competent investigator of these problems to by-pass it as nonexisting, and especially to make claims of discovering a new region, new methods, and new uniformities in this field. Such a procedure is but another case of the discussed "amnesia" so typical of many recent "researchers" in the psychosocial sciences.

Let us now turn to a critical examination of other results of Bavelas' study. Can they be regarded as valid uniformities? For instance, can we say that all the straight-line and the inverted *Y* patterns invariably solve their problems faster and with fewer errors than the circular arrangement? Can we regard as a scientific uniformity the proposition that morale under the "democratic" circular pattern tends always to be more cheerful and happy than morale under the autocratic arrangements? Bavelas himself correctly points out that the speed of solving the problem, the number of errors, and the morale depend upon many conditions besides the factor of the pattern: upon the interest, insight, and ability of the members, and so on. For this reason alone the results of the experiments cannot be viewed as uniformities. Even more, the results cannot be extended much beyond the small group experimented with. The autocratic pattern of communication does not always solve its problems faster and with fewer errors, and have a lower morale than the democratic (circular) pattern, and vice versa.

Historical experience well supports these conclusions. When thoughtfully studied, history gives us thousands of "autocratic" communication groups of all sizes with fast and slow, and correct and erroneous solutions to their problems, with high and low morale—groups that are stable and unstable, short-lived and durable. The same can be said of "democratic" communication groups. To sum up: the discussed results are temporary and local, in no way universal or general uniformities.

One more remark: Bavelas' conclusion that the person in the central position (in the straight-line and the inverted *Y* arrangements) invariably becomes the leader, should also be taken with a serious limitation, and in no way can be viewed as a uniformity. The rise to leadership of such a person is seemingly due to the greater number of messages that pass through his hands, and to the greater ease with which he sends and receives messages with respect to the other members. First, such an advantage becomes a disadvantage if the messages are inaccurate and the information is misinformation. Under these conditions the person in the middle position becomes the most misinformed member with the least chance to rise to leadership. Actually, many heads of states or business corporations, or other groups, are frequently in this position of being the most misinformed person, in spite of the overabundance of information they have. This fact alone deprives Bavelas' conclusions of any general significance.

Second, even when the information is correct, the advantage discussed is at best only one of the factors facilitating leadership, in no way sufficient by itself to bestow it, because other more important conditions are necessary for one to become an actual leader even in the small group under experiment: intellectual capacity, comparative knowledge of the problem, lucky guessing, co-operation of other members, and so on. Otherwise, if the number of messages, or the information, were the decisive factor, the secretaries of many business, political, scientific, religious, and other leaders would have become the leaders instead of their bosses, because secretaries often have better, richer, and fuller information than their bosses. For the same reason, the great leaders in science and the arts, business and politics, philosophy and religion would have been "walking encyclopedias," the persons with the vastest amount of information in a given field, and in all fields of human activity. We know well that the real situation has been very different: the "walking encyclopedias" rarely emerge as the great leaders. More frequently than not the great leaders have been less erudite than many an encyclopedic mediocrity.

The necessary and most important factor for becoming a great leader in any creative field is the mysterious gift called genius, talent, grace of God, "supraconscious intuition," "divine inspiration," and so on.[42] And genius is something basically different from being a "walking encyclopedia" or from passing through one's hands an enormous mass of informational material.

These remarks explain why Bavelas' conclusions concerning leadership cannot be generalized—nor do they throw a real light upon the mystery of creative leadership. His study hardly even touches this difficult problem.

Finally, he deals only with one—and not the most important—trait of the phenomena of communication and organization. Geometric arrangement is inapplicable to many communication systems, and where it is applicable—mainly in small groups at their meetings—it plays a modest role in the total sum of the characteristics of organized communication in the group.[43] These characteristics are not touched at all in Bavelas' study. As a result it gives a wrong perspective of the total problem by concentrating our attention on only a single—and secondary—trait and by forgetting to outline the whole system of communication and organization, as the matrix of this trait.

The above criticisms show the meagerness of the real contribution made by studies like that of Bavelas to our knowledge of the phenomena of communication, control, and leadership. After his study we know as little about these phenomena as before. If other investigators follow his neglect of the vast fund of knowledge accumulated in this field by the experience of preceding centuries; if they forget to consult thousands of historical facts concerning these problems; if they study only one unimportant trait torn from the total system, then the actual results of their studies are likely to be negative. "Amnesia," the rediscovery of the long-ago-discovered table of multiplication, and many other errors, are bound to result from this sort of research, no matter what methods are used and how carefully the experimentation is done.

The preceding criticism of the cybernetic variation of physicalistic interpretations of psychosocial phenomena is sufficient to warrant a cautious attitude towards such studies. So far, they have promised much more than they have accomplished. The goods they have delivered are, so far, meager and of doubtful quality. The explicit and implicit errors they have committed are already considerable. Until their big promissory notes have been redeemed, we are entitled to refuse to exchange them for real scientific cash.

# *Chapter Ten*

# The Wonderland of Social Atoms and Small Groups

*Humpty Dumpty sat on a wall;*
*Humpty Dumpty had a great fall;*
*All the King's horses and all the King's men*
*Couldn't put Humpty Dumpty together again.*

## 1. The Search for Social Atoms and Elementary Particles

Since the pre-twentieth century physics dealt with atoms as the simplest units of physical phenomena, our physicalistic sociologists and psychologists had also to imitate the physical sciences in this important point, and had to find the social counterpart of these simplest units. Accordingly, they started several expeditions in search of social atoms or the simplest units of psychosocial phenomena. And they are still preoccupied with this task, especially with mutual dispute as to the nature of the looked-for atoms and elementary particles.

"Some . . . find this 'unit' in the individual. Others define it as a 'socius' of 'fellowship.' Still others . . . conceive it as the 'role' or 'action' which the individual performs. Many identify it with 'social relationship'. . . . [Still others] look for the simplest unit in the 'most elementary society,' meaning thereby either the family, or 'the most primitive society,' or a 'small group.' "[1]

While this hunt for the elusive "humpty-dumpties" has been going on, a few voices have been warning the zealous explorers about the possible futility of their search. "Your social atoms and simplest units may be mere phantoms of your imagination and misinformation as to the structure and role of atoms or elementary particles in physics. For this reason only your hunt for social atoms may easily be fruitless." In a more developed form such a warning was also sounded by this writer:

> A study of the structural aspect of sociocultural phenomena begins with an analysis of the *generic* properties common to all sociocultural phenomena—past, present, and future. By the *"generic sociocultural phenomenon" is not meant "the simplest unit."* Imitating the poorly understood natural sciences, sociologists are still looking for the "simplest unit" of social phenomena analogous to the atom in physics and the cell in biology. . . . This quest for the simplest social unit is based largely upon a misconception. 1) Physics and general biology begin their study of structural properties with the atom and the cell, respectively, as the *generic* elements of physical and biological structures—not *because they are the simplest units.* Every physicist and biologist is fully aware of the extremely complex structures of atoms and cells. Again, these disciplines begin their study . . . not with this or that specific atom or cell, but with the atom and cell in the generic form common to all atoms and cells. 2) [None of the suggested social atoms or simplest units is acceptable, for several reasons.] An individual, or even a million isolated individuals do not constitute social phenomenon, or society, to say nothing of its simplest unit. An individual represents a complex physical, biological, and psychological, but not social, phenomenon. He can become the object of study of a physicist, biologist, or psychologist, but not of a sociologist. Nor can an isolated individual perform any "social role" or "social action." Without a drama there can be no "role," or "social action" for a social role or a social action is possible only in the context of all the roles or actions of the play. . . . Only in the social matrix can the role or the action become an element of a social phenomena, just as a chromosome is a constituent of a cell or an electron a constituent of an atom; but neither the role as such, nor an electron or chromosome *per se* is the simplest unit of the social, physical, or biological structures. On the other hand, an individual taken as a *socius* or the total personality is one of the most complex of social phenomena. To say that the total individual or a *socius* is an ultimate, irreducible unit is equivalent (as E. C. Hayes rightly observes) to calling a bouquet of flowers the simplest and ultimate unit of plant structures. . . . Likewise, the family is not the simplest or generic social phenomenon. [Its structure and functions are among the most complex of all social groups.] The same is true of primitive societies—the postulated "simple societies" of H. Spencer and E. Durkheim—and of Malinowski's "institution" as a unit. [None of these and of the other social phenomena, offered by

various physicalistic sociologists, meets the qualifications of social atom or simplest unit.] [2]

2. Moreno's Social Atom

This criticism is fully applicable also to the "small group" which constitutes Moreno's "social atom." Recent studies of small groups will be discussed in the next section. For the present we shall briefly examine Moreno's conception of the social atom. The following lines sum up the essentials of his several definitions of it.

> The social atom is the nucleus of all individuals toward whom a person is emotionally related or who are related to him at the same time [emotional relatedness means attraction or repulsion]. It is the smallest nucleus of an emotionally toned inter-personal pattern in the social universe.[3]
>
> The social atoms are the centers of attraction and rejection.[4]
>
> It is the social atom which is the smallest social unit, not the individual. [The individual] has from birth on already a structure of relationship around him, mother, father, grandmother, and so forth. The volume of the social atom is in continuous expansion as we grow up: it is within it that we live most concretely. . . . These social atoms change from time to time in their membership, but there is a consistency in their structure. . . . The social atom is simply an individual and the people to whom he is emotionally related at the time.[5]

A careful examination of this conception of social atoms discloses several peculiar features. First, it considers only the emotional tone of social relations and completely ignores the intellectual, the volitional, and the affective aspects (if we distinguish the emotional aspect from the affective one, as many psychologists correctly do) of social relationships. In other words, out of many aspects of the relationships between an individual and others, and between others and the individual, Moreno selects only one—the emotional—and on this aspect exclusively builds his social atom.

Second, even out of a wide diversity of emotions, Moreno takes only attraction and repulsion and ignores dozens of other emotions which cannot be viewed strictly as attraction or repulsion—such as forgiveness, compassion, empathy, cheerfulness, depression, generosity, stability, instability, joy, sorrow, apathy, ecstasy, peace of mind, and so on. Of course, Moreno is perfectly entitled to build his social atom out of whatever constituents he pleases to choose. But when his social atom is built of only one very narrow trait out of hundreds of different qualities of social relationships, such a social atom obviously cannot cover most social relationships and, therefore, cannot describe them or be their generic representative or their common constituent. All social relationships which lack emotional attraction or repulsion do not contain or are not made up of his social atoms; on the other hand, those social relationships which have the quality of either attraction or repulsion, are far from being specified and differentiated from one another by Moreno.

Third, in regard to nonemotional social relationships, Moreno's atom is not an atom at all, because they are not made up of it but of qualities —intellectual, volitional, affective, etc.—different from Moreno's atom. In regard to emotional social relationships, his atom plays at best the role of an outmoded Linnean botanical classification based on the number of stamens and pistils, that is, upon only one differential characteristic of plants among many important ones irreducible to it. Contemporary botanical and zoological taxonomy have completely replaced such an inadequate, unilinear classification by a complex classification based upon a combination of important—genetic, anatomical, physiological—characteristics.

Fourth, in these respects Moreno's social atom has hardly any similarity to the atom of physics and chemistry. The physical atom was viewed as the smallest unitary constituent of *all* physical structures. Moreno's social atom is a constituent of not *all* but only of a portion of social relationships (emotional). There are some ninety different physicochemical atoms, according to the ninety-odd elementary substances, like hydrogen, oxygen, iron, gold, uranium, and so on. And these atoms differ from one another not by one trait only, such as mass or weight, but by several characteristics, particularly by the number and arrangement of the electrons about the central nucleus.[6] Moreno's different "social atoms" are distinguished from one another by one trait only: either by emotional attraction or rejection (or indifference). In these basic respects the atom of physics and the social atom of Moreno have practically nothing common with each other. There is no good reason for Moreno to borrow the term *atom* from physics and give to it a meaning devoid of even a superficial similitude to its meaning in physics.

Fifth, still more serious are the shortcomings of the social atom from the logical and psychosociological standpoints.

*a*) First of all, it is not the smallest social unit, especially in regard to the totality of emotional relationships of such individuals as a monarch, a president, a dictator, the prime minister of a big state, the Roman Catholic Pope, a patriarch of a vast religious organization, a military leader of large armies, an important captain of industry and finance, or the world-famous writer, artist, composer, and so on. Each of these persons has emotionally colored (as by attraction or repulsion) relationships to thousands and thousands of persons scattered over the whole earth; and the emotional relations of others toward such a person involve millions of individuals. The total network of emotional relatedness in such a social atom is, in fact, one of the vastest and most complex webs of social relationships in the whole universe of emotional interactions of human beings. Only euphemistically can such complex networks be called "the smallest," or "the simplest." Obviously, Moreno's social atom does not meet at all his own condition for the smallest or simplest unit. This is true even in regard to the network of emotional relatedness of most ordinary individuals: the emotional web of each of them is also quite complex and extensive. Only, perhaps, the web of a hermit or recluse or member of a pre-literate tribe is comparatively small and consists of few attractions and repulsions in regard to few individuals.

*b*) The physical atom of hydrogen or of any of the ninety-odd elements remains identical to itself in all its important traits. Moreno's atom incessantly changes with respect to the same individual—it shrinks and expands, now involving a few, now many individuals. In this point, Moreno's atom again radically differs from the physical atom.

*c*) The preceding remarks show that Moreno's social atom embraces a long series of quantitatively and qualitatively different networks of social (emotional) relationships. The social atom centered around pope or monarch or world-celebrity is quite different from the social atom centered around a hermit or peasant in simple society. It is an elementary scientific rule to call by the same term only those phenomena that are essentially similar to one another, and to call by different terms the phenomena that are essentially different. From this standpoint Moreno's use of the term "social atom" for notably different phenomena is hardly justifiable.

*d*) The atom of the physical sciences always remains the smallest unitary constituent of physical structures. It never covers a vast and complex aggregate of physical phenomena. It is regularly distinguished from a molecule and from the aggregates of atoms or molecules. The same atom, say of hydrogen, is never inflated and "stretched out" to the extent that the total hydrogen contained in a body of water is considered as *one* hydrogen atom. On the contrary, the total hydrogen of even a small body of water in a little cup is viewed as an aggregate of millions of atoms of hydrogen. Meanwhile, the vastest emotional web of relationships, such as that of a monarch or pope, is, in Moreno's atomic theory, just one social atom. In this point, again, Moreno's term "the social atom" is a striking misnomer.

*e*) A physicist or a chemist shows convincingly that all physical or chemical bodies are made of specific combinations of atoms. Out of his atoms he constructs any and all of the infinite variety of physical or chemical compounds and the whole physical universe. In this respect Moreno's social atom is again quite different from the physical atom. Moreno's atom covers only a part of the emotional aspects of social relatedness, and does not cover at all the intellectual, volitional, and affective aspects. As these aspects are numerous, important, and ever-present in the universe of social relationships between individuals and groups, Moreno cannot construct many "social compounds," nor, with his atoms, can he construct the social universe. Neither can he decompose or dissolve the total social universe into his atoms. The nonemotional aspects of this universe are neither made of, nor can be analyzed into, Moreno's emotional atoms. In regard to the social universe his social atom fails again to fulfill the functions which the physical atom does in regard to the physical universe.

*f*) Moreno's atom does not give a sufficiently detailed analysis and classification of his attractions and repulsions. There are hundreds of qualitatively and quantitatively different attractions and repulsions. Each of these has different intensities, extensities, durations, purity, and a series of qualitative differences [7] through which one form of attraction radically differs from the others. It is true that Moreno somewhat differentiates various forms of attraction or repulsion: attraction or repulsion to A as a roommate, to B as a coworker, to C as a playmate, to D as sex-mate, and a few additional differentiations. But these few differentiations in no way exhaust the rich diversity of attractions or repulsions. Even such a seemingly simple attraction as love of man for woman covers, by the same term "love," very different emotional experiences ranging from, say, the "platonic" love of Dante for Beatrice, or of Don Quixote for Dulcinea where the sexual element is almost totally absent, through "love" for a woman as an incarnation of beauty, wisdom, comradeship, virtue, and loyalty, up to purely sexual love. Even the sexual love itself has again various forms of emotional attraction—masochist, frigid, mutually orgasmic, satisfied with the same mate or striving for ever new partners, and so on. The same is true of repulsion. Insofar as Moreno's differentiation of various forms of attractions and repulsions is limited to five or six variations only, his analysis of the central "stuff" of his atom is quite insufficient. It reminds one of classifications of elementary substances by ancient philosophers who reduced them to water, fire, air, earth, and so on. Modern chemistry has, instead, some ninety-odd elementary substances irreducible to one another. The insufficient differentiation of various forms of attraction and repulsion makes inadequate Moreno's analysis of these emotional relationships and, through that, of the forms and properties of social relatedness, regardless of whether or not we call them "the social atom."

*g*) Finally, the sociometric study of attractions and repulsions has hitherto been confined mainly to investigating the vocal answers (through interviews or questionnaires) of the questioned persons as to who among a set of certain individuals would be their first or second choice as a roommate, as a coworker, as a playmate, and so on. Most of the sociometric investigations have dealt not with the overt actions of the respondents but with their preferences, wishes, and desires as expressed in their written or vocal speech-reactions. To this extent, the sociometric universe of social atoms has been not so much the total world of behavioral or actual attractions and repulsions, as a wonderland of wishful choices, aspirations, and preferences in the dreamland of imaginary attractions and repulsions. Though such a wonderland is one of the aspects of the total social universe, nevertheless, out of such "dreamy and wishful atoms" nobody can construct the total, real universe of social relations, manifested in overt acts of attraction and repulsion.

For constructing the real and total social and physical universe, the respective atoms have to be more than imaginary constructs or merely wishful vocal utterances; they must be real atoms—in our case the actually performed attractions and repulsions—at least roughly corresponding to the wishful vocal preferences, or to imaginary first or last choices. Ordinarily there is a notable discrepancy between the wishful vocal reactions and the overt actions of the same individual. The concentration of sociometric studies of social relatedness on the wishful, largely imaginary, rapidly changing, and always uncertain aspect, greatly limits, and often makes impossible, an adequate study of all the important aspects of the total universe of real social relatedness or of the social world of real attractions and repulsions.

The above criticisms warrant the following conclusions: (1) Moreno's "social atom" does not resemble the physical atom in its structure or functions or basic properties. (2) For this reason the term "social atom" is a misnomer for the network of emotional attractions and repulsions radiating from one individual to other individuals and coming from the others to the individual. (3) Moreno's concept of social relatedness is unduly limited to purely emotional relations and even to a part of emotional relations. For this reason, it does not cover all the nonemotional relationships that occupy quite a large place in the total universe of social—interpersonal—relationships. (4) Even that part of emotional attractions and repulsions that makes up Moreno's "social relatedness" is limited by an unfortunate concentration on the wishful, imaginary, or "daydreaming" speech-reactional aspect of the total phenomenon of social relatedness. Even a most careful, sociometric study of this "wonderland" of wishful preferences, and of hypothetical and vocal attractions and repulsions, could not help but miss most of the real aspects of social relatedness realized in overt actions of attractions and repulsions. (5) For these reasons, sociometric study gives us a picture of a mainly imaginary, hypothetical, wishful web of social relatedness, and not an integral knowledge of the actual, total web of social relations.[8]

### 3. Atomic Humpty Dumpty Had a Great Fall

The *coup de grâce* to all searches for the social atom as the smallest and simplest unit of social phenomena has been given by modern physics itself. Physical theories of the atom and of elementary particles have undergone a profound change in the last few decades. The net result of this change is that the atom has ceased to be viewed as the simplest unit of physical phenomena, and its place is being taken by an ever-increasing number of progressively smaller and smaller elementary particles. The essentials of this profound transformation can be summed up as follows:

Before the twentieth century the atom was viewed as the elementary particle. About 1930 the electron and the proton replaced the atom. Then the largely "non-material" photon was added to these "elementary particles." By 1932 their number had been further augmented by the neutron and the positron. In 1935 two kinds of mesons, and during subsequent years the neutrino, the antiproton, the antielectron, the antineutron, and the antineutrino increased the number of nature's ultimate constituents. With this increase, the very terms "elementary" or "ultimate particle" had either to be abandoned or to be changed in their meaning. "Elementary now seems to mean the equivalent of cryptic, arcane, perplexing, enigmatic, inscrutable." Since many of these enigmatic particles lack most of the characteristics of "matter," the term "material" has also become inapplicable to them and has had to be largely abandoned.[9]

As a rule our psychosocial imitators of the physical sciences have a limited, sometimes bizarre, knowledge of these disciplines. In this case, also, they seem to have entirely overlooked the radical transformation of atomic and particle theories in modern physics. While the physical sciences have already abandoned the atom as the elementary unit, and have found that an ever-increasing number of the elementary particles are of a less and less "material" nature, our "home-made physicists" are still playing with atomic marbles, still looking for social atoms as the simplest and smallest units of psychosocial phenomena. If indeed they are anxious to build sociology or psychology on the model of the physical sciences, they should imitate not the antiquated but the modern atomic theories of physics. This means abandoning the search for "social marbles." In this, as well as in many other points, the theories of modern physics entirely coincide with the warnings, quoted above, from real sociology and psychology.

## 4. Perambulations in the Wonderland of "the Small Groups"

This warning equally concerns the psychosocial dealers in "the small groups." Following the old precept that a study of the structures and evolutions of organisms should begin with their simplest and smallest forms, a number of investigators have "discovered" in recent years that "a small group" is the elementary social unit. Accordingly, they have concentrated their exploratory energy on a study of "the small groups," not only as the most fruitful field *per se,* but also as the most promising approach for discovering generalizations valid for larger groups and for the whole universe of psychosocial phenomena.

Directly or indirectly a recent impetus to the study of the small groups has been given by J. L. Moreno and K. Lewin. Under their influence a considerable number of younger researchers—like the proponents of "Group Dynamics," R. Bales, A. Bavelas, G. C. Homans, and others—have enthusiastically engaged in the study of the small groups, have succeeded in obtaining considerable funds for their research, have published a sizable number of papers and books, and for the time being have made such study fashionable. Along with the development of this movement the claims of its partisans have mounted concerning the revolutionary character of their discoveries, the exceptionally scientific nature of their studies, and so on, up to the contentions that a truly scientific study of social groups was really only begun by recent investigators of small groups, and that before their research the psychosocial sciences were nothing but "speculative theorizing."

In order to accurately appraise the movement, its discoveries and its grandiose claims, we can ask the following questions: (a) What precisely is the small group, and is there a sound logical or factual basis for making "the small groups" a distinct class of social groups? (b) Is a small group the simplest unit of social groups and social phenomena generally, and should a scientific study of social groups always begin with the small groups? (c) What sort of groups have actually been studied by the recent missionaries of the small groups? (d) Is it true that psychosocial thinkers of the preceding centuries and decades neglected a study of the small groups? (e) Is it true that the recent investigators of small groups have made revolutionary discoveries and enriched our knowledge of psychosocial phenomena by new, significant theories, new and valid generalizations, new uniformities, new methods, new techniques, and new insights?

*a*) The answer to both parts of the first question has to be in the negative. So far, the theorizers of the small groups have not given a satisfactory definition of a small group, nor have they been able to supply an even remotely adequate reason for considering the small groups as a distinct class of social groups. R. Bales' definition of a small group is about as good as any given by the devotees of this movement, and, as such, it can serve as an example for our examination: "A small group is defined as any number of persons engaged in interaction with one another in a single face-to-face meeting or a series of such meetings, in which each member receives some impression or perception of each other member distinct enough so that he can, either at the time or in later questioning, give some reaction to each of the others as an individual person, even though it be only to recall that the other was present. . . . According to this definition a number of persons who have never interacted with one another do not constitute a small group." A number of persons present at a lecture, or a number too large and too scattered, communicating with one another indirectly or not clearly aware of the presence of others, do not make a small group.[10]

Thus, according to this definition, a meeting of some twenty-five persons who do not know one another and who cannot receive a clear perception and "in any discernible way" be aware of the presence of all twenty-four members of the meeting—be it an incidental cocktail party, a spontaneous political gathering, or a religious revival—is not a small group. On the other hand, a series of meetings of 600 members of a parliament where each member knows all other members, and all members have a clear "impression" and "perception" of one another, is "a small group," though it is twenty-four times larger in number than the meeting consisting of twenty-five persons. The Republican or the Democratic convention with more than 1,000 members is also "a small group," because the delegates of the convention are usually well acquainted and interact face-to-face with one another. According to this definition, then, many groups large in membership miraculously become "the small groups," and many small groups turn out to be large groups. Such a use of the terms "small" and "large," in senses almost opposite to their regular meanings, can hardly be condoned on logical, semantic, and scientific grounds. It certainly does not contribute to the clarity of the definition of a small group. If anything, it hopelessly confuses the issue. Especially when, according to Bales, even a single individual, talking to himself, or feeling ashamed, also constitutes a small group. As almost every individual thinks of, talks of, has various feelings about, himself, then practically every single individual is a small group. This makes the confusion hopeless.

If the number of interacting persons is not a specific characteristic of a small group, the *differentia* given by Bales are certainly less successful in differentiating it as a distinct class of social groups. Thus Bales' "face-to-face interaction" cannot serve as a distinct mark of a small group because "face-to-face" interaction occurs in a milling and shouting crowd of hundreds of persons and in a meeting of two lovers; in a parade of a regiment where soldiers know and mutually influence one another, and in a meeting of an executioner and his victim; in the highly organized large groups like the above-mentioned parliamentary session and in the small organized group like the family, or the teacher and his pupil. One-sided face-to-face interaction occurs between the actor of a television show and the millions in his audience, and between a lecturer and his small class. Face-to-face interaction takes place between murderer and his victim, and between a person saving the life of his friend and this friend. In brief, the face-to-face characteristic is found among the most heterogeneous groups, beginning with semi-nominal plurels, passing through unorganized groups and ending with the highly organized groups; beginning with the deadly inimical and ending with the most altruistic interaction; beginning with the interaction of one or two persons, and ending with that of hundreds, thousands, and even millions of persons (in especially one-sided interactions).

Instead of giving to us a homogeneous class of social groups, the face-to-face characteristic delivers in fact a veritable motley of groups as different from one another as the groups can be. One can put into this sort of "small group" almost any group he pleases. Such a class is not class at all. And such a definition is in fact a lack of any definition. The main reason for this utter confusion is a complete disregard of the logical canon for making a satisfactory definition, and a lack of the elementary differentiation of groups. Under the pretext of face-to-face interaction, one cannot throw into the same basket the nominal plurels, unorganized, semi-organized, and organized groups; inwardly antagonistic and solidary groups; the vast and the small groups, and so on.[11] Otherwise, following Bales' and other's definitions of a small group, the zoologist can easily make a "nosey species" out of all organisms which have a nose, and on this ground can put man and dog into the same species; or such a zoologist can easily make "the species of game" out of all organisms hunted by man. Likewise, a botanist can create "the species of vegetables" because all plants of this species have the common trait of being edible by *homo sapiens*. Fortunately for zoology and botany, their taxonomy does not have any species cut out according to the precept of Bales. And sociology, unfortunately, still abounds with such illogical definitions, concepts, and classifications. The definers of the small groups suffer from this disease particularly strongly. Almost all of them fail to make an elementary distinction between organized and unorganized groups, between a real group and a nominal plurel, and between other fundamentally heterogeneous groups which cannot be put into one class under the pretext of having in common a small or a large size, a face-to-face or an indirect interaction, the trait of "receiving impression or perception of each other" (this characteristic is also quite vague and undefined), or some other single trait.

The ideologists of the small groups seem to be unaware that there exist fairly well-developed taxonomies of social groups, and that there are a large body of investigations of this problem. Their naïveté is so striking that they do not even see the series of complex problems involved in classifying social groups and in defining these classes. One could have envied their *sancta simplicitas,* if it were not a mere *sancta ignorantia.*

To sum up: the theorizers of the small groups display poor logic and a still poorer knowledge of elementary taxonomic principles, not to mention their failure to make a preliminary differentiation of basic classes of social groups. No wonder they have not succeeded in even a rough delineation of a small group as the object of their study. Since the investigator does not know exactly what he is studying, and what place the object of his study occupies in the larger universe of which it is a part, no wonder that his study does not yield fruitful results. Further on, we shall see the accuracy of this prognosis.

The answer to the first part of our first question largely predetermines the answer to its second part. There is no logical or factual basis for making "the small groups" a special, distinct class of social groups. The preceding analysis makes this clear. The crucial evidence for this answer is the very fact that the devotees of the "small groups" study have failed to satisfactorily define their class. To the reasons given, the following consideration can be added. What would the botanists say if some adventurous and not too competent innovator in botany introduced the class of "small plants from 2 to 25 inches high as a distinct species"? What would the zoologists say if some innovator added to the existing classification of animal species a new species of "small animals from 1 to 20 pounds in weight"? Such taxonomic innovations would have no chance of being accepted in botany and zoology. For the same reason, the species of "the small groups" cannot be taken seriously by any competent sociologists or social psychologists. If it is accepted by a considerable number of psycho-social researchers, the fact signifies only the immaturity of their sociology and psychology. Such fads and delusions occur from time to time in many disciplines. However, they are short-lived and eventually are put in the place where they belong—in the cemetery of human errors.

This does not mean that specific forms of small groups cannot or should not be studied. On the contrary, such small groups as "the dyads," "the tryads," "the family," "an exclusive political or religious small sect," "a small minority," "a royal dynasty," the small business firm or union, and so on, have been fruitfully studied. However, they have been investigated not just as small groups generally but as specific groups whose structural, functional, and dynamic properties cannot be extended over all groups with small membership. The basic properties of the family cannot be generalized and applied to all the dyads or tryads or small business, political, religious, recreational and other groups quite different from the family; and especially not to the incidental, semi-nominal meetings of the "discussion group," or to unorganized groups. The same can be said of any other small group. As a specific form of a group with small membership, it has been, is, and will be studied, but not as a typical example of all the heterogeneous groups of small size. To extrapolate the properties of the husband-wife-child group to all three-member small groups, or to all groups of a comparatively small size, is to make a gross blunder. And exactly this blunder is committed by the cultists of the small groups generally.

*b*) Since the theorizers fail to give even a roughly clear definition of a small group, it is impossible to answer definitely our second question: Is a small group the simplest and smallest unit of social groups and structures? Moreover, a clear-cut answer cannot be given for the lack of precision in the question itself: because of the earlier-mentioned failure of the theorizers to distinguish the organized, semi-organized, and unorganized groups, the real and semi-nominal groups, from one another, the question does not specify the sort of group of which a small group is or is not the simplest unit. It is one thing to ask if a small group is the simplest unit of all organized groups. And it is another matter to view a small group as the simplest unit of all the unorganized, or of all the real, or of all the semi-nominal groups, or of all the groups of all the kinds. Likewise, to make the question precise, it must also be specified whether the small group is an organized or unorganized, real, or semi-nominal group. As long as such specification is lacking, the question and the answer are both indeterminate and meaningless.

If a small group is assumed to be the simplest social unit for the reason of its small membership—as some of the theorizers indeed assume—the assumption is unwarranted. Such a small group as the strong family is a group incomparably more complex in its structure and functions than many a national and international association with millions of members, like the National Association of Manufacturers or the American Federation of Labor, and so on. Structurally,

> the family as a socially sanctioned union of husband(s) and wife (wives), parents and children is bound together by an enormous number of bonds (interests, values, needs): a) the satisfaction of sexual needs of husband and wife; b) procreation; c) procuring for the members the means of subsistence; d) the socialization and education of especially the younger generation in linguistic, religious, moral, mental, physical, occupational values, and activities to fit the children for adult life; e) the protection of the life, integrity, and values of the members from enemies and violators; f) the mitigation of psychosocial isolation; g) promotion of the members' well-being and happiness. In other words, it is a multibonded group made up of a unique compounding of heterogeneous and supplementary sex + age + race + kinship + territorial propinquity + language + culture + religious + occupational + economic + educational + moral + recreational bonds. . . . For this reason its solidarity embraces the whole life-experience and life-values of its members, resulting in the merging of their activities and their individual selves into a single close-knit collectivity. As such it is the only true *Gemeinschaft,* the only all-embracing (encyclopedic) "community" of bodies and souls, of minds and activities. It is, indeed, as the great Roman lawyer, Modestinus, defined it, *"consortium omnis vitae, divini et humani juris communicatio."* [12]

Compared with the family an enormous number of large national and international groups are comparatively simple bodies. Structurally their members are bound together by only one or two bonds: economic, occupational, political, religious, recreational, scientific, or moral, and so on. Functionally the activities of these vast groups are also much less encyclopedic, and much more narrow and specialized than the activities of the family. Many of the vast groups carry on only one of many activities of the family. Thus, though the family is a small group, it is "anatomically and physiologically" a much more complex body than many a large group with millions of members. Many other small groups are also much more complex than many a vast group. So far as the real communities (*Gemeinschaften*) are ordinarily of a small size in comparison with many specialized associations (*Gesellschaften*), and so far as the total activities of the communities are more diverse and encyclopedic than those of the specialized associations, the small communities are frequently (but not always) more complex in their structure and functions (activities) than the vast associations.

These considerations suffice to dissipate the myth that the small groups are simpler bodies than the large groups, and especially the myth that the small group is the simplest unit of collectivities.

If a small group is not the simplest unit of social groups, then the study of social groups must not necessarily begin with the small groups and pass to an investigation of larger and larger social bodies. Moreover, the precept itself, that a study of all phenomena should always begin with the simplest forms and pass to those which are more and more complex, is not to be taken as a universal rule. Aristotle's opposite precept that if one wants to know all the properties of an oak, one should study these properties, not on an acorn but on a fully grown oak, is as valid as the precept "from the simplest to the most complex." Both rules are relative and are to be applied to the problems to which they are applicable. So much on this point.

*c*) The haphazardness with which their recent "discoverers" approach the study of small groups comes out particularly clearly in the kind of groups they select for their research. Most of the selected small groups do not meet either of the two outlined methodological precepts: they are neither simplest units ("acorn-groups"), nor are they the fully grown "oak-groups." The bulk of the groups studied represents incidental, semi-organized collections of students or soldiers, or workers, or dwellers in an establishment (room, apartment, several small houses, factory room, classroom, etc.), or of members of a street gang, and so on. Often the real purpose of researching is not disclosed to the members of these semi-nominal plurels. Instead, they are told some yarn as to why they are gathered together and have to answer the questions or participate in discussion, and the investigators naively assume that their yarns fool the drafted or semi-drafted participants. Further, this incidental collection of individuals is often made up of complete strangers to one another, quickly corralled together into a pen of semi-organized discussion or interviewing. These collections now and then are replaced by studies of a few heterogeneous organized groups, like the family in Tikopeia, or a metropolitan club group, or a well-organized political clique, or a small religious sect. In brief, "the small groups" studied are mainly unorganized or semi-organized collections indiscriminately mixed up with a few organized groups and studied with the same procedures and techniques. If the investigators were making a special study of unorganized or semi-organized "small groups", they would be justified in selecting samples of unorganized or semi-organized groups, respectively. Likewise, if they were studying the organized groups, they should have selected samples of organized collectivities. Instead of this, they indiscriminately pick up most heterogeneous unorganized, semi-organized, and organized groups for a study of small groups generally. No wonder that their net, in trying to catch all sorts of fish, in fact does not catch any.

For catching the real "social fish," Aristotle's precept is appropriate to follow here. If we want to know the properties of the important classes of small groups, the shortest way is to study the most important organized small groups, especially those which are found in almost all populations of the past and present, and which have been most powerful in conditioning the behavior, mentality, culture, and institutions of their populations and in determining their historical destiny. The powerful organized groups, in their totality, have exerted much greater influence upon the respective populations than the totality of unorganized and semi-organized groups. Methodologically, the organized groups are like Aristotle's full-grown oak: they display all the important properties and processes of a certain class of small groups, which are not visible and not developed, as yet, by the unorganized or semi-organized small groups.[13] From these effective and methodological standpoints, a selection of mainly incidental, *ad hoc,* hastily-put-together semi-organized and unorganized groups is possibly the least fruitful, the longest, and the most hazardous way for obtaining knowledge of the small groups.

Besides this haphazard approach, the fact that an overwhelming majority of the studies of the incidental small groups have been limited to investigation of mainly speech-reactions, and particularly speech-reactions telling about the wishes, desires, choices, and preferences of the group members, is an additional eloquent demonstration of the superficiality and fragmentariness of studies of this sort. How the members of such groups overtly behave in real life, how and why they do what they do, how and why the given group lives and functions amidst other groups, what is the *raison d'être* of its emergence, existence, change, and continuity of structure—these are realities which the criticized studies of small groups hardly touch. Instead, they choose the path of least resistance and merrily preoccupy themselves with semi-mechanical registration of what this or that member said in replying to what was said by another member or the investigator; what words were used, and how many times each member used them, during an hour or a half-hour session of incessant chattering with one another; what wishful desires each participant expressed; and so on, and so forth. These studies hardly go beyond the registration, arbitrary classification and statistical summary of the speech-reactions of the members of a small group, and they hardly give an analysis of the behavioral facts of the group.

To sum up: the kind of small groups selected by our investigators for their study clearly reveal a haphazard, unfruitful and most confused approach to the problem. It is one of the least scientific approaches possible.

*d*) Similarly, the claims of the ideologists of the small groups, that until their research a study of the small groups was largely neglected, and that they are the pioneer-explorers in this field, are also largely baseless. In contrast to the haphazard selection of heterogeneous and unimportant small groups by the recent "explorers," the social thinkers of the past soundly selected for their investigation mainly the important and well-organized "small groups," now and then supplementing their study by including a few unorganized or semi-organized bodies. The family and the household, dyads like moral teacher and pupil, tryads like the judge with accused and accuser, a small *Bruderschaft* or blood-brotherhood, a small monastic community, a kinship group, a small caste, a small guild, a cottage industry group, a village or a small cooperative community, a small professional association, a royalty and an aristocracy, a small military or priestly organization—these and other small groups were well investigated, experimented with, and actually built by past investigators from ancient times on up to the present century. The studies of the family and of other small groups by the authors of the *Law of Hammurabi* in Babylonia; by Confucius, Mo-ti, Mencius, and others in China; by the anonymous and the known authors of the Indian Puranas, Tantras, Arthasastras,

Nitisastras, Dharmasutras, Smritis, including the law books, like the *Laws of Manu, Gautama, Instituts of Vishnu, Brihaspati,* etc., and by such authors as Kautalya; the classic analyses of the family, the household, the village, the city, the state, cliques, and factions, by Plato and Aristotle (whose *Politics* begins with a study of the small "domestic group," then systematically passes to an investigation of the society of several families, then of the city, and finally ends with a study of the state as a self-sufficient social group); by, especially, the great Roman jurists (whose works were incorporated into the *Corpus Juris Civilis*), who studied in detail all the important small and large groups and defined in the clearest possible way their structure, functions, rights, duties, and change, with a precise definition of the *status civitatis, status libertatis* and *status familiae* of each member of each group; these and hundreds of other works, especially the enacted codes of law regulating in detail the organization and activities of each of the groups in a given population and the status, behavior and relationship of each member of these groups, are a few examples of the large number of studies of small groups in the remote past.

Still more important is the fact that some of these studies—like the Confucian study of the family and the filial piety, or Aristotle's study of a household, or especially the Roman jurisconsults' painstaking analyses of practically all social groups, small and vast, existing in the Roman Empire—still remain unexcelled and unrivaled by the "puny" study of small groups in the present time. Instead of superficially registering the vocal reactions of the members of hastily put together "chatterbox groups," without a serious study of their behavior and life, of the place of the group in the universe of other groups, and so on, the ancient investigators studied such groups and their members in all the important structural and dynamic, speech-reactional and behavioral aspects; and the integral study of each of these groups included a thorough investigation of the whole universe of the groups amidst which the studied group lived, functioned, and mutually interacted. And what is still more important, the ancient investigators of all sorts of small groups had to formulate their findings in the clearest possible definitions, because these findings and concepts were transformed into law-norms, which by their nature have to be unambiguous and clear (otherwise they would not serve their social task). It is precisely the scientific qualities of the ancient investigators which account for the wide diffusion and the immortality of their findings. For instance, the concepts, the definitions, the generalized formulae of the Roman law, like its definition of *Status* (ascribed to R. Linton by ignorant authors of recent studies), of *Potestas, Imperium, Majestas, Manus, Commercium, Consensus, Cessio, Beneficium, Dominium, Proprietas, Possessio, Nuptio,* and so on; or the definition of the main social institutions, organized groups, and social relationships—these were not only taken into the law of the European continental countries, but they still constitute the main framework of contemporary constitutional, criminal, civil, and international law in Europe and Latin America.

These brief remindings are sufficient to demonstrate the utter fallacy of statements that the small groups were not studied until recent times, and that our investigators of the small groups are pioneering in this virgin field. Only complete ignorance of the past history of these studies, or the "amnesia" of the contemporary Columbuses, make these childish claims possible—the America they claim to have discovered was discovered and well explored long ago.

*e*) No less childish are the claims of modern investigators of small groups as to the revolutionary character and importance of their discoveries. Going carefully through their publications, I did not find any original theory, or new valid generalization, or new uniformity, or new method, or new technique. Instead, I found the following categories of pseudo-contributions: (1) "amnesia" in the sense of an almost complete ignorance of the study and experience of the social thinkers of the preceding centuries; (2) purely verbal innovations in the sense of the "defects of speech-behavior" discussed above; (3) pseudo-experimental and pseudo-objective methods and techniques; (4) painfully elaborated platitudes and poorly reiterated generalizations, discovered long ago and defined more accurately by the preceding social thinkers; (5) sterile tautologies of the kind *A* is *A,* instead of fruitful propositions of the type *A* is *B;* (6) a number of errors, semi-truths, and dogmatic assertions; (7) narcissistic self-admiration and overconfidence; (8) the policies of mutual back-patting in which "a cuckoo praises the rooster because the rooster praises the cuckoo," and the whole company thus inflates its virtues and achievements; (9) finally, a few real discoveries of small importance.

Let us now substantiate and illustrate these points.

1) As to the "amnesia," the preceding section, as well as the first chapter, have given sufficient evidence of it. Additional proofs are supplied by

almost complete lack of references in the publications of the "small groups" theorizers to the theories of preceding investigators. A mere glance at the index of authors in the books of our Columbuses is enough to see the "amnesia." Once in a while a few names of predecessors are mentioned, but mainly in the form of the condescending remark that though a previous investigator touched the problem he did not investigate it seriously. Not only the predecessors of the past centuries, but even the contemporary sociologists and psychologists who have fruitfully studied the problems of the small groups and whose theories have often been "borrowed" by our theorizers—even such contemporary scholars are rarely mentioned by our "amnesiacs." With these rare exceptions, the recent investigators of the small groups form a closed and exclusive referential club in which they mutually and complimentarily refer only to one another.

2) Chapter Two has given a number of examples of verbal innovations made by the members of "Group Dynamics" and by other investigators of small groups: "valence" instead of "attraction," "locomotion" in place of "change" or "mobility," "cohesion" in lieu of "solidarity" or "integrity," and so on. The same chapter has shown that practically all of these innovations are either innoxious puerilities or obnoxious "disorders of speech behavior." They certainly do not add anything to our knowledge of psychosocial phenomena or of the small groups and are, all in all, a big liability rather than a contribution.

3) Nor is anything new displayed in the methods or techniques of the recent investigators of the small groups. Mainly they use the ancient method of asking questions and registering the answers. The inquiries are made, now in the form of straight oral questions, now in the form of oral interviewing, now in that of written questionnaires. The oral or written answers of the respondents make up the main, often the only, stuff of their information. Since this method of getting information was used by mankind even in its "prehistoric age," the method obviously cannot be regarded as a new scientific approach.

Again, there is nothing new in the several variations of this method, such as "directed" or "undirected," "closed" or "open" interviewing, the use or non-use of false pretences in questioning the respondents, wording the questions in this or that way, trying to get a representative or incidental sample of respondents, and so on. All these variations are again very old and have been used since time immemorial.

Perhaps something new has been invented in the florid embellishments of the discussed method, such as the "operational," "observational," "experimental," "instrumental," "objective," and "statistical" decorations with which our theorizers impressively ornament this ancient method? Hardly. When seriously examined, these embellishments are found to be merely an imitative veneer, superimposed upon the essentially subjective and incidental "hearsay stuff" of the main procedure. All the criticisms given in the preceding chapters, and showing the pseudo-operational, pseudo-experimental, pseudo-objective, pseudo-precise and inadequate testing methods current in the modern psychosocial sciences, are particularly applicable to the procedures of the recent investigators of small groups.

Let us take, for example, R. F. Bales' instrumental procedure [14] as one of the best of these ornamental techniques imposed upon the essentially arbitrarily treated "speech-reactional" stuff manufactured in his "chatterbox" ("discussion") groups. At first glance, Bales' setting and procedures impress one as truly instrumental and objective. His "discussion group" meets in a special room equipped with a one-way mirror and a sound recorder, which permits the observer to see and to record what is going on in the room without being seen by the members of the "experimental group." Then there is another gadget—"the interaction recorder"—which enables the observer to record each "unit of speech" of each participant, and to place it into one of the twelve categories of speech-units which supposedly exhaust all the possible kinds of speech-units or actions of the members of "discussion" or "problem-solving group." These categories are as follows: (*1*) "shows solidarity; (*2*) shows tension release; (*3*) agrees; (*4*) gives suggestion; (*5*) gives opinion; (*6*) gives orientation; (*7*) asks for orientation; (*8*) asks for opinion; (*9*) asks for suggestion; (*10*) disagrees; (*11*) shows tension; (*12*) shows antagonism." The first three categories are labeled "social-emotional area: positive reactions"; the next three categories cover "task area: attempted answers." Categories *7, 8,* and *9* represent "task area: questions." The last three categories are again "social-emotional area: negative reactions." From another standpoint, categories *6* and *7* embrace "the problems of orientation"; *5* and *8,* "the problems of evaluation"; *4* and *9,* "the problems of control"; *3* and *10,* "the problems of decision"; *2* and *11,* "the problems of tension-management"; and, finally, *1* and *12,* "the problems of integration."

Armed with the interaction recorder, seeing and hearing everything that goes on in the one-way mirrored room, the observer objectively records every "speech-unit," indicating who uttered it and to whom it was addressed; simultaneously, he puts each speech-unit into one of the twelve categories. At the end of the session he has at his disposal a full record of all the speech-units of all the members. The total sum of recorded and classified speech-units also gives the observer the number and the time order of the speech-units in each category. These data enable the observer to analyze statistically the total sum of speech-units from several standpoints.

The studied groups fluctuated in size from two to ten and from three to six. Most of the groups consisted of Harvard undergraduates, obtained through the Harvard employment bureau. The students did not know each other prior to the first meeting. Each group had four meetings for discussion of a "human relations case."

This setting and procedure seemingly have all the earmarks of an objective, strictly observational, even experimental and quantitative study. Such details as a one-way mirror, a sound recorder, and an interaction recorder give a finishing touch to the apparently careful scientific nature of the investigation.

And yet, the slightest examination of the whole procedure with all its gadgets and other trimmings shows that it remains essentially subjective, superficial, inadequate and, as we shall see, often pointless. To begin with, Bales' "speech-unit" is neither given objectively as a real objective unit, nor is it defined clearly. Shall we regard as a "speech-unit" every single word or two or three or more words? Is it every single proposition consisting of subject, copula and predicate? Or is it a series of propositions dealing with the same subject? or a series of propositions showing similar emotional tension? or tension-release? or agreement? or disagreement? or evaluation? or what? If a speech-unit can be a series of propositions, how long can this series be? And so on, and so forth. This central concept (like the concepts of equilibrium and other basic concepts used by Bales) remains undefined. As a result, which words make a speech-unit is quite arbitrarily decided by the observer, according to his subjective notions and fancy. Since this central concept is undefined, the whole huge analytical and statistical superstructure built upon it remains a foggy mirage suspended in air.

If we ask, further, on what objective basis the incessant and rapidly flowing stream of vocal utterances of the members of the group—sometimes talking simultaneously—is cut into the "speech-units" and at the same time hastily pigeonholed into one of the twelve categories, the answer is that in many cases this also is done by an arbitrary, hasty, and impulsive fiat of the observer. Unlike electronic mathematical calculators, Bales' "interaction recorder" does not automatically classify speech-units. This is done by the observer in a great hurry, having no time for carefully analyzing whether the words belong to the category of "gives suggestion," or of "gives opinion," or of "gives orientation"; whether the words fall into the category of "disagrees," or of "shows tension," or of "shows antagonism." Even when an observer has plenty of time to determine correctly to which of the twelve categories certain words belong, he often is incapable of doing so correctly, for—as indicated above—the categories are often so similar and so overlapping that in many cases they are synonymous and do not permit a distinct choice. Then, "disagreement" is frequently expressed with "tension" and "antagonism." In such cases the observer cannot put such speech-units into any one of these three categories.

The net result is that, if not all, then a majority of the utterances incessantly pigeonholed by the observer into his categories, are placed there by subjective decisions made in a great rush, without carefully considering to which category each unit belongs, especially when he has to choose one of very similar categories. This means that not only the "speech-units" but even their categories are largely the products of the arbitrary and impulsive opinion of the observer. If these two basic things are thus subjective, all the main data of the study become subjective also. As a result, all the conclusions and results of the statistical analysis of this arbitrary mass of unreliable data also become subjective and doubtful. This brief analysis is sufficient to show the pseudo-objective, pseudo-experimental, pseudo-quantitative, and pseudo-scientific nature of these procedures. No gadgets, no one-way mirrors, no long series of figures and indices can hide this subjectivity.

To these defects we can add several others. I have already mentioned one of the important shortcomings of the set of twelve categories: even a careful investigator with plenty of time often cannot determine which words belong to which category, and whether these categories themselves are different from one another. From the standpoint of logical canon, Bales' classification is clumsy: it distinguishes categories that in fact and in the ordinary meanings of their terms are very similar (like "disagrees," "shows antagonism," and "shows tension," or "gives opinion," "gives suggestion," and "gives orientation"), and it unites into one category, like "gives orientation," such different meanings as "information, repetition, clarification and confirmation." "Repetition" is evidently not synonymous with "information," and "clarification" means something very different from "confirmation." For this reason, all the "typical" percentages of "speech-units" in each category allegedly occurring in discussion groups of various kinds, as well as some time-order uniformities dealing with the succession of categories, are practically meaningless, so far as such percentages and time-orders are supposed to reflect realities.

Furthermore, a mere glance at the categories shows that, at best, they aim to describe only the speech reactions of the participants. Bales' and other studies of small groups, omitting entirely the overt behavior of the participants and all the real motives of their actions, glide on the vocal surface. In this sense the studies dodge the real problems of group phenomena. This is an additional reason why the results of their studies are so meager, as we shall see in the next section.

Finally, the studied groups, usually made up of total strangers recruited through the employment service or by the order of the authorities, are unorganized or only slightly organized groups, whose members are not bound together by any durable and strong ties. The groups are momentarily put together and, after four sessions, as suddenly disappear. Such semi-nominal groups do not possess most of the main characteristics of the fully organized groups, and with them one consequently cannot observe and study most of the important properties of organized and even of unorganized groups. Therefore, there is not the slightest ground for extending the findings of a study of such plurels over the whole class of the organized, semi-organized, and unorganized groups. Bales and other investigators claim that the results of their studies can be generalized and applied to all discussion groups, planning groups, policy forming and executive committees, boards, panels, diagnostic councils, seminars, classrooms, teams and work groups, the family and household groups, children's play groups, adolescent gangs, cliques, clubs, recreational groups, "and small associations of various kinds." These grandiose claims are without foundation. A most superficial study of the "speech-units" of the family gathering, or of a boys' gang, or of work groups, would show at once that in content, frequency, time-order, and so on, the vocal behavior of such gatherings is very different from that of Bales' semi-nominal groups.

The totality of the above criticisms shows that Bales' method and procedures are very old; that various scientific trimmings of the old method are a mere veneer over the essentially subjective, arbitrary, and defective body of the old speech-reactional method, registering undefined "speech-units," classifying them into poorly defined categories, and statistically computing nobody knows exactly what sorts of units, what kind of vocal utterances, and so on.

These conclusions are fully applicable to the still more ancient, more superficial, more subjective method of "questions and answers" of other investigators of the small groups. They have neither discovered nor used any new method for a study of these groups, nor even any new scientific technique.

4) Since our investigators suffer from "amnesia" and "disorders of speech"; since their method of study is hoarily old, subjective, and defective; since the studied groups are mainly incidental and semi-nominal plurels, such studies can hardly yield important scientific results. Contrary to the ambitious claims of the investigators, this contention is well borne out by an examination of the results obtained by recent researchers of small groups.

The "discoveries" of our investigators of small groups consist of a large number of laboriously elaborated and ponderously formulated platitudes —right and wrong—of tautological propositions, of vaguely worded familiar statements, of "revelations" discovered long ago and more precisely formulated by the previous social thinkers, of fallaciously presented old generalizations, of distorted transcriptions of the propositions and uniformities of physical science, and of plain errors. Here are a few examples of these "discoveries" randomly picked up from the works of our investigators. These examples can be multiplied *ad libitum*.

"Interaction is a process consisting of action followed by reaction." [15] What a marvelous tautology of the type *A* is *A!* "[For leadership] there must be a group with a common task . . . and at least one must have responsibilities which differ from those of the other members" (R. M.

Stogdill).[16] How true! and almost as new as the discovery that "after the spring comes the summer, and after the summer, the fall," and so on. However, as often happens with platitudes, the statement forgets that sometimes the group and its common task are created by a leader.

"Some members [of a group] may be regarded as rating higher than others in leadership" [because they have responsibility for making the decisions].[17] An extraordinary new discovery, not a bit older than five thousand years.

"A significant aspect of our society is that persons desire membership in groups" (L. Festinger).[18] What a revelation this is, especially after Aristotle's "man is a naturally political animal" and "there is in all persons a natural impetus to associate with each other." [19]

No less striking are other of Festinger's "discoveries" about "why people seek membership in groups." The answer is that "groups frequently [help in] the attainment of important individual goals." The activities of the group are frequently attractive to the member. And they are attractive because people have needs that can be satisfied only in groups.

And so on. Proclaiming these platitudes, the author forgets to mention several important limitations of these verities, like the fact that millions of persons become members of a group automatically, regardless of their wishes; e.g., state citizenship automatically imposed upon all those born from the citizens of the state; and sometimes many individuals, such as prisoners of war and criminals, are coerced into belonging to the prisoner of war group or to the group of inmates in a prison, contrary to their wishes. And such "automatic" and "undesirable" memberships play a much more important role in the life of hundreds of millions than the voluntary or sought for memberships.

"[In the groups] we have the simultaneous existence of forces tending to move the people in and out of groups and forces restraining such movement. Groups differ in their attraction for members, and members differ in how satisfying the group membership is for them." [20]

Again, how primitive and vague this generalization is in comparison with the much more developed, analyzed, even empirically documented and statistically measured, theory of the general and differential metabolism of groups elaborated by the "old-fashioned sociologists" [21] long before the investigators of the small groups.

The same conclusion applies to Festinger's "discoveries" about the relationship between friendship (or enmity) and territorial and "functional" propinquity and about the conditions of successful community action, and to practically all of Festinger's conclusions, allegedly derived from his "experimental" studies of the Regent Hill and Westgate groups. Each of his roughly sound conclusions was incomparably better formulated, developed, and demonstrated by investigators of the preceding generations. What is still more important, the older scholars not only gave more generalized formulae but also most of the important limitations and main variations of these formulae, ordinarily absent in the vague conclusions of the recent "observers" of small groups.

Let us now take the discoveries concerning the "cohesiveness" of groups. The term "cohesiveness" means "the total field of forces which act on members to remain in the groups" (John Thibaut).[22] The term, as well as its definition, is a distorted version of mechanical propositions borrowed from physical science. For many a freshman in the social and physical sciences it may sound quite scientific. For a senior in these disciplines, it is an extremely vague and inadequate statement to apply to the forces which maintain the unity, identity and continuity of social groups. Without a preliminary differentiation between the kinds of the groups whose "cohesiveness" is studied, no real understanding of the forms and "forces of cohesiveness" is possible. The point is that there are "voluntary" and "coercive groups"—or, more exactly, the "familistic," the "contractual," and the "compulsory" groups. The basic difference of these groups from one another manifests itself also in the fundamental difference between various "forces of cohesiveness" in each type of group. The factors which unite the members of a good family into one unity and which maintain its identity, "cohesiveness," and continuity are quite different from the factors of cohesiveness that cause the inmates of a prison "to remain in the group." The forces that keep together the employees and the employer of a business firm are again different from those of the family, of a prison group, or of the American Sociological Society.

This differentiation of the types of groups and the types of bonds that keep the members of various types together is not made at all in the studies of Thibaut and others. As a result, all their industrious efforts to study the cohesiveness of small groups scientifically have not yielded a single new significant discovery. Taken together all the studies of group cohesiveness by the apostles of "Group Dynamics," and by other investigators of small groups, have not promoted our knowledge of this old problem at all. In comparison with the existing body of knowledge in this field, their theories, their "discovered" uniformities, and their total grasp of the problem in all its main ramifications, still remain at a primitive stage, passed long ago by the psychosocial sciences.[23] Their "discoveries" represent either a rediscovery of the table of multiplication, or the discovery that the law of gravitation is applicable not only to Camel cigarettes but also to Chesterfields.

Here is a further example of a largely meaningless statement taken from the physical sciences. "The attraction to the group is a function of the resultant forces acting on the member to belong to the group." [24] What "resultant forces"? and how do they act on the members? In mechanics all these terms are strictly defined and measurable. Here they remain just vague words. Being apparently unacquainted with the vast existing body of careful studies of "cohesiveness" in the psychosocial disciplines, our explorers can hardly help but make discoveries of this kind. Here, as in other similar cases, "it does not pay to be ignorant."

Let us continue to examine the "discoveries" of our "pioneers." Here are further examples of tautology.

"The term [group] cohesiveness refers to phenomena which come into existence if, and only if, the group exists." How wonderful!

The more a group is needed for satisfaction of the needs of an individual, the greater is the valence (attraction) of the group. "Any reduction in the ability of the group to meet the needs of a member will decrease the attractiveness of the group for him" (Cartwright).

Or, "The members of a group who are . . . friends . . . are likely to be more interested in one another as persons, perhaps more supportive of each other, more cordial in interpersonal relations." What a revelation again! and note especially an extreme "scientific" caution in this remarkable "perhaps." Until now we naively thought—without any "perhaps"—that "friendship" implies the mutual interest, cordiality, and support of the friends.[25]

"The more prestige a person has within a group, the more will he be attracted to the group" (Cartwright). "Kelly found that the high status job with the implied threat of demotion, and the low status post with the impossibility of promotion, were the most undesirable positions." "For the group members a cooperative relationship is more attractive [than a competitive one]." [26]

Reading these revelations I am inclined to borrow G. Saintsbury's expression: "O clichés! O tickets! O fudge!" [27]

But let us continue: "An increase in the frequency of interaction between persons may increase the strength of their favorable sentiment toward one another." [28] So the more frequently German and American soldiers fight (interact), the more favorable will be the sentiment they develop toward one another. Consequently, the fighting and hating interaction is as good a means for the development of mutual admiration, sympathy, and altruism as is mutual help. Fortunately for Homans, at the end of the paragraph stating and developing this "scientific" generalization, he seems to have grasped its one-sided fallacy and has therefore added, in just four words, two other possible consequences of frequent interaction, namely, development "of respect or, worst, antagonism." Like other members of small-groups "specialists," Homans entirely passes over the enormous literature on this question. These previous studies formulated, with fair precision, under what conditions an increase in the frequency of specified types of interaction leads to mutual friendship or "favorable sentiment," and under which conditions it leads to mutual indifference or to mutual antagonism.[29] But let us proceed with our examples.

"Splinter-group formation will disrupt the larger organization when the goals of the smaller group are incompatible with those of the larger." Again, what a beautiful tautology! Splinter-groups tend to splint or disrupt! But, as happens with many tautologies, the statement in this form is inadequate because instead of disrupting the larger group, the splinter-group more frequently is suppressed by the larger group. Empirically one-sided also is the statement that "the tendency to break apart would be more likely, the larger the group." [30] If the generalization were true, no large groups like great empires, world religious organizations, or large labor unions, could emerge and have a long life-span. As a matter of fact, during the historical existence of mankind there have always been large groups, and they have had much longer life-spans than the small groups.[31] Schism in large groups is often counterbalanced by the influx of many small groups desirous of the advantages and protection of the large groups, not to mention the considerable resourcefulness of the large groups in suppressing or curing the schisms of splinter-groups. In passing, it can be noted that in the works of Toynbee and some other "armchair philosophers" one finds a much deeper and more scientific analysis of schism or of splinter-groups than in all the "scientific" studies of the investigators of small groups taken together.

Here are further examples of the "discoveries" discussed. Bales and his associates start their paper with the usual "amnesiac" claim:

> The frequencies of communication between members in small face-to-face groups show certain striking regularities which have not previously been described. . . . The detection of these regularities represents a significant gain in our knowledge about the distribution of communication in small groups, and provides a basic framework of order within which many more detailed analyses of the interaction process may be made.[32]

Quite a modest claim! Now let us see what the discovered "striking and significant regularities" are. Since they concern units of acts, we have to learn what is meant by "the unit of act." The answer is:

> If the act is verbal, the unit is usually the simple subject-predicate combination. If the act is non-verbal, the unit is the smallest overt segment of behavior that has "meaning" to others in the group.[33]

The definition of the unit of act seems to be clear. And yet, it is not helpful at all. In verbal acts, shall I view as one unit the following utterances? "Help!" "Kiss me!" "I was saying, but forget it!" "And although religion teaches us much on this subject [the nature of our souls and their immortality], nevertheless, I confess in myself an infirmity which seems to be common to the greater part of mankind; namely, that though we wish to believe and even think we believe strongly all that religion teaches us, yet, are we not usually so touched by it as by what has been brought home to us by natural and clear reason" (Descartes).

The exclamatory utterances do not have any subject or predicate; therefore, according to Bales' definition, they are not units of verbal acts. Descartes' statement consists of many words and has several grammatical subjects and predicates; and yet, its meaning is grasped only when the whole statement is read. Shall we take the whole statement as one unit? or shall we divide it into several units? If so, on what basis?

These examples show that Bales' definition of the verbal unit hardly defines it at all and leaves the whole matter to the arbitrary decision of a "surveyor of verbal units."

Still worse is the definition of the unit of the non-verbal act. How many act-units are produced by the uninterrupted writing of an individual for 5 or 15 or 50 minutes? One? Five? Fifty? or what? How many act-units are there in the action of a person who wants to sit down and who, for that purpose, takes three steps to the chair, grasps the chair and moves it, then bends his knees, adjusts his trousers, and finally sits down? One unit, or as many units as there are different observable motions: three steps, grasping the chair, moving it, bending the knees, adjusting the trousers, and sitting down? If we take all these actions as one unit of one meaningful action of sitting down, then, assuming that the person sits down in order to read a book, what hinders us from taking as one unit all the numerous actions, including sitting down, that are components or means-actions for the one meaningful action of reading the book? If reading the book itself is one of the means-actions for an investigation of, say, small groups, then what keeps us from considering as one unit all the various actions necessary for realization of one action of research? Each of these means-actions for the end-action (research) acquires its real meaning only when it is taken in the total set of actions involved in the task of research. Such a "macroscopic" interpretation of the act-unit is in agreement with Bales' definition.

On the other hand, if one wants to take as a unit each elementary microscopic action, then one can make not only eight units from the above action of sitting down, but a much larger number of units because one can break into several units each step made, extension of a hand to grasp the chair, motion of fingers to grasp, grasping, turning the body, and so on, breaking each of eight units into several more elementary units. Such microscopic units will also be in agreement with Bales' definition of the unit of act.

These considerations mean that in reality Bales' definition does not define the unit of act at all. According to one's fancy, one can inflate this unit to a magnitude consisting of many actions, and one can deflate it to the extent of the motion of a single muscle or gland or a part of the body. When such an inflating-deflating balloon of act-unit is made the foundation of quantitative research, all the complex computations, and all "the striking uniformities" derived from these computations, automatically become arbitrary and fictitious.

Having cleared this basic point, let us glance now at "the striking uniformities" discovered by the authors. Here they are:

> The findings reported indicate that if participants in a small group are ranked by the total number of acts they initiate, they will also tend to be ranked: (1) by the number of acts they receive; (2) by the number of acts they address to specific other individuals; and, (3) by the number of acts they address to the group as a whole.[34]

In plain words these ponderous "uniformities" mean that in a discussion group the persons who talk more frequently, and so initiate more suggestions, tend to talk more frequently to the other members and to the group as a whole, and are more frequently talked back to by the members whom they address. Or, to express the whole matter still more concisely: the most talkative members of a group talk more frequently and are talked back to more frequently than the less talkative members. From this beautiful tautology we can derive an additional "striking and significant uniformity" overlooked by Bales: the persons who are silent, talk less frequently, and are talked back to less frequently than the talkative persons.

However, Bales' tautology can, in no way, be considered a general empirical rule for all groups. In the courtroom group consisting of the judge, the accused, the prosecuting and the defense attorneys, and the jury, most of the talks—contrary to Bales' uniformity—are addressed to the jury and the judge. The jury, as a rule, remains silent, instead of talking most; even the judge ordinarily talks less than the attorneys. A lecturer, a preacher, a commander of a platoon issuing orders, are the only talking members of their respective groups. In a large number of groups, all the talking members address themselves to "Mr. Chairman!"; and Mr. Chairman often talks the least in the group. And so on.

Bales' "uniformities" are exceptions rather than rules, from the standpoint of the real processes of talking in the overwhelming majority of small and large groups. And what is still more important, no painstaking and misleading research of Bales' type is necessary for discovering the order, frequency, and the kind of talks by various members of almost all organized groups: all this can easily be found in the constitution of such groups. The laws and bylaws of each organized group supply incomparably more accurate information on all these points than the vague and largely fictitious uniformities of the investigators.

Let us close these examples with what appears to be an "epoch-making discovery," achieved by the cooperative effort of an investigator of small groups and of the producers of "theoretical frameworks" for all "social actions" and all the psychosocial sciences of all times. Here are the first two of the four discoveries of this sort.

> The Principle of Inertia: A given process of action will continue unchanged in rate and direction unless impeded or deflected by opposing motivational forces.
>
> The Principle of Action and Reaction: If, in a system of action, there is a change in the direction of a process, it will tend to be balanced by a complementary change which is equal in motivational force and opposite in direction.[35]

One can ask, what are the reasons for, and the sense of, these distorted transcriptions of Newtonian principles, or of the D'Alembert-Lagrange principle of "virtual displacement—work-velocity," or of the Bernoulli-Cournot principles of oscillation? If the reason is mere transcription, then the principles of these great physicists should be transcribed exactly as they are formulated by Newton, D'Alembert, Lagrange, Bernoulli, and Cournot (though I doubt that Parsons, Bales, and Shils know these principles). If Parsons' and Bales' propositions aim to be the basic principles of human or social action, then they are either meaningless or outright fallacious. They are meaningless because without units of space, time, change, direction, or vector and force, neither the change of action, nor the rate of its change, nor its direction, nor its motivational force, nor "equal" and "opposing" force can be determined, defined, and measured. Since the authors give none of these units, their first proposition is void. It is mere imitative verbiage. If we try to squeeze from it a vague meaning, namely, that without impeding or deflecting forces a given action will continue unchanged for an indefinitely long time, then the proposition is empirically fallacious. Concretely it means that if one starts to eat or to micturate, providing there is no interference of external deflecting or inhibiting forces, one will be forever eating or micturating at the same "rate" and in the same "direction" to the end of his life—except that there would be no end to his life, because his eating or micturating "will continue unchanged in rate and direction," forever and ever! Besides the empirical absurdity of their "principles," the authors of these "striking laws" evidently forget two basic principles: that of immanent change of a system and that of limit. According to the principle of immanent change, any system, even in a constant environment, incessantly changes "from within" for the reason that the system is a going concern.

The idling motion of the best automobile engine in the best constant environment cannot help changing the engine in due time for the reason of its running. The healthiest organism, put in a constant environment, also cannot help changing from childhood to old age, for the reason of its being a going concern. So, also, any real social or cultural system changes immanently because it is a going concern. The second principle forgotten by our authors is "the principle of limit." According to it, for any change in a certain direction there always is a limit. When a system reaches this limit, it either changes the direction of its previous change, or radically transforms itself or disintegrates.[36]

In the light of these principles and of empirical evidence, Parsons' and Bales' Principle of Inertia is logical and empirical nonsense. The same is true of their "principle of action and reaction." It is again a poorly understood and distorted transcription of the principles of physics. As long as the authors do not give any unit of space, of direction, of change, of force, and so on, their principle remains mere verbiage. If we try to take the words of the proposition for what they mean, then no change can take place in any system of action, because any tendency to change will be counterbalanced by "the opposite and equal motivational force." Consequently, all actions will be forever frozen in the form in which they either appeared or were created for the first time. If one's primordial prototype action was eating or chopping wood, one will forever be eating or chopping wood, unless some external force interferes. Thus one of the surprising conclusions of the authors' principle is that no change of any action is possible and, unless some external force interferes, we are, like a marble statue, damned to be frozen forever in our primordial state.

These remarks make unnecessary a criticism of Parsons' and Bales' subsequent "principles of effort and of system-integration."[37] If anything, they are still more meaningless or fallacious than the principles of their "home-made" inertia and action-reaction. One general remark is, however, advisable. In all their four principles and in a special paper of Bales ("The Equilibrium Problem in Small Groups"), the authors supposedly deduce these principles from the basic principle of equilibrium. They fail, however, to define clearly this basic concept. From their vague statements one gathers that by equilibrium they mean one of the five different meanings this term has; namely, equilibrium "as a tendency of a social system, when disturbed, to return to its previous status, or to hold its 'normal' trend or level." [38] Groping around this concept of equilibrium, they do not understand fully its real meaning in physics, are unaware of the four other quite different meanings of "equilibrium," and, what is most important, do not realize that none of these five different concepts is applicable to psychosocial systems and congeries. Used by many economists, sociologists, psychologists, political scientists, and so on, the term has only an analogical value, and more often than not it becomes meaningless or conveys fallacious notions.[39] The same is true of the use of "equilibrium" by other "social physicists," by investigators of small groups, by a whole legion of physicalistic sociologists and psychologists, and by social scientists generally. As a result of this basic defect, a multitude of meaningless or wrong "principles" are manufactured daily.

It is high time to humbly ask the manufacturers of this sort of "laws" to study, before promulgating their spurious "principles," what the imitated principles really mean in the physical sciences, then ponder a little to what extent they can be applied to the study of psychosocial phenomena, and, if in some form they may be applied, what their psychosocial modification can really mean, and how they can be empirically verified and measured. Until this sort of preparation is made, no social scientist can offer a useful transcription of the principles and laws of physical sciences.

If there were need, one could go, page by page, through the published studies of the recent investigators of small groups. On almost every page one would find the "discoveries," concepts, definitions, and theories represented by the given examples. Carefully reading these works I have not found any single new discovery of even tertiary importance. And I have found a superabundance of "pseudo-discoveries". More specifically, one can make the following observations about these researches:

The investigators are strikingly ignorant of the most important studies in the fields of the problems they are investigating.

In spite of the strong penchant of our explorers to ponderous "conceptualization," or "theorizing," their concepts, definitions, hypotheses, and formulations are conspicuously clumsy, vague, and defective—logically, semantically, and empirically. Very rarely, if at all, do they display a minimum of clarity, logic, or enlightening insight.

Their discoveries abound with platitudes, both right and wrong; with a multitude of tautological propositions; with valid propositions laboriously arrived at but discovered long before them; with numerous one-sided conclusions partly true but mainly false, in spite of the fact that adequate formulations have been made by previous psychosocial investigators; with a plethora of "rouge and powder"—pseudo-experiments, pseudo-quantitative indices, pseudo-scientific terminology, pseudo-gadgets, etc.—hiding the defective body of their theories and procedures; and, finally, with a superabundance of very ambitious claims concerning their pioneering role, and with a superabundance of mutual compliments between the members of this "closed club." Factually walking in a well-cultivated park they picture themselves as great pioneer-explorers opening hitherto unknown land.[40]

With this summary our exploration of the explorers of the small groups can be concluded.

# *Chapter Eleven*

# Predictability and Scientific Theory

## 1. Predictability as Evidence of a Theory's Validity

Above, in the chapter on operationalism, it has been shown why predictability is neither the necessary nor the sufficient evidence that a theory is true or scientific. Almost all propositions regarding the history of man, of animal species (biological evolution), of the earth, and of the heavenly bodies deal exclusively with the past and the present, and rarely, if ever, with the future. As such the historical propositions do not predict anything, insofar as prediction means forecasting a future event. In spite of this, most of the statements of historical science are found to be scientifically correct. Even an addict of predictability cannot find an error in historical statements like the following one: "On the evening of the 16th (of December, 1773) some 8,000 people assembled in and near Boston's Old South Church [and] disguised as Mohawk Indians rushed to Griffin's Wharf, boarded the tea ships, and dumped all the tea (342 chests) into the harbor." The statements of historical science thus present a vast body of propositions which have no relationship to prediction; and yet, these statements are scientific. Likewise, practically all mathematical statements contain propositions which have the highest possible validity and which, again, have little to do with predictability. The statement: "two times two is four" is valid for the past, the present, and the future; it has nothing to do with a time-factor, especially with a prediction of the future event; therefore, it is not a "predictive" proposition. There are a vast number of statements in the various sciences that are true but still are free from predictive elements. The total body of such propositions and theories occupies a very large place in the total system of scientifically true propositions. This means that correct prediction is *not* a necessary characteristic of a scientific or true theory.

On the other hand, correct prediction is insufficient evidence for making a proposition or theory scientific. Side by side with a legion of wrong predictions, innumerable correct forecastings have been made by the oracles, prognosticators, astrologers, crystal gazers, prophets, and medicine men of different societies and periods on the basis of wrong theory or of no theory at all. In our time many lucky forecasts are made daily, but they are sheer guesswork, without any theory, or with wrong theory as the basis of the guess. A lucky prognostication is not evidence that a wrong theory is scientific.

Moreover, now and then a scientific theory yields a wrong prediction, either because the theory is misinterpreted in making the forecast or because, being valid within its stipulated conditions, the theory fails to consider the possibility of interference by unforeseen, powerful factors that neutralize the predicted effects. Facts of this kind indicate again that right or wrong prediction is insufficient evidence of the scientific or unscientific nature of a theory. Consequently, the contention of our empiricists on this point becomes invalid. And if this is invalid, there is a great lessening of importance and scientific content in the elaboration of innumerable tests, statistical devices, mathematical formulae, the weighing and ranking of different variables, factor-analysis, and other impressive paraphernalia for predicting happy marriage, or success in school, or the results of election, or business conditions, or the recidivism of a probated criminal, and so on.[1]

This does not mean that correct predictability is unimportant theoretically or practically. It means two things: first, as we have said, predictability is not a necessary or sufficient criterion of a theory being scientific; and second, though correct forecasting is very important practically, it meets so many and such great difficulties, that a correct prediction of especially complex, rarely repeated, important psychosocial processes becomes hardly possible. No matter how impressive the statistical, experimental, and mathematical paraphernalia of such predictions, if and when they are made, they always are a sort of adventurous guess rather than a true scientific prediction. As a guess they may or may not come true.

Note, this statement concerns complex and infrequently repeated processes and events. Predictions of endlessly repeated processes—such as the prediction that "every human being will die," or that "if an individual lives a full human life, he will pass from childhood to maturity and senility"—are quite possible, but no scientific research is needed for such platitudes. Likewise, predictions of frequently repeated mass-processes, like the next year's birth, marriage, death, and divorce rates for a given population, are also possible with a certain degree of accuracy, provided no extraordinary unforeseen factors interfere. Prediction becomes increasingly uncertain: (a) as we pass to more vast and complex processes, infrequently or irregularly repeated, or not repeated at all, or repeated under very different conditions; (b) as the future time-moment of the predicted event becomes increasingly removed from the present; and (c) as the number and heterogeneity of the various forces involved progressively increase. In regard to such processes or events hardly any scientific prediction is possible, because at the present moment there are no solid scientific bases for predictions of this sort. As early as 1936 I stressed the lack of these necessary bases.[2] Since that time, the developments of physical science have greatly reinforced my arguments. The arguments of my paper, supplemented by today's position of physical science, and by typical examples of "lucky" and unlucky predictions, will clarify my statement.

## 2. Uncertainty of the Bases of Prediction

Theoretically we can distinguish three types of predictions according to their bases: *causal, probabilistic,* and prediction on the basis of the *immanent self-regulation and self-determination of a sociocultural system or of the integrated individual.* In regard to the individual, it often assumes a form of *voluntaristic prediction* followed by active efforts to make it true.

*Causal prediction* is based upon two main assumptions: first, that definite causal laws determine sociocultural processes or events; second, that a perfect knowledge of these causal laws is possible.

*Probabilistic prediction* views most events and processes as chance phenomena. Among these it distinguishes the single, unique, unrepeated phenomena and the large aggregates of repeated phenomena. Most of the unique and unrepeated chance phenomena do not show any visible order or uniformity; therefore, they cannot be predicted. The large aggregates of repeated phenomena often manifest a certain order or uniformity. According to the probability theory, the greater the number of the observed uniform repetitions of a given event or process, and the lesser the number of exceptions to the observed uniformity in these recurrences, the higher the probability of the recurrence of the observed uniformity; the more certain the prediction. Probabilistic predictions view the predicted phenomena as chance congeries.

*Predictions on the basis of the self-regulation and self-direction of a sociocultural system or of the integrated individual* deal only with systems and not with congeries. Viewing a sociocultural system as a logically or aesthetically consistent meaningful unity in which each part tangibly depends upon other parts and the whole, and the whole depends on each and all of the parts, predictions of this kind require a thorough knowledge of the structural and dynamic properties of a given system, and especially of its meaningful component, of the main phases of its whole life cycle and of the properties unfolded in each phase. This thorough knowledge of the system is supplemented by observation of other systems of the same kind and of their life cycles recurring under similar and under different conditions. On the basis of this knowledge, which combines, in a sense, the causal and probabilistic analysis and supplements it with an analysis of the meaningful component of the system, an investigator is equipped to predict a number of things that may occur with the system in the future.

*Voluntaristic prediction* is a specific form of this type of prediction. Viewing an individual or an organized group as a meaningful system, consciously trying to realize its goals or its "manifest destiny," voluntaristic prediction believes especially in the all-important role of human volition and effort. Voluntaristic prediction is the purposive setting of a future goal, accompanied by a decision to achieve it by the efforts of the predictors or of other specific persons and groups.

Thus we have the following assumptions for these types of prediction:

(a) The principle of causal determinism; (b) the principle of chance; (c) belief in the possibility of a complete knowledge of the factors and conditions of the predicted phenomena; (d) the principle of immanent self-determination of a system, supplemented by a belief in the decisively important role of human volition and effort in determining the course of sociocultural processes and of individual life.

How solid are these bases, and to what extent can they be used for the purposes of prediction?

*a*) As to the *principles of determinism and indeterminism,* both are of uncertain validity. My study of the comparative domination of each of these theories from 580 B.C. to A.D. 1920 shows that they alternate in their rise and decline and in their domination. For instance, indeterminism dominates over determinism, in the sense of being viewed as a truer theory than determinism, from the sixth to the twelfth centuries A.D. Determinism dominates over indeterminism in the centuries from the third to the first B.C., and from the seventeenth to the end of the nineteenth century A.D.[3] This means that both of these principles are still a matter of belief rather than proven scientific theory. As a matter of belief they can hardly serve as a solid foundation for any certain prediction. If in the nineteenth century the deterministic credo was fairly generally accepted as the last word of science, at the present time this credo has lost a large part of its prestige and is being increasingly replaced in the physical sciences by the principle of chance and probability. The change has been so great that some physicists, like H. Margenau, call it "causal catastrophe." Quantum mechanics and subatomic physics have substituted Heisenberg's principle of uncertainty and principle of chance for all sorts of causal determinism. "The laws of physics and chemistry are statistical [or probabilistic but not causal] throughout," is the way the situation is summed up by E. Schrödinger, one of the eminent leaders of today's physical science.[4]

> The experimental facts and the nature of the theory by which we are best able to cope with them unite to convince us that the extrapolation from large scale experimental work on the basis of which the dogma of absolute physical determinism has been formulated is not legitimate. . . . The physical universe is ultimately only partly deterministic. The principle of causality is of limited scope. Quantum theory views the principle of determinism as an invalid extrapolation from experience. . . . In the microscopical world of modern physics [there are no causal uniformities; instead there are ambiguity, uncertainty and discontinuity].[5]

Such is the summary of the situation by another eminent physicist.

In the microcosm there reigns "lawlessness," "atomic uncertainties," "chance." "No theory has yet been proposed to render the vagaries [of the individual atomic system] understandable in detail, none is able to predict it. Indeed, Heisenberg's principle says precisely that such predictions are impossible"—so is the standpoint of modern physics formulated by still another leading physicist.

He views historical events as "reaching by their roots the chaos of microcosm" and, therefore, in part being chance phenomena. In historical events we have "the multitude of immediacies over which physical causation has lost its direct control. A sensation, a will, an action, psychological introspection belong to this class." In such a historical universe there is a place for "voluntaristic decision" as an important factor of historical processes.

> The new physics . . . leaves greater room for [voluntaristic] action. Because what is now dynamically determined is a probability, not a necessity. There is no cause for fatalism, but accentuated need for action . . . Decision fits neatly into the spaces presented by the semi-deterministic honeycomb of historical reality. . . . Along with these developments, man has been transformed from a spectator [observer] to an active participant in the drama of becoming. Room has been made for decision and choice, which had no place in the older scheme of things. What was formerly fate has become history.
>
> Causality can fail for various reasons. Chief among them is the use of states so top-heavy with variables as to be useless for prediction. Such is the predicament in which many of the social and biological sciences are caught at present.[6]
>
> [The law of chance is] the most fundamental and indispensable of all physical laws [and all predictions in the physical sciences are based upon] the assumption of noncorrelation of the behavior of individual particles, which is derived from the law of chance.[7]

The pendulum has moved again away from the principle of universal causal determinism towards the principles of chance probability and voluntaristic decision of man. This signifies that no certain prediction is possible on the basis of such an uncertain principle as universal causal determinism. Finally, this shows again the antiquated theory of our psychosocial determinists endeavoring to predict and control sociocultural phenomena on the basis of the causal determinism of the two preceding centuries. We again find them thinking in terms of what was believed before and what has been largely relinquished by today's physical science. If, instead of causal determinism, "we try to lean in our predictions upon indeterministic assumptions, the situation becomes still worse, because the very concept of indeterminism implies a denial of any uniform or definite relationship between two or more variables. By its very nature indeterminism in its application to human affairs rules out of existence all causal and functional uniformities. In one case A may be followed by consequence B; in another, by C; in a third, by D; and so on. . . . Under such circumstances no forecasting of the future upon the basis of the past is possible." [8]

*b*) With the replacement of causal determinism by *"colorless probabilities"* microphysics has found that in large aggregates of atoms the unpredictable continuity of the "motion" of single or small numbers of atoms between "jumps" is replaced by a sort of probabilistic order which can be calculated and predicted. "Probabilities congeal to certainties when the masses in question become large." This suggests that if sociocultural events cannot be predicted on the basis of causality, perhaps they can be predicted as chance phenomena on the basis of probability theory. If we cannot predict the behavior of single or small aggregates of psychosocial phenomena, can we, perhaps, predict these phenomena with high probability when they are taken on a mass scale, in large aggregates?

The idea seems to be reasonable and in part it has already been used by the social sciences in their statistical observation and probabilistic prediction of such mass phenomena as death, birth, marriage, divorce, and suicide rates, business conditions. In these fields, *short-time* predictions have been moderately successful, more frequently right than wrong. However, even in these few fields the predictions now and then have failed. In a large number of other fields either no predictions have been attempted or, if ventured, they have failed at least as frequently as they have come true. In subsequent sections of this chapter typical examples of recent wrong predictions will be given.

The reasons for the failures of such predictions are at hand. In physics, by large aggregates of atoms are meant aggregates consisting of millions, billions, and still larger numbers of units. In the psychosocial sciences we still do not know what a "large aggregate" of psychosocial phenomena means, and how large it must be for the purposes of predictions. One hundred events or persons of the same kind? A few thousands? A few millions? In statistics we talk of "representative samples," but a statistical "representative sample" is something very different from the large aggregate of psychosocial phenomena sufficient for manifesting some uniformity and thereby for the purposes of predictions. Even the problem of a "representative sample" still remains an unsolved problem for many mass phenomena. Such are the initial uncertainties we have to face in our probabilistic predictions of complex psychosocial phenomena.

The second difficulty is still more formidable. The greater the number of observed recurrences of a uniformity, and the fewer the observed exceptions to it, the higher the coefficient of probability. When the number of the observed recurrences of a certain uniformity is practically unlimited, and no exception to the rule is observed, the probability becomes equal to 1 and turns into a certainty. For instance, the alternation of day and night has been observed millions of times by millions of human beings and, so far, no certain exception to this uniformity has been noticed. For this reason one can predict with certainty that after this night there will come tomorrow, and this alternation is likely to continue hundreds and thousands of years from now, as long as the sun and the earth remain essentially the same as they are now. Also, of course, the fewer the recurrences of an observed uniformity, and the greater the number of observed exceptions to it, the lower the probability index.

Most of the complex psychosocial phenomena—like war and peace, revolution and stable order, prosperity and depression; the creative growth and decline of nations, cultures, civilizations, religions, sciences, fine arts; the emergence, organization, and disorganization of social groups; fluctuations of monarchical and republican governments, of totalitarian and democratic regimes, of classicism and romanticism, of materialism and idealism, of monogamic and non-monogamic marriage, of sexual chastity and licentiousness, of increases and decreases of criminality and mental disease—these and thousands of other sociocultural phenomena have recurred only a limited number of times in known human history, and of these recurrences a still smaller number have actually been observed and recorded. Moreover, they have recurred irregularly in time and space, under different conditions—each monarchy or republic has been different from other monarchies or republics. Such recurrences are too small in number, too heterogeneous in character and conditions, too non-periodical in the time span of recurrence, too scattered in physical and social space, to be satisfactory material for calculating their probability. If, in a very rough way, the calculation is made, the coefficient of probability is bound to be too low to have a real predictive value. With proper modification, the same can be said of the predictions concerning rarely repeated events in the life of an individual, especially when the change is predicted to occur in a remote future.

It must be stressed that not only the smaller number of recurrences or units of an aggregate of sociocultural phenomena, but also their heterogeneity and the diversity of the conditions of their recurrence, make their prediction much less certain than predictions applied to large aggregates of atoms in the physical sciences. There, all atoms of hydrogen or oxygen are assumed to be identical. In the psychosocial universe each human individual, each marriage or murder, each revolution or war, each monarchy or republic, are different from other phenomena of the same class. And each of these phenomena occur under conditions tangibly different from those under which other phenomena of the same class happen. These are additional difficulties for accurate prediction of the complex psychosocial and historical phenomena.

Add to this the exceptionally dynamic variability and creative character of many psychosocial processes. Creativity means an unforeseen, masterly realization of a new discovery, hitherto unknown and unpredicted. It is always a miracle, unexpected and often undreamed of by any except the creator. Sometimes it is a surprise even for the creator himself. Other conditions being equal, phenomena which vary highly and irregularly are less predictable than phenomena which vary little and vary regularly. Truly creative processes largely defy any prediction. Facing such processes —for instance, observing Beethoven starting to write a new symphony— the predictor can hardly even guess what kind of notes Beethoven will be putting on paper. The predictor is totally helpless in forecasting this "little matter" if he is entirely ignorant of the previous compositions of Beethoven. But even if he knows these compositions, he still would be unable to predict the general character of the new symphony—for instance, whether it is going to be the *Eroica* or the *Pastoral* symphony—and the overwhelmingly larger part of the score. If he were able to do so, then he and all predictors would have been Beethovens or Bachs. The total creativity of historical processes is still more complex than Beethoven's creative activity. This creative dynamism of human history, alone, makes the prediction of important historical events almost impossible. The dynamism and creative nature of historical or sociocultural processes—taken together with the small number of observed uniformities, the irregular character of their occurrence in time and space, the heterogeneity of units within the same class or aggregate of units, and the diversity of conditions under which the unit-recurrences occur—do not allow either certain or high-probability prediction concerning many events and processes in the life of an individual, group, nation, culture, and mankind. As a matter of fact, hardly any probabilistic predictions of events or processes of this sort can be much different from the sheer guess of a common sense observer.

These considerations explain why the principle of chance probability has some, but limited, use in predicting complex, rarely repeated, creative, psychosocial or historical phenomena, when they are sociocultural congeries but not systems. If the only bases for predicting sociocultural events were causal determinism and chance probability, the predictors would do well to close up shop except for a couple of hours one day a week: there would not be enough honest prediction-business to do for the rest of the week. (This does not exclude a great demand for fraudulent prediction-business and for various quack predictors. These, however, do not concern us here.)

*c*) As for belief in the possibility of a sufficient knowledge of all the important factors and processes involved in, and necessary for, accurate prediction, such a belief pertains more to things hoped for than to the actual situation. Existing knowledge is especially insufficient with regard to predicting complex, irregular, infrequently repeated events, processes, and phenomena. Here the door is wide open to the intrusion of all sorts of unforeseen and unsuspected factor-visitors. The roots and branches of such complex processes spread so widely that they cannot help but come into interaction with the roots and branches of many other processes, agencies, or variables. Only an omniscient mind could possibly know all the factors involved in the process or phenomenon whose future course, direction, tempo, position, and properties are to be predicted. An experimental study shows that even the much simpler and better known phenomena cannot be predicted accurately. Each person knows himself and his own behavior possibly better than others, and others' behavior. We are equipped with better knowledge to forecast our own behavior than to forecast the behavior of others. Yet, our study shows[9] that one cannot forecast it with accuracy even for the next twenty-four hours; and the error increases with an increase of the time span. One hundred and six unemployed persons were asked to write on a special sheet each evening how they were going to spend the next twenty-four hours, listing as exactly as possible every activity and the duration of each activity. On the next day, with the aid of special supervisors, they had to check how they actually spent the twenty-four hours. For more than three months such forecasting and checking continued, extending for each of our subjects through some 2,000 hours, and for all together through more than 200,000 hours. In a similar manner they forecasted how each would spend "the day after tomorrow," then "the day one week hence," then "the day one month hence." The main results of the study are as follows. (1) The prediction of tomorrow's behavior for each of the 106 cases erred, on an average, by 305 minutes per day, an error of fully one-fifth of the day. (2) The prediction for "the day after tomorrow" erred by an average of 353 minutes, or almost 6 hours of the day. (3) The prediction for "the day one week hence" erred by 331 minutes. The slight decrease is probably due to a certain rhythmical routine in the way we spend our Mondays or Tuesdays from week to week. (4) The error of the prediction for "the day one month from now" came to an average of 494 minutes per day per individual. (5) The error increased to 536 minutes in the prediction for "the Sunday one month from the coming Sunday."

Of other results of the study the following can be mentioned: (6) Activities consisting of satisfaction of physical and economic needs—sleep, meals, personal care, work, etc.—were predicted with greater accuracy than pleasurable, artistic, intellectual, and religious activities, like reading, talking, visiting, radio, movies, etc. (7) The further in the future the day predicted, the larger the error of prediction. (8) With an increase in the age of the individual, the error of prediction tends to decrease. (9) The married and the men gave a smaller error of prediction than the single and the women. (10) Persons with a greater income predicted more accurately than those with a lower income. (11) The accuracy of prediction is little correlated with school education from grade school to college. (12) The more stable and routine the social life in which an individual lives and acts, the higher the accuracy of prediction. (13) One tends to predict one's own behavior more accurately than that of other persons, and among these others the behavior of a well-known friend better than that of an unknown person.[10]

If we cannot predict accurately our own behavior during the next 24 or 48 hours, still more insufficient is our knowledge for accurately predicting complex individual, group, and historical processes and, therefore, still greater is bound to be an error of such predictions. This conclusion is well corroborated by the relevant facts, if and when predictions are made on the basis of either causal determinism or probability treating the predicted phenomena as congeries or as a mere aggregate of respective units. Contrary to the wide-spread opinion that predicting the future of groups and organizations is easier than predicting the future of individuals, the enormous mortality of groups and organizations convincingly repudiates such a belief. Organized groups are started with an expectation that they will develop and live a long life. As a matter of fact, American small business organizations, like drug and hardware stores, live an average of only 3 years; larger economic organizations live about 10 years on the average, the largest ones about 28 years; literary and cultural organizations of a local character have an average life-span of around 2 or 3 years; most families live less than 100 years as a distinct social unit; most of the small religious denominations appear and disappear within some 10 to 20 years; even the age of most of the existing states is under 100 years. And so on.[11]

This high mortality of groups and organizations demonstrates how optimistically wrong the founders and promoters are in their expectations and predictions. The facts of history offer endless evidence of the impossibility of an accurate knowledge of forthcoming events. If somebody in 1914 had predicted a small fraction of the happenings since that time, he would have been branded crazy. And yet, madder things have happened than could be predicted by such a "crazy" forecaster. The cup of history has been filled to the brim by the unforeseen and "improbable" surprises. When in the nineteen-twenties I forecast the end of the modern Sensate era and the coming of bigger and more terrible wars, of a multitude of revolutions and revolts, of anarchy, destruction and misery, of a decline of democracy and the rise of dictatorial, totalitarian governments, of the emergence of a demoralized and disintegrated man-the-killer as "the worst of the beasts," and so on and so forth, the forecastings being published in several of my works and in full form in the four volumes of my *Social and Cultural Dynamics* (1937)—many of my colleagues and students, and especially the "leading scientific authorities," branded my forecastings as "utterly impossible" and myself as a somewhat "loony" person. Alas! These "utterly impossible" things have come to pass, and, so far, historical processes have been unfolding according to my "schedule."

On the other hand, most of the "scientific predictions" of my critics about the course of historical processes, war and peace, democracy and progress, etc., have been thrown into history's garbage can.

The history of recent "scientific" forecastings of the statistical-probabilistic type is replete with wrong forecasts, due evidently to an insufficient knowledge and insufficient consideration of the above difficulties. And what is important is the fact that these wrong forecastings have been for a near future, separated sometimes only by a few weeks or a few months, rarely by a few years, from the moment of prediction. Thus one of the most eminent American economists, W. Mitchell, in 1927—two years before the crash of 1929—forecast that from then on no crashes were to be expected in the development of American business and prosperity, and that, in fact, the amplitude of business fluctuations was going to become progressively narrower until a smooth, "streamlined" progress of business was achieved. A few weeks before the crash of 1929, the Harvard Business Bureau and most of the economic forecasters were similarly predicting a glorious course of business progress. The crash of 1929 was so sharply contradictory to these predictions, that the Harvard and other agencies of economic forecasting had to close their shops. If one goes through the bulk of prognostications on political and international relationships, particularly in respect to war and peace, democracy and totalitarianism, communism and capitalism, as they were predicted by hundreds of scientists and scholars in the nineteen-twenties and thirties, one finds that the overwhelming majority of these forecasters were painting the future in the most cheerful colors: prosperity, peace, international cooperation, expansion of democracy, the near end of communism and totalitarianism, the further humanization of mankind, progress in the arts and sciences, further improvement of the standard of living, and so on—a veritable cuckoo-Utopia was guaranteed by the "scientific" forecasters. The real historical process strikingly repudiated these predictions and sent them into the museum of human errors. The same may be said of the predictions (from 1920 to 1937) of our scientific demographers about the birth-rate, the size of population, the size of the family in this country, and several other "social trends."

If one compares the expected results of a new law or of a new governmental policy with the actual consequences, one finds, as a rule, a striking discrepancy. Sometimes the actual effects are quite contradictory to the forecasted ones; sometimes, side by side with the expected results, a host of unforeseen effects takes place, making the total effects of the measure quite different from the expected ones. The initiators of the Volstead prohibition act did not foresee that it would create a large-scale bootlegging industry and gangster-type criminality. The initiators of the Dawes-Young plan did not expect that it would contribute to the rearmament of Germany, and to the Second World War. Likewise, the initiators of the Marshall plan did not expect many of the consequences which have already happened. Hitler's government and its experts did not foresee the destruction of the Nazi regime and of the Third Reich as a result of their policy of aggression. Lenin and other communist leaders did not expect a legion of the actual consequences of their revolution—mass executions, famine, poverty, an enormous increase in mortality, the destruction of a large area in Russia during the civil war, and so on, up to the present cold war. Few, if any, governmental leaders of various countries expected, even in 1941-42, that the cooperation of the communist and the allied governments in the Second World War would lead to the deadly cold war between the communist and democratic blocs of nations.

If one turns from these forecastings and expectations to more narrow ones, like planned governmental financial budgets for the next year, a discrepancy between the planned and actual budgets is nowadays something "normal." A large deficit is the ordinary form of the discrepancy.

With slight modification, these statements are applicable to the expectations, forecastings, and plans of various institutions and private agencies: religious, cultural, business, up to private families and persons. All in all, their expectations and plans, often counseled by scientific experts, fare no better than the current predictions of weather. Not infrequently scientific forecastings of social events just a few days or weeks in advance go strikingly wrong—as witness the predictions of the presidential elections in 1948 by the Gallup and other polls.

Another example is given in "the best possible forecasts of the kind of problems which would confront the command [of the American Army] after the capitulation of the German War machine." These predictions were made in the summer of 1944, when the defeat of the German coalition was quite certain and many consequences of this defeat were perfectly obvious. Putting aside the platitudinal predictions which any intelligent person could forecast without any specific research, and turning to the less platitudinal forecastings, we find that most of these were wrong. The authors duly acknowledge this: "some of the predictions made in the 1944 memorandum were completely borne out [mainly platitudinal ones], others were not. . . . The forecast was particularly inadequate in not anticipating that the French, rather than the British or Russians as well, would be primary targets [at the present time even this "correction" of the initial prediction has turned out to be wrong: now the Russians are the hated target of the cold and hot war]. The forecast overestimates the increase of hostility toward home and skepticism about the war." The forecast did not anticipate at all either the Korean and Indo-China wars, or the cold-hot war against the Russian-Chinese bloc, or the United Nations, or the NATO, or the Marshall Plan, or the communist governments in China and other countries. In brief, it foresaw hardly any of the world-shaking events and changes. In spite of the correctness of its "predictions" of such "important" events as that after the victory there would likely appear "a desire for celebration," the total prediction is a conspicuous failure.[12] If need be, the list of the total or partial failures of "scientific predictions" can be continued *ad libitum*. Hundreds of pages can be filled with these "obituaries." Similar partial or total failure quite frequently attends the plans and expectations of individuals. The above study of the forecastings of their own activities for tomorrow, etc., by 106 forecasters well confirms this.

All these failures demonstrate a lack of the necessary knowledge for scientifically forecasting most of the important sociocultural and individual processes. Discrepancies between the forecasted and real events also confirm the difficulties of probabilistic forecastings of such processes.

The discussed failures of the forecastings do not, however, mean that all such forecastings are wrong. It is certain that now and then a portion of predictions comes true. But if the predictions were based on an adequate knowledge and were really scientific, wrong forecasts either should not have occurred at all, or their number should have been insignificant and much lower than in the case of forecasts not based on scientific knowledge. Since a partial discrepancy between forecastings and actual reality seems to be common to almost all predictions of complex processes, and since the total failure of forecastings is also fairly frequent, the portion of wrong predictions apparently is very large, possibly larger than that of correct predictions.

On the other hand, in the unscientific forecasts of the Oracle of Apollo at Delphi, of various prophets, seers, prognosticators, crystal gazers, and so on, not all forecastings were wrong; a part, and possibly a large part of their "reading of the future" was correct. Otherwise, such forecasting agencies and institutions would have not functioned for decades and centuries; their invariable failure would have been exposed, their prestige undermined, and they would have been abolished in a short time. There are no data for comparing the percentages of right and wrong forecasts by these "unscientific agencies" with those by contemporary "scientific" forecasters. I, for one, would not be surprised at all if the predictions of the Oracle of Apollo had, at least, as high a per cent of correct predictions as that of the contemporary scientific pollers and forecasters; perhaps, an even higher one.

The above considerations justify a very conservative or even skeptical position in regard to the possession or availability of sufficient knowledge for scientific forecastings. The actual knowledge is sorely inadequate for most psychosocial and cultural predictions. We must humbly acknowledge our ignorance and either abstain from "scientific prediction" or offer it with warning for what it really is: mainly a guess sprinkled here and there by "scientific pepper."

Summing up what has been said of causal and probabilistic predictions and of belief in the existence or availability of adequate knowledge for these predictions, we come to the conclusion that these three bases of prediction are largely uncertain, unusable, and insufficient. At best they permit one to make roughly accurate predictions in regard to routine, platitudinal, frequently recurrent processes or events. In regard to more complex, irregular, rarely recurrent, important social, cultural, and personal processes, they are not very helpful. All in all their positive service is about the same as that rendered by common-sense judgment. We are, as yet, very far from the era of truly scientific predictions.

*d*) As to predictions on the basis of *"the meaningful-causal" principle of the immanent self-determination of social, cultural, and personal systems,* the eminent physicists explicitly reserve, under different terms, a special place for predictions of this sort in the field of meaningful, conscious phenomena—both personal and sociocultural. While, according to A. Eddington, "the law of chance is the most fundamental and indispensable of all physical laws," "the manifestations of consciousness or life" are "governed by objective law of direction instead of being wholly a field of chance."[13] Max Planck states, similarly, that the fields of "ego," "free will," and conscious, meaningful processes are exempt from causation or chance.[14] N. Bohr,[15] F. G. Hopkins, Charles E. Guye, E. Schrödinger, and many others express similar views.[16] In the preceding chapter, Schrödinger's analysis of a small aggregation of atoms in the genes, as definitely determining the structural and dynamic properties of the future organism, has been given as an example of the immanent self-determination of a living system, quite different from either chance probability or mechanical causation.

These remarks aim to show especially to our self-appointed "natural science sociologists and psychologists" that this "meaningful-causal" method of analysis and prediction of psychosocial phenomena is not a fanciful invention of the present writer but that, as a matter of fact, it has been one of the most fruitful methods used by the eminent past investigators of the psychosocial universe, and is well acknowledged by the leaders of the modern natural sciences.

An adequate analysis of what is here called the "meaningful-causal" or "integral" method of understanding and predicting personal, social, and cultural phenomena requires considerable time and space. It is out of place in this work. Since it has been done in my other works,[17] the reader can simply be referred to these works and a short summary of the high points of the method must here replace its detailed analysis. Following are some of the main points.

1) Empirically rooted sociocultural or superorganic phenomena are made up of three components: first, meanings (values, standards of conduct) superimposed upon physical and biological phenomena; second, vehicles—material, sensory objects and energies, such as sound, light, color, and motion, and electrical, thermal, and other agencies—through which the "immaterial" meanings and values are "objectified" and "communicated" to others; third, human beings—both individuals and groups—who create, use, communicate, and interchange the meaning-values through their vehicles. By the component of meaning-values, sociocultural phenomena differ basically from physical and biological phenomena: these do not have the component of meaning-values, superimposed on their biological and physical properties.

2) The component of meaning-values establishes a tangible interdependence or "causal nexus" among all the main vehicles of a given system of meanings. On the basis of their purely physical or biological properties, the vehicles often do not have this tangible interdependence or "causal nexus," and vice versa. The component of meanings sometimes eliminates the "causal interdependence" existing among the vehicles due to their physical or biological properties.

3) All sociocultural phenomena fall into two main classes: congeries, and systems. By congeries is meant two or more sociocultural phenomena which do not belong to each other meaningfully and "causally." The sociocultural phenomena "Stalin," "azalea," "quantum mechanics," "whisky," "Middletown" are an example of a congeries. A broken beer bottle, a worn out shoe, and a copy of *Look* lying side by side on a sidewalk, furnish another sample of a congeries. Congeries phenomena are not bound together by meaningful and interdependent ("causal") ties. They are just chance-phenomena unrelated to each other in a meaningful-causal way.

A collection of strangers or an unorganized plurel of individuals is an example of a social congeries.

In contrast to the congeries, the social or cultural system consists of sociocultural phenomena united by logically or aesthetically consistent meaningful bonds and by "causal" ties of interdependence in which each part (meaning, vehicle, human member) tangibly depends upon the other parts and the whole (its total system of meanings, all its main vehicles and human agents), and the whole depends tangibly upon each and all important parts. This meaningful and tangible empirical interdependence makes out of all the part-phenomena a single meaningful and causal system or unity. Such a system radically differs from the congeries of sociocultural phenomena, which consists of a mere heap—whether spatially adjacent or scattered in space and time—of phenomena not bound into a unity by any ties of meaningful consistency or "causal" interdependence.

An organized group—be it family or labor union or state—is a social system. An organized institution—be it the Roman Catholic or other church, a university, a Supreme court, an army, and so on, is again a social system. A logically or aesthetically consistent system of meanings—such as mathematics or physics, a philosophical system like Plato's or Kant's, a religious credo, a law-code or ethical system, a masterpiece by

Beethoven or Michelangelo, the epic of Homer, or Shakespeare's dramas, all objectified by their vehicles and used and communicated by human beings—is an example of a cultural system.

4) Sociocultural systems in regard to one another are: in a relationship of subordination, one system being a subsystem in a larger system, as arithmetic is a subsystem of mathematics; or in a relationship of coordination, as are algebra and geometry, or literary, musical, and dramatic representations of essentially similar topics; or in the relationship of congeries, like Calvin's theological treatise, quantum-mechanics, and car advertising; or in the relationship of antagonism, like atheistic and religious credos, and like the communist and capitalist "philosophies."

5) Since a system has a triple interdependence of part upon other parts and upon the whole and the whole upon its parts, all parts of a sociocultural system function and change "in togetherness."

6) As any real unity, a sociocultural system is to a large extent a self-directing individuality in its functions and life history. Following its "conception" or "emergence," the essential forms of its future development are implicit in the system itself, as its inherent properties and potentialities. Its development consists largely of unfolding its potentialities into actualities. A system has a margin of autonomy from the forces external to it. This margin is different for different systems. The principal role of the external factors is to accelerate or retard, facilitate or hinder the unfolding of the system's inherent properties and potentialities. Sometimes the external forces can mutilate or even destroy the system, but they cannot change its essential nature, e.g., turn religion into mathematics, turn an army as an army (not its individual members) into apostles of non-violence, or turn a symphony concert into a football match. If such "transformation" occurs, it means simply a complete substitution of one system for another which is totally different.

After this "digression" we can return to our topic.

7) Meaningful-causal prediction deals only with sociocultural systems; it does not concern itself with sociocultural congeries. These chance phenomena are to be studied and predicted by the probabilistic method and not by the meaningful-causal method. Likewise, the latter does not deal directly with purely causal or chance relationships based on purely physical or biological properties: among sociocultural phenomena there are hardly any purely "causal" relationships. If they are found in human organisms

and material vehicles, they are there as purely physical or biological phenomena, and as such are to be studied by the physical and biological sciences by their methods of investigating purely causal or chance connections.

The essential steps in the meaningful-causal analysis and prediction of the future state of a given system or of a constellation of systems are in brief as follows.

A) The first step consists of finding out whether a given group of sociocultural phenomena is a congeries or a system. The investigator must remember that a system has a logically (or aesthetically, in fine-arts phenomena) consistent and mutually dependent set of meaning-values, whereas a congeries is only a dump of unrelated meaning-values. The meaning component gives us the first and most important clue as to whether a given set of phenomena is a congeries or a system. If the meanings of the phenomena studied exhibit a logical or aesthetic consistency and unity, like the propositions of Euclidian geometry or the articles of the Christian Credo, this is a strong indication that in their component of meanings they belong to one meaningful system. Their meaningful unity suggests that in their vehicles and human members, the phenomena are also interdependent and make one empirical, interdependent system.

The meaningful aspect of sociocultural phenomena permits logic and intuition to play a vastly greater role in ascertaining the existence of meaningful-causal relationships between the phenomena variables than is possible in the field of purely natural phenomena, which are devoid of meaningful components. With only empirical observation at our disposal, we should not be able to grasp—especially in discrete and spatially dispersed sociocultural phenomena—any connections except congeries or chance relationships. Even the meaningful aspect of these can hardly be "observed" in the narrow sense of the term—that is, through the sense organs.

In brief, if we had only had empirical observation of "externalities" at our disposal, sociocultural reality would have been but a chaotic mass of congeries. Perhaps we should have been able to observe that a few of the variables which frequently coexist or change together were somehow connected with one another. But they would have been very limited in number and confined to very narrow, concrete, material phenomena adjacent in space and in time. The vast majority of sociocultural phenomena, particularly those separated by space and time, would never have been apprehended as "causally or probabilistically connected." Fortunately, their meaningful aspect permits us to realize that in millions of cases, dispersed over the whole planet, there may be or actually is a connection between them—as, for instance, between the various activities of scattered communist agents, since they represent the same meaningful system (the Communist party).

Through purely empirical observation of external things, we could never apprehend the fact that demonstrations conducted by motley crowds of individuals of both sexes, widely divergent in age and race, attired in the most diverse costumes, speaking a multitude of different languages, living under the most disparate climatic and geographic conditions, constituted a joint manifestation of protest on the part of the Roman Catholic Church against the persecution of Catholics. Nor could we guess that a bill introduced in Congress to sever diplomatic relationships with aggressive anti-Catholic governments, the visit of a diplomat to the Vatican, a Papal encyclical, the collection of money for victims of the persecution, and hosts of other externally heterogeneous phenomena, were not chance phenomena vis-à-vis one another but articulations of one—the Roman Catholic—system and were therefore meaningfully and causally connected with one another.

On the basis of purely inductive, empirical, external observation, we should certainly conclude that all such phenomena, separated as they are in space, were independent of one another; because they do not conform to the inductive laws of agreement, difference, concomitant variation, and "residue." Even if, by chance, we should suspect that they were connected, there would be no substantial reason for insisting upon their connection or uniformity. If, however, we know—and know with certainty—that they are connected, as diverse manifestations of the same system, through its vehicles and agents, this is because we know the system as an objectified and socialized system of meanings. Knowing the system—its meanings, its vehicles, and its agencies—we throw a net of "meaningful-causal" relationship over thousands of discrete phenomena that look empirically independent of one another; and in most cases, our deductions are borne out by subsequent observations.

In brief, by considering the meaningful aspect of sociocultural phenomena, we can, through intuition, logic, and then observation, easily solve the problem of whether a given variable is a congeries or a system.

B) Having obtained our first—and most important—clue through analysis of the meanings of the variables, and knowing the three-component structure of sociocultural phenomena, we must ascertain whether the given complex of meanings has its vehicles and agents; and, if so, what they are, and whether the three components of each variable show a tangible interdependence. If these tests suggest that a given variable is a system, we must ascertain, furthermore, whether it shows other properties of systems as analyzed in detail in *Dynamics* (vol. IV, chaps. 1 and 2). If it shows these properties, the investigator must determine the degree of interdependence between the three components of the system: Do the vehicles and agents objectify and socialize the system of meanings adequately, or do they perceptibly disfigure and distort it? How marked is the conductivity of the system from component to component? What are the physicochemical and biological properties of the vehicles and agents? By what forces are they, as purely physicochemical and biological entities, particularly influenced? And, under the pressure of these external forces, may their system of meanings in its empirical manifestation be influenced retroactively?

To complete his preliminary study of the system, the investigator must ascertain precisely what its system of meanings is: Does it contain congeries? Is there an inner tension (*Spannung*) which might lead to a split or modification of the system of meanings, by virtue of its implicit contradictions? Moreover, if the type of the system is known, what are its potentialities, the rhythms and phases of its existence, and the tempo of its changes, and at what stage or phase is it at the moment of investigation?[18] Finally, is the system a subsystem in a larger system, with what systems is it coordinated, and amidst what systems and congeries (in its sociocultural milieu) does it exist and function?

C) *In exploring the interrelationships of systems, the meaning component and the "meaningful induction" are again paramount.* Without them, we should be unable to grasp most of the meaningful-causal relations between the systems, and especially between important system variables. (The reason is that the principal sociocultural systems are never identical, but differ from one another in respect to a series of secondary points even when they belong to the same class. Examples are afforded by the Christian, Hindu, Confucian, and Mohammedan religions; and by the Greco-Roman, medieval, and modern economic systems.)

Since a given system is never repeated under identical conditions, to apply the rules of an external induction becomes exceedingly difficult—indeed, virtually impossible.

Fortunately, we have at our disposal the meaning component of the systems. It gives us the first clue and then steadily guides us in our orientation in the jungle of causal and chance relationships. It permits us to discover quite validly which relationships among sociocultural systems are accidental and which are causal-meaningful. It enables us frequently to detect the causal or empirical interdependence between phenomena (systems and processes) which are repeated only a few times, appear quite dissimilar from the perceptional standpoint, occur under the most diverse conditions, and are scattered in space and time—in brief, among phenomena where any externalistic induction is utterly useless.

A pertinent example is the causal relationships between the heterogeneous phenomena in which the aforementioned protest of the Catholic Church manifests itself. Another, and perhaps much more significant, example is the discovery of the interdependence—static and dynamic—among the enormous number of systems and processes that constitute the ideational, idealistic, and sensate supersystems of culture, their rise and their decline. Perceptionally and externally, there is certainly no resemblance between the impressionistic style of painting, materialistic philosophy, empirical epistemology, secular government, utilitarian ethic, nominalistic and singularistic mentality, the improvement of the material standard of living, and the contractual and compulsory character of social relations. Externalistically observed, these phenomena reveal no "causal" dependence or interdependence. A strict behaviorist and "operationalist" could not even surmise that a "causal" interdependence existed between such heterogeneous variables. In my work, *Dynamics,* however, I have shown the existence of a very definite interdependence between these and many other variables. As the articulation of the sensate supersystem of culture, they function and change together, each variable depending upon the other subsystem or parts of the sensate supersystem, each part depending upon the whole, and the whole supersystem depending upon its parts. The same is true of the vast number of subsystem variables that make up the ideational and idealistic supersystems. Only through the clue of the relationship of the meanings of each of these subsystems was one able even to conceive of their possible interdependence.

Once discovered and empirically tested, the meaningful-causal method permitted the detection of a vast network of "causal" interrelationships between the principal variables—systems of science, religion, philosophy, fine arts, law and ethics, economics and politics, with a multitude of other important sociocultural variables (subsystems). In its totality, the nexus of causal-meaningful relations between the variables (systems and subsystems) that make up the sensate, idealistic, and ideational supersystems of culture, and that determine their interdependent rise and decline, enable us to comprehend the structure and dynamics of a huge section of sociocultural life. They supply us with *a knowledge of static and dynamic meaningful-causal relationships unattainable through externalistic induction.* Let us elucidate this point a little further.

*Static meaningful-causal relationship.* Knowing the essential character of our *A,* say, of the sensate supersystem (or the sensate phase in its dynamic aspects), we can say: if the sensate phase of the system (*A*) is given, then such and such *B, C, D, E,* · · · *N* will be given, because *A* and *B, C, D, E,* · · · *N* are meaningfully and causally connected. Concretely, if the sensate system (*A*) is given, then, with a reasonable degree of certainty, we can predict that its art will be predominantly visual (*B*), with all the essential characteristics of such an art (*b, c, d, e, f*), as depicted in Volume I of *Dynamics;* that its system of truth (*C*) will be predominantly empirical, with concentration on the natural sciences and technological inventions, and other characteristics of such a system, as analyzed in Volume II of *Dynamics;* that supersensory religion will play a very modest part, while business and empirical science will have an enormous role in such a culture (*D*); that its ethics and law (*E*) will be predominantly utilitarian, hedonistic, expedient; that its government (*F*) will be secular, led by military, rich, or professional groups; that its literature (*G*) will be predominantly "realistic," sensual, in part erotic, with common types of people as its main personages, mixed liberally with the "glamour girl," criminal, prostitute and other subsocial types; . . . and so forth, down to the minutest details, like the presence of quantitative colossalism, "progressivism," a "linear conception of historical process," and so on. The same is true of the ideational or idealistic systems. When either one of these is given, we can predict a large number of the forms which would be assumed by its art, philosophy, religion, ethics, social organization, and so on, since this *A* and its *B, C, D, E,* · · · *N* are connected causally and meaningfully.

Thus we find ourselves in *possession of a meaningful-causal relationship between an enormous number of most important sociocultural phenomena or variables,* which otherwise, being in "stochastic" relationship with one another, cannot be grasped if mechanically treated as mere "variables" or congeries. These meaningful-causal relationships concern, not only the relationship of *A* (supersystem) with its *B, C, D,* · · · *N,* but also the relationship of *B* with *C, D, E,* · · · *N,* of *C* with *B, D, E,* · · · *N,* of *N* with *B, C, D, E,* and so on, if and when they are part of the supersystem. This means that *B, C, D, E,* · · · *N* are also connected "causally" in the strictest sense of static causal relationship: when *B* is given, *C, D, E,* · · · *N* are given; when *N* is given, *B, C, D, E* are given.

So far as the discovery of a meaningful-causal relationship is possibly the supreme aim of any study, we find ourselves in possession of a large number of such relationships discovered through our "meaningful-organic" approach, guided by the meanings and through the method of system and supersystem, rhythm and super-rhythm. From this standpoint, our method has all the predictable value which any genuine causal connection has: if *A* is given, *B, C, D,* · · · *N* will be there; if *A* is absent, *B, C, D,* · · · *N* will be absent. In addition, the meaningful-causal relationship here concerns, not merely two variables, but a bunch of many variables from all the main compartments of culture, and a large number of the variables within the same system (or compartment) of culture. Such a result is certainly one of the richest crops that any method can give.

*Dynamic meaningful-causal relationship* means a relationship between *A* and *B,* according to the formula: If *A* varies, *B* varies. In our case, it means, not only that if *A* varies *B* varies, but also that *C, D, E,* · · · *N* vary respectively and concomitantly (in togetherness). We thus have a super-rhythm dominating the sensate, ideational, and idealistic supersystems: if the supersystem passes from, say, the ideational phase to the idealistic (*A*), then all the embraced rhythms and all their subrhythms also pass from the ideational to the idealistic phase. If someone states that, in such and such a culture, its ideational supersystem or phase begins to pass into the idealistic supersystem or phase, with this datum we can fairly certainly predict what kind of transformation will be undergone by the fine arts of the culture and by its system of truth—religion, philosophy, science; what trend will prevail in scientific discoveries and inventions, in law and ethics, in the economic well-being of the population, in the movement of war and revolutions, and in all the subsystems of the supersystem studied.

If we assume, for instance, that at the present time our culture has entered a transition from its dominant sensate phase to the ideational phase, this datum is quite sufficient to predict hundreds of trends in our culture, such as an increase in war and revolutions in the transitory period —because, in such a period, war and revolutions uniformly increase—a decrease in economic well-being, for the same reason; a progressive depreciation of most of the sensate values, beginning with money and the prestige of the rich classes as such; a heightening tempo of increase in destructive scientific discoveries and inventions; a decline of contractual relationships; an increasing role for supersensory religion; a decreasing empiricism, in all its varieties, an increasing mysticism, religious rationalism, fideism, and so on; a decline of utilitarian and hedonistic ethics; a tranformation of law in the same direction; a decline of visual, sensate, sensual, and erotic forms and contents in the arts, and so on . . . All these trends will be given if the major premise is accurately diagnosed.[19]

The fruitfulness of this meaningful-causal method in studying the relationship of systems, and the comparative sterility of methods that attempt to study sociocultural phenomena as congeries, from the standpoint of an external observer and without use of the meaningful clues, is apparent. When one mechanically, externalistically, and probabilistically studies the relationships between most of the sociocultural phenomena and takes, for example, the relationship between the movement of quantitative nudity in pictures and that of nominalism, treating both as chance variables (congeries), one can find hardly any relationship; one can hardly even guess that, in some way, they may be interdependent. Still less possible is it to find, through such a mechanical procedure, any relationships of interdependence between the thousands of phenomena—meanings, vehicles, and human agents—that make a sensate or ideational supersystem and the thousands of processes of which the life of the supersystem is made up. No inductive method in its mechanical application, no statistical correlation technique, can even be applied to such a task. If such methods are applied, they cannot give anything except blunders, for the same reason that they cannot find any relationship of interdependence between a piece of heart, a piece of lung, and a piece of gland all cut from the same organism. When this or that style of art and this or that philosophical current, plus the amount of pig iron produced, are taken mechanically, as mere chance variables, they disclose as little interdependence as the above pieces of heart, lung, and gland. What is interdependent in a system is not so outside of it.[20]

When one takes such variables as the high frequency of prostitutes, gangsters, hypocrites, or glamour girls as the chief personages of fiction, the predominantly utilitarian character of legal and ethical codes, and the multiplicity of technological inventions, and studies their relationships mechanically through statistical or other techniques, obviously no genuine relationship of interdependence can be detected. Considered not as embodiments of the same system, but as isolated variables, they cannot exhibit either positive or negative correlation; nor can they offer any other inductive basis that would suggest and support the existence of the relationship which, in fact, they possess as articulations of the same sensate system, and which, when grasped in that setting, is supported by the *a posteriori* inductive test.

### 3. Summary

*a*) Correct predictability is neither a necessary nor a sufficient criterion of the scientific nature of a theory. A vast number of scientific propositions in the total body of science are not predictive. Many correct predictions are made on the basis of a nonscientific theory. A number of wrong predictions are made on the basis of scientific assumptions. The contention of many sociologists and psychologists that predictability is a most important evidence that a theory is scientific is untenable, so far as it makes predictability a necessary and universal characteristic of all scientific propositions.

*b*) The prevalent views about causal determinism as the only basis for scientific predictions are also untenable. First of all, in the sociocultural universe we hardly deal with a "naked causality" based exclusively on the physical and biological properties of sociocultural phenomena. Such a causality may be found in physical and biological phenomena as one of the components of psychosocial phenomena; but as purely physical or biological phenomena, isolated from the component of meanings, they are dealt with by the physical and biological sciences, not by the psychosocial sciences. Instead of "naked" causal relationships, sociocultural phenomena have meaningful-causal ones, due not only to the purely physical and biological properties of these phenomena, but especially to their three-component structure in which the component of meaning-values plays a particularly important role. The presence of this component in psychosocial phenomena transforms the purely causal relationship into the meaningful-causal one. A complete disregard of this cardinal fact is one of the reasons for the untenability of the prevalent view that causal determinism (or indeterminism) is the only foundation for scientific predictions.

The second reason for the untenability of these views is the obsolescent conception of causality maintained by the bulk of modern sociologists and psychologists. They have overlooked a basic change in modern physical science on this point; namely, the substitution of a chance-probability relationship for a strictly causal determinism in the whole "lawless" region of subatomic, and in a considerable part of macrophysical phenomena. In this, as well as in other points, the "home-made" physics and biology of our partisans of "natural science sociology and psychology" is simply pseudo-physics and pseudo-biology, repudiated and transcended by the modern natural sciences.

*c*) So far as sociocultural congeries are chance phenomena, the probabilistic method is the proper one for their investigation and prediction. Using it we can detect some chance-uniformities among the congeries and make some correct predictions about them. However, the application of this method for purposes of predicting sociocultural congeries is confined mainly to routine, comparatively simple, and frequently repeated chance phenomena. In regard to predicting the complex, rarely and irregularly repeated, sociocultural phenomena, particularly the sociocultural systems, the probabilistic method is either largely inapplicable or fruitless.

*d*) The sociocultural systems and their relationships can be most fruitfully studied and predicted by the meaningful-causal method, assisted wherever possible by the probabilistic method. Only the meaningful-causal method has given and can give the best possible understanding of the main body of sociocultural phenomena (systems) and can serve as the best basis for predicting important changes in the psychosocial universe.

*e*) The validity of these conclusions is well corroborated by—among other proofs—the excessively high per cent of total and partial failures among so-called scientific predictions concerning important sociocultural phenomena (systems). These failures decisively repudiate E. W. Burgess' boastful statement that "prediction works." [21] The routine, platitudinal phenomena are as correctly forecast by mere common sense and routine experience as by "scientific predictions." But, as we have seen, in regard to the complex, unrepeated or rarely repeated, and highly variant phenomena, the bulk of "scientific predictions," including some of Burgess' predictions concerning the family and the happiness in marriages, do not work at all or work very poorly. In correctly predicting these phenomena "partial and multiple correlation, matrix algebra, factor analysis, and mathematical equations" [22] do not help much, and their use or misuse by psychosocial researchers has not prevented the failure of most of their predictions. As long as the pseudoscientific forecasters cling to their obsolescent views on causality, their smattering of mathematical and probabilistic methods, their evasion of a serious analysis of the difficulties of forecasting sociocultural phenomena, their superficial conception of the nature and forms of these phenomena; particularly, as long as they neglect the component of meaning, the difference between sociocultural congeries and systems, and, finally, the meaningful-causal method as the specific method of the psychosocial disciplines—just so long will their predictions continue to fail, and just so long will it be useless to expect real progress in this matter.

# *Chapter Twelve*

# Obsolescent Philosophy and the Theory of Cognition of the Modern Psychosocial Sciences

## 1. The Prevalent Senescent Empiricism

The preceding chapters pointed out several diseases of modern sociology and psychology. These defects, and those to be treated hereafter, are largely due to their faulty philosophy and theory of cognition. The majority of contemporary psychosocial investigators profess the philosophy of empiricism in one of its primitive variations. It is often called by the names of "positivism," "logical positivism," "instrumentalism," "operationalism," "scientific approach," and so on. Its senescent theory of cognition or "scientific knowledge" can be outlined as follows. There is the researcher—the subject of cognition, or the knower; and there is the phenomenon studied—the object of cognition, the known. The knower is an outsider to the known and the known is a phenomenon external to the knower. Both are mutually independent and separated by a chasm from each other. They never merge into each other, never lose their separateness, and never unite into one indivisible whole.

The process of cognition consists of observation of the phenomenon by the knower. Observation is made through the sense organs and their extensions, the microscope, the telescope, and other gadgets. The observer is a photographer; his sense organs play the role of a camera reinforced by various attachments and accessories; the object of study is the landscape or person photographed—in our case psychosocial phenomenon. The task of observation consists of photographing as accurately as possible the object of study. To accomplish the task, the photographer-knower must make not one but many repeated shots; wherever possible he is advised to "experiment" with his object by arranging and re-arranging its position and conditions in the ways demanded by the "experimental method." Now he should make the shots of the object in a constant environment where only one condition is varied; now under the conditions of "identity"; now of "difference"; now under those of "concomitant variations." To be sure that his camera does the job adequately, our photographer-investigator should take repeated shots of his object, and he should invite other photographers to verify the accuracy of his shots by taking their own. When the photographer-knower wants to get not so much an individual portrait of his object, but a typical picture of the whole class to which his object belongs, he must take many shots of many objects of the same class and then, through statistical processing, make a "composite photo" of the whole class, eliminating the unique differences of each object and bringing to light the traits, relationships, and uniformities typical for the whole class of phenomena studied. His "composite picture" is a replica of the summary tables which are derived from a statistical investigation of the mass-phenomena of the same class.

Through "the lenses of our sense organs" our empirical investigator observes and photographs the external object of his study. The sense organs, reinforced or not, are the only "camera" through which he can observe the object. According to him, there are no other cameras—such as the alleged "super-sensory" or "extra-sensory" cameras of intuition—that can do the job. The "intuitional" and the "rational" cameras either do not exist in reality or represent merely a poor, decrepit "camera of senses" or a dark box of unconscious urges that cannot photograph anything. Our belated empiricists firmly believe in John Locke's famous statement: *Nihil esse in intellectu quod prius non fuerit in sensu.* (There is nothing in the intellect that was not perceived before through the senses.) Since the camera of the senses can photograph only sensory objects existing in space and time, our empiricists do not admit any supersensory reality: it is also a mere myth, or, if it exists in some form, it cannot be photographed (perceived) by our sense camera. Therefore, this "unknowable" is equivalent to the non-real ("agnostic empiricists"). Scientific knowledge has nothing to do with it.

When the correctly photographed data of observation are ready, they have to be put together, arranged as a "film of observations," and then "developed" according to the techniques prescribed by logical or mathematical canon: the data are to be analyzed, conceptualized, computed and measured, and, finally, formulated into a series of propositions almost automatically following from the data. The logical and mathematical canons themselves are not independent from observations, but are, rather, particularly helpful forms of the same "routine of perception."

As an additional test of the correctness of observation, and of the logico-mathematical "development" of the films of observation, our empiricists recommend strongly the test of prediction. Following Comte's dictum *"Savoir pour prevoir,"* they assert that scientific knowledge of given phenomena enables us not only to restore their past history, but also to predict their future course. For our operationalists predictability is possibly the most important test of the scientific nature of the conclusions reached, or of the accuracy of sense-observation and of conceptual "development" of the "films" of the phenomena studied.

Since, according to empiricism, the rules of inductive, deductive, and "abductive" (mathematical) logics are but "the routine of perception," the whole empirical theory of cognition is sensory. It starts with sense-perception or observation, proceeds with sensory refinement of the accuracy of observation, with the "development" of the film of observation according to the logico-mathematical "routine of perception," and ends with the sensory test of predictability. It denies all nonsensory or supersensory ways of cognition, as well as the autonomy of logical and mathematical cognition: ultimately mathematical inferences and the deductions of logic are either mere tautologies or a mere "consolidated routine of perception." Apart from the data of sensory perception they are useless. As such they are to be distrusted rather than trusted. This emphatic denial of the intuitional or supersensory way of cognition, and this profound distrust of purely logical thought as an independent way of knowing, are particularly conspicuous among modern sociologists and psychologists.

This explains the logical clumsiness, and some other characteristics, of their studies. For the present, we shall examine to what extent this theory of cognition is valid. How solid is its claim to be the scientific theory of knowledge? And is it indeed the only theory unanimously supported by today's science, and by the physical sciences in particular?

## 2. The Obsolescence of the Prevalent Theory of Cognition

In answering these questions I am not going to repeat the crucial criticisms of empiricism given many times by the great philosophers, epistemologists, and methodologists of science. These criticisms can be found in any substantial history of philosophy and there is no need to transcribe them in this work. Any philosophically trained scholar knows that the main criticisms have not been answered satisfactorily by empiricism. If they do not destroy its validity, at least they seriously limit its claims and demote it from the position of a monopolistic theory of cognition to that of one of several theories of knowledge. For the thoughtful scientist or philosopher an acquaintance with the criticisms is sufficient to insulate him well against a credulous acceptance of a radical empiricism.

In our simile of the empirical observer-photographer we can ask the empiricist a number of embarrassing questions: If there is a chasm between the observer and the external phenomena, how can he know the phenomena to which he is an outsider? How can he throw the line of communication so as to observe and understand phenomena totally different from him and his sensory camera? How can he be sure that his sensory camera can "photograph" the objects studied and can do it accurately? How can he be certain that his sense-camera is not playing a trick on him and that, instead of a genuine picture of the object studied, he is not receiving grotesque shadows of shadows of the phenomena? What are the guarantees that his camera is not out of order, is not misfocused, or does not give a black-and-white picture where there should be a colored one? or does not register one aspect instead of the many aspects, or only an insignificant number of "frequencies" in place of the innumerable frequencies of the studied object? In brief, how can he be sure that his sense-camera is fit to reproduce correctly the external objects?

After these embarrassing questions concerning sensory observation, the empiricist faces a legion of still more difficult questions about the conceptual arrangement and development of his "sensory snapshot." If the logical rules are a mere routine of perception, is not the empiricist, in the logical arrangement and development of his sensory data, merely going in a vicious circle? If the validity of photographing is doubtful, how can a processing through the same routine of photography change the doubtful into something valid and scientific? If each photographing is uncertain, how can this uncertainty be turned into certainty by merely multiplying the operation by statistical mass-observation? Mere mass-repetition of the "observation" that "two plus two makes seven" does not change it into a valid proposition. How can we be certain that our definitions, inferences, and measurements, including our coefficients of correlation, do not mislead us and give us fallacies instead of valid knowledge? Can we, indeed, without our concepts, even observe any concrete phenomenon, and, especially, can we describe it even in the most primitive way? Does not each word we use mean a concept? Is even such a sense-observation as "this paper is white and firm" a pure observation-photograph? Is it not rather a collection of several concepts centered around one point? "This" is a concept; "paper" is a concept; "is" is a very abstract concept; "white and firm" are concepts. Thus, what is supposed to be a pure sense-photograph, free from any concepts, in fact turns out to be a "heap of concepts thrown together" and giving an illusion of "a concrete, single, empirical object" perceived by our "sense organs."

Thus, the basic belief of empiricism in the possibility of a pure, correct perception of objects, not contaminated by any concept, is largely an illusion. What is thought to be a mere derivative "routine of perception" happens to be the necessary precondition without which neither the perception nor the description of the object are possible. These, and many other criticisms, serve to puncture empiricism's inflated claims.

After these general remarks we can turn to examine a few specific contentions of contemporary empiricists in the psychosocial sciences. In the first place we shall ask: are they valid in their claim that the only channel of cognition is the sensory channel, and that there are no supersensory (intuitional) or purely rational (logico-mathematical) channels of knowing different from sense-perception? And, if our empiricists insist on their claim, is such a claim supported by today's science, particularly by the physical sciences whose authority and sanction they regularly invoke?

The answer to both of these claims is in the negative. In spite of an emphatic denial of the supersensory, intuitional way of cognition by the overwhelming majority of our sociologists and psychologists; notwithstanding their semicontemptuous dubbing of it as a delusion of confused mystics, or as a prerational and nonlogical superstition, or as a mere lucky hunch, or as unconscious, instinctual groping—still, the existing body of scientific evidence, as well as the position of scientists on this problem, shows, with a reasonable degree of certainty, that the intuitional and the rational (logico-mathematical) ways of cognition were discovered long ago and have functioned fruitfully for millennia. This is being increasingly recognized by today's science. The anti-intuitional and antirational position of our psychosocial empiricists is obsolescent.

Here is a brief summary of the situation in regard to intuitional cognition. By it is meant a momentary, unpredictable enlightening that gives to the knower, or to a creative genius, the essence of the problem studied or the solution of a creative task. Supersensory intuition is basically different from sensory perception-observation, as well as from rational (logico-mathematical) analysis and inference.[1] The supersensory and superrational intuition is the very opposite of the unconscious with which it is regularly confused. While the supersensory intuition is above the rational, conscious level of mentality, the unconscious or subconscious is below this level. While any cognition, discovery, or creative achievement is always done consciously or superconsciously, the unconscious, by definition and by fact, cannot consciously discover or create anything other than the instinctively automatic. The all too familiar identification of the superconscious with the unconscious is a gross blunder, no matter how often and by whom it is done.

As in other basic problems, our self-appointed guardians of scientific sociology and psychology have hardly ever seriously studied the problem of intuitional cognition and creativity. And for the last half-century they have largely missed the important changes in science in regard to this problem. They seem to be unaware that the very leaders of "scientific positivism," like Comte and John Stuart Mill, regarded intuition as the ultimate ground on which all inductive and deductive scientific methods are based. Our anti-intuitionalists also do not seem to know that the overwhelming majority of great scientists and technological inventors have asserted that intuition is the origin of their discoveries and inventions. Our empiricists seemingly do not realize, either, that the term "genius" is another name for the superconscious intuition, and that "genius" cannot be accounted for without the superconscious. They are also apparently ignorant of the fact that the superconscious intuition has been the main source of practically all of the greatest achievements in science, technology, religion, philosophy, fine arts, ethics, law, economics, and politics. They have missed the great body of evidence showing that intuition is, *sui generis,* distinct from rational thought (logico-mathematical), from sensory perception, and from the unconscious instinctual impulses. Likewise, they have hardly noticed the increasing conversion of their contemporary leaders in "scientific standpoint" into pro-intuitionalists. R. Carnap's most recent statement on this point is typical for a number of leading "scientific or logical positivists." "The task of inductive logic is not *to find* a law for the explanation of given phenomena. This task cannot be solved by any mechanical procedure or by fixed rules; *it is rather solved through the intuition, the inspiration, and the good luck of the scientist.* The function of inductive logic begins after a hypothesis is offered for examination." [2] This statement asserts the reality of intuition and of its important role in discovering scientific laws and in creative achievement generally.

In the next section of this chapter, the shift toward intuitional cognition among several other leaders of our anti-intuitionalists, like P. Bridgman, will be described. Our belated empiricists are hardly cognizant of such facts as the emergence and growth of the intuitional school in mathematics; as the pro-intuitional standpoint taken by an ever-increasing number of leading scientists, including those in the physical and biological sciences. The evidence for this last point will be supplied by the next section of this chapter. Finally, our self-appointed "mouthpieces of science" hardly know the long life-history of intuitional cognition and creativity. They seemingly are unaware that a large number of great creators in all fields of culture have been the explicit or implicit partisans of supersensory and superrational intuition, and have regarded themselves as instrumentalities, and their masterpieces as manifestations of intuitional genius or grace. Lao-Tse, Buddha, Mahāvīra, Moses, Christ, Mohammed, and practically all the great religious and ethical creators; the anonymous authors of the Upanishads, the Yogas, the Bhagavad-Gita; Sankara, Patanjali, Plato, Aristotle, Plotinus, St. Augustine, Al Ghazalli, Al Hallaj, Abu Said, Erigena, St. Thomas Aquinas (of the later period of his life), Master Eckhardt, Nicolas of Cusa; J. S. Bach and Beethoven, Phidias and Michelangelo, Homer and Dante, Galileo, Isaac Newton; recent and contemporary thinkers like E. Husserl, H. Bergson, N. Hartmann, N. Lossky, A. Whitehead; or scientists like G. Birkhoff, I. Langmuir, E. Schrödinger, C. Sherrington, and most of the physicists and biologists —these are just a few names among the many intuitionalist discoverers and creators of great masterpieces of culture in all its departments.[3] A mere acquaintance with this long and glorious history of intuitional thought is sufficient to prevent the foolishly contemptuous attitude toward it so frequently expressed by our pedestrian pseudoscientific sociologists and psychologists.

Still more untenable are their interpretation of the rational, logico-mathematical modes of thought as a mere routine of perception, and their denial of the intuitional basis of the rational rules of thought. Especially baseless is their distrust of the cognitive role of logical deduction and mathematical inference or "abduction." As has been pointed out above, without logico-mathematical concepts, deduction, and inference, no adequate observation, description, and definition of a single empirical fact is possible. Likewise, the all-important role of deductive and "abductive" thought—the role of "theoretical" thought versus "the operational method"—in the development of the physical sciences has been indicated in the chapter on operationalism. This role is so well ascertained at the present time, that there is no need to argue the point. The common use of statistical and superficially mathematical methods by our empiricists, their insistence on the quantification and measurement of phenomena, is additional evidence against their own theory, and against their distrust of the logico-mathematical mode of cognition. Contradicting their own practice, their denial of the autonomy and importance of the rational mode of cognition is hopelessly antiquated and untenable. It is directly contradicted by today's science and by the physical sciences particularly.

To sum up: in spite of their noisy claims, our home-made "scientific" sociologists and psychologists have not followed the recent changes in the natural sciences in regard to superconscious intuition and logico-mathematical cognition. The primitive form of the empirical theory of cognition they hold is strikingly obsolescent from the standpoint of today's natural sciences. It is untenable in the light of existing evidence. The self-appointed guardians of "scientific" sociology and psychology do not have any ground for their pretentious claims, and especially for their monotonous incantations that all intuitional and rational theories of cognition and creativity are unscientific.

The same verdict holds in regard to the relationship of the knower and the known in the process of cognition, and in regard to the "objective" nature of scientific propositions as they are stated by the prevalent empirical theory of our sociologists and psychologists. According to their contention, the scientific observer and the phenomenon remain as much strangers to each other as the camera and the landscape. They do not and cannot merge into one unity in which the chasm between them becomes obliterated, and the very separateness of the knower and the known disappears. As a result of this premise, scientific cognition can consist only in an objective observation and description of the observed object by the outside observer. No properties, categories, principles, biases, estimations, or other characteristics of the observer must enter into this observation and description of the object. The observer must be as impartial as a camera. Only that theory or description which is entirely free from the knower's subjective properties can be a scientific theory. Such is the position of our empiricists in this matter.

Consistent with this position, they view the intuitional theory of cognition as utterly unscientific. In contrast to the empirical, the intuitional theory of cognition asserts: (a) that it is possible for the knower and the known to merge into one unity; (b) that some degree of merging is necessary for any even approximately accurate cognition of an object; (c) that a complete merging is the only way for the adequate cognition of the ultimate or true reality; (d) that since this reality is infinite—quantitatively and qualitatively—intuitional knowledge of it cannot be expressed by any words, concepts, definitions, measurements or other external means of communication. Such an adequate cognition of the true reality becomes "unutterable," "inexpressible," "undefinable" by any words or figures. It can only be symbolized or, in exceptional cases, be intuitively communicated by merging the minds of the communicants.

(e) Words, concepts, definitions, categories of our thought—like time, space, subject, object, what, who, causality, and so on—are applicable to and can describe only the limited, the finite, the differentiated ripplings of an infinite ocean, but they are inapplicable to and cannot describe the infinite qualitative and quantitative properties of the undifferentiated ocean itself. Only the complete union with the ocean-God, Tao, Brahman, the Oversoul, the True Reality, the *coincidentia oppositorum,* the Unutterable, and so on—can adequately convey the manifold infinity of the ocean. J. S. Erigena's "God Himself does not know *what* He is because God is not *what*" pointedly expresses this view: the categories of what, who, time, space, person, spirit-matter, and so on, are not applicable to God or the true reality. Each worded proposition, definition, concept, equation, or theory defines only one of the countless differentiations of the infinite ocean; but it cannot define the ocean itself. Each worded scientific proposition throws a pinpointed light at an infinitesimal speck of the infinite ocean, but it leaves unlit the infinite darkness that surrounds the speck. An empirical description is "a finger pointing at the moon," but no description is the moon itself.

(f) So far as any empirical or logico-mathematical cognitions are explicitly or implicitly the worded cognitions, expressed in the worded descriptions, concepts, definitions, propositions, equations, and theories, to that extent only can the worded cognitions give us a limited notion of a few of the "specks" surrounded by darkness. They can never give us an adequate knowledge of the darkness itself. In this sense, they deliver to us only shadows of real, many dimensioned phenomena, or knowledge of a few momentarily differentiated ripplings of the infinite ocean. Herein lies the inadequacy, superficiality, and relativity of sensory and logico-mathematical knowledge. (g) But even this knowledge of the ripplings our sense-perception and logico-mathematical reasoning can "deliver" only if in the process of cognition some remote but real identification of the knower and the known occurs. Otherwise, when they remain complete strangers to each other, mutually external and having no "line of communication" between them, no approximate knowledge of even the ripplings of the ocean is possible: there can be no accurate observation, no accurate description, and no remotely adequate logico-mathematical analysis.

(h) As a result of this "remote and imperfect merging of the knower and the known" in sensory and logico-mathematical cognition, any scientific proposition is always a "function of two variables: the properties of the knower and those of the known." This is contrary to the empiricists' contention that a scientific theory is a pure description of the properties and relationships of the object studied, unmarred by any properties of the observer.

Such, in black and white, are the contrasting points of the prevalent empiricistic and intuitional theories of cognition.

Before examining their validity, let us stop for a moment at what is meant by the intuitional identification or merging of the knower and the known into oneness.

One example of it is given by the mental concentration of a genuine yogin who, after a long and strenuous training, reaches the state of *samadhi* or of a superconscious transcontemplation.

> In this stage the duality of the subject and object disappears and both become one: mind becomes transformed to the form of the object of contemplation. . . . It is a concentration pushed beyond anything we can imagine, and divided into three periods. In the first, the attention is fixed upon a chosen object (a body organ, a feeling, a philosophical object, etc.). It is a struggle against automatic mechanisms which have a tendency to distract the attention from it. The attention has to maintain itself upon the chosen object for a period of time determined by will. It is the concentration of diffused attention and a focusing upon a single point ("the single-pointedness of mind"). The elements making up this period are triple: subject, object, and act of concentration.
>
> In the second period, consciousness loses awareness of effort and the inhibition of the unconscious processes is complete. The self (it is different from the intellect or "the mind-stuff" according to the Yoga philosophy: the mind is a more delicate form of a material substance or, in our terms, of the physiological mechanism, while "the self" is the superconscious, egoless part of the true reality, purusha, or Brahman) has before it only the chosen object upon which the concentration, now happy and easy, can last indefinitely. There is now only a duality of subject and object; the feeling of effort disappears.
>
> In the third period (samadhi), this feeling of duality of subject and object in turn disappears. The conscious being is indissolubly united to the object of its contemplation, melts into it and becomes identical with it. Being identical with the object, the Samadhi-Yogin knows it fully, without any mediation of discursive logic or sensory observation and other "fingers pointing at the moon." Instead, it becomes identical with the moon itself.
>
> The thing in this state does not appear as an object of consciousness, but the consciousness being divested of all "I" or "mine," becomes one with the object itself, so that there is no such notion here as "I know this." . . . This state brings to us the real knowledge of the thing divested of false and illusory associations, which instead of explaining the real nature of the object, serve only to hide it all the more.[4]

This gives an idea of direct and adequate cognition, or "enlightenment" (*prajna* or *jnana*), in contradistinction to the purely discursive, indirect, logical and observational knowledge of the intellect ("the mind-stuff"). Purely intellectual knowledge does not annihilate the unbridgeable chasm between the knower and the known. "When in opposing the subject and object, intellectual theory abstracts them both from Being (reality), it makes the apprehension of Being impossible. To oppose knowledge and Being is to exclude knowledge from Being." The knower, being put outside of Being, cannot obtain a real knowledge of Being. All this was well understood by the great Hindu and Buddhist logicians: Nagarjuna, Asanga, and Vasubandhu, and partly by Gotama, Dignaga and Dharmakirti (all of whom lived between the first and the seventh centuries A.D.). With brilliant dialectical logic they demonstrated that the nature of the true and whole reality "forbids every formulation by concept or speech, since they can only bifurcate reality and never directly seize it," and that "the real Buddha (or reality) can be grasped only directly by intuition," and that sensory and discursive knowledge is in reality very imperfect knowledge or even ignorance (*avidya*) that always leads to self-contradiction in empirical and logical thought.[5]

The intuitional transcontemplation of Yoga is essentially identical with the process of union with "Godhead," "the Unutterable," "the Divine Nothing," "the Unconditional," etc., of all the real mystics, sages, saints, seers, and prophets. The creative intuitional flashes of the great geniuses, that in "the twinkling of an eye" reveal to them the essentials of a scientific discovery, or of a creative masterpiece, are also of the same nature as the state of *samadhi* of a genuine yogin. In Chapter Six of *The Ways and Power of Love,* I have given a great amount of the testimony of the great thinkers and creators on how they create and how the central idea of their masterpiece originates. Unanimously they assert that the creative or discovery process is started as an unforeseen and superrational intuitional flash. This flash cannot be predicted, willfully produced, and rationally achieved. In such moments any consciousness of their "ego," or "I" disappears, they become totally absorbed by, or united with, the discovery, and are transformed into a mere instrumentality of a superpersonal creative *X* called "God," "*nous,*" "Cosmic Mind," "creative grace," and so on. The terms used are different, but they all point to the same supersensory and superrational *X*.

The great scientists of the past and of the present assert this role of the supersensory intuition and a complete union with the known during the flash of discovery no less emphatically than the great creators in the fields of religion and philosophy, fine arts and ethics, creative politics and economics. The empiricists are thus contradicted by a vast body of empirical evidence, by logical reasons, and by a large and ever-growing number of modern scientists. The criticized theory does not have any serious basis for claiming to be scientific generally and monopolistically scientific particularly.

Our empiricists become hopelessly obsolescent when they contend that real cognition is possible under the conditions of a complete separateness of the knower and the known. Untenable, also, is their claim that scientific theory always incorporates only the objective properties of the phenomena studied, and does not and should not contain the properties of the knower —or, to put this in familiar terms, that "any scientific proposition is the function of only one variable: the properties and relationships of the object studied." The statement is not supported at all by the modern physical and biological sciences.

During the past few decades, especially after the discovery of quantum mechanics, the physical and biological sciences have undergone a radical change in respect to this problem. R. Godel describes the change perhaps as tellingly as anyone. Quotations from his study[6] will serve well to introduce us to the viewpoint of today's physical science.

> While the oriental truth seeker makes his way toward the interior of his own being, the occidental savant is endeavoring to question the world outside. In the substance and order of the cosmos should be situated the reality of which he hopes to get the formula. The "real" for him is the object, the thing *(res)*, circumambient phenomenology. To know reality he must penetrate into the intimate structure of surrounding matter by process of analysis and by efforts at reconstruction endlessly repeated in progressive syntheses. Man thus acquires knowledge of the laws which each moment shape the shifting configuration of the world.
>
> But now suddenly—around a bend of quantum mechanics—exploration of the objective field brings the theorist of the physical sciences to a most disquieting position; before him appears an ambiguous universe where the observer and the phenomenon observed are inextricably commingled. So close is their confrontation that each is reflected in the other, powerless to separate or to fuse.

In this realm of indetermination, all the symbols and formulas familiar to our experience of things vanish. Notions of energy and of matter require so profound a transformation as to lose their original meaning; energy condenses into matter, matter dematerializes into radiation. The waves associated with the propagation of light quanta need no substratum in order to propagate in space-time; they undulate neither in a fluid, nor in a solid, nor yet in a gas. Only the unreal thread of analogy links them to the image of a wave rippling the surface of water. They are in fact waves of probability, waves of consciousness which our thought projects afar: curvilinear variation of an abstract function. To each point in the curve there corresponds a variable coefficient of probability in favor of the presence of photons: chance maximal at the crest, minimal at the trough.

On this advanced horizon of the scientific spirit, the play of phenomena is still graspable under the aspect of complementary terms. But the reign of duality is here only an appearance, since the jointly and severally paired antinomic poles are reciprocally determined and mutually resolved. Their relative opposition corresponds to the mode of approach to an idea that its own investigative dynamism limits. The reality is beyond this superimposing of dualistic attributes; to attain it requires breaking with temporo-spatial forms of apprehension and letting atemporal cognition, present in us without our knowing it, arise of its own free will. In this nondimensional focus of consciousness all display of appearances ceases.

The investigator of physical sciences resolves, however, to explore another domain. What interests him is the natural order of the world about him. The spirit of research incites him to penetrate deep into the complex web of phenomena. Every step opens new perspectives to him; because his thought proceeds by analysis, it carves out and suscitates a transfinite diversity of mental images. But of necessity he also remains caught in the meshes of relativity. Even if he succeeds in grouping as a synthesis, however comprehensive, the multitude of elements that the analytic spirit has set gushing, he still remains captive to the form. All his efforts will carry him no farther. This we should know: that neither the synthesizing spirit nor analysis can provide access to cognizance of the Real. This final end of the search requires for its accomplishment another mode of realization irreducible to the dynamisms of informational thought.

Yet the gains of the contemporary sciences, limited as they are, teach us one valuable lesson. They break down the fictive barrier that our corporeal *I* has improperly established between the "objective" world and "subjectivity." Upon careful consideration of the facts, every presentation of our senses and of the intellect bears, inextricably within itself, elements borrowed from externality and from our own internality. Things as they appear to us are the products of our modes of apprehension and of our activity. As P. Rousseau aptly expresses it, "objectivity vanishes." The atomic world removes from our old idea of objectivity all reason for being. . . . Is not an atom an object no less real than a watch, since it too may be weighed (in the Wilson chamber) and since this same apparatus permits us to see it, hence to locate it in space? Yet when hard pressed this supposed reality slips through the fingers and vanishes. Seen in the light of wave mechanics and the matrix calculus, the electron dissipates into a vague metaphysical nebula.[7]

Arrived at the foot of the electronic ladder, our thought renounces all habits which exercise of the senses had imposed upon it; appearances are different at this level. Terms such as the concrete, the full, the empty, space, time, causal connection—as familiar as they are inexact—are no longer applicable. People persist in employing them, but this is an abuse of language. In sum, the world of sense appearances has been wiped out to give place to an aspect of the universe irreducibly different.

While the physicist thus despoils his field of research of so many attributes and qualities, he fails to perceive that it is himself—his own modes of apprehension—that he is in process of despoiling. To the exact extent to which the object of his investigation loses the characteristics of objectivity, the observer himself rejects his veinstone to tend toward the impersonal. "The Tensor Calculus," said Langevin, "knows physics better than the physicist himself."[8] While the development of an equation is progressing through the play of mathematical thought, the operator is nothing but the impersonality of a norm in process of being expressed. Such is his conscious field—filled by action of the impersonal. From this normative quality proceeds the whole value of the formula produced.

In taking cognizance of the microphysical aspects characteristic of an intra-atomic field, the investigator illuminates the corresponding function in his own internality. He penetrates into himself, parallel with his penetration into the object, down to some deeper spiritual level where the structures of atom and nucleus become conceivable. Within him are revealed articulations of thought homologous to the configurations of the material studied. On this plane, the categories of object and subject are more joined in a system of close interrelation than opposed. The active thought of the theorist-experimenter and his material of study here form an indissoluble plexus whose web is projected as on a screen in the conscious field of work. It is then himself—or rather his own mental functions mingled with what was their object—that the observer discovers. He witnesses his own initiation into a disconcerting world from which are banished all the usual notions of time, space, causality, identity, and individuality, of external and internal, of simultaneity and succession of motion, of matter and energy, of mass, of body. He recognizes the relativity of all variable and impermanent appearances to different points of view, the complementarity of the dualistic antinomies.

This spiritual ascesis familiar to the physicist might very profitably be used in the search for a knowledge of ourselves. It is readily applicable to the examination of our biological being.

If occidental man decides to follow to its normal conclusion the philosophy implied in the contemporary sciences, he will of necessity tend to reach a perspective where the antinomy which sets the objective world over against subjectivity is wiped out.

Time, space, causality, indeterminacy, and the dualistic aspect which circumambient phenomena and his own biological dynamisms assume will appear to him as categories derived from the joint relativity of his own spirit and of things. His bodily image, his sensory system, his emotions, and even his intellect will rejoin the cosmos to which they belong.

What will be left of him at the end of this epistemological discrimination? A singular evidentness, irreducible to any appellation. To be sure, such a realization exempt of content is likely to seem rather pale to anyone who has not experienced it. But it undoubtedly compensates for the disappearance of outlines and of shadows by the incommensurable intensity of its flash. Of this unqualifiable knowledge nothing can be said, however, for no formula crosses its threshold.

In contrast to the occidental inquirer whose steps are turned toward the "external world," it is within himself that the Hindu sets out for reality. He has been on his way for over twenty-six centuries; and this gives him a real start on us. His peregrination has long since taught him that the words "external," "internal," "subject," and "object" lose their significance from a certain point of view. We in the Occident have barely begun to suspect this elementary truth. For the sage—or *freed-alive,* according to the Vedantist expression—the Real is permanent axis of our being, and not the perception which our senses evoke or the concept erected by the intellect. It is the intimate experience of individuality; it is revealed in transcendence of all qualification. Dialectic is vain when it would give to That—the unnameable—a name.

Thus the Hindu, choosing the shortest road, the direct way, reached the finish of the race, while the occidental inquirer was lost in the mazes of cosmology. Socrates, however, more perspicacious than his predecessors or his contemporaries, knew enough to abandon these circuitous routes in time, and probed inward. He was evidently right.

In our time, however, because an intimate bond is being forged between the physical sciences and the biological, the cosmological way might well cease to be the interminable and aberrant route that it was of old. Yet there is still need that a sound and sane epistemology should light the way and that the wanderer should renounce his delight in the relativity of points of view.

The subsequent quotations from the works of the modern physicists well confirm Godel's conclusions.

> Nineteenth Century natural science conceived of man as a detached spectator of an objective universe. It held the spectator-spectacle polarity to be genuine and fundamental. During the present century, discoveries concerning the nature of atoms rendered this doctrine untenable. The nucleus of a new philosophy of nature emerged with Heisenberg's principle of uncertainty, whose basic meaning implies a fusion of the knower with the known. The theory grew with amazing speed and success; it led to a mathematical formalism which, in order to attain its purpose, namely lawful description of experience, has to speak of probabilities rather than unique events. Individual events are no longer related in causal fashion, although the domain of probabilities still reigns. . . . Thus has been introduced another, more significant principle of division than the old spectator-spectacle bifurcation: the distinction between physical and historical reality. . . .[9]

The boundary between "external-internal," "objective-subjective" worlds is very relative and "is no longer clear-cut." Both are the world of our experience and of our projection or extrapolation. If there is any tenuous difference between the objective-subjective, external-internal worlds, it is this: the external world of objects is a projection of that part of our experience which is comparatively more stable, less variant, and more easily sharable with others, while the inner or subjective world is a projection of a more changing, variant, and less easily sharable part of our experience. But even this tenuous difference is perfectly relative and ever shifting, and, after quantum mechanics, it tends to be more and more obliterated. Any scientific theory is thus a projection of our experience in which the objective and the subjective elements are fused together.[10]

Even such a leader of our empiricists as P. Bridgman seems to have notably changed his position on this problem.

> Naked sense impressions simply do not occur, and the traditional analysis of our conscious experience into naked sensations as building blocks is palpably bad description. Perceptions we have always had with us, but they are so ubiquitous that we have not been aware of their presence. . . . We cast the world into the mold of our perceptions. . . . We all of us perceive the world in terms of space and time. . . . We cannot help wondering whether perceiving the world in terms of space and time is a good way to perceive it.
>
> These common sense notions [of time and space] have failed in the microscopic domain of quantum phenomena. . . . In the quantum domain we

> are beyond the reach of direct perception and the "space" and "time" of this domain are constructions made and extrapolated by us. . . . Out of all the detail emerges the one stark fact that we can never get away from ourselves [neither in a profound philosophical theory, nor in the vision of a mystic, nor in common sense philosophy of the man in the street, nor in Einstein's theory]. Wherever we go [and whatever scientific theory we construct] we find ourselves. . . .[11]

The standpoint of modern physical science, outlined by these statements, is quite different from that of our empiricists and comes quite close to the standpoint of the intuitionalists. Here, as in many other points, the "theories" under criticism are but antiquated yarns.

Finally, *"predictability"* as a most important pragmatic evidence for the scientific nature of a theory has already been "weighed and found wanting."

# *Chapter Thirteen*

# In the Blind Alley of Hearsay Stuff and Negativism

## 1. The Sham Objectivism of Modern Sociology and Psychology

Infected by a narcissistic sense of superiority over the "old-fashioned" sociological and psychological "armchair philosophers," a great number of modern sociologists and psychologists pride themselves with many virtues, and especially with ushering their disciplines into a scientific-objective, quantitative and experimental stage. The preceding chapters have shown the vanity of most of these claims. In this chapter we shall expose the hollowness of their claim of being the builders of *objective* sociology and psychology. Actually, instead of fostering objective study of the basic, trans-subjective psychosocial phenomena, they have driven these disciplines into a blind alley of subjective mirages, evanescent trivialities, arbitrary rankings, and fleeting shadows of the essential psychosocial realities. Rarely if ever before, have sociology and psychology so greatly neglected the study of objective and basic psychosocial facts, and been so excessively preoccupied with a minute investigation of "hearsay" trivialities, especially those of a wishful character.

On what sort of phenomena have recent sociology and psychology been doing "research"? Speech-reactional utterances mainly. How have these utterances been obtained? By speech-reactional interviews and questionnaires. What have the investigators asked their respondents in their interviews, questionnaires, and recordings? (a) Predominantly about their wishes, desires, preferences, tastes, evaluations, and similar wishful dreams; (b) in part about what the respondents would prefer to do under various imaginary or hypothetical conditions, a, b, c, d · · · —for instance, if the respondent should see his chum cheating in an examination; (c) in part, in "projective techniques," the respondents are asked about their dreams, word-associations, and interpretations of ink-blots, about some "traumatic" events, and especially about all the possible and impossible details of their sex experiences; (d) or the respondents have to answer a long list of questions allegedly revealing their intelligence, temperament, attitudes, aptitudes, and all sorts of imaginable and unimaginable mental, volitional, emotional, and other qualities; (e) or they are asked—in sociometric tests—with whom they hypothetically would prefer to work, to play, to eat, to live in the same room, and so on, up to with whom they would prefer to go to bed; (f) or they are asked to talk and act out a certain role in a make-believe situation, with imaginary co-actors; (g) or the respondents are forced to answer thousands of questions about tens of thousands of facts, hypothetical mirages, momentary impressions, and other fantastically diverse items about which they often know nothing; (h) or the respondents are closeted in a small room and are there made to talk about any topic which the fanciful observer happens to impose upon the members of his "problem-solving" or "Group Dynamics" group or upon soldiers and pupils delivered by their authorities for the tortures of questioning and interviewing by the indefatigable executioner-investigators.

In brief, the bulk of recent psychosocial research deals with speech-reactions, gathered by speech-reactional operations, centered around wishful, hypothetical, "syndromatic," and subjective utterances, rarely checked for their accuracy, sincerity, and correspondence to the facts. This sort of "hearsay" is the material out of which most of the recent psychosocial theories and "research conclusions" have been manufactured, by mechanically processing the "stuff" through the calculating gadgets of the statistical routine. As indicated in the preceding chapters, in this processing phase perfectly arbitrary decisions (rankings, scorings, classifications, etc.) are made throughout the whole processing operation while the "hearsay stuff" moves along on the statistical assembly belt. The result is the mass-manufacture of doubly subjective products which are then thrown in great quantities on humanity's mental stock-exchange.

It is enough to take a random dozen of recent volumes in sociology or psychology, or a dozen recent issues of sociological or psychological journals to see, roughly, the accuracy of the picture we have outlined. To be sure, there are exceptions to this pattern of research, but the exceptions do not repudiate the rule. One of the symptomatic details confirming the rule is the recent glorification of books whose main virtue consists in containing the largest number of verbal responses to the greatest number of questions put to a crowd of respondents. Whether such volumes are filled with the obligatory responses of military men, or with the "juicy" utterances of voluntary sex-exhibitionists or "sincere" prostitutes, is of secondary importance. What is important is the fact that a volume, in order to be valued as "a great contribution to the science of sociology or psychology," has to be filled with thousands of tables and diagrams summing up such stuff.

The preceding chapters have shown the trivial, unreliable, short-lived, and ever-changing character of these speech-reaction "snapshots." At best, these snapshots depict situations only as they are at the moment of answering. Often the speech-reactions give insincere and hypothetical results. No careful scholar can take these vocal utterances as typical for any category of population beyond the group questioned. Nor can any real scholar take the snapshots as true pictures of the respondents' constant opinions. We know well how rapidly wishful opinions and speech-reactions change. Even for the respondents, the picture is representative only for the moment of registering their answers. We have also seen that hardly any speech-reactional tests—intelligence, temperament, projective, sociometric, psychodramatic, and so on—test the qualities they are supposed to be testing. The testing speech-reactional stuff is also unreliable and of small cognitive value.

The research factories manufacturing such products have become the dominant industry of sociological and psychological research. Their products are manufactured on a mass scale, moving along the assembly-line almost as mechanically as automobiles. As a result, scientific journals, texts and monographs are filled mainly with this sort of research. Its total volume has already become so large that nobody, except "the All-Remembering, All-Indexing, and All-Tabulating Electronic Robot," can know, remember, and use this cosmic mass of research. Human scholars and scientists can hardly master it: after all, human memory is limited, and human life is too short. Moreover, it is not certain whether these products are worth remembering. Many real scholars refuse to waste their time and energy in plodding through miles and miles of this monotonous research. What cognitive value can possibly be gained from the "findings" that 87.68 per cent of the soldiers of platoon A of regiment B of army C, questioned on February 7, 1942, at 2:00 P.M., answered that on the front line they did not have enough sleep and were dirty; or that the prostitutes of establishment X serve, on an average, 11.6 customers per 24 hours in the summer and 9.4 in the winter; or that 96.78 per cent of the wives of the class of 1928 of X University answered they were satisfied with their husbands as lovers, though 47.23 per cent of these wives wanted to be *la femme fatale et perdue*. These and similar "findings" only glut our minds with all sorts of odds and ends. Nor does the indexing, cross-indexing, and crisscross indexing help much, either. In these conditions a scholar is inclined to repeat Hobbes' dictum: "If I had read [these research papers] as much as other men, I should have known as little." Preoccupation with this time-and-fund-consuming research leaves little time for the researchers to study more important sociocultural phenomena, or to acquaint themselves with the vast fund of real knowledge accumulated by hundreds of eminent social thinkers. In this research industry the researchers have hardly any time even for seriously thinking about the problems studied and still less time for cultivating intuition or incisive rational thought, or for developing their minds generally. As a result of this mechanized research industry, we have a vast army of "research-factory hands" who, in the terms of Lao-Tse, "are never wise men, while wise men are never researchers." No wonder, therefore, that this vast army has not enriched our knowledge by many new discoveries or verities.

Such, in brief, is one of the important characteristics of today's sociology and psychology. Whether we like it or not, both disciplines are in a blind alley of subjective and evanescent hearsay trivia. In our courts most of this "hearsay stuff" is rejected as evidence. And rightly so. At the present time we already have so many of these products that we do not know what to do with them. The further expansion of this research-industry will, if anything, drive these disciplines deeper and deeper into the blind alley of creative sterility and pseudoscience. The only real way out of this situation is the way of integral sociology and psychology, based on an integral theory of truth and artfully using the combined intuitional, logico-mathematical, and empirical ways of cognition. However difficult this royal road to truth and scientific knowledge is, there is no other way to a creative renaissance of these disciplines.

## 2. Negativistic Proclivities

Preoccupation with the above trivia, and the failure to cultivate enlightening intuition and penetrating thought, together with the generally negativistic mentality of the distintegrating Sensate culture of our time, are responsible for the prevalence of negativistic interpretations of man and of social and cultural phenomena in modern sociology and psychology. The neglect of intuition and of deep, consistent thought results in an inability to discern what is real and what is merely apparent in the enormous mass of data collected for analysis; to discern what is important and what is trivial, which factors or variables are primary and which are secondary or fictitious.

This poorly-discerning state of mind in the psychosocial sciences is subjected to the incessant pressure of the disintegrating Sensate culture, as suggested above. In my *Social and Cultural Dynamics* a vast body of evidence is given to show that the dominant Sensate supersystem of Western culture has entered such a phase of disintegration. On the basis of this evidence, I ventured, as early as the nineteen-twenties, to predict terrible wars, revolutions, and anarchy; the utter atomization of all religious, moral, aesthetic, political, and other values, with the attendant rise of rude force—assisted by fraud—to the position of supreme arbiter of inter-individual and intergroup relationships; tornadoes of destruction, bestiality, and inhumanity; further dissolution of the family and marriage; the vulgarization and disintegration of the hitherto magnificent Sensate literature, music, painting, sculpture, etc.; the increasingly destructive trend of scientific discoveries and inventions; the progressive mechanization of scientific research; and so on and so forth. And I also predicted and stressed an increase of negativistic proclivities. At its disintegrating phase, Sensate mentality becomes increasingly "pathological," "negativistic," and "dirty." It mortalizes the immortals, uglifies the beautiful, identifies genius with insanity, the saint with the superstitious maniac, the great masterpiece with the best-seller. In such a culture the bigger replaces the better, and technique supplants creativity; and all values are dragged into the muddy waters of the social sewers.[1]

The science, and particularly the psychosocial sciences, of a disintegrating Sensate culture cannot help but be stamped with the same negativistic marks. Most of the discussed shortcomings of modern psychology and sociology are due to the disintegrating Sensate culture in which these disciplines live and work. Breathing the negativistic air of this culture, they have also become negativistic in their interpretations of man and the sociocultural universe.

In the atmosphere of our Sensate[2] culture we are prone to believe in the power of the struggle for existence, of selfish interests, egoistic competition, hate, the fighting instinct, sex drives, the instinct of death and destruction, in the all-powerfulness of economic factors, rude coercion and other negativistic forces. Yet we are highly skeptical in regard to the power of creative love, disinterested service, unprofitable sacrifice, mutual aid, the call of pure duty and other positive forces. The prevalent theories of evolution and progress, of the dynamic forces of history, of the dominant factors of human behavior, of the "how" and "why" of social processes unanimously stress such negativistic factors as the above. They view them as the main determinants of historical events and of individual life courses. Marxism and the economic interpretation of history; Freudianism and its libidinal-destructive explanation of human behavior; instinctivist, behaviorist, and physiosomatic theories of personality and culture; Darwinistic and biological theories of the struggle for existence as the main factor of biological, mental, and moral evolution; even the prevalent motto of the chambers of commerce that "rivalry and competition made America great"—these and similar theories dominate contemporary sociology, economics, psychology, psychiatry, biology, anthropology, the philosophy of history, political science, and other social and humanistic disciplines. These ideologies have an enormous appeal to the prevalent Sensate mind, are eagerly believed by Sensate man, and are considered by him as "the last word in modern science."

On the other hand, the Sensate mind emphatically denies the power of love, sacrifice, friendship, cooperation, the call of duty, the unselfish search for truth, goodness, and beauty. These appear to us as something epiphenomenal and illusory. We call them "rationalizations," "self-deceptions," "derivations," "beautifying ideologies," "opiates of the people's mind," "smoke screens," "idealistic bosh," "unscientific delusions," etc. We are biased against all theories that try to prove the power of love and other positive forces in determining human behavior and personality; in influencing the course of biological, social, mental, and moral evolution; in affecting the direction of historical events; in shaping social institutions and culture.

This penchant to believe in the power of negative forces and to disbelieve the influence of positive energies has nothing to do with the scientific validity of either type of theory. It is mainly the result of the congeniality of the "debunking theories" and the noncongeniality of the positive "idealistic" theories with our negativistic and decaying Sensate culture. The negativistic theories are "the flesh from the flesh, and the bone from the bone" of the negativistic Sensate world. As such they are at home in that culture and appear to be valid to the Sensate mind. They easily infect Sensate individuals, including Sensate scientists and scholars. Their "facts" appear to be convincing, their logic persuasive, their "evidence" undeniable: hence the success of these theories in the Sensate sociocultural world.

Because of their noncongeniality, the positive "idealistic" theories are doomed to be stepchildren in this Sensate culture of ours. They are destined to be unpopular and unsuccessful; they appear to be unconvincing, unscientific, prejudiced and superstitious to Sensate society and Sensate man.

When both kinds of theories are carefully tested, their comparative validity becomes quite different from that determined by the extrascientific, existential factor of their congeniality or noncongeniality with the dominant Sensate culture.

The foregoing does not mean that some of the negativistic theories are totally wrong. A part of truth they certainly contain. But this part is much more limited than is thought by the bulk of modern scholars, and even this part needs many reservations and qualifications to make it true. If there is to be a creative revival of the psychosocial sciences, one of their immediate tasks is to cleanse themselves of their fallacious negativistic beliefs. It is urgently needed, also, for the moral and aesthetic ennoblement of man himself and of his social and cultural life. Whether we like it or not, the fallacious portions of the negativistic theories have tangibly contributed to the present degradation of man and of all the great values from the supreme value called God (or some other name) to the values of truth, love, beauty, creative genius and sainthood, and, finally, to those of fatherhood, motherhood, the family, duty, sacrifice, and decency in treatment of man by man. The negativistic ideologies have debunked, degraded, and poisoned these values and thereby contributed their share to today's inter-human strife, with its bestiality, cruelty, destruction, and misery. The destructive science of the dying Sensate culture, and its negativistic psychosocial disciplines, are largely responsible for this tragedy. The latter, in the name of science, have infected the minds of our intellectual, governmental, business and other leaders, as well as the minds of the masses of the led, with various negativistic notions, nihilistic dogmas, cynical beliefs, and debunking ideologies. These have undermined the great values, and supplied an easy justification of anything—if one can get away with it. Directly and indirectly, the negativistic ideologies have notably helped in the mental, moral, and social disorganization of humanity, and in bringing about the existing tragedy.

This tragedy begins now to threaten the very existence of man and the continuation of his creative mission, including man's scientific creativity. A thorough self-cleansing of the psychosocial disciplines thus becomes the paramount necessity for the survival and growth of the disciplines themselves. If this ultimatum of destiny is not heeded by science generally and by psychosocial sciences particularly, they may, by their unresponsiveness, write their own death verdict. *Volentem fata ducunt, nolentem trahunt.*

### 3. The Nemesis

Perhaps the most convincing corroboration of the discussed foibles of modern sociology and psychology is the fact of their insignificant creativity. Although hundreds of thousands of researchers have been working in psychosocial fields for more than a quarter of a century; notwithstanding millions of hours and an untold amount of energy spent in sociological and psychological investigations; despite millions of dollars invested in these researches and thousands of courses and seminars given in these disciplines in universities; in spite of a prodigious expansion of the psychosocial research industry; the net creative results have been disappointing.

Let us survey the creative achievements of the period mentioned. Has this big-scale research-industry produced, during the last thirty years, a new, great, and valid theory or a truly significant conceptual framework for social and psychological phenomena? Hardly! A few significant theories have been formulated [3] but mainly in the field of "philosophy of history" or "philosophy of culture," or "social philosophy," and mostly by the nonsociologists and nonpsychologists. For this reason we can here pass them by without further discussion. As to the theories of the psychosocial theorizers and conceptualists and of the natural science sociologists and psychologists, none of them can be called new, great, and important. Many sociologists and psychologists have failed to produce a coherent theory for the simple reason that they view any theory as armchair philosophy or metaphysical speculation. Instead of theorizing they have preferred to be busy with fact-finding, interviewing, questionnairing, making pleasant field trips, and then counting and calculating. Of course, this antitheoretical position is also a sort of theory; but our "antitheoretical theorists" seem to have been unaware of this simple fact and, therefore, have not attempted to set forth a comprehensive "antitheoretical theory."

The natural science sociologists and psychologists have not produced any original and significant conceptual framework, because they have been busy with imitating and bootlegging poorly understood theories from physical sciences. Even a competent imitation of a model-theory remains an imitation and not an original creation. Incompetent imitation is mere distortion; as such it has no chance to be original, or great, or even "skillful in its art of imitation." Instead of building a new theory, many modern sociologists and psychologists have candidly used the previous sociological or psychological theories, like those of K. Marx, S. Freud, Max Weber, E. Durkheim, F. Tönnies, G. Tarde, L. von Wiese, G. Simmel, W. Stern, E. Spranger, W. Wundt, I. Pavlov, W. G. Sumner, L. Ward, C. H. Cooley, E. A. Ross, V. Pareto, W. I. Thomas and F. Znaniecki, F. Giddings, R. Park, O. Spengler, C. G. Jung, and so on. In some cases they used these theories in their original form, in other cases in a diluted form, but in no case did they pretend to have created their own theory.

Other modern sociologists and psychologists have preferred to make an eclectic hash of some of these theories, and—without any pretensions to be systematic theorizers—in their texts and research papers they have referred now to one, now to another theory for explanation of their problems. For obvious reasons neither of these groups have created a new framework for these sciences.

Finally, there remain a few sociologists and psychologists who have been ambitious enough to build their own "analytical framework," to create a new general theory of social action or interaction, or of social or cultural system, which would serve as a foundation, as a referential system, and as a guide for a large body of special research. These ambitious "theorizers" have dreamed they are the Newtons of sociology and the Galileos of psychology, and they have earnestly endeavored to create a new sociological *Principia* or a new psychological *Prolegomena* that would direct the bulk of future research in these fields for some two hundred years, as Newton's *Principia* did.

In spite of their commendable purpose, the new Newtons and Galileos have failed dismally. Instead of the great *Principia* they have only delivered abortive intellectual concoctions. These concoctions are marked by an absence of consistent and elegant logic, of penetrating thought, of enlightening intuition, of any original idea; nor does any significant empirical material mar their monotonous pages. On the other hand, the would-be *Principia* are conspicuous for their abundance of ponderous platitudes; and for a plethora of new terms needlessly replacing the older and better ones. Still more conspicuous in these pretentious theories is eclecticism, vagueness, and lack of logic. Instead of a logically developed system, they give a hash of various odds and ends taken from preceding psychosocial thinkers like A. Comte, H. Spencer, M. Weber, F. Tönnies, E. Durkheim, V. Pareto, S. Freud, and others. The borrowed fragments are neither unified into a real system, nor, as a rule, are their authors mentioned. Instead of a magnificent cathedral of sociology or a resplendent palace of psychology, our system-builders have thrown together a mere sociological shack, a primitive psychological tourist cabin devoid of modern conveniences.

If one subtracts from the shack or the cabin the parts pilfered from the noble buildings of previous sociologists and psychologists, only the debris of empty ponderosities and the rubbish of scattered platitudes remains.

This eclecticism is accompanied by a notable vagueness of thought and scantiness of logic in our "analytical theorists"; and this, despite their sincere efforts to define, analyze, classify, and develop their ideas "rigorously and scientifically." They solemnly start to define the problem *X*. They define it by a "first approximation" through references to the unknowns *A, B, C* · · · Instead of one unknown, *X*, the definition introduces several unknowns, *A, B, C* · · · This necessitates defining *A, B, C* as a "second approximation." In defining *A, B,* and *C,* "the operational definition" of one unknown *X* by several unknowns, *A, B, C* · · · is repeated as a "third approximation." *A* now is defined through the unknowns *a, b, c; B* through the unknowns *d, e, f; C* through the unknowns *g, h, i.* Then each of these—*a, b, c; d, e, f;* and *g, h, i*—undergoes similar splitting into several unknown "variables," the unknowns increasing with each approximation in geometric ratio. The more "rigorously" they endeavor to define their *X,* the greater becomes the need of "the definition of definitions," of "the definition of the definitions of the definitions" and so forth, *ad infinitum.* The more precisely they endeavor to define, the more undefined the problem remains. As a result of this peculiar logic of definitions, the reader has to track the multiplying pathways and byways until he is lost in the bewildering and endlessly branching maze of unknowns. Utterly exhausted in this hopeless search for a clear definition of *X,* he returns empty-handed to his point of departure, and finds the unknown *X* more undefined than before the searching expedition. In other cases our definition-makers and builders of analytical conceptual frameworks solve their problems by the short cut of *obscurum per obscurius,* in which the dark problem is defined through reference to a still darker one. In other instances they do not give any clarification of their mysterious *dicta,* leaving it to the reader to find out what, if anything clear, the dicta mean.

Thus, for instance, in some of the pretentious works several basic concepts are defined through reference to the concept of equilibrium. This concept is used in the loosest of ways in the psychosocial disciplines and has at least five different meanings.[4] If one tries to find the author's meaning, one either does not find any at all or finds a mere transcription of one of the meanings of this term in physics—a meaning which is meaningless in application to the social problems discussed. In another would-be *Principia* the concepts of "means and ends," of "goal and goal-directed activity" play a basic role in the scheme of the authors. If one wishes to get the exact meaning of these principles and terms, one does not find any. The point is that since the Aristotelian four-fold classification of causes—the material, the efficient, the formal, and the final—the principles and terms of means and ends, of goal and goal-directed activity, can have several different meanings: (a) the antecedent and the consequent; (b) the cause and the effect; (c) the consciously set purpose and consciously arranged means for its achievement; (d) the unconscious drive towards a certain objective and the instinctive set of actions to obtain it; and several others. If we refer to the principle of means and ends without further specification, we say something vague or meaningless or something that has several different meanings. As a matter of fact, our "theorizers" do exactly that: they leave it at the state of this indeterminacy. If need be, the examples of this monotonously ponderous but invariably dull and artless "analytical reasoning" can be supplied *ad libitum*.

The same semblance of logic is shown in numerous classifications of our theorists. They seem to be very fond of classifying, pigeon-holing, dividing and subdividing their notions into various classes, sub-classes, and sub-sub-classes, with side-line deviant categories thrown in as bonuses. When, however, one carefully examines these classifications, one is strongly impressed by their nonlogical character as well as by their fruitlessness for understanding psychosocial phenomena or for guiding empirical research. They do not have any logical *fundamentum divisionis,* nor do they follow the principle of definition and classification *per genus et differentia specifica* or any other logical or mathematical rules of sound division and taxonomy. Instead, they represent an incidental, inadequate pigeon-holing of things into a lopsided set of fictitious or semi-fictitious verbal classes.[5] In their totality these verbal classes contain only a portion of the classified phenomena, but not their whole universe (*A*); on the other hand, the total set of these classes contains also the phenomena of an entirely different universe (*B*) which do not belong to universe *A*. No logic can sanction such classifications. The following classifications give an idea of the defects discussed. "All human beings fall into four main classes: (1) Protestants, (2) Females, (3) Negroes, (4) Fascists." "The orientation of man to his surroundings can be divided into the following classes: (1) The Cognitive, (2) the Cathectic-affective, (3) the Evaluative, (4) the Appreciative-affective, (5) the Moral." "All human actions can be divided into the following classes: (1) Pleasurable, (2) Universal, (3) Goal-directed, (4) Aggressive, (5) Particular." "Mechanisms for solving external problems are as follows: (1) Integrative, subdivided into cognitive learning and reality testing; (2) Allocative, subdivided into substitution, displacement, fixation, and cathectic learning."

This type of classification, with variations, is endlessly repeated in sub-classifications and sub-sub-classifications stretching like sand dunes through the arid pages of the works discussed. In comparison with this lifeless scholasticism of undefined definitions and nonlogical classifications, even the withered scholasticism of the late Middle Ages appears quite elegant and lively. If we further examine how well the basic principles of each of the systems are mutually harmonized, and to what extent they give a real unified system of sociology or psychology, we are again bound for a disappointment. In the eclecticism of the would-be system, the different principles continue to squat side by side in all their unassimilated separateness and irreconciled contradiction. Thus the principles of sociological or psychological realism and nominalism, universalism and singularism; of the sensory, rational, and intuitional ways of cognition; of materialism and idealism; the principles of immanent and nonimmanent change; of the old-fashioned macrophysical and the probabilistic "causality"; of Max Weber's "rationalism" and "preponderant role of religion," and S. Freud's "libidinism" and negative position toward religion; of "meaningful sociology" and "social physics"; of "expectation" as a criterion for nondeviant lawful conduct, and the concept of "lawful conduct" having no relationship to "expectation"; of the nominalistic reification of "actor and role" as the central axis of the system, and the realistic conception of "actor and role" as merely one of many characteristics of an organized social system; these and dozens of other basic principles continue to appear at random in the eclectic hash of the would-be system. If most of the current introductory texts in sociology and psychology can be defined as collections of amazingly diverse bits of information bound together mainly by the binding of the book, the pages and chapters of the systems discussed have, besides the binding of the volume, additional bonds: ponderosities, newly introduced terms, misdefining definitions, misclassifying divisions, and the all-pervading eclecticism. In spite of these "bonds," the systems still remain eclectic congeries of irreconciled principles and notions taken from the works of previous social and psychological system-builders.

To sum up: from the epistemological and logical standpoints the would-be systems are nonlogical, artless congeries. They do not benefit our understanding of psychosocial phenomena; nor are they graced by a penetrating insight in the mysteries of the psychosocial cosmos and of its central being—human personality; nor do they furnish us with a set of principles on which we can build the temple of knowledge of social and psychological phenomena; nor are they entertaining and enjoyable as artistic masterpieces.

But perhaps these systems offer newly discovered empirical uniformities? or causal-probabilistic correlations of empirical variables? or a set of empirical facts of a highly important nature? or a remarkable interpretation of empirical data? Alas! They do not offer any empirical knowledge of this kind, for the simple reason that they have almost no empirical material. Pretending to be empirical and empirically tested, the theories move in a superempirical kingdom of abstractions rarely touching the prosaic empirical region. From the standpoint of empirical, fact-finding exploration they do not add anything to our knowledge of psychosocial empirical facts and relationships.

From the above examination, we must conclude the recent period has not produced anything remarkable in the field of general systems of sociology and psychology.

But how about special monographs dealing with special classes of social or psychological phenomena? Have not outstanding monographs been published, and have they not offered new and remarkable theories concerning their special topics? There is no doubt that a number of monographic studies of some value have appeared; but they are not of the kind that become the immortal landmarks in history of sociology or psychology. Likewise, they are not the masterpieces that exert a lasting influence on subsequent studies in their field. For a short time they may establish a fad, but after a few months or years they fade into oblivion as all mediocre studies do.

There also have been published, during the period examined, a number of sensationally successful best-sellers. Each of these is acclaimed, not only by the publishers' blurbs but by many a sociologist and psychologist, as "one of the greatest contributions of all times" to these disciplines. Untempered glorification of sensational things, including the books in the social sciences, especially when they become best-sellers, is one of the characteristics of the decaying Sensate culture. We regularly fool ourselves, and inadvertently the others, with this sort of misjudgment and misvaluation. However, as Lincoln correctly observed, we cannot fool all the people all of the time, or, as Hegel no less correctly stated: *Die Weltgeschichte ist das Weltgericht*. The historical process conducts a constant and pitiless evaluation and selection of all values created by man, and its verdicts are well balanced. The average life-span of contemporary best-sellers is about six months to one year. Their life may linger a few more years, but beyond that, with very few exceptions, they go with the wind into oblivion. *Die Weltgeschichte ist das Weltgericht,* indeed. Similar is the fate of the recent, sensationally successful best-sellers of a sociological and psychological nature. Most of these "greatest contributions of all times" are already forgotten; others are still lingering in their movement toward oblivion. Hardly any of the recent "greatest contributions" has a chance to survive longer than a decade or two, and none of them can escape the unavoidable oblivion.

To sum up: the period has produced a number of scholarly and, on a small scale, valuable studies. But they are pedestrian works of industrious mediocrity. None of them is marked by the stamina of a genius or of a great sociological or psychological creator.

Thus surveying the general and special theories in the psychosocial field for the period mentioned, we come to the sad conclusion that the period has indeed been one of pedestrian mediocrity, an age of psychosocial shacks and tourist cabins, not one for the building of immense pyramids, great cathedrals, immortal Parthenons, or even of Empire State buildings. This sterility is the Nemesis which has pursued modern sociology and psychology because of their erring ways.

Being infertile in the field of general and special theories, the period has, perhaps, made important contributions to the methods and techniques of psychosocial research, and has discovered important empirical uniformities in psychosocial processes? Before making our conclusion final, we must examine the possible contributions in these areas.

If we ask what *new important empirical uniformities* have been discovered by psychosocial research for the period considered, the answer is: hardly any. To be sure, a legion of "correlation-uniformities" have been discovered and their coefficients calculated. But we have shown earlier that different coefficients of correlation or of least squares between the same variables are quite discordant and often contradictory and are, therefore, unreliable. The respective association-uniformities therefore become uncertain. It has also been pointed out that practically all the allegedly new real uniformities were discovered before the modern period. Sometimes, the claim of having discovered a new uniformity becomes plainly ridiculous. Thus, during the period examined, we read of such important discoveries as that the average height and weight of the rich classes tend to be greater than those of the poor classes; that broken homes and disorganized families contribute a larger share of juvenile delinquents than happy homes and harmonious families; that group decision is more effective in changing behavior in certain fields than a mere lecture; that an active participation of the employees in management, and especially in designing the changes to be made in the distribution of jobs in a factory, tend to decrease labor-management tensions; and so on, and so forth. Many other allegedly new uniformities have been mentioned in various chapters of this book. On the other hand, some of the partly new uniformities happen to be very doubtful, often wrong, in the unqualified and unlimited formulation in which they are presented. Thus, for instance, the uniformity of greater tension in the experimental "autocratic" than in the "democratic" groups (K. Lewin and others) is questionable, if and when it is formulated as a universal rule. Some democratic groups have much greater inner antagonism than do some autocratic groups. As with many other "new" uniformities, the uniformity discussed was also discovered and more precisely formulated by such "speculative" thinkers as Plato and Aristotle, or by such historians as Thucydides and Polybius. They clearly set forth the specific conditions under which the democratic group is inwardly harmonious, and the conditions under which such a group becomes a house divided against itself, "full of variety and disorder." [6]

The same can be said of several other "uniformities" supposedly discovered during the period considered. The essentials of these uniformities were well known to the social thinkers of the past. Some details of such uniformities are new, but the new variations are often questionable in their unqualified and unspecified formulations. Whether we take the uniformities in death, birth, marriage, divorce, suicide, and morbidity rates; or those in the phenomena of migration and mobility; or in organization and disorganization of social groups; or in the movement of criminality; or in the fluctuation of peace and war, order and disorder, prosperity and depression, totalitarian and liberal regimes; or in the increase and decrease of the amount and forms of freedom, or in mobility and diffusion of culture—if we take practically any known uniformity in any of the main fields of psychosocial and cultural phenomena it will be found in works published before the recent period and, as a rule, will be formulated more accurately, analyzed more thoroughly, and corroborated more adequately, than in the works of the period considered. The recent period has not been fortunate in the discovery of new important uniformities.

No better is the record of the period in devising *new methods and new techniques of psychosocial research.* The preceding chapters have dealt with practically all the main methods of modern sociology and psychology. All these methods were known and used before: deductive, inductive, "operational" or experimental, mathematical and statistical, not to mention historical, "clinical," and generally observational. The same is true of the techniques, if by this term we mean something different from "method"; namely, the concrete details of application of a given method. For example: what person or group is to be studied by a given method; in what concrete conditions; what sort of actions of the subjects are to be observed or experimented with; what kinds of gadgets are to be used, and so on. These technical minutiae always vary from study to study, from investigator to investigator. In this sense, no basically new techniques have been used by psychosocial researchers of the recent period. The only new feature they have added to the old techniques is the practice of administering various mechanical tests on a mass-scale—that, and an extraordinary faith in the adequate testing power of these mechanical tests. The preceding chapters have shown, however, that this faith in the revealing power of the tests is largely unwarranted.

The same goes for various "refinements" of different, particularly quantitative, methods. If there have been real refinements of the mathematical part of these methods, this is due to the mathematicians rather than to the routine statisticians whose mastery of mathematics is too elementary for them to discover new mathematical verities. Other attempted improvements of statistical or quantitative methods, like the discussed efforts to make unscalable variables scalable, and so on, have been, so far, unsuccessful. Finally, there remain the improvements in various tools, especially of the quantitative method: better calculating machines, better paper and pens, better "scalogram boards," and so on. Thanks to the improvement of the technological part of our culture, the recent period of psychosocial research has, indeed, had much better means, instrumentalities, and gadgets for research than the previous periods. It is obvious, however, that the possession of better tools of research is insufficient for accomplishing better research. Moreover, the refinement of these tools is due to the engineers and manufacturers of the research instruments, rather than to sociologists or psychologists. Thus in the field of methods and techniques, modern sociology and psychology have precious little to boast about.

Finally, there remains a *mountain of elementary and advanced texts* by modern sociology and psychology. The mass production of text books is possibly the most conspicuous characteristic of the period considered. Perhaps the creative genius of the period has found its best expression in the exceptionally high scientific standards of these texts? Unfortunately, the answer to this question must be in the negative. A careful dissection of these texts shows that their scientific standards are peculiar rather than high.[7] For historically minded scholars these texts bear the typical marks of the uncreative Alexandrian period of Greek culture and science. In the terms of our modern culture, the texts strikingly reflect the current mass-mania of quiz shows and "information" entertainment. The texts are filled mainly by an enormous mass of information about the most diverse physical, chemical, biological, psychological, sociological, philosophical, theological, ethical, and artistic items, presented pictorially, diagrammatically, statistically, and in any way you please. The diversity of the topics and information in the texts is so rich that often it is only the cloth which holds the chapters together. The elementary texts serve up this potpourri of informative odds and ends in a sketchy but well chewed and even overchewed form easy to swallow and digest without any mental effort on the part of the students. The advanced texts furnish a much bigger mass of informative material and present it in a drier eruditional way. The advanced texts also give somewhat more space to "analytical thought" than do the introductory texts. But both classes of texts are largely devoid of a consistent systematic development of their discipline, of "phenomenological" and logical analysis of their problems, and especially of any sparks of originality and philosophical "speculation." Thus, although they supply some information—partly relevant, partly irrelevant—about psychosocial phenomena, they contribute little to the cultivation and development of psychosocial thought and of sociology and psychology as unified systems of knowledge of psychosocial phenomena. Moreover, being written mainly by the beginners in these disciplines, the texts can hardly have high scientific standards; as with any creative achievement the writing of great texts requires long study and a mature knowledge which the novitiates seldom have.

Since a mere compilation of various bits of information is not a particularly creative achievement—otherwise the compilers of encyclopedias would be the greatest scientists and scholars—the modern texts in sociology and psychology do not display a creative genius for the period. They are, rather, stamped by characteristics typical for periods of decline. In times of decline, information ordinarily replaces penetrating thought; technical erudition substitutes for genius; quantity for quality. Our texts are marked by these ominous signs.

The preceding survey of the achievements of modern sociology, and partly of psychology, shows that these achievements have been very modest. Our sociological and psychological research industry is efficiently manufacturing, on a big scale, a large quantity of standardized mediocre products. But, so far, it has been unable to create real masterpieces of psychosocial science. We seem to be a generation of competent technicians rather than of great discoverers and creators. And if the existing "assembly-line" system of our research is going to grow, an ever-increasing number of our research-technicians will become mere "research factory hands." With this change, research itself would tend to become progressively narrower, shallower, and less and less significant for purposes of understanding the psychosocial universe, as well as for serving the daily mental, moral, and social needs of human beings. The first symptoms of the Nemesis of creative sterility are already noticeable in today's sociology and psychology. If these disciplines do not free themselves from the erring assumptions, dogmas, methods, and techniques which have been discussed in this book, the sterility is likely to grow until it turns the living, knowing, and creating body of psychosocial science into a dried up mummy. We must not forget that *die Weltgeschichte ist das Weltgericht.*

## 4. From the Blind Alley to the Royal Road of Integral Sociology and Psychology

The creative renaissance of our disciplines requires a basic reconstruction of the prevalent conceptions of sociology and psychology. The central task of this reconstruction consists of replacing the prevalent defective views on what constitutes psychosocial reality, what is valid knowledge of it, and what are the methods of its cognition, by more adequate conceptions of these fundamentals. Prevalent psychosocial science views psychosocial reality as purely sensory phenomena; an adequate knowledge of it as a systematized body of propositions, describing sensory observations; and sensory perception in all its forms—plain observational, clinical, experimental, statistical—assisted by logico-mathematical reasoning, as the only way in which cognition of the total psychosocial reality can be gained.

From these assumptions almost all the characteristics of today's psychosocial science follow. To the same assumptions are due practically all its shortcomings discussed in this book.

For a creative renaissance of our disciplines these invalid assumptions must be replaced by what can be called the integralist conception of reality, knowledge, and ways of cognition. The integralist conception views psychosocial reality as a complex manifold in which we can distinguish at least three different aspects: sensory, rational, and supersensory-superrational. The sensory aspect is present in all psychosocial phenomena that can be perceived through our sense organs. The rational aspect is present in all the rational phenomena of the psychosocial universe: in logically and mathematically consistent systems of science, philosophy, religion, ethics, fine arts, up to the rationally motivated and executed activities of an individual or group. The supersensory-superrational aspect of psychosocial reality is manifested by the highest creative activities and created masterpieces of genius in all fields of cultural creativity: by the great creative achievement of a genius-scientist, philosopher, founder of religion, great law-giver, great apostle of unselfish love, genius-writer, poet, painter, sculptor, composer, architect, and so on. Newton and Galileo; Sankarāchārya, Plato, Kant; Beethoven, Bach, Mozart; Phidias, Michelangelo, Raphael; Homer, Shakespeare; Buddha, Jesus—these and their likes are the human incarnations of the supraconscious in the psychosocial universe.

Viewing thus the manifold psychosocial reality, the integralist conception of its knowledge consists of an adequate knowledge not only of the sensory aspect of this reality, but also of its rational and supersensory-superrational aspects.

In accordance with this, the integral science contends that this many-sided reality can be cognized not only through the channel of sensory perception-observation, but also through the channel of rational, logico-mathematical thought and through that of supersensory-superrational intuition. The sensory channel should be used mainly for cognition of sensory phenomena; the rational channel for cognition of rational phenomena; and the intuitional channel for cognition of the superrational-supersensory phenomena-noumena in the psychosocial universe.

A roughly adequate knowledge of psychosocial reality requires a concerted use of all three channels. This concerted use gives us knowledge of all three aspects of our reality, while the use of only one channel gives knowledge of only one aspect. In the integrated utilization of all three channels, the knowledge obtained through one channel is supplemented and checked by the knowledge from the other two channels. This mutual checking is an additional insurance against the errors of one-channel knowledge and an important guarantee of fuller validity for our cognition. The history of human knowledge is filled with wrong observations, fallacious reasonings, and false intuitions. Mutual checking of the knowledge obtained through one channel by that acquired through the other two reduces this danger.

Such, in skeleton form, is the integralist conception of psychosocial reality, of its adequate knowledge, and of the method of its cognition.[8] So conceived, the integral study of the psychosocial world contains in itself all the main methods of investigating and understanding psychosocial reality: the empirical, the logico-mathematical, and the intuitional. To each of these methods it assigns for study its proper aspect of the integral reality: in cognition of the empirical aspect, the empirical method in all its variants is the legitimate method of study; in cognition of the rational and superrational aspects, the logico-mathematical and intuitional methods are the proper methods of investigation and understanding; finally, for the integral cognition of the total, "three-dimensional" psychosocial reality, the unified system of all three main methods is to be used. In all these respects the integral approach to the understanding of the psychosocial universe is fuller and more adequate than any single method of cognition.

The prevalent empirical psychosocial science has delivered, especially during the sixteenth, seventeenth, eighteenth, and nineteenth centuries, important knowledge of man and of his sociocultural universe. Helped in part by the logico-mathematical method, this empirical science has labored strenuously for several centuries. At the present time it is tired and has become somewhat neurotic and less creative. It urgently needs much greater help from the other two methods of cognition. This means there should be the closest cooperation and unification of all three methods into one integral conception of reality, an integral system of truth, and an integral method of cognition. Only such an integral way can lead today's psychosocial science out of the blind alley onto the royal road of a recreated sociology and psychology.

# *Notes*

# Notes

## Chapter One

1. D. Cartwright, in the symposium: D. Cartwright and A. Zander, *Group Dynamics* (Evanston, Illinois, 1953), p. ix. (By permission of Row, Peterson and Company.)
2. *Ibid.,* p. 14.
3. *Ibid.,* p. 39.
4. *Ibid.,* p. 65.
5. *Ibid.,* pp. 52 ff.
6. *Ibid.,* p. 319.
7. *Ibid.,* p. 249.
8. For similar assertions see pp. 144, 191-203, 231, 249-50, 306, 307, 308 ff., 319, *et passim.*
9. J. L. Moreno, *Who Shall Survive?,* new edition (New York: Beacon House, Inc., 1953), pp. lxi-lxii. Ivan Pavlov used to complain that what these people did was to "first, poorly master, then appropriate" his theories. (By permission of J. L. Moreno.)
10. Moreno, *ibid.,* pp. c-cii.
11. S. A. Stouffer and others, *Studies in Social Psychology in World War II* (Princeton, 1949), vol. I, pp. 38-39, 43, 125. (By permission of Princeton University Press.)
12. *Ibid.,* vol. II, p. 3.
13. *Ibid.,* vol. IV, pp. 4, 46, 61.
14. E. D. Chapple, *Measuring Human Relations* (Provincetown, 1940), pp. 9-10.
15. G. C. Homans, *The Human Group* (New York, 1950) pp. 1-2, *et passim.*
16. R. Merton's Preface to Homans' *The Human Group,* p. xvii.
17. S. C. Dodd and J. Nehnevajsa, "Physical Dimensions of Social Distance," *Sociology and Social Research,* 38 (1954), p. 287.
18. A. Rapoport, *Operational Philosophy* (New York, 1953), p. vii.
19. *Ibid.,* pp. viii, 6, 9, 14, 153.
20. Cf. Th. Tscherbatsky, *The Buddhist Logic* (Leningrad, 1932), 2 vols., *passim,* and chaps. 1-4.
21. S. A. Stouffer, "Measurement in Sociology," *Amer. Sociol. Review,* XVIII (1953), pp. 591-92.

22. For further details on the law-codes' measurement of actions see P. Sorokin, *Society, Culture, and Personality,* chap. 4.
23. I can but wonder at the profound ignorance and neglect of law-phenomena among sociologists busy "measuring" values, attitudes, and role-obligations, by use of fanciful questionnaires and interviews collecting and counting the incidental speech-reactions of incidental respondents in incidental, often hypothetical, conditions. They concoct all sorts of cumbersome and arbitrary "techniques" and "theories"—which, to the uninitiated, sound "very, very scientific"—while ignoring the objective social realities available to them.
24. Stouffer, *ibid.,* pp. 591, 597.
25. R. W. White, "Interpretation of Imaginative Productions," in J. McV. Hunt (ed.), *Personality and the Behavior Disorders* (New York, 1944), pp. 214-15. (By permission of the Ronald Press Company.)
26. See the evidence in P. Sorokin, *The Ways and Power of Love* (Boston, 1954), chaps. 20, 21; and P. Sorokin (ed.), *Forms and Techniques of Altruistic and Spiritual Growth* (Boston, 1954), *passim.*
27. J. G. Miller, "Introduction," in *Symposium: Profits and Problems of Homeostatic Models,* Chicago Behavioral Sciences Publications, No. 1, 1953, pp. 3-5.
28. R. Linton, *The Cultural Background of Personality* (New York, 1945), pp. 2, 28, and others.
29. B. Malinowski, *A Scientific Theory of Culture* (Chapel Hill, 1944), p. 4, *et passim.*
30. See these theories in P. Sorokin's *Contemporary Sociological Theories* (New York, 1928), chap. 11.
31. Cf. R. Linton (ed.), *The Science of Man in the World Crisis* (New York, 1945), pp. 123-42. Cf. a full development of the principle of limit and of its earlier formulations in P. Sorokin, *Social and Cultural Dynamics* (New York, 1941), vol. IV, chap. 14.
32. Cf. A. H. Leighton, *The Governing of Men* (Princeton, 1945), Part II.
33. C. Kluckhohn and W. H. Kelly, "The Concept of Culture," in Linton's *The Science of Man,* quoted, pp. 78-106.
34. C. Kluckhohn, *Mirror of Man* (New York, 1949), pp. 2, 3, 180-81, 187, 222-23, 229, 262.
35. Cf. A. Kardiner, *The Individual and His Society* (New York, 1939); A. Kardiner, R. Linton and others, *The Psychological Frontiers of Society* (New York, 1945); and Kardiner-Linton's "The Concept of Basic Personality Structure," in *The Science of Man,* quoted.
36. Cf. H. Ozanne, "Synthesis in Social Science," *Sociometry,* VIII, pp. 208-215 (1945).
37. E. Faris' review of Parsons' *Social System* (Glencoe, Illinois, 1951), in *American Sociological Review,* 18 (1953), p. 18.

38. Cf. L. von Wiese, "Ein Neues Amerikanisches Sammelwerk," *Kölner Zeitschrift für Soziologie,* 5 (1952-53), 87-98.
39. *Ibid.,* pp. 97-98.
40. Some two hundred mimeographed copies of it were sent to American and European social scientists almost all of whom responded by confirming my statements.
41. Answering the criticisms of Faris and others, Parsons had to acknowledge his indebtedness to Sumner, W. I. Thomas, G. H. Mead, Cooley, Pareto, Simmel, L. J. Henderson, W. B. Cannon, and many others (except myself). He, however, insists on his own contributions. Here they are: "If I made one contribution . . . it was the demonstrations that all these men [Pareto, Simmel and other European sociologists] . . . had been converging on a single theoretical scheme." Cf. T. Parsons, "Some Comments on the State of the General Theory of Action," *Am. Soc. Review,* 18 (1953), pp. 619-31. This "contribution" is quite questionable. The logic of this contribution is as follows: "man has nose and dog has nose; therefore, man and dog have been converging on a single type of species." The theories of Pareto, Max Weber, F. Tönnies, Durkheim, A. Marshall, and W. Sombart—which Parsons considers as "converging"—in reality converge as little "on one single theoretical scheme," and remain as different from one another as the above man and dog. For an excellent criticism of Parsons' theories, see G. Gurvitch, "Le concept de structure sociale," *Cahiers Internationaux de Sociologie,* XIX, 1955, 21-31.
42. Cf. Parsons, "Some Comments," quoted, pp. 621 ff.
43. Cf. P. Sorokin, *Society, Culture, and Personality* (New York, 1947), chaps. 3-9, *et passim.*
44. *Social Mobility in Great Britain,* edited by Glass (London, 1953), p. v.
45. *American Sociological Review,* 18 (1953), 387-97.
46. Published in *Am. Soc. Review,* 10 (1945), 242-49.
47. Compare Davis' and Moore's paper with pp. 11, 100-106, 182, 327, 346, *et passim* of my *Social Mobility.*
48. To serve as examples of this reiteration of my conclusions (without reference to them) are the statements that American society is not classless, but is a stratified body with a greater vertical mobility than is found in European societies; that this greater vertical mobility is due to the differential birth-rate, the opening of new lands, increase of standard of living; that there was a vast upward mobility of soldiers during the war; that college men and other men of ability were more successful in promotion than non-college and less able men; and so on. Cf. Stouffer, *Studies,* vol. I, pp. 231-32, 243-44, 258: "The modern democracies do not present any exception to the rule [of universal stratification]. Though in their constitutions it is said that 'all men are equal,' only a naive person would

infer from this that there is no social stratification within these societies. It is enough to mention the gradations: from H. Ford to a beggar; from the President of the United States to a policeman; from the president of a university to a janitor; from a commander-in-chief of an army to a soldier; from a chairman of board of directors of a corporation to its common laborer, and so on." Sorokin, *Social Mobility,* pp. 14 ff.

"One of the most conspicuous characteristics of the so-called 'democratic societies' is [not an absence of social stratification, which is often even higher than in the non-democratic societies, but] a more intensive vertical mobility compared with that of the non-democratic societies." *Ibid.,* pp. 137-38.

After giving the data showing an exceptionally high mortality in the upper strata and in the higher army ranks in the Greek, the Roman, the Mediaeval and the modern wars and revolutions; and after demonstrating that these wars and revolutions caused a vacuum in the upper classes, *Social Mobility* concludes that "during such periods the infiltration of newcomers from the lower strata into the higher ones is especially intensive" and that this intensified vertical mobility has a fairly general uniformity. *Ibid.,* p. 359, and the whole of chapter 15.

"In present Western societies, the schools represent one of the most important channels of vertical circulation. . . . Without university graduation, an individual cannot factually (often not even juridically) be appointed or obtain any prominent place; and, contrarywise, a graduate with a brilliant university record is easily promoted and given a responsible position." And so on. *Ibid.,* pp. 170 ff.

In brief, practically all the conclusions drawn from the study of social mobility in the American Army during World War II corroborate the formulations which I have made and documented in *Social Mobility.*

The situation is different with such writings as those of T. Parsons and W. L. Warner, including Parsons' "An Analytical Approach to the Theory of Social Stratification" (*Amer. Journ. of Sociology,* XLV, 1940, pp. 849-62) and his "Revised Analytical Approach" (in B. Bendix and S. M. Lipset, *Class, Status, and Power,* Glencoe, 1953). These works deal with hardly any of the empirical facts of stratification and mobility, and represent mainly a speculative "taxonomy" of factors and forms of stratification, which is logically incidental, empirically incomplete, questionable in its dogmatic dicta, and largely useless for empirical research in these fields. In the "Revised Analytical Approach" the problem of stratification and mobility is submerged in a sea of ponderous ruminations without re-emerging with any clear form and substance.

What is valid in Warner's *Yankee City Series* (New Haven, 1941), *Democracy in Jonesville* (New York, 1948), and other works, is mainly a reiteration of three basic forms of stratification—occupational, economic, and politico-cultural—already developed in my volume. What is specifically Warner's represents a questionable mixture of his own arbitrary evaluations and criteria with those of a modest number of questioned individuals. And yet the mixture is offered as an objective basis for his still more arbitrary "six-layer cake of stratification," which does not exist in social reality. This theory of stratification is the first important mistake in Warner's works. His second serious error consists of identifying stratification with social class. Like many others, he seems to be unaware of the substantial difference between these two concepts and phenomena. There is not only inter-class, but also intra-class stratification. On the other hand, there are social classes which are basically different without any of them being "higher" or "lower" than the others. Nobody can objectively state whether a class of farmers or of industrial laborers is higher or lower than the other; whether the class of big landowners or that of the capitalists is "superior" to the other. But, in spite of the fact that such classes are not stratified in regard to each other, they do exist as different classes in the objective universe of social groups. On these points see my *Society, Culture, and Personality,* chaps. 14, 15. The third important mistake of Warner's is his effort to find clear-cut social classes and a hierarchy of social strata, where in fact they do not exist in populations like those of Yankee City or Jonesville. What really exists is either a blurred multiplicity of discordant stratifications or the as yet non-crystallized and incessantly changing beginnings of social classes and of social stratification. Similar remarks are applicable to many other studies on social stratification, social mobility, social classes, and the general theory of social groups.

49. A. H. Hobbs, *The Claims of Sociology: A Critique of Textbooks* (Harrisburg, Penn., 1951), p. 16.
50. A. H. Hobbs, *op. cit.,* p. 16.

## Chapter Two

1. L. Kanner, "Behavior Disorder in Childhood," in J. McV. Hunt (ed.), *Personality and Behavior Disorders* (New York, 1944), p. 783. An uncharitable critic can diagnose these speech disorders, in the words of N. Cameron, as "metonomic, i.e., lacking in precise definitive terms for which approximate but related terms or phrases are substituted . . . many of these being personal idioms," and as "varied, shifting, and usually inadequate verbal generalizations," *Ibid.,* p. 891. (By permission of Ronald Press Co.)
2. R. B. Cattel, in Cartwright and Zander, *op. cit.,* pp. 14 ff. (By permission of Row, Peterson and Company.)
3. Cattel, *Ibid.,* p. 22.

4. *Ibid.,* p. 21.
5. *Ibid.,* p. 26.
6. "Group Cohesiveness: Introduction," Cartwright and Zander, *op. cit.,* p. 74.
7. Cf. these theories in P. Sorokin, *Society, Culture, and Personality* (New York, 1947), chaps. 4-7.
8. Cartwright and Zander, *op. cit.,* pp. 76-77.
9. Cf. on this, P. Sorokin, *Contemporary Sociological Theories* (New York, 1928), chap. 1.
10. Cartwright and Zander, *op. cit.,* p. 306.
11. L. Festinger, "Informal Social Communication," in Cartwright and Zander, *op. cit.,* p. 199.
12. M. Deutsch, "The Effects of Cooperation, etc.," *Ibid.,* pp. 321 ff.
13. J. F. Brown, "On the Use of Mathematics in Psychological Theory," *Psychometrika,* vol. I (1936), nos. 1 and 2. See also K. Lewin, *Principles of Topological Psychology* (New York, 1936); J. F. Brown, *Psychology and Social Order* (New York, 1936). See other literature of this "topological-locomotional" kind and criticism of these theories in P. Sorokin, *Sociocultural Causality, Space, Time* (Duke University Press, 1943), chap. 3.
14. T. Parsons and E. Shils (eds.), *Toward a General Theory of Action* (Cambridge, 1951), p. 5. (By permission of Harvard University Press.)
15. *Ibid.,* pp. 5, 10, 68, 164, 294, 337, 449, 453.
16. T. Parsons, *The Social System* (Glencoe, 1951), p. 7; Cf. also pp. 45-51, *et passim.* (By permission of the Free Press.)
17. T. Parsons, *The Social System,* p. 39.
18. E. A. Tolman, "A Psychological Model" in Parsons-Shils, *Toward a General Theory of Social Action,* pp. 323, 340, 341. The whole paper of Tolman is rich with speech disorders of this sort.
19. *Amer. Sociol. Review,* 18, p. 106 (1953).
20. J. G. Miller, E. B. Holt, in *Chicago Behavorial Sciences, Symposium,* No. 1, 1953, pp. 8, 16, 41.
21. K. S. Lashley, "The Behavioristic Interpretation of Consciousness," *Psychological Review,* XXX (1923), pp. 327, 329.
22. W. S. Hunter, "The Problem of Consciousness," *Psychological Review,* XXX (1924), 1-31; and, "Psychology and Anthroponomy," *Psychologies of 1925,* p. 91.
23. G. A. Lundberg, *Foundations of Sociology* (New York, 1939), pp. 12-14.
24. G. A. Lundberg, *Foundations of Sociology* (New York, 1939), p. 115; G. K. Zipf, *Human Behavior and the Principle of Least Effort* (Cambridge, 1949), pp. 212, 253, 327-28. (By permission of Addison-Wesley Press.)

## Chapter Three

1. H. Poincaré, *La science et la méthode* (Paris, 1920), p. 95; H. Poincaré, *Dernière pensées* (Paris, 1913), pp. 38 ff.
2. H. Poincaré, *La science et la méthode,* pp. 96-104.
3. L. Lecornu, *La Mécanique* (Paris, 1918), pp. 6-8. See also J. C. Maxwell, *Matter and Motion* (London, 1882), p. 20; P. Appel et S. Dautheville, *Précis de mécanique rationelle* (Paris, 1924), chaps. 1, 2; E. Mach, *The Science of Mechanics* (Chicago, 1902), pp. 226 ff.
4. Cf. P. W. Bridgman, *The Logic of Modern Physics* (New York; Macmillan, 1927); and *The Nature of Physical Theory* (New York; Macmillan, 1936); also Bridgman's "Some General Principles of Operational Analysis," *Psychol. Review,* 52 (1945).
5. R. B. Lindsay, "A Critique of Operationalism in Physics," *Philosophy of Science,* 4 (1937), p. 456. (By permission of R. B. Lindsay.)
6. E. G. Boring, "The Use of Operational Definitions in Science," *Psychological Review,* 52 (1952), pp. 243, 269; S. S. Stevens, "The Operational Basis of Psychology," *Am. Jour. of Psychology,* 47 (1934), p. 323.
   See, on the rapidly increasing operationalism in psychology, G. Allport's *The Nature of Personality* (Cambridge, 1950), pp. 57-58. (By permission of Addison-Wesley Press.)
7. On the role of suprasensory and supralogical intuition in scientific discoveries, technological inventions, and creative achievements in religion, philosophy, fine arts, ethics, and other fields of creativity see P. Sorokin's *The Ways and Power of Love* (Boston, 1954), chap. 6. P. Sorokin (ed.), *The Forms and Techniques of Altruistic and Spiritual Growth* (Boston, 1954); K. W. Wild, *Intuition* (Cambridge, 1938); R. Ulich, *Man and Reality* (New Haven, 1948); F. S. C. Northrop, *The Meeting of East and West* (New Haven, 1948); E. W. Sinnott, *Two Ways to Truth* (New York, 1953). See other literature in P. Sorokin's quoted works.
8. R. B. Lindsay, *op. cit.,* p. 457. See also H. Margenau, *The Nature of Physical Reality* (New York, 1950).
9. Cf. many other facts of this sort in Lindsay's paper, quoted, pp. 456 ff.
10. G. Allport, *op. cit.,* pp. 68-69. Also H. Blumer, "The Problem of the Concept in Social Psychology," *Amer. Sociol. Review,* XLV (1940), pp. 710 ff.
11. Lindsay, *op. cit.,* pp. 457-58.
12. H. Margenau, "Physical Versus Historical Reality," *Philosophy of Science,* 19 (1952), p. 203.
13. Lindsay, *op. cit.,* p. 458.
14. At the present time the intuitional origin of most scientific discoveries and great creative achievements in all fields of culture can be regarded

as quite sufficiently proved. See the body of the empirical evidence on that in P. Sorokin, *Social and Cultural Dynamics,* vol. IV, chap. 17; P. Sorokin, *The Ways and Power of Love,* chap. 6.

15. Cf. Lindsay, *op. cit.,* 459 ff. R. B. Lindsay and H. Margenau, *Foundations of Physics* (New York, 1936); F. S. C. Northrop, *The Meeting of East and West* (New York, 1946), chap. 12, *et passim.*
16. Lindsay, "A Critique of Operationalism," p. 470. See also A. C. Benjamin, *Operativism* (1955).
17. C. Kirkpatrick, "A Methodological Analysis of Feminism," *Amer. Journal of Sociology,* XLIV (1939), p. 332.
18. Cf. L. M. Terman, *Psychological Factors in Marital Happiness* (New York, 1938); E. W. Burgess and L. S. Cottrell, Jr., *Predicting Success or Failure in Marriage* (New York, 1939); E. W. Burgess and H. J. Lock, *The Family* (New York, 1945), pp. 458 ff.; P. Wallin and H. M. Vollmer, "Marital Happiness of Parents," *Amer. Soc. Review,* 18 (1953), pp. 424-31; J. Bernard, "An Instrument for the Measurement of Success in Marriage," *Publications Amer. Sociol. Society,* 27 (1933), pp. 94-106.
19. Cf. S. A. Stouffer and associates, *The American Soldier* (Princeton, 1949), vol. II, pp. 36 ff. This sort of "operational method" is used throughout all four volumes of Stouffer's and associates' *Studies in Social Psychology in World War II* (Princeton, 1949-50). (By permission of Princeton University Press.)
20. Cf. the treatment of the numerous theories of social physics in P. Sorokin, *Contemporary Sociological Theories,* chap. 1; and in Sorokin's *Sociocultural Causality, Space, Time* (Duke University Press, 1943), *passim.*
21. S. C. Dodd, "A System of Operationally Defined Concepts for Sociology," *Am. Sociol. Review,* 4 (1939), pp. 620-22. (By permission of S. C. Dodd.)
22. E. Shanas, "Comment," *Am. J. of Sociol.,* XLVIII (1943), p. 491. Cf. also E. Shanas, "A Critique of Dodd's Dimensions of Society," *Am. J. of Soc.,* XLVIII (1942), pp. 214-30.
23. See H. Blumer's criticism in his "The Problem of the Concept in Social Psychology," *Am. J. of Sociol.,* XLV (1940), pp. 710-12.
24. S. C. Dodd, "Operational Definitions Operationally Defined," *Am. Journ. of Sociology,* XLVIII (1943), pp. 482-89.
25. See the evidence for the development of this uniformity in P. Sorokin, *Social and Cultural Dynamics,* vol. IV, chap. 5.
26. See "the law of three phases in the genesis of cultural systems" in P. Sorokin, *Society, Culture, and Personality,* chaps. 35-38.
27. See F. Cumont, *L'Egypt des astrologues* (Bruxelles, 1937), pp. 177 ff.
28. S. A. Stouffer, "Intervening Opportunities: A Theory Relating Mobility and Distance," *Amer. Sociol. Review,* V (1940), pp. 846-47.

29. S. A. Stouffer does not mention at all the dozens of quantitative theories and formulae of migration-mobility of his predecessors. Only E. G. Ravenstein's classic study is mentioned. Contrary to Stouffer's claim that his theory and formula constitute "a modest formulation of a new sociological law," both are at best only slight variations of previous theories and formulae. Besides the theories and formulae of Ravenstein, P. M. Meuriot, and others, E. C. Young's formula $M = K\frac{F}{d^2}$ (where M is the movement of the population, F the force of attraction by a given city or territorial group, D distance, and K a constant) takes care not only of the variable of distance, but also of that of attractions or intervening opportunities. See various theories of migration and respective formulae in P. Sorokin, C. C. Zimmerman, and C. J. Galpin, *A Systematic Source Book in Rural Sociology* (Minneapolis, 1932), vol. III, pp. 515 ff.
30. M. L. Bright and D. S. Thomas, "Interstate Migration and Intervening Opportunities," *Am. Sociol. Review,* VI (1941), pp. 773-88.
31. *Amer. Soc. Review,* 18 (1953), pp. 612-17.
32. *Ibid.,* pp. 616-17. I do not know whether Hart himself performs operational manipulations to test the "reliability" of various definitions of "operation" seriously believing in his operational procedures, or whether he does this with tongue in cheek to show the unreliable character of statistico-operational procedures. Whichever is Hart's real attitude in this matter, it is to be noted that his analysis of "operation" involves several arbitrary assumptions on his part, such as the division of the judges into "the better" and "the poorer"; his assumption that the majority vote is the correct and reliable one; his arbitrary ascription of points for computation of the total score; his identification of the meaning of the word *"operation"* with reliability or unreliability; and so on. All these operations are but statistical computation of the number of the respondents giving one of the four meanings to the word *"operation."* This computation has no relationship to the validity or reliability of any of the four meanings of the word. Nevertheless, Hart's paper demonstrates the conclusions concerning the lack of a precise meaning for the term "operation" in the works of operationalists.
33. Cf. S. C. Dodd, "On Classifying Human Values," *Am. Soc. Review,* 16 (1951), pp. 645-53; "Can the Social Scientist Serve Two Masters," *Research Studies of the State College of Washington,* 21 (1953), pp. 195-213. What is valid in this study concerns the physical and spacial distribution of leaflets thrown from airplanes, a distribution which, from the time of Galileo, has been well-known to the physical, mathematical, and meteorological scientists. Dodd's generalized conclusions concerning the diffusion of information in the human universe hardly even touch upon the problem, and in no way can be accepted as a uniformity, except for

platitudes like "the more leaflets dropped, the greater the number of persons who are likely to see them."

Cf. G. A. Lundberg, Mirra Komarovsky, and Alice M. McInerny, *Leisure: A Suburban Study* (New York, 1934); G. A. Lundberg, *"Human Values—A Research Program," Proceedings of the Pacific Sociological Society* (Pullman), September, 1950.

34. See Cartwright and Zander's *Group Dynamics,* quoted, *passim.*

35. A. Rapoport's attempt to define operationalism, operational definition, and operational philosophy utterly fails in this task. He gives many, and quite different, definitions of operationalism: "a study of relationship between doing and thinking," "a philosophy of science," a "fruitful study of what man does vs. what man is," "a study of the relationship of language to human experience." Now operational method is identified with experimental method; now with inductive and postulational deductive method; now with all these, plus intuitive grasp of the phenomena studied; now with measurement; now with a study of the invariants in common experience; now with predictability; now with "parsimony," and so on. In several places he describes operational definition as a "description of operations to be performed so that the thing defined (or its effects) will be observable." In other places he finds that observability of "the thing" or of its effects is not necessary for operational definition. Now operationalism is described as "an attitude which views thought and action inseparable; which defines 'truth' in terms of predictive content of assertions, and ethics in terms of action-directed goals." In other places neither predictability nor "the attitude" are regarded indispensable for operationalism. The net result of this confusion is that his "philosophy of operationalism" represents a hash of various odds and ends, beginning with Plato's philosophy and idealistic ideologies, or of W. Occam's nominalism, and ending with mathematical logic, experimental method, Korzybski's semantics, "logical positivism," "statistical measurements," and what not. This failure to give at least a roughly clear analysis of operationalism by a good bio-physicist is a warning against, and evidence for, the insolubility of this false problem of operationalism. Being a phantom-problem, mistakenly taken for a real problem, operationalism does not permit a clear definition of itself, or its method, or its philosophy. Cf. A. Rapoport, *Operational Philosophy* (New York, 1953), pp. viii, 4, 6, 14, 15, 23, 27, 28, 49, 50, 75, 78, 150, 230; also A. C. Benjamin, *op. cit., passim.*

## Chapter Four

1. In *L'Année Psychologique,* 1905-11.
2. See L. J. Cronbach, *Essentials of Psychological Testing* (New York, 1949); *The Third Mental Measurements Yearbook* (New Brunswick,

1949); F. S. Freeman, *Theory and Practice of Psychological Testing* (New York, 1950); H. H. Remmers and N. L. Gage, *Educational Measurement and Evaluation* (New York, 1943); H. Gulliksen, *Theory of Mental Tests* (New York, 1950); E. F. Lindquist (ed.), *Educational Measurement* (Washington, 1951); L. M. Terman and M. A. Merrill, *Measuring Intelligence* (Boston, 1937); E. L. Thorndike, *The Measurement of Intelligence* (New York, 1927). For a critical analysis of the tests, W. I. Thomas and D. S. Thomas' *The Child in America* (New York, 1928) is still quite good. See also K. Eells, A. Davis, R. J. Havighurst, and others, *Intelligence and Cultural Differences* (Chicago, 1951).

3. See a much more detailed list of such tests in Ch. V. and M. E. Broadley, *Know Your Real Abilities* (New York, 1953), pp. 228 ff.
4. On this subject, see P. Sorokin, *Society, Culture, and Personality,* chap. 4.
5. See P. Sorokin, *Social Mobility* (New York, 1927), chap. 2 *et passim.*
6. *Ibid.,* chaps. 7-9.
7. See the details of these tests in P. Sorokin, *The Ways and Power of Love: Types, Factors and Techniques of Moral Transformation* (Boston, 1954), chaps. 20-21.
8. *The Essays of Michel de Montaigne* (London, 1913), vol. I, p. 5.
9. For instance, the bulk of the questions of sociometry and of many works like Stouffer's *The American Soldier,* quoted, are of these two kinds.
10. S. A. Stouffer and others, *Studies in Social Psychology in World War II* (Princeton, 1949), v. III, pp. 34 ff.

## Chapter Five

1. Cf. "Intelligence and Its Measurement: A Symposium," *Journal of Educational Psychology,* 12 (1921): 123-47, 195-216.
2. W. I. and D. Thomas, *The Child in America* (New York, 1928), pp. 332-35. (By permission of Alfred A. Knopf.)
3. E. L. Thorndike, *The Measurement of Intelligence* (New York, 1927), p. 1.
4. See an analysis of this problem, its history, and the literature in K. Eells, A. Davis, R. J. Havighurst, V. E. Herrick, R. Tyle, *Intelligence and Cultural Differences* (Chicago, 1951).
5. The same is true of numerical scoring of examinations. For many years my assistants in grading examination papers of students used to bring them to me with each question neatly graded by a precise numerical value: 67, 74, 93, or 88. I used to ask the graders how they arrived at such precise values? and why in one examination the same question was graded, say, 76, while in another 79? I never received a satisfactory explanation. As a matter of fact, it could not be given because the figures were based largely on the subjective impressions of the graders and on

their belief in a prescribed "normal curve of grade distribution." In the many years of my university teaching and grading, I never have been able to grade any written or oral exams so precisely. Instead, I have tried to sum up my total impressions about all the student's performances—in examinations, discussions, informal chats, essays (and, in a given examination, my total impressions from the examination book)—and on the basis of this total knowledge of the student I have given the required grades: A, B, C, D, E, never trying to numerically evaluate each answer to each question. If it depended upon me, I would replace most of the examinations by a substantial thesis or essay on which the student could spend several weeks of the semester and which he could write under normal conditions. He could then best show how well he knows the field, and how much originality or consistent thought he has.

6. L. M. Terman and M. H. Oden, *The Gifted Child Grows Up* (Stanford, 1947), pp. 2-4. (By permission of Stanford University Press.)
7. *Ibid.,* pp. 4-14. For a detailed account of the testing and its results see L. M. Terman, *Genetic Studies of Genius,* vol. I, *Mental and Physical Traits of a Thousand Gifted Children* (Stanford, 1925); vol. II, C. M. Cox, *The Early Mental Traits of Three Hundred Geniuses* (Stanford, 1926); vol. III, B. S. Burks, D. W. Jensen and L. M. Terman, *The Promise of Youth: Follow-up Studies of a Thousand Gifted Children* (Stanford, 1930).
8. See the evidential data in P. Sorokin, *Social Mobility* (New York, 1927), chap. 10. Terman's comparisons of the gifted group with the general population is grossly misleading. Since more than 81 per cent of his group come from *professional and well-to-do business classes,* the comparisons should be made with the population of these classes, and not with the general population.
9. See the evidence in *Social Mobility,* quoted, chap. 11. A somewhat lower rate of suicide in the "gifted group" is deduced from very conjectural computations and doubtful comparisons with the fragmentary data on the general population.
10. L. M. Terman and M. Oden, *The Gifted Child Grows Up,* p. 112.
11. The rate of delinquency may be lower in the gifted group than in the general population; but this again is a fairly uniform characteristic of the professional and business classes in many societies. See P. A. Sorokin's *Social Mobility,* chaps. 11, 12.
12. Terman-Oden, *op. cit.,* pp. 138-39.
13. *Ibid.,* p. 148.
14. See the data in Sorokin's *Social Mobility,* chap. 12.
15. Terman-Oden, *op. cit.,* p. 155 and chap. 13.
16. *Ibid.,* p. 191 and chap. 14.
17. *Ibid.,* p. 192.

18. *Ibid.,* pp. 361 ff.
19. See P. Sorokin, *Social Mobility,* pp. 283 ff. for additional data and the sources of these figures.
20. See P. Sorokin, "Leaders of Labor and Radical Movements," *Amer. Journal of Sociology,* XXXIII (1927), pp. 395-98; P. Sorokin and C. Zimmerman, "Farmer Leaders in the United States," *Social Forces,* VII (1928), pp. 33-45.
21. *Assessment of Men. Selection of Personnel for the Office of Strategic Services by the OSS Assessment Staff* (New York, 1948), p. 5.
22. *Ibid.,* p. 8.
23. *Ibid.,* p. 392.
24. *Ibid.,* chap. 9.
25. *Ibid.,* pp. 423 ff.
26. *Ibid.,* p. 425.

## Chapter Six

1. On this triadic personality structure and the supraconscious see P. Sorokin, *The Ways and Power of Love,* chaps. 5 and 6; P. Sorokin (ed.), *Forms and Techniques of Altruistic and Spiritual Growth: A Symposium* (Boston, 1954), *passim.*
2. On this see P. Sorokin, *The Ways and Power of Love,* chaps. 5, 6.
3. See on the projective tests of monastic orders and other ancient tests in P. Sorokin, *The Ways and Power of Love,* chaps. 19-21; *Forms and Techniques of Altruistic and Spiritual Growth,* passim; R. Pettazoni, *La confession des pêches* (Paris, 1931), 2 vols.; J. T. McNeill and H. M. Gamer, *Medieval Handbook of Penance* (London, 1938).
4. In passing, it can be noted that theories of dreams as wish-fulfillment, or as expression of sex-wishes are very old. They can be found in the Hindu, Tibetan, and Buddhist Yoga texts; in the theories of the Monastic Fathers, like St. Basil the Great, St. John Cassian, and others. See, for instance, John Cassian, *De Institutis Coenobiorum,* VI, 11. Here again is an example of "amnesia."
5. S. Freud, "The Interpretation of Dreams," in *The Basic Writings of S. Freud* (New York, 1938), p. 391.
6. S. Freud, *A General Introduction to Psycho-Analysis* (New York, 1949), pp. 138-40; "The Interpretation of Dreams," quoted, p. 388.
7. J. Brozek, H. Guetzkow, M. D. Baldwin, R. Cranston, "A Quantitative Study of Perception and Association in Experimental Semi-Starvation," *Journal of Personality,* 19 (1951), pp. 245-64; also, P. Sorokin, *Man and Society in Calamity* (New York, 1943), chaps. 1-3.
8. G. W. Allport, "The Trend in Motivational Theory," *Amer. Journ. of Orthopsychiatry,* XXIII (1953), p. 109.
9. *Ibid.,* p. 108.

10. J. W. Getzels, *The Assessment of Personality and Prejudice by the Methods of Paired Direct and Projective Questionnaires.* Unpublished Thesis. Harvard College Library, Cambridge, 1951.
11. See G. W. Allport, *op. cit.;* S. Rosenzweig, "Levels of Behavior in Psychodiagnosis," *Amer. Journ. of Orthopsychiatry,* 20 (1950), pp. 63-72; J. C. Whitehorn, "Psychodynamic Considerations in the Treatment of Psychotic Patients," *Univ. of West Ontario Medical Journ.,* 20 (1950), pp. 27-41. A. A. Low, *Mental Health through Will-Training* (Boston, 1954); V. E. Frankl, *The Doctor and the Soul* (New York, 1955); K. E. Appel, "The Present Challenge of Psychiatry," *Am. J. of Psychology,* July, 1954, pp. 1-12; J. L. Moreno, "The Significance of the Therapeutic Format," *Group Psychotherapy,* April, 1955, pp. 7-19; C. R. Rogers and R. F. Dymond, *Psychotherapy and Personality Change* (Chicago, 1954); R. Assagioli, *Psycho-Synthesis* (Florence, 1955); also the works of E. Straus, L. Binswanger, M. Heidegger, and others.
12. On the supraconscious region of personality and on the "intuitional" method of its study see P. Sorokin, *The Ways and Power of Love,* chaps. 5, 6.
13. See P. Sorokin, *The Ways and Power of Love,* chaps. 15, 19, 20, 21.
14. For details, *ibid., passim.* Also P. Sorokin (ed.) *A Symposium: Forms and Techniques of Altruistic and Spiritual Growth, passim.*
15. By the "by-their-fruits" test, the psychoanalytic treatment of mental disorders is increasingly shown to be the poorest method, and other psychiatric treatments are also shown to be not very effective. One of the latest investigations of this problem shows that "patients treated by means of psychoanalysis improve to the extent of 44 per cent; patients treated only eclectically improve to the extent of 64 per cent; patients treated [occasionally] improve to the extent of 72 per cent. There thus appears . . . the more psychotherapy, the smaller the recovery rate." H. J. Eysenck, "The Effects of Psychotherapy: an evaluation." *Journ. of Consult. Psychology,* 16 (1952): 319-24. Cf. also A. A. Low, *op. cit.,* pp. 11-15; V. E. Frankl, *op. cit.,* pp. 1-26; G. W. Allport, *Becoming* (New Haven, 1955), chap. 20.
16. For a criticism of all these theories and tests see P. Sorokin, *Contemporary Sociological Theories,* chaps. 3, 5, 6; P. Sorokin, *The Ways and Power of Love,* chap. 11; P. Sorokin, *Social and Cultural Dynamics,* vol. IV, chap. 10.
17. P. A. Sorokin, "Concept, Tests, and Energy of Spontaneity-Creativity," *Sociometry,* 12 (1949), pp. 215-17; see there a development of these ideas. As a real scholar J. L. Moreno frankly acknowledged: "I am in full agreement with Sorokin that the concept of spontaneity(s)-creativity(c) is in need of further elaboration." *Ibid.,* p. 252. For a further

development of Moreno's and Sorokin's views on this, cf. *International Sociometry,* No. 1, 1956.

CHAPTER SEVEN

1. Erwin Schroedinger, *What is Life* (Cambridge University Press, 1947), p. vii. By permission.
2. See the details in P. Sorokin, *Contemporary Sociological Theories,* chap. 1.
3. A. Lysen, "Anorganisches und Organisches in den sozialen Erscheinungen," *Kölner Vierteljahrshefte für Soziologie,* XI (1932), pp. 139-53.
4. Kurt Lewin, *Field Theory in Social Sciences: Selected Theoretical Papers* (New York, 1951), pp. 100, 239-40.
5. S. C. Dodd, *Dimensions of Society. A Quantitative Systematics for the Social Sciences* (New York, 1942), frontispiece. (By permission of the Macmillan Co.) S. C. Dodd, *Systematic Social Science (A Dimensional Sociology)* (American University of Beirut, 1947).
6. E. T. Bell's review of Dodd's "Dimensions of Society," *Amer. Sociol. Review,* VII (1942), pp. 707-709.
7. G. Lundberg, *Foundations of Sociology* (New York, 1939), p. 118.
8. Concerning the multitude of different meanings for Time, Space, Causality, etc., see P. Sorokin, *Sociocultural Causality, Space, Time* (Duke Univ., 1943); G. Gurvitch, *Déterminismes et Liberté Humaine* (Paris, 1955).
9. One of the reasons for this and other shortcomings is an ambivalence of the purposes of the S-theory. In some places Dodd seems to view it as a practical device for pigeonholing *printed* or *written material* (tables, maps, graphs, prose paragraph, etc.) in the field of the social sciences. In other places he views it as a general formula for the classification and quantification of *all social phenomena.* Fluctuating between these radically different tasks, Dodd failed in both.

   Similar ambivalence exists in regard to the quantitative functions of the S-theory. In a number of places Dodd explicitly states that its purpose is systematization and quantification of the science of sociology. In these statements he regards his "formulae" as quantitative and mathematical ones. In other places he seems to consider the S-theory as a sort of convenient device for describing social phenomena and only remotely mathematical.
10. See a concise factual history of "social physics," "social mechanics," and "social energetics" in P. Sorokin, *Contemporary Sociological Theories,* chap. 1.
11. See an analysis of various meanings given to the term "equilibrium" in the psychosocial sciences and the inadequacy of all these meanings in P. Sorokin, *Social and Cultural Dynamics,* vol. IV, chap. 14.

12. A. Portuendo y Barceló, *Essais de mécanique sociale* (Paris, 1925), pp. 7-8, 20-21, 121.
13. See criticism of them in P. Sorokin, *Contemporary Sociological Theories,* pp. 13 ff. P. Sorokin, *Sociocultural Causality, Space, Time,* chap. 3. "They have been doomed to failure, because of a too literal imitation of physics." N. Rashevsky, *Mathematical Theory of Human Relations* (Bloomington, 1947), p. v.
14. J. F. Brown, "On the Use of Mathematics in Psychological Theory," *Psychometrika,* I (1936), pp. 80-81. K. Lewin, *Principles of Topological Psychology* (New York, 1936), and Lewin's *Field Theory,* quoted.
15. On the main forms of motivations and respective actions see P. Sorokin, *Society, Culture, and Personality,* pp. 44 ff. L. Petrazycki, *Law and Morality* (Harvard University Press, 1955), chap. 2.
16. Brown, *op. cit.,* p. 81.
17. George K. Zipf, *Human Behavior and the Principle of Least Effort* (Cambridge, 1949), pp. ix, 3, 5-8. (By permission of Addison-Wesley Press.)
18. *Ibid.,* pp. 20-22.
19. *Ibid.,* p. 212.
20. *Ibid.,* pp. 327-28, 253, *et passim.*
21. For details on these periodicities see P. Sorokin, *Social and Cultural Dynamics,* vol. IV, chap. 9; vol. II, pp. 353-84.
22. Cf. L. F. Richardson, "Variation of the Frequency of Fatal Quarrels with Magnitude," *Journal of Amer. Statistical Association,* XLIII (1948), pp. 523-46; L. F. Richardson, "Contiguity and Deadly Quarrels: the Local Pacifying Influence," *Journal of the Royal Statistical Society,* CXV (1952), pp. 219-31.
23. C. R. Shaw and H. D. McKay, *Juvenile Delinquency and Urban Areas* (Chicago, 1942), pp. 111-12.
24. *Cornell University Agriculture Experiment Station Bulletin* No. 426, pp. 27 ff.
25. W. Firey, *Land Use in Central Boston* (Harvard University, 1947), p. 327.
26. See L. Guttman's and P. F. Lazarsfeld's investigation in S. A. Stouffer, L. Guttman, P. F. Lazarsfeld, and others, *Studies in Social Psychology of World War II;* vol. IV: *Measurement and Prediction* (Princeton, 1950).
27. *Ibid.,* vol. IV, pp. 103-21.
28. *Ibid.,* vol. IV, pp. 157-58. (By permission of Princeton University Press.)
29. *Ibid.,* vol. IV, pp. 141-42.
30. For a full development of the theory of sociocultural systems see P. Sorokin, *Social and Cultural Dynamics,* all four volumes, and volume IV especially. Criticized at the time of its publication, this theory of socio-

cultural systems, even its terminology, is now repeated by most sociologists, usually without reference to my works.

31. For a discussion of this logical and factual adequacy see P. Sorokin, *Contemporary Sociological Theories,* pp. 34 ff.
32. *Ibid.,* vol. IV, pp. 5-7.
33. Cf. on the quantum theory and its relationship to biological and "historical" or psychosocial phenomena in the works of such eminent physicists as: E. Schrödinger, *What is Life* (Cambridge, 1947), *passim;* H. Margenau, "Physical vs. Historical Reality," *Philosophy of Science,* 19 (1952), pp. 193-213; E. C. Kemble, "Reality, Measurement and the State of the System in Quantum Mechanics," *Philosophy of Science,* 18 (1951), pp. 273-99; C. W. Churchman, *The Theory of Experimental Inference* (New York, 1948).
34. *Ibid.,* vol. IV, p. 45.
35. *Ibid.,* p. 63.
36. On the difficulty of measuring incommensurable variables in a multiple causation see P. Sorokin, *Sociocultural Causality, Space, Time,* pp. 47 ff.

## Chapter Eight

1. *Positive Philosophy,* tr. by Martineau, vol. I, p. 30.
2. N. Rashevsky, *Mathematical Theory of Human Relations* (Bloomington, 1947), pp. iii-xi, *et passim.* (By permission of Principia Press.) N. Rashevsky, *Mathematical Biology of Social Behavior* (Chicago, 1951), pp. iii-ix, chap. 27, *et passim.* A. Tarski, *Introduction to Logic* (Oxford, 1946), chap. 6; J. von Neumann and O. Morgenstern, *Theory of Games and Economic Behavior* (Princeton, 1947); I. Fisher, "The Application of Mathematics to the Social Sciences," *Bulletin of Amer. Mathem. Society,* 36 (1930); R. R. Bush and F. Mosteller, "A Model for Stimulus Generalization and Discrimination," *Psych. Review,* 58 (1951), pp. 413-23; R. Fisher, "The Expansion of Statistics," *American Scientist,* 42 (1954): 275-82.
3. R. R. Bush and F. Mosteller, *Unpublished volume on Mathematical Models,* Introduction, p. 1; N. Rashevsky, *Mathematical Theory of Human Relations,* "Preface and Explanatory Remarks."
4. S. Karlin, *A Mathematical Treatment of Learning Models,* Research Memorandum No. 921, Rand Corporation, 1952; H. G. Landau, "Note on the Effect of Imitation in Social Behavior," *Bull. Mathem. Biophysics,* 12 (1950), pp. 221-36; H. D. Landahl, "Mathematical Theory of Imitative Behavior," *Bull. Mathem. Biophysics,* 12 (1950), pp. 207-13; L. F. Richardson, "Generalized Foreign Policies," *British Journ. of Psychology,* Monog. Suppl. No. 23, 1939. A. Rapoport and L. I. Rebhun, "On the Mathematical Theory of Rumor Spread," *Bull. Math. Biophysics,* 14

(1952), pp. 375-83; S. C. Dodd, "Can the Social Scientist Serve Two Masters?" *Research Studies of State College of Washington,* XXI (1953), pp. 195-213.

5. A. Comte, *System of Positive Polity* (London, 1875), vol. I, p. 30.
6. *Bulletin of Mathematical Biophysics,* 15 (1953), pp. 197-234.
7. See the extensive literature on the role of shore line, ocean, rivers, in C. Vallaux, *La mer* (Paris, 1908), appendix: "bibliographie." See also P. Sorokin, *Contemporary Sociological Theories,* chap. 3.
8. For evidence of these changes in scientific, technological, religious, artistic, and other forms of leadership of different nations see P. Sorokin, *Cultural and Social Dynamics,* vol. II, chaps. 2, 3. P. Sorokin, *Society, Culture, and Personality,* chaps. 37-41.
9. H. Margenau, "Physical Versus Historical Reality," *Philosophy of Science,* 19 (1952), pp. 201-202. (By permission of H. Margenau.)
10. P. Sorokin, *Reconstruction of Humanity,* p. 74; C. F. Chassell, *The Relationship between Morality and Intellect* (New York, 1935), pp. 25-133, 377-470.
11. See the data in L. M. Terman and associates, *The Gifted Child Grows Up,* pp. 13-14; P. Sorokin, *Contemporary Sociological Theories,* Ch. 12; Sorokin-Zimmerman-Galpin, *A Systematic Source Book in Rural Sociology* (Minneapolis, 1932), vol. III, chap. 20; and the works quoted in Chapter Seven in this work.
12. Compare, for instance, the conclusions and the coefficients in the following studies: K. Pearson, *Grammar of Science* (London, 1902), pp. 431 ff.; C. A. Anderson, "Our Present Knowledge of Assortative Mating," *Rural Sociology,* III (1938), pp. 296-302; H. E. Jones, "Homogamy in Intellectual Abilities," *Amer. Journ. of Sociology,* XXXV (1929), pp. 369-82; E. Burgess and P. Wallin, "Homogamy in Social Characteristics," *Am. Journ. of Sociology,* XLIX (1943), pp. 102-124; H. M. Richardson, "Studies of Mental Resemblance between Husbands and Wives," *Psychol. Bulletin,* XXXVI (1939), pp. 104-120.
13. Compare, for instance, the coefficients of correlation in analysis of the factors of happy marriages given by L. M. Terman's *Psychological Factors in Marital Happiness* (New York, 1938), pp. 19 ff.; those given by E. Burgess and L. Cottrell, Jr., in *Predicting Success or Failure in Marriage* (New York, 1939), pp. 50 ff.; and those given by E. Burgess and P. Wallin in the above mentioned "Homogamy in Social Characteristics." For several factors the coefficients of Terman's study are comparatively high, while those of Burgess-Cottrell's book are low, and *vice versa.* The same is true, especially with the factor of agreement in religion, about the coefficients in Burgess's two studies. Cf. also G. Karlsson, *Adaptability and Communication in Marriage* (Uppsala, 1951), p. 107; P. Benson, "Familism and Marital Success," *Social Forces,* 1955, pp. 277-80.

14. S. A. Stouffer and others, the *American Soldier,* quoted, vol. II, p. 12.
15. For summarized coefficients of correlations obtained in various studies, see P. Sorokin, *Contemporary Sociological Theories,* pp. 549 ff. See there also the sources and the literature. About the relationship between economic variables and revolution-war phenomena see P. Sorokin, *Society, Culture, and Personality,* chap. 33.
16. Several times I have suggested compiling a special card catalogue of the available coefficients of correlations between all the studied psychosocial and biosocial variables in the libraries of universities and research institutions. Such an inventory would have saved an enormous amount of energy and time for psychosocial researchers, and would be useful in many other ways. For example, such an inventory would be a convincing warning to the devotees of the correlational faith who claim that the infallibility of statistics saves one from all the sins of the nonstatistical heretics and schismatics.
17. S. Stouffer, the *American Soldier,* vol. II, p. 165.
18. *Ibid.,* p. 108.
19. *Ibid.,* vol. II, p. 108.
20. J. D. Unwin, *Sex and Culture* (Oxford, 1934), p. 8.
21. *Ibid.,* p. 8.
22. With some reservations Stouffer acknowledges this frankly in the *American Soldier,* vol. I, pp. 40-41.
23. The *American Soldier,* vol. II, pp. 174-75.
24. The *American Soldier,* vol. I, pp. 44 ff.
25. H. Margenau, "The Meaning of 'Elementary Particle,' " *Amer. Scientist,* 39 (1951), p. 424.
26. E. C. Kemble, "Reality, Measurement, and the State of the System in Quantum Mechanics," quoted, p. 294. (By permission of E. C. Kemble.)
27. H. Margenau, "The Meaning of 'Elementary Particle,' " quoted, p. 424.
28. H. Margenau, "Physical Versus Historical Reality," quoted, pp. 195-99. See similar statements in E. Schrödinger's *What is Life,* pp. 77-80, *et passim;* Schrödinger, *Uber Indeterminismus in der Physik* (Leipzig, 1932); W. Heisenberg, *Wandlungen in der Grundlagen der Naturwissenschaft* (Leipzig, 1935); P. A. M. Dirac, *The Principles of Quantum Mechanics* (Oxford, 1935); E. C. Kemple, "Reality, Measurement and the State of the System in Quantum Mechanics," quoted; L. de Broglie, "Continuité et individualité dans la physique moderne," *Cahiers de la nouvelle journée,* XV (1929). G. Gurvitch, *Déterminismes sociaux et liberté humaine* (Paris, 1955).
29. E. C. Kemble, *op. cit.,* pp. 294-96.
30. Cf. G. Allport, *The Nature of Personality,* pp. 63-64; G. Capograssi, "Incertezze sul'individuo," *Scritti di Sociologia e Politica in Onore di L. Sturzo* (Bologna, 1953), vol. I, pp. 255-91.

31. E. Schrödinger, *What is Life,* pp. 2, 19-20. (By permission of Cambridge University Press.)
32. O. Spengler, *Decline of the West* (New York, 1947), vol. I, pp. 117-24.
33. For a detailed analysis of the integrated personality, the organized social group and the unified cultural system in contrast to the unintegrated or disintegrated personality, the unorganized social group and eclectic congeries of cultural phenomena, see P. Sorokin, *Society, Culture, and Personality,* chaps. 4, 17, 18, 19, *et passim;* P. Sorokin, *The Ways and Power of Love,* chaps. 5, 6, 7; P. Sorokin, *Dynamics,* vol. IV, *passim.*
34. For further details on the constant and inalienable characteristics of all personal, social, and cultural systems, see P. Sorokin, *Society, Culture, and Personality,* chaps. 8, 17, 18, 19.
35. *Ibid.,* pp. 696-97. In order that these statements may be fully understood, one needs to know well my theory of sociocultural systems and congeries, fully developed in my *Dynamics, Society, Culture, and Personality, The Ways and Power of Love,* and *Social Philosophies of An Age of Crisis.* In the words of an eminent sociologist of our time, "as yet, the only thorough and consistent effort to integrate all specialized nomothetic cultural sciences into a general theory of culture is that of Sorokin. . . . [H]is basic concept is that of system. Although this concept has been used by specialists . . . yet nobody before him extended it to all categories of cultural phenomena." F. Znaniecki, *Cultural Sciences* (University of Illinois Press, 1952), p. 377. Recent works like C. C. Homans' *The Human Group* (New York, 1950) independently repeat what is more fully stated in one chapter (the eighth) of my *Society, Culture, and Personality.* Other works which began to use the concept of social and cultural systems, like T. Parsons' *The Social System,* or Parsons' and Shils' (eds.) *Toward a General Theory of Action,* also reiterate in a somewhat defective way the essentials of my theory of social and cultural systems. This "convergence" of the imitative and independent conclusions of an ever-increasing number of sociologists and psychosocial scientists towards my systematic analysis of sociocultural and personal systems and congeries is one of the evidences of its validity and cognitive value.
36. This, precisely, is one of the main reasons for the superficiality, fruitlessness, and meaninglessness of a large part of modern statistical studies of psychosocial phenomena. Their authors hardly had a direct coliving, coexperiencing and intuitional identification with the phenomena studied; and they hardly "understood" the nature of the systems of ideas and values they counted and measured. No wonder, therefore, that a legion of books and courses on general education do not contribute much to general education, because they are written and taught by persons who themselves do not have the direct experience of general education. Similarly, we have a multitude of books on the family and marriage written by per-

sons who never married and had children; a plethora of studies of industrial sociology, executed by persons who hardly ever had an experience as a factory hand or foreman or manager; and so on and so forth. As a result, despite the ever-rising tide of statistical figures, tables, indices, coefficients and formulae in modern sociological and psychological studies, our knowledge of these phenomena has increased little, if at all. The dead and meaningless figures are weeds that progressively drive out the good grass of knowledge from the "lawns" of sociology and psychology.

37. P. Sorokin, *Society, Culture, and Personality,* p. 644. See there, and especially in my *Sociocultural Causality, Space, Time,* a detailed development of this criticism, pp. 67 ff., *et passim.*
38. W. L. Warner and P. S. Lundt, *The Social Life of a Community* (New Haven, 1941).
39. W. L. Warner and P. S. Lundt, *The Status System of a Modern Community* (New Haven, 1942).
40. See the analysis and criticism of these theories in P. Sorokin, *Social Philosophies of an Age of Crisis* (Boston, 1950), chaps. 3, 4, 5, 12.
41. See the detailed analysis of the componential structure of sociocultural phenomena in P. Sorokin, *Society, Culture, and Personality,* chaps. 3, 4. Cf. for a detailed criticism of the dichotomic theories *ibid.,* chap. 44; *Social and Cultural Dynamics,* vol. IV, chap. 4. In these works all the varieties of dichotomic theories are analyzed and criticized.
42. On this order of change, see P. Sorokin, *Society, Culture, and Personality,* pp. 580 ff.
43. See *Society, Culture, and Personality,* chaps. 38, 43-45, *et passim.*
44. Cf. P. Sorokin, *Social and Cultural Dynamics* and *Crisis of Our Age.*

## Chapter Nine

1. H. Margenau, "Physical vs. Historical Reality," *Philosophy of Science,* 19 (1952), pp. 212-13. A. Einstein's letter quoted in E. F. Molnar's *Human Action* (1955), p. 23.
2. Cf. on inductive and experimental method J. S. Mill, *A System of Logic* (London, 1843), book 3, *et passim;* J. Venn, *The Principles of Empirical and Inductive Logic* (London, 1889); the good survey of the literature on inductive-deductive and experimental methods given in P. H. Furfey, *The Scope and Method of Sociology* (New York, 1953); F. Znaniecki, *The Method of Sociology* (New York, 1934); P. Sorokin, *Sociocultural Causality, Space, Time.* See also R. Carnap, "Inductive Logic and Science," *Proceedings of the Amer. Academy of Arts and Sciences,* 80 (1953), pp. 189-97.
3. Cf. F. S. Chapin, *Experimental Designs in Sociological Research* (New York, 1937); E. Greenwood, *Experimental Sociology* (New York, 1945).

4. Cf. G. and L. B. Murphy, *Experimental Social Psychology* (New York, 1931, or its later editions).
5. Cf. for a brilliant analysis of these difficulties and probable errors in A. A. Tschuprow, *Ocherki po teorii statistiki (Studies in Statistical Theory),* (St. Petersburg, 1909), pp. 111 ff.
6. *Studies in Social Psychology in World War II* (Princeton, 1950), vol. III.
7. *Ibid.,* vol. III, pp. 5-30.
8. *Ibid.,* pp. 254-73.
9. Most of these studies can be found in D. Cartwright and A. Zander, *Group Dynamics,* quoted earlier.
10. On these works and on psychological obstacles in experimental research, see D. J. Ingle, "Psychological Barriers in Research," *American Scientist,* 42 (1954), 283-93.
11. See P. Sorokin and others, "An Experimental Study of Efficiency of Work," *Amer. Journal of Sociology,* 35 (1930), pp. 765-82; these experimental studies represent as near an approach to real experimental investigation as any experimental study of psychosocial phenomena known to me. P. Sorokin (ed.), *Explorations in Altruistic Love and Behavior* (Boston, 1950), pp. 33 ff.; J. B. Maller, *Cooperation and Competition: An Experimental Study in Motivation* (New York, 1929).
12. B. A. Wright, *Selfishness, Guilt-Feeling, and Social Distance;* and *Fairness and Generosity* (unpublished theses, University of Iowa, 1940 and 1942). A possible reason for the peculiar results of Wright's studies is that they met experimental conditions much less rigorously than my experiments, and the choice of toys in her experiments was imaginary and speech-reactional only, not the actual giving of toys to the strangers and the children's friends.
13. See the basic differences between these groups, aggregates, and plurels in P. Sorokin, *Society, Culture, and Personality,* chaps. 4, 5, 8, 9.
14. "Experimental studies" of S. Schachter, L. Festinger, L. Killian, L. Coch, J. R. P. French, Jr., J. Levine, and others in D. Cartwright and A. Zander, *Group Dynamics,* quoted earlier, gives spectacular examples of this sort of rash extrapolation and generalization.
15. By a very rough estimate, at least 90 per cent of allegedly experimental studies in psychology and sociology belong to the sham-experimental kind. Of these no less than one-half suffer from violation of logical laws, poor observation and, especially, from a multitude of questionable, sometimes bizarre, assumptions.
16. P. W. Bridgman, *The Intelligent Individual and Society* (New York, 1938), pp. 7, 8, 12, *et passim.* Cf. also Bridgman's "The Task Before Us," *Proc. Amer. Acad. of Arts and Sciences,* 83 (1954): 97-112. (By permission of P. W. Bridgman.) In contrast to Bridgman's stand upon it Albert Einstein states that "it is in my opinion a great danger for psychology if concepts of physics are used there instead of those concepts which have

developed in psychology itself." A. Einstein's letter, Feb. 3, 1942, in E. F. Molnar's *Human Action,* 1955, p. 23.

17. See P. Sorokin, *Contemporary Sociological Theories,* chap. I.
18. J. Q. Stewart, "A Basis for Social Physics," *Impact of Science on Society,* 3 (1952), pp. 110, 118. (By permission of J. Q. Stewart.)
19. *Ibid.,* pp. 122-23.
20. *Ibid.,* pp. 116-18.
21. These remarks are probably unclear to most modern sociologists and psychologists, who hardly ever have studied the meaning—forms—and functions of time and space, and especially their sociocultural forms. A clarifying analysis of sociocultural time and space can be found in P. Sorokin, *Sociocultural Causality, Space, Time,* chaps. 3, 4; *Social and Cultural Dynamics,* vol. IV, chaps. 9, 10, 11. G. Gurvitch, *Déterminismes Sociaux,* quoted.
22. *Ibid.,* pp. 118-29. In a personal letter to me, Professor Stewart states that "as the point of view of social physics develops further, you would be willing to consider that the dimensions of reason, feeling, and authority offer sufficient description of many sociocultural phenomena. This would leave time, distance, and mass as purely physical." Letter, May 26, 1953.
23. On these matters, *cf.* the best texts in economics, sociology, demography, psychology, anthropology.
24. Among these studies, my study on the "Influence of Occupation Upon Behavior and Psychological Processes" ("Vliianie professii na povedenie ludei"), *Journal Psichologii i Nevrologii,* No. 1, 1921, pp. 397-424, showed a tangible influence of occupation and occupational values upon perception, attention, memory, association of ideas, etc., essentially similar to the results of Bruner and Associates' investigations. Cf., J. S. Bruner and C. C. Goodman, "Need and Value as Organizing Factors in Perception," *Journal of Abnormal and Social Psychology,* 42 (1947), pp. 33-44; L. Postman, J. S. Bruner and E. McGinnies, "Personal Values as Selective Factors in Perception," *Ibid.,* 43 (1948), pp. 142-54.
25. J. S. Bruner, R. Tagiuri, and R. R. Blake, "Some Determinants of the Perception of Positive and Negative Feelings in Others," *Journal of Abnormal and Social Psychology,* 48 (1953), pp. 585-92.
26. Cf. E. F. Borgatta, "Analysis of Social Interaction," *Sociometry,* 17 (1954), pp. 7-31; D. P. Ausubel, "Reciprocity and Assumed Reciprocity," *Ibid.,* 16 (1953); R. Dymond, "A Preliminary Investigation of the Relation of Insight and Empathy," *Journ. of Cons. Psychology,* 4 (1948), pp. 228-33. For a good criticism of mechanistic theories of perception, see F. H. Allport, *Theories of Perception* (New York, 1955).
27. Cf. P. Sorokin, *Society, Culture, and Personality,* chaps. 5, 6. See there the literature and an analysis of various forms of solidarity, friendship, etc., in the works of M. Scheler, E. Durkheim, F. Tönnies, L. von Wiese, G. Gurvitch, Aristotle, P. Lavrov, F. LePlay, G. Davy, Cooley, and others.

28. See N. Wiener, *Cybernetics or Control and Communication in the Animal and the Machine* (Cambridge, 1948).
29. F. D. Barrett and H. A. Shepard, "A Bibliography of Cybernetics," *Proceedings of the American Academy of Arts and Sciences,* 80 (1953), pp. 204-22.
30. N. Wiener, *The Human Use of Human Beings. Cybernetics and Society* (Boston, 1950), pp. 9, 15, 16. (By permission of Houghton Mifflin Co.)
31. D. M. MacKay, "On Comparing the Brain with Machines," *American Scientist,* 42 (1954), pp. 261-68; Cf. also J. O. Wisdom, R. J. Spilsbury and D. M. MacKay's paper in *Symposium on Mentality in Machines, Proceedings of Arist. Society, Supplement,* 1952.
32. Cf., for a fairly full bibliography of various cybernetic social and psychological theories, the cited paper of Barrett and Shepard.
33. See further details and the references to the works of Descartes, Leibnitz, Hobbes, and others, in P. Sorokin, *Contemporary Sociological Theories,* chap. 1; Condillac, *Treatise on Sensations,* tr. by G. Carr (Los Angeles, 1930), chap. 1.
34. Charles Sherrington, "Mystery of Mysteries: the Human Brain," *New York Times* Magazine, December 4, 1949, pp. 19-20. (By permission of the *New York Times.*)
35. D. M. MacKay, *op. cit.,* pp. 259-60.
36. On the component of meanings as the main component of all psychosocial phenomena as different from physical and biological ones, see P. Sorokin, *Society, Culture, and Personality,* chap. 3.
37. See S. C. Dodd, "Can the Social Scientist Serve Two Masters?" referred to earlier. Also Dodd's "Diffusion Is Predictable," *Amer. Sociol. Review,* 20: 392-401 (1955). (By permission of S. C. Dodd.)
38. See P. Sorokin, *Social and Cultural Dynamics,* vol. IV, chaps. 5, 6, 7, for an analysis of these problems and for the vast literature in this field.
39. For an analysis and for the literature of these problems see P. Sorokin, *The Ways and Power of Love, passim; Reconstruction of Humanity,* and *Society, Culture, and Personality,* chaps. 35-48.
40. Cf. A. Bavelas, "Communication Patterns in Task-Oriented Groups," *Journal of the Acoustical Society of America,* 22 (1950), 725-30. A. Bavelas and D. Barret, "An Experimental Approach to Organizational Communication," *Personnel* (April, 1951); H. J. Leavitt, "Some Effects of Certain Communication Patterns on Group Performance," *Journ. of Abnormal and Social Psychology,* 46 (1951), pp. 38-50.
41. See a few patterns of communication systems in the Islamic rituals of the dzirk and the Rahmaniya, in the Zen-Buddhist sesshin in E. Dermenghem's and Kita's and Nagaia's papers in P. Sorokin (ed.), *Forms and Techniques of Altruistic and Spiritual Growth* (Boston, 1954), pp. 109-143

42. See P. Sorokin, *The Ways and Power of Love,* chaps. 6, 7, 8.
43. On the essential structural and dynamic traits and factors of organized groups, the forms of their emergence and organization, their stability and longevity, their modes of self-maintenance, and so on, see P. Sorokin, *Society, Culture, and Personality,* chaps. 4, 5, 6, 8, 21-24.

## Chapter Ten

1. P. Sorokin, *Society, Culture, and Personality,* p. 39.
2. P. Sorokin, *ibid.,* pp. 39-40, *et passim.* See there a development of these remarks and evidence of the extreme complexity of the total individual, the family, a primitive society, and other alleged social atoms.
3. J. L. Moreno, *Psychodrama* (New York, 1946), vol. I, pp. 184, 229. (By permission of J. L. Moreno.)
4. J. L. Moreno, *Who Shall Survive* (Washington, 1934), pp. 77 ff., 96.
5. J. L. Moreno, "The Social Atom and Death," *Sociometry,* 10 (1947), pp. 80-84.
6. Cf. W. H. Furry, E. M. Purcell, and J. C. Street, *Physics* (New York, 1952), pp. 148, 252, *et passim.*
7. On the five main aspects—intensity, extensity, purity, duration, and adequacy—of such "emotional relatedness," as love or hatred, see P. Sorokin, *The Ways and Power of Love,* chaps. 1-4. These five aspects, irreducible to one another, compose the very minimum of aspects of any emotional relatedness. If one takes only one of these aspects, one practically misses the very essence of emotional attractions and repulsions. Any unidimensional definition of emotional relationship radically distorts its nature, and fails to grasp its heart and soul.
8. Concerning other, particularly nominalistic, shortcomings of Moreno's concept of the social atom, see G. Gurvitch, "Microsociology and Sociometry," *Sociometry,* 12 (1949), pp. 1-31. Gurvitch's friendly criticism of Moreno's sociometrical system is, so far, the best among all the criticisms I have read.
9. Cf. E. Fermi, *Elementary Particles* (New Haven, 1951); E. Schrödinger's article in *Endeavour,* 9, No. 35, 1950; H. Margenau, "The Meaning of 'Elementary Particle,'" *Amer. Scientist,* 39 (1951), pp. 422-31.
10. R. F. Bales, *Interaction Process Analysis* (Cambridge, 1950), chap. 2. (By permission of Addison-Wesley Press.) Other investigators of the small groups, like G. C. Homans, mention the family, childhood gang, school and college cliques, clubs, and teams, as the small groups. The small groups "mediate between us and the leviathans. [They are] the commonest, the most familiar, of social units." G. C. Homans, *The Human Group* (New York, 1950), pp. 1-2. Cf. also P. Hare, E. F. Borgata, R. F. Bales (eds.): *Small Groups* (New York, 1955).

11. For definition and classification of the basic categories of social groups, see P. Sorokin, *Society, Culture, and Personality,* chaps. 4-9.
12. P. Sorokin, *Society, Culture, and Personality,* p. 246.
13. On the importance of powerfulness of groups, criteria of group-powerfulness, and the classification of social groups from this standpoint, see P. Sorokin, *Society, Culture, and Personality,* chap. 9.
14. R. F. Bales, "A Set of Categories for the Analysis of Small Group Interaction," *Amer. Soc. Review,* 15 (1950): 257-63; R. F. Bales, "The Equilibrium Problem in Small Groups," in T. Parsons, R. F. Bales and E. A. Shils, *Working Papers in the Theory of Action* (Glencoe, 1953); R. F. Bales, *Interaction Process Analysis* (Cambridge, 1950).
15. R. F. Bales, "The Equilibrium Problem in Small Groups," T. Parsons, R. F. Bales, and E. Shils, *Working Papers in the Theory of Action* (Glencoe, 1953), p. 121.
16. D. Cartwright and A. Zander, *Group Dynamics,* p. 42.
17. *Ibid.,* p. 49.
18. *Ibid.,* p. 93.
19. Aristotle, *Politics,* 1253 a.
20. Cartwright and Zander, *op. cit.,* p. 94.
21. See the analysis and the literature on this problem in P. Sorokin, *Society, Culture, and Personality,* chaps. 9, 24, 25, *et passim.*
22. Cartwright and Zander, *op. cit.,* p. 103.
23. See the state of this problem in today's sociology and vast literature in P. Sorokin, *Society, Culture, and Personality,* chaps. 5, 6, 7, 8, 21, 22.
24. Cartwright and Zander, *op. cit.,* p. 77.
25. *Ibid.,* pp. 76-79.
26. *Ibid.,* pp. 80-81.
27. G. Saintsbury, *A History of Criticism and Literary Taste of Europe* (London, 1900), vol. I, p. 128.
28. G. C. Homans, *The Human Group,* p. 444.
29. See the literature and the main generalizations in this field in P. Sorokin, *Society, Culture, and Personality,* chaps. 6, 7, 31-33; P. Sorokin, *The Ways and Power of Love* (Boston, 1954), *passim.*
30. Cartwright and Zanders, *op. cit.,* pp. 86-87.
31. On the life-span, mortality and resurrection of various groups see P. Sorokin, *Society, Culture, and Personality,* chap. 34.
32. R. F. Bales, F. L. Strodtbeck, T. M. Mills, and M. E. Roseborough, "Channels of Communication in Small Groups," *Amer. Sociol. Review,* 16 (1951), pp. 461, 465.
33. *Ibid.,* pp. 461-62.
34. *Ibid.,* p. 468.
35. T. Parsons, R. F. Bales, and E. A. Shils, *Working Papers,* p. 102. (By permission of the Free Press.) "Laws" of this sort were formulated many

times earlier by "social physicists" of the seventeenth and subsequent centuries. Cf. P. Sorokin, *Contemporary Sociological Theories,* chap. 1.

36. On the principles of immanent change and of limit, see P. Sorokin, *Society, Culture, and Personality,* chap. 46; P. Sorokin, *Dynamics,* vol. IV, chaps. 12-16.
37. Parsons, Bales, Shils, *Working Papers,* pp. 102-103.
38. P. Sorokin, *Dynamics,* vol. IV, p. 689.
39. See an analysis and criticism of all five concepts of equilibrium in *Dynamics,* vol. IV, pp. 677-93.
40. For a further criticism see L. A. Coser, "The Functions of Small-Group Research," *Social Problems,* July, 1955.

## Chapter Eleven

1. An example of such predictive paraphernalia is given in P. Horst, P. Wallin, L. Guttman, *et al., The Prediction of Personal Adjustment* (New York, 1941). See a criticism of this work in *Amer. Journ. of Sociology,* XLVIII (1942), pp. 61-86.
2. See P. Sorokin, "Is Accurate Social Planning Possible?" *Amer. Sociol. Review,* I (1936), pp. 13-25.
3. For further details, see P. Sorokin, *Dynamics,* vol. II, chap. 9.
4. E. Schrödinger, *What Is Life?* quoted, p. 2, *et passim.*
5. E. C. Kemble, "Reality, Measurement," etc., quoted earlier, pp. 273-78, 294-96. (By permission of E. C. Kemble.)
6. H. Margenau, "Physical vs. Historical Reality," pp. 195-98; H. Margenau, "The Meaning of Elementary Particle," p. 425. (By permission of H. Margenau.)
7. A. Eddington, *Philosophy of the Physical Sciences* (New York; Macmillan, 1940), pp. 61, 89, 90, 180-84. See also the works of other eminent physicists like M. Born, A. Boutaric, P. Bridgman, N. Bohr, R. Millikan, P. Jordan, H. Weyl, L. de Broglie, F. Oppenheimer, and others, quoted, in P. Sorokin, *Sociocultural Causality, Space, Time,* pp. 32-33.
8. P. Sorokin, "Is Accurate Social Planning Possible?" quoted earlier, p. 15.
9. See P. Sorokin and C. Berger, *Time Budgets of Human Behavior* (Cambridge, 1939), chap. 13.
10. *Ibid.,* chaps. 13, 14.
11. See details in P. Sorokin, *Society, Culture, and Personality,* chap. 34.
12. S. A. Stouffer and others, *The American Soldier,* quoted earlier, vol. II, chap. 12, pp. 549 ff.
13. A. Eddington, *op. cit.,* pp. 89-90, 181-84, 221.
14. M. Planck, *Where Science Is Going* (New York, 1932), pp. 145-69.
15. N. Bohr, "Causality and Complimentarity," *Philosophy of Science,* 1937, pp. 289-90.

16. See an historical and systematic outline of the problem and reference to the leading thinkers in P. Sorokin, *Dynamics,* vol. IV, chaps. 12, 13; vol. II, chaps. 9, 11.
17. See *Dynamics,* particularly vol. IV, *passim;* vol. I, chaps. 1, 2, 3; vol. II, chaps. 9, 11; *Sociocultural Causality, Space, Time,* chaps. 1, 2; *Society, Culture, and Personality,* chaps. 4, 8, 17, 18, 19, 35, 36, 38, 43, 46.
18. An analysis of the rhythms, phases, periodicities, and tempi of sociocultural systems is given in Sorokin, *Dynamics,* vol. IV, chaps. 8-11.
19. Sorokin, *Dynamics,* chap. 4, pp. 430-33.
20. *Ibid.,* chap. 4, pp. 433-34.
21. E. W. Burgess, "Rejoinder," *Amer. Journ. of Sociology,* XLVIII (1942), p. 85.
22. *Ibid.,* p. 86.

CHAPTER TWELVE

1. See the definition and properties of the supersensory intuition, the body of empirical evidence for its existence and functioning, and for its being the main source of the greatest creative achievements in human culture, and the literature on this problem, in P. Sorokin, *Dynamics,* vol. IV, chap. 16; P. Sorokin, *The Ways and Power of Love,* chaps. 6, 19; P. Sorokin (ed.), *The Forms and Techniques of Altruistic and Spiritual Growth,* chaps. 1, 16, *et passim.* In the present work only a summary of the conclusions from this evidence is given.
2. R. Carnap, "Inductive Logic and Science," *Proceedings of Amer. Acad. of Arts and Sciences,* 80 (1953), p. 195.
3. See the long list of creative intuitionalists (under the term, "mysticism") in the history of the Greco-Roman and the Western cultures in P. Sorokin, *Dynamics,* vol. II, pp. 639-42.
4. T. Brosse, in P. Sorokin, *The Ways and Power of Love,* pp. 363-64. See there a comprehensive analysis of intuitional cognition and creativity, chaps. 6, 19.
5. See on this *ibid.,* pp. 364 ff.; and especially the unique and unrivalled study of Buddhist logic in Th. Tscherbatsky, *Buddhist Logic* (Leningrad, 1932).
6. R. Godel, "The Contemporary Sciences and the Liberative Experiences of Yoga," in P. Sorokin (ed.), *Forms and Techniques of Altruistic and Spiritual Growth,* pp. 1-12. See there also T. Brosse's experimental study of the influence of the supersensory *"nous"* on the activities of the heart, the organs of breathing, and other organs of our body, chap. 16.
7. Pierre Rousseau, *La Conquête de la Science* (Paris, 1945), pp. 279, 280.
8. Cited by M. G. Bachelard, *Le Nouvel Esprit Scientifique,* p. 54.
9. H. Margenau, "Physical Versus Historical Reality," quoted, p. 212.

10. E. C. Kemble, "Reality, Measurement, and The State of the System in Quantum Mechanics," quoted, pp. 273-79.
11. P. W. Bridgman, "The Task Before Us," quoted, pp. 104-106. (By permission of P. W. Bridgman.)

### Chapter Thirteen

1. For the evidence see *Dynamics,* all four volumes.
2. P. Sorokin, *The Ways and Power of Love,* pp. 47-48.
3. Most of these theories are analyzed in P. Sorokin, *Social Philosophies of An Age of Crisis* (Boston, 1950).
4. See its analysis and criticism in P. Sorokin, *Dynamics,* vol. IV, pp. 677-93.
5. See an analysis and criticism of inadequate classifications, in P. Sorokin, *Contemporary Sociological Theories,* pp. 29-37.
6. See Plato, *The Republic,* Book VIII.
7. See A. H. Hobbs, *The Claims of Sociology: A Critique of Textbooks* (Harrisburg, 1951).
8. See the developed theory of the integralist system of reality, truth, and cognition in P. Sorokin, *Social and Cultural Dynamics,* vol. II, chaps. 1-12, vol. IV, chap. 16; P. Sorokin, *Sociocultural Causality, Space, Time,* chap. 5; P. Sorokin, *The Ways and Power of Love,* chaps. 5-8; P. Sorokin (ed.), *Symposium: Forms and Techniques of Altruistic and Spiritual Growth,* chaps. 1, 16.

# *Name Index*

# Name Index

## *Name Index*

# Name Index

# Name Index

# Name Index